365 Magical Moments

A Daily Spiritual Journey Through All Things Disney

Albert Thweatt

Editor: Bob McLain
Layout: Artisanal Text

ISBN 978-1-68390-331-4
Printed in the United States of America

Theme Park Press | www.ThemeParkPress.com
Address queries to bob@themeparkpress.com

This book is dedicated to all Disney Cast Members, past and present, who work tirelessly every day to keep Walt's dream alive and provide magic to all of us kids, both young and old, around the world.

Monthly Devotional Themes

January:	DISNEY MUSIC
February:	WALT AND THE HISTORY OF DISNEY
March:	DISNEY RIDES
April:	RESTAURANTS, RETAIL AND REFRESHMENTS
May:	PIXAR
June:	DISNEY QUOTES
July:	DISNEY SHOWS
August:	DISNEY CHARACTERS
September:	DISNEY RESORTS
October:	DISNEY CLASSIC FILMS
November:	DISNEY FUN FACTS
December:	MISCELLANEOUS MOUSEDOM

Introduction

Okay, so I lied. I admit it, and I apologize. But I promise it wasn't intentional. You see, I said in the introduction to *Disney Devotionals: Book 3* that I was done, that I wasn't writing anymore and that it was my grand finale. And I fully intended it to be. Three was enough, and I was out of ideas. That was until the early part of 2021 when another one just popped into my head. I guess the fact that I told God I really enjoyed writing and would love to do it again some day may have been a factor. But He answered so quickly! Way faster than I expected, presenting me with another idea and the means to get another devotional book published. So here we go!

Now this one is a bit different than the previous three, so maybe I didn't lie. Maybe I meant I was done with the format of 100 Disney devotionals covering one broad topic with each two-page entry because this book is instead 365 devotionals, one for each day of the year, and they are much shorter, each just a page in length. And I decided to do a different Disney theme every month, meaning 12 themes in all. Each devotional contains several parts: 1) the date, 2) a Biblical passage I strongly suggest you read first, 3) the title and topic, 4) a related verse that may or may not be from the main passage, 5) a brief devotional and spiritual thought related to the Disney topic at hand, 6) a suggested prayer and finally 7) a daily challenge. I offer each of these as tools to aid in your daily devotion time with God. But please do whatever works best for you. For example, if you prefer to say your own prayer or spend more time in that area, by all means please do so. What I offer are mere suggestions to guide you, but you should make your time with God your own and do what's best to help make it a daily habit that will strengthen and advance your relationship with the Father. There is one additional part I wish I had room for, and that is journal lines. **Therefore, I also strongly suggest buying a daily journal and pairing it each day with these devotionals.** After reading the Scriptural passage and the message presented, I suggest taking some time to reflect and put your thoughts, takeaways, thanksgivings, struggles, confessions, requests and prayers into your own words. It's just a suggestion, but I think it would really be a beneficial addition to help focus and organize your thoughts for reference and spiritual growth.

One disclaimer I will offer as there is a lot of Disney information found in the following pages. The main purpose of this book is to aid you in spiritual growth, but I do hope you'll enjoy learning even more about Disney as well. However, writing about 365 different Disney topics was, to put it nicely, not an easy task. I did my very best to research and report only accurate information, but I can't promise perfection. None of us can. It is quite possible that a very small portion of the facts and information found in the pages to follow are either incorrect or have changed since I wrote the entry. As you know, Disney changes often. I tried my best to go back and update entries that changed even while I was writing, but it's possible I missed something. Some of the attractions listed may not even exist anymore or there are plans to refurbish and change them in the near future. Any Disney author will tell you it's extremely difficult to keep informational books current with the constant changes happening every day. But I do sincerely apologize if any information is inaccurate. I assure you I did my best to prevent that from happening.

I once again want to give a huge shout-out and thanks to my amazing family, especially my wife, Susan. She has been nothing but supportive in allowing me to tackle another book, one that took even more of my time than the previous three and caused a greater bit of stress and struggle. After I got a little more than half-way through with this one, I admit I went through a bout of anxiety and severe writer's block which I now know is a very real thing. For some reason, I lost my creative ability and motivation for a few weeks in the process of writing this book. There were even a few days I wanted to quit or severely postpone its release, and I never would have been able to get back on track and re-discover my inspiration and imagination without my wife. She even helped me write a few of these, giving me ideas and offering constant love, prayers and assurances that everything would be okay. In all honesty, her name should most definitely be on the front of this book too! And of course, even more than that, I never could've gotten through without the inspiration, support, guidance and love of my Father in Heaven who never ceases to amaze me with what He can and continues to do in my life.

I hope and pray this book, like the others, can help and benefit you in what is most important in life. Don't forget that very little on this Earth really matters. The hectic life, the time crunches, the deadlines, the to-do lists, the material possessions, the stress, the struggles, the work, the school...it's all meaningless and will eventually, like our bodies, pass away. The only thing that is truly important is your relationship with God and the path you are currently traveling. There is only one, narrow road that leads to Him, and you can only find that route through

Jesus Christ. The whole point of this and my other books is to help you discover that path. It is never too late to find it, get on it and stay on it forever. You can't even begin to imagine what's in store for you if you do. Keep reading to find out what I'm talking about. Daily time with God is vital and so important in achieving that ultimate, eternal goal. Strive diligently and work hard to maintain time for Him each and every day this year. Eventually, it will become a habit as well as your favorite time of the day. As always, I love you all and pray fervently for your success, your soul and your salvation. May God truly bless you all and please let me know if I can ever assist in any way.

Albert (albertruns@gmail.com)

JANUARY THEME

DISNEY MUSIC

JANUARY 1 **Read PSALM 51:10-19**

A NEW BEGINNING

Disney Music – "Start of Something New"—*High School Musical*

"Remember not the former things, nor consider the things of old. Behold, I am doing a new thing..."
—*Isaiah 43:18-19*

Happy New Year! It may seem an odd choice to start this book and your year of devotionals with a song from *High School Musical* (HSM). Not exactly a Disney classic, right? However, the title of the song, "Start of Something New" is just too perfect for a January 1st devotional. This song at the beginning of the film is also appropriately titled representing the beginning of what would become the HSM franchise and start of "Troy" and "Gabriella's" relationship, played by Zac Efron and Vanessa Hudgens. Did you know that Zac Efron didn't actually sing much at all in this first film? His voice was considered too low at the time and so another actor sung most of Troy's parts. Efron would go on to sing all his parts in the next two HSM films.

In Psalm 51, David asks God to create a clean heart inside him, also requesting a renewed spirit and restored joy. David is basically asking God for a restart. We all need occasional restarts in life. We often make mistakes, find ourselves caught in sin or heading down the wrong path, away from God. The good news is that we can always get a restart with God. And what better time than right now...on the first day of the year. Decide today to restart your life with God this year. Make a list of anything standing in your way of being right with Him and make a true effort to get rid of those things. Tell God about them and ask His help in purging them from your life. Make this year truly the "start of something new" in your relationship with God. Keep your faith and bond with Him strong every single day. It will lead to a wonderful year and eternal future with God always beside you.

PRAYER—Dear God, like David, please renew my life with You. Help me to get rid of anything standing in the way of a deep and faithful relationship with You. Help this year to be one where I find Your purpose for me and use me to do Your will. In Jesus' name, Amen.

TODAY I WILL...make a list either mentally or physically of anything standing in the way of a meaningful relationship with God and make a plan to eliminate these things from my life.

JANUARY 2 **Read EPHESIANS 4:17-27**

THE PAST IS IN THE PAST

Disney Music – "Let It Go"—*Frozen*

"...to put off your old self, which belongs to your former manner of life and is corrupt through deceitful desires, and to be renewed..."
—Ephesians 4:22-23

Now this is more of a Disney classic, right? *Frozen* hit theaters in 2013 and became an instant blockbuster raking in over $1.2 billion worldwide. Its sequel did even better! One of the most beloved parts of the original is this song, sung by Queen Elsa on the mountaintop as she builds her ice palace. This hit tune was written in one day with the voice of Elsa, Idina Menzel, specifically in mind. It was the first Billboard top ten hit for an animated Disney film since "Colors of the Wind" from 1995's *Pocahontas*. It also won the Oscar for Best Original Song. In the film, it is during this song that Elsa accepts her powers, throws off her fears and "let's go" of the past. In fact, you may remember the lyrics, "I'm never going back. The past is in the past."

As mentioned yesterday, we all make mistakes. Like Elsa, we have parts of our past we want to forget. I certainly do. In today's passage from Ephesians, we see Paul reminding the people that once we are in Christ, having adhered to the instructions God set forth in the New Testament, we put off our old self, are renewed, and put on a new self as a follower of God. This means as Christians, we can talk to God about those past mistakes and "let them go" once and for all. If we are sincere in our repentance, the Bible says He forgives our past sins and remembers them no more. Don't dwell on past errors! I say again, "let it go!" Ask God for forgiveness, accept it, move on and strive harder to follow Him daily! Trust that He has forgotten those things and take comfort. He doesn't remember them so why should you?

PRAYER—God, there are parts of my past I'm not proud of. Please forgive me of these things and help me not to focus on them anymore. Thank You for forgiveness! In Jesus' name, Amen.

TODAY I WILL...make a list of any past mistakes I can't seem to let go of, talk to God about them, ask for and accept His forgiveness, destroy the list and dwell on them no more.

JANUARY 3 **Read 2 CORINTHIANS 11:16-33**

WORTH YOUR WHILE

Disney Music – "Go the Distance"—*Hercules*

"I do not account my life of any value nor as precious to myself, if only I may finish my course and the ministry that I received from the Lord Jesus, to testify to the gospel of the grace of God."
—Acts 20:24

This is one of my favorites. I may have even belted it out a few times while driving, although there's no proof. "Go the Distance" was one of two songs written for Hercules to sing in this film bearing his name. However, the other song, "Shooting Star" didn't make the final cut and can only be heard on the soundtrack. Roger Bart was the singing voice in the film, but Michael Bolton recorded the pop version of this song while Ricky Martin of "Livin' la Vida Loca" fame sang a Spanish adaptation. You can probably guess the message without looking at the lyrics. Through this song, Hercules shares his determination to keep pressing on despite difficulties standing in his way. In the chorus, he sings, "I know every mile will be worth my while."

If you want a Biblical example of someone that "went the distance," Paul is an easy choice. In today's reading, Paul describes all he suffered while teaching the Gospel, mentioning prison, beatings, shipwrecks, being stoned, lost at sea, hunger, thirst and much more. Through it all, he never stopped striving for his goals. In fact, look at what he said above in Acts. He believed his life was worth nothing unless he finished his goal of testifying the Gospel. What an amazing example! Hopefully none of us ever face that level of hardships, although the Bible does promise suffering and persecution for Christians. Like Paul, we must never stop striving for our spiritual goals no matter what life throws at us. The Bible is clear what awaits if we continually strive and follow God's Word throughout our lives, and it will definitely be "worth our while!"

PRAYER—Dear Father, life is hard, but I know that being Your faithful servant means inevitable struggles and tough times. Please help me through and keep me always striving. I can't wait for my eternal reward. In His holy name, Amen.

TODAY I WILL...redefine my spiritual goals, write them down and place them in a prominent place. I will bring them before God asking for his strength in accomplishing them.

JANUARY 4 **Read JOHN 15:12-17**

HIS FRIENDSHIP WILL NEVER DIE

Disney Music – "You've Got a Friend in Me"—*Toy Story*

"You are my friends if you do what I command you."
—John 15:14

Think about the friendships in your life. What makes your best friends the best? What are some words you'd use to describe your closest friends? This song from the original *Toy Story* has become representative of the franchise and the various friendships made throughout the series. Whether Woody and Andy, Buzz and Woody or any of the other lovable characters, this song's lyrics perfectly sum up the close bond shared during the four films many memorable scenes. Did you know that composer Randy Newman wrote this song in just one day, and that Tom Hanks (Woody himself) sang a version in a scene from *Toy Story 2*? It was nominated for an Oscar and Golden Globe but lost both to "Colors of the Wind" from *Pocahontas*. Take time to look up these lyrics. I wish I had room to print them all here as they beautifully describe true friendship.

I believe Jesus has an even better definition of friendship in today's passage from John 15, describing it as loving one another just as he demonstrated love. He further states friendship includes laying down one's life for another. The people then didn't realize that was exactly what he would later do for them...and for us as well. Finally, Jesus says that we're His friends if we follow His commandments. Don't you want Jesus as your friend? Isn't it incredible to know that He desires to have you as a friend and gave His life to show it? Let us work hard to follow His commandments and show Him in return that we truly want to be his friend. Read this lyric from today's song out loud imagining Jesus saying it directly to you, because I promise He is. "...none of them will ever love you the way I do. It's Me and you..."

PRAYER—Father, thank you so much for sending Your Son to be my Savior, guide, example and friend. He is the best friend I could ever have. Thank you for the sacrifice of His life for mine. In His beloved name, Amen.

TODAY I WILL...commit to being a friend to Jesus by following His commands. I will also pledge to read often about His life in the Gospels so I can know what those commands are.

JANUARY 5 **Read PROVERBS 3:5-8**

DREAM WITH FAITH AND FOCUS

Disney Music – "A Dream is a Wish Your Heart Makes"—*Cinderella*

"Be not wise in your own eyes; fear the Lord and turn away from evil. It will be healing to your flesh and refreshment to your bones."
—Proverbs 3:7-8

Once again, I suggest you look up the lyrics to today's song. Cinderella sings it to various creatures in the early morning, encouraging them to follow their dreams despite any obstacles in the way. She urges them to have faith and keep striving as fulfilling dreams will heal the heartaches of life. Cinderella was originally voiced by Ilene Woods who suffered from Alzheimer's later in life and didn't recall playing the role. However, as she neared life's end, it's said she was very comforted whenever nurses would play this song. In 2020, Demi Lovato and Michael Buble` performed a version of this song for a Disney family sing-along special.

Re-listening to this song and its lyrics reminded me of today's reading. Cinderella sings, "In dreams you will lose your heartaches...no matter how your heart is grieving, if you keep on believing, the dream that you wish will come true." Do you see how similar that is to the proverb above? Solomon writes one of my favorite passages here encouraging us to continually trust in God as we won't always understand His plan (v 5-6). But he goes on to say that fearing God and turning from evil will be like healing to our bodies. Cinderella makes the same claim singing that following dreams cause you to lose heartaches and heal your grieving heart. What happens when dreams don't go the way you've planned? The answer is to press on, trusting in God's timeline and not your own. You may not understand God's path, but if you keep your focus on Him without giving up, He will show you the way, heal your heartaches and comfort your soul. As Cinderella sings, "Have faith in your dreams and someday your rainbow will come smiling through." God will provide that rainbow if we keep our faith strong.

PRAYER—Holy Father, I have many dreams I want to accomplish. Help me to trust in Your plan and path to success. Thank you for the healing caused by keeping my faith strong in Your will for my life. In Jesus' name, Amen.

TODAY I WILL...talk to God about my dreams and desires whether spiritual or not. I will trust in His timeline and path to those wishes and never give up my faith and focus on Him.

JANUARY 6 **Read MATTHEW 5:13-16**

BE A LIGHTHOUSE

Disney Music – "Candle on the Water"—*Pete's Dragon*

"...I am the light of the world. Whoever follows me will not walk in darkness but will have the light of life."
—John 8:12

I gladly admit that *Pete's Dragon* has been my absolute favorite Disney film since I was a kid. I absolutely love the story and music, including this song sung by Helen Reddy who plays Nora, the affable lighthouse keeper who takes Pete in. She sings it from the top of a lighthouse as she remembers her lost fiancé, Paul and longs for his return. The song was originally intended to be the only song in the film but was so well-received that it alone caused the entire film to be turned into a musical. Helen Reddy claims she was told by the song's writers that they deliberately placed spiritual symbols within the lyrics. Another song in *Pete's Dragon* mentions God as well, maybe another reason I love this film. Oh, to be back in the good ole' days!

The symbolism in this song compared to today's reading from Matthew is obvious. In his famous "Sermon on the Mount," Jesus tells us to be set apart from the world encouraging us to be salt and light. In the song, Nora wants her true love to be guided home through the dark and scary waters by not only the literal lighthouse she calls home, but also the burning flame inside her. Similarly, we should have a passion for Christ burning inside that others recognize and follow. We must be the candle, lighthouse or whatever light image you visualize that others see in the evil and darkness of the world. Jesus was our ultimate example of how to be a light even calling Himself the "light of the world." Just like Him, we must let our light shine before others, so they recognize our dedication and faith and desire to follow God themselves (Matt. 5:16).

PRAYER—Father, Help me, like Jesus, to have passion and boldness so that I too can be a light in this dark world. Send me souls to save and give me courage to do so. In His name, Amen.

TODAY I WILL...ask God's help in actively seeking one person I can be a light to. I will make it obvious that I'm a Christ follower and try to guide that person closer to God.

JANUARY 7 **Read ISAIAH 9:2-7**

A PRINCE'S GIFT OF PEACE

Disney Music – "Someday My Prince Will Come"—*Snow White and the Seven Dwarfs*

"And let the peace of Christ rule in your hearts, to which indeed you were called in one body. And be thankful."
—Colossians 3:15

I'm sure you're aware that *Snow White and the Seven Dwarfs* was Walt Disney's first animated feature-length film and began the legacy that continues today of some of the greatest films ever made. This film also began Disney's epic and forever-loved music library that also continues in the present age. Today's song is sung by Snow White as she laments how the prince she once met will one day return for her. Snow White was voiced by 18-year-old Adriana Caselotti when she interrupted a phone conversation her father was having. He was talking with a talent scout looking for someone to play this role, and Caselotti grabbed the phone and recommended herself. Walt Disney loved that her voice sounded like a 14-year-old and cast her for the iconic role.

In today's reading from Isaiah, we see one of many prophecies of the first coming of our Lord and Savior, Jesus Christ, in which He is given many memorable titles including "Prince of Peace." Not only did Jesus bring peace the first time, but He left us with this peace until He returns. In John 14:27, He assures us He left His peace so our hearts need not be troubled. I know from experience that God will give this peace in difficult times if you only seek and ask for it. Accepting Jesus in your heart provides this peace that passes all understanding (Php 4:6). Snow White sang this song dreaming of her prince returning someday. Our Prince has come once, but rest assured, He will also return again someday. In the meantime, He has left us with an amazing gift of peace that helps us greatly throughout life in this often-difficult world. What an amazing gift we should thank God for!

PRAYER—Dear Lord, I can't wait for my Prince to return and take me home. While I anxiously wait, thank you for the peace He left me by accepting Him into my heart. Please continue to provide me with this peace, especially in troubling times. Through Him, Amen.

TODAY I WILL...make a list of 10 Biblical titles given to Jesus including "Prince of Peace." I will then take the time to thank God for Him and the comfort that each title provides.

JANUARY 8 **Read EPHESIANS 4:1-13**

A FIGHT TO UNITE

Disney Music – "Let's Get Together"—*Parent Trap*

"Iron sharpens iron, and one man sharpens another."
—Proverbs 27:17

I've always found it amazing when movies or TV shows turn one actor into twins. Sometimes it's done so well, it's hard to believe it's the same person, especially when they interact or pass behind one another. Disney was a pioneer of this technology when they released the classic *Parent Trap* in 1961. This well-known included song was written by the infamous Sherman Brothers and featured young Hayley Mills singing with herself. It was done using double-tracking, an impressive feat this early on in filmmaking. When the song was released as a single, it rose all the way to #8 on the Billboard Top 100 chart.

In this comedic and clever live-action story from Disney, Hayley Mills sings this song with her "twin sister" as entertainment for their parents in an effort to reunite them. The lyrics speak of coming together in unity, an issue the twins must deal with themselves at the beginning when they meet for the first time and don't get along. Once they realize they're sisters, they form a strong bond working together to reunite their parents. Similarly, God's desire is that we "get together" in unity with our Christian family. In today's passage, Paul urges the Ephesians to maintain unity in the Spirit reminding them there is one faith, hope, baptism and Father. He preaches that unity is a goal we should all work diligently to attain. There are many other verses that attest to the benefits of Christians coming together in unity and love. We need each other to lean on, listen to and learn from. It's God's desire that we unite and build each other up instead of clashing in unnecessary disagreement and petty differences. Let's honor God by uniting with our spiritual brothers and sisters and by bringing as many others as possible into the family.

PRAYER—Most Holy Father, I thank you for my Christian family. Help us to come together in Your name, unite in love and use each other to lean on and strengthen our faith during hard times. In Jesus' holy name, Amen.

TODAY I WILL... decide at least one person to invite into God's family before January ends.

JANUARY 9 **Read I PETER 3:13-22**

IS YOUR ANSWER READY?

Disney Music – "Be Prepared"—*The Lion King*

"...honor Christ the Lord as holy, always being prepared to make a defense to anyone who asks you for a reason for the hope that is in you."

—I Peter 3:15

I've loved *The Lion King* since I first saw it in the theater...and then saw it a second time less than a week later. I love the story, music and characters as well as the Animal Kingdom show and Broadway musical that have evolved from it. There are many great songs included. This one might be slightly lesser known, but it's still a catchy tune with a clear message. "Be Prepared" is sung by the evil Scar to all his minion hyenas as he anticipates being king. In the film, the song was sung mostly by Jeremy Irons, the voice of Scar. However, Jim Cummings, the voice of Ed the hyena, had to sing some of the parts due to Irons' voice giving out during recording. As mentioned, the meaning is quite obvious. Scar is trying to rally the hyenas and motivate them to be ready and excited for what's coming next...his plan to steal the kingdom.

In a similar, but more positive way, we are told to anticipate something important. In today's reading, Peter teaches us to be prepared at all times to give a defense as to why we are so full of excitement and hope. As believers in Christ, we should be openly enthusiastic about the hope and joy we have being God's children. It should be so outwardly evident that others notice, become curious and ask the reason for our happiness and confidence of eternal life. We need to make sure we're always prepared to give that answer, one that will bring the same joy and excitement to others and give them a valid reason for wanting to serve God and accept Jesus as their Savior. So be prepared! Someone may be asking you soon. Is your answer ready?

PRAYER—Heavenly Father, thank you for the joy I have being Your child and the hope I receive through Your Son. Help it to be evident to others through my actions and words. Prepare me at all times to give a defense for my happiness and faith. Through Jesus, Amen.

TODAY I WILL... plan my defense! I will take time to prepare and possibly write out what I'm going to say when someone asks about my outward joy and evident hope in Christ.

JANUARY 10 **Read MATTHEW 7:1-5**

WHAT DO YOU SEE?

Disney Music – "Reflection"—*Mulan*

"As in water face reflects face, so the heart of man reflects the man."
—Proverbs 27:19

I heard a statistic that 75% of people don't like what they see in the mirror. That surprising and downright depressing high number most likely refers more often to what people see outwardly. What do you think the number would be if it referred to what's inside? In today's classic film, Mulan sings this well-known song reflecting on herself and who she is inside. Through the lyrics, she expresses feelings that she's a better person inside than how she appears to others. Did you know that this song gave rise to a certain young pop star by the name of Christina Aguilera? Just 17 at the time, Aguilera recorded a pop version which became very successful, funded her first album and provided notability among recognized writers and producers. Since that start, she has won multiple Grammys, is ranked among the world's best-selling artists and has a star on the Hollywood Walk of Fame.

So how's your reflection? Again, not so much on the outside, but what does your inside look like? Mulan knew deep down she was a good person with a lot of potential but had a hard time at first figuring out how to show it. In today's reading from Matthew, Jesus warns us not to judge the actions of others before reflecting on our own inside first. We often find fault with others without realizing an even bigger imperfection within ourselves. Before going around talking to others about the Word of God and His expectations, we must make sure we're right with Him ourselves. As the Proverb above states, what's inside our hearts reflects outwardly to show others who we truly are. Take time today to make sure your heart is pure, and you are reflecting nothing but Jesus outwardly to others. Then you can truly be proud of what you see in that mirror and know that God is too!

PRAYER –Lord, help me to reflect daily on who I am. Through self-evaluation, help me to make changes to keep my heart pure and reflect Christ to others. Through Him, Amen.

TODAY I WILL... look in a mirror for several minutes reflecting on who I am inside. If there are changes that need to be made, I will change today and be proud of what's staring back at me.

JANUARY 11 **Read I CORINTHIANS 11:23-26**

DO THIS IN MEMORY OF ME

Disney Music – "Remember Me"—*Coco*

"And they remembered his words..."
—Luke 24:8

How good is your memory? We all tend to remember things differently. For instance, I'm pretty good at remembering important events and dates while my wife is better at remembering people and names. As time goes by, we all tend to struggle with remembering certain things. Today's song come from my favorite Pixar film and is basically the theme of the whole movie. It's sung many times by several different characters but most notably by young Miguel near the end as he tries to persuade his great-grandmother, Coco to remember her life and family. The song was written by the incredibly talented team of Robert and Kristen Lopez who developed the music for *Frozen* and "Finding Nemo – the Musical." This song won an Oscar making Robert Lopez the only two-time EGOT (Emmy, Grammy, Oscar, Tony) winner in history!

If you've seen *Coco*, you no doubt remember the ending scene where Miguel sings this song, desperately hoping his great-grandmother will remember her father so he won't disappear forever in the Land of the Dead. It's important to remember certain things from our past... the instructions of parents, the lessons of teachers and the advice of mentors. But remembering everything about Jesus is no doubt most important. In today's passage from I Corinthians, Paul reminds us that Jesus Himself set up communion as a way to remember Him and the sacrifice He made for us. In 2 Timothy 2:8, Paul advises again to remember Jesus and His resurrection from the dead. It is vital in our spiritual walk to not only get to know Jesus and learn everything about Him, but to also remember always His life, His love, His words and His death. Keeping Him in the forefront of our minds will guide us always in the right direction.

PRAYER—Holy Father, help me to remember Jesus in all I do. Thank you for Your Word that tells me about Him and His teachings which are the guidebook for my life. Help me to never forget what He did for me on that cross. I love You and Your loving Son. In His name, Amen.

TODAY I WILL... remember and write down at least 5 things Jesus said to us. I will focus on these and all His teachings daily.

JANUARY 12 **Read LUKE 21:29-36**

DON'T CLOSE YOUR EYES

Disney Music – "Stay Awake"—*Mary Poppins*

"Therefore, stay awake, for you do not know on what day your Lord is coming."
—Matthew 24:42

What's the longest you've stayed awake? I have friends that claim to have stayed awake for nearly 48 hours. Not me! I think 24 is my record, but I probably even dozed briefly during that time. I find it quite difficult to stay awake for long periods of time. Today's song may be unfamiliar, although it certainly comes from a well-known, beloved film. "Stay Awake" is a lullaby sung by Mary Poppins, played by Julie Andrews, to the children after they protest going to bed. The song, of course, lulls them to sleep by the end. There were plans to delete this song completely from the film until Andrews fought back. She wrote a letter of concern to the author of the *Mary Poppins* books who insisted the song remain. Andrews also wanted to sing it in a particular soothing, soft voice and used nearly fifty takes to get it perfect.

Part of the lyrics read "stay awake, don't close your eyes." In today's passage from Luke's Gospel, Jesus also warns us to "stay awake at all times," reminding us that one day this world will end, and we'll all have to stand before Him in judgement. Obviously, He doesn't expect us to literally never sleep. Instead, He's advising us to always be prepared for His return, the world's end and our transition into eternity. Scripture makes it clear that when that happens, all people will be divided into two groups: those that are eternally saved in Heaven and those that are forever condemned to hell. We must "stay awake" by always keeping our lives right with God since we don't know what that ending date will be. Make sure you're always ready no matter when Christ returns, and don't fall asleep to following God's Word at all times.

PRAYER—Father, help me to always stay awake and be prepared for Your Son's return. Keep me from falling asleep and giving in to the evils of this world. I can't wait to see Jesus returning. Thank you for that promise and hope. In the name of Christ, Amen.

TODAY I WILL...make sure I am ready for Christ's return. Will you be excited if He comes by today's end? Do you know where He will send you? Are you awake and always ready?

JANUARY 13 **Read I PETER 4:7-11**

ARE YOU USING ALL YOUR GIFTS FOR HIM?

Disney Music – "Something There"— *Beauty and the Beast*

"Do not neglect the gift you have..."
—I Timothy 4:14

What are you good at? We all have areas of talent where we shine, but have you ever really explored ALL the skills God gave you? Once again, we are focusing on a lesser-known song from a very popular film. "Something There" was actually used as a last-minute replacement for "Human Again," a song cut from the original film that was later added back for the stage and live-action versions. Today's song is sung by several characters but mainly Belle and the Beast, the only time where we get to hear him sing. During this song, they begin to realize feelings for each other and see things in each other previously unrecognized.

This leads to a question for you to consider...are there abilities you have that you've never recognized or used before? Are there hidden talents, skills, or strengths you could use to serve God that you haven't even explored yet? In today's reading from I Peter, we are told to not only use the gifts God gave us to serve but also to figure out where we shine best and use it to His glory. God made us all different on purpose, each with various gifts. It's our job to figure out what those gifts are and how best to use them for Him. As Paul said in the verse above, don't neglect any of the gifts or talents God has blessed you with. There may be something you don't even realize yet that you can do to serve Him. Try some new things, explore your strengths and glorify God daily in as many ways as possible.

PRAYER—Dear God, help me to discover all the talents You've given me. If there's something I can do better to serve You, please give me the courage and boldness to find and use it to the fullest extent. Thank you for the gifts you've blessed me with. In Jesus' name, Amen.

TODAY I WILL...make a list of my known strengths and gifts. Beside each one, I will write down how I'm using it to glorify God. I will also explore at least one new talent to see if I might be able to use it in His service.

JANUARY 14 **Read PSALM 32:1-11**

GET BACK UP

Disney Music – "Try Everything"—*Zootopia*

"The Lord…is patient toward you, not wishing that any should perish, but that all should reach repentance."
—2 Peter 3:9

Have you ever fallen? I remember one time falling down a flight of stairs leading to my basement. It hurt pretty bad and even caused me to pass out when I tried to get up. But guess what? I did get back up and still take those stairs daily. Today's song from *Zootopia* is all about that concept. The title is slightly deceptive as most of the lyrics speak of getting back up after you've fallen. In fact, part of the lyrics read, "I keep on falling down. I keep on hitting the ground. But I always get up now to see what's next. Birds don't just fly. They fall down and get up. Nobody learns without getting it wrong." I love the *Zootopia* scene where this song is first played while new officer, Judy Hopps rides the train through the different lands toward the big city. The song was nominated for a Grammy and sung by Columbian singer, Shakira.

The Bible speaks often about this song's theme, getting back up after you fall…into sin that is. It's called repentance. Today's psalm is also one of repentance. David wrote it remembering his sin. At first, he kept silent and was plagued with guilt. However, when he got up, repented and confessed, he was able to feel the Lord's forgiveness and some much-needed relief. We all sin. The important thing is not to let sin ruin your life. When you find yourself caught up in it, stop, change directions and get back on the right path. Like the song says, you don't learn without sometimes getting it wrong. We're so blessed to have a loving God offering forgiveness upon repentance. He's always willing to take us back not wishing any to perish in sin.

PRAYER—Lord, I want to get back up and repent from all sin today. I want to be always right with you remaining on the narrow path to Heaven. Forgive me of all sin. Through Jesus, Amen.

TODAY I WILL…Repent and confess any sins aloud to God. I will promise Him to always get back up when sin knocks me down and never give up on my relationship with Him.

JANUARY 15 **Read PSALM 104:1-24**

MY, OH MY, LOOK AROUND!

Disney Music – "Zip-a-Dee-Doo-Dah"—*Song of the South*

"He has made everything beautiful in its time."
—Ecclesiastes 3:11a

Do you enjoy hiking? Exploring? Walking around in nature? Today's song is hopefully more familiar and speaks fondly of the beauty in what we see each day. "Zip-a-Dee-Doo-Dah" was written for the 1946 film, *Song of the South*. The word itself was supposedly invented by Walt Disney who had a fondness for nonsensical words. If you think hard enough, you may be able to remember some other silly Disney song titles (hint—think *Cinderella* and *Mary Poppins*). This song was only Disney's second ever Oscar win for Best Original Song after *Pinocchio's* "When You Wish Upon a Star." It is sung by Uncle Remus in a memorable scene, one of the last shot during production. There was apparently little money left in the budget, and so Walt himself suggested a close-up shot of Uncle Remus with various lighting, saving both time and money.

These devotionals have already mentioned the evils and darkness of the world, especially when you consider the amount of sin and disobedience of God's Word. But the physical world itself is stunningly beautiful and a wonderful blessing and gift from God. There are so many incredible and majestic landscapes God has created for us to enjoy, and sometimes we just need to get out and appreciate what He's made. Today's psalm is a bit lengthy but read it carefully. It speaks fondly of the Earth's beauty with some wonderful descriptions of picturesque scenery. It also reminds us just how many different and breathtaking sights God has made. Make sure you take time often to just stop and look around. Go exploring. Visit some new places of beauty you've never seen. No matter what, spend time daily thanking God for giving us this amazing and magnificent world to enjoy during our short time here.

PRAYER—Dear Lord, thank you for giving me such a beautiful world to enjoy. Help me to take the time to look around and appreciate it. In Your Son's name, Amen.

TODAY I WILL...take an extended walk. Try to find some beautiful scenery or place in nature where you can walk, look around, pray and thank God for what you are seeing.

JANUARY 16 **Read JOHN 13:1-15**

THE SHADOW GAME

Disney Music – "I Wanna Be Like You"—*Jungle Book*

"Be imitators of me, as I am of Christ."
—I Corinthians 11:1

Ever played the "shadow game," copying what someone else says or does. I used to drive my two sisters crazy growing up with it. Maybe I need to do a reboot and bring it back at our next family function. I'm sure they'd enjoy that. That game may be annoying to the victim but is the idea behind today's song and spiritual thought. This song from the Disney classic, *The Jungle Book,* is sung by King Louie as he tells the boy, Mowgli he wants to be just like him. You may know the lyrics, "Oobee do. I wanna be like you. I wanna walk like you, talk like you too." Written by the Sherman brothers, it has been covered by many different artists since. I actually prefer the version from the 2016 live-action film. The original was also used in a British anti-smoking commercial showing children mimicking their parents. Check it out on YouTube.

I love the story in today's reading from John. It demonstrates the fact that Jesus came here to serve and show compassion on man. Philippians 2 assures us of that. Washing the feet of 12 other men would've been a filthy job that would've surprised all in the room...except Jesus. We even see that Peter didn't want Jesus touching his feet. But Jesus did it anyway to demonstrate to the Apostles, and to us, how we are to act as His followers. That doesn't mean we have to wash feet necessarily, but we do have to constantly look for ways to serve others and subsequently spread the message of Christ. We should desire each day to be more like Him and do everything in our power to imitate Him including this incredible act of service. Play the shadow game with Jesus every day! You should wanna walk like Him and talk like Him too!

PRAYER—Lord, help me to imitate Christ in all I do. I want to do everything He did. Help me to discover ways to serve others and "wash feet" daily. In His name, Amen.

TODAY I WILL...wash feet! Before I sleep tonight, I will serve someone new whether it be a physical act, an encouraging word or letter, a friendly call or even monetarily.

JANUARY 17 **Read REVELATION 12:7-12**

YOU'D BETTER BEWARE

Disney Music – "Cruella De Vil"—*101 Dalmatians*

"He was a murderer from the beginning, and does not stand in the truth, because there is no truth in him. When he lies, he speaks out of his own character, for he is a liar and the father of lies."

—John 8:44

I bet you could've guessed the Biblical application of today's song without even reading the passage. After all, the name is right there in the song's title. Cruella De Vil is of course the villain from 1961's *101 Dalmatians*. She's been notoriously ranked as one of Disney's most evil and terrifying villains. She's been played by notable actors Glenn Close, in the 1996 live-action remake, and Emma Stone in a recent 2021 reimagining. She was originally voiced by Betty Lou Gerson who mostly worked on radio as a voice actress but was also heard as the narrator in Disney's original *Cinderella* and a small acting role in *Mary Poppins*.

Today's reading from Revelation describes the battle in Heaven when Satan was defeated and thrown down to this world to take over and deceive man. He is unfortunately alive and well today, still trying to pull us away from God any chance he gets. If you read the lyrics to today's song, they certainly describe the vile Cruella, but they also nearly perfectly describe our real-life villain who is even more terrifying. Look at some of them: "If (s)he doesn't scare you, no evil thing will. All innocent children had better beware. (S)he's like a spider waiting for the kill." It's a perfect depiction of the enemy of God who watches us and waits to pounce when we are most vulnerable. He is active in constantly tempting us and working hard to lead us to sin. I promise you he exists, is energetic and extremely evil; and he's coming after you and me. Resist him! Don't let him control your life by falling into any temptations he throws your way. Lean on God and ask His help to defeat the advances of the deceitful and devious "DeVil."

PRAYER—Dear God, please don't let the devil win in my life. Help me to realize, recognize and resist his attempts on me. Keep me strong and grounded in my dedication to You. In Jesus' name, Amen.

TODAY I WILL...examine my life and make sure Satan doesn't have a hold of any part. If he does, I will actively work immediately to remove him and stand up to his future efforts.

JANUARY 18 **Read JOHN 15:18-27**

TOO MANY THINGAMABOBS

Disney Music – "Part of Your World"—*The Little Mermaid*

"Do not love the world or the things in the world. If anyone loves the world, the love of the Father is not in him."
—I John 2:15

Do you have any collections? I have a large Disney collection I'm quite proud of. In today's song, Ariel, (a.k.a. the Little Mermaid) sings about all her "gadgets and gizmos" collected from the surface but makes it quite clear it's not enough. She wants more and even longs to be a part of the world where all that "stuff" is from. This was of course originally sung by the voice of Ariel, Jodi Benson, who requested the lights in the studio be dimmed so she could imagine singing it underwater like Ariel. The song was almost cut for fear it would be too boring to children. Thankfully, it remained and has proven to be one of Disney's most beloved songs.

There's nothing wrong with enjoying the things of this world. However, if we, like Ariel, desire to be a part of it too much, it can cause problems as it did for her. This world is not our permanent home. It's just a short stop on our journey to Heaven. We're instructed clearly not to love this world or anything in it. In today's passage, Jesus Himself reminds us we're not part of the world and even tells us to expect the world to hate us because of it. Too many people get caught up in worldly desires, always craving more, and forget it's the next world they should be more concerned about. Conforming to the world and the unfortunate evils within will only lead to destruction. Yes, like Ariel, I want more for my Disney collection, but in the end, that stuff won't matter. Instead, I must desire more to build up my collection of treasures in Heaven which will be much better than anything found down here. I wish to be, plan to be and will be a part of God's world. Please join me!

PRAYER—Lord, I want to be a part of Your world in Heaven forever. Help me to get there and not love this world so much that I forget about You and my true purpose. In Christ, Amen.

TODAY I WILL...make sure I'm not part of this world. I will begin a new collection building up treasures in Heaven (Matt 6:20) and keep either a physical or mental list of what's in it.

JANUARY 19 **Read REVELATION 21:1-7**

A NEW WORLD BEYOND COMPARE

Disney Music – "A Whole New World"—*Aladdin*

"For he was looking forward to the city that has foundations, whose designer and builder is God."
—Hebrews 11:10

You may have noticed we're still in January and have already focused several times on the world...both positively and negatively. Make no mistake, the world is both. It's a beautiful creation and blessing from God for us to enjoy as we do His work. At the same time, it's also full of evil, and we must be careful not to love it too much as discussed yesterday. Today, we're just gonna leave it altogether. This iconic song from one of my favorite movies not only won an Oscar but was the only Disney song ever to win the Grammy for "Song of the Year." Aladdin and Jasmine sing this memorable duet while soaring high above the Earth on a flying carpet. They harmonize about experiencing a "whole new world" together since they've now found each other. We instead are discussing a completely different world...one that's more incredible than you could ever imagine.

Today's passage from Revelation describes beautifully the "whole new world" I'm referring to and just how amazing it will be. How anyone could read those words about Heaven and not do everything in their power to get there is beyond me. The dwelling place of God where He will be with His people! No tears or mourning! No death or pain! And it will all be eternal. Forever! Don't you want to be there to experience that?! Yes, there are many blessings in this world including times of happiness, laughter, joy and fulfillment. But I'm telling you, the whole new world God has waiting for us will be so much better and won't even compare to this one! Study His Word daily so you know how to get there. Just don't miss it!

PRAYER—Holy Father, thank you for this world. I am blessed and appreciate so much the times of happiness here. However, I know there is a whole new and much better world waiting for me with you someday. Help me to get there. That's all that matters. In Jesus' name, Amen.

TODAY I WILL...write down the three most beautiful places I've ever seen on Earth. I will then realize and thank God that a new world is available to me that will always top that list.

JANUARY 20 **Read PROVERBS 1:8-19**

BE WEIRD!

Disney Music – "Stand Out"—*A Goofy Movie*

"Do not be conformed to this world..."
—Romans 12:2

We kinda had a "world" theme going on the last couple days I didn't plan on. But let's go with it and complete the trilogy today. Two days ago, we discussed the dangers of wanting to be part of this world. Yesterday we focused on a better world awaiting us. Now we're coming back down to Earth to talk more about God's desires for us while here. Today's film and song may be unfamiliar. "Stand Out" is performed by Goofy's son, Max, to impress his schoolmates and especially his love interest. The song was actually sung by R&B recording artist, Tevin Campbell who performed two songs for the soundtrack. Check out YouTube to watch Max singing this song and notice a hidden Ariel when the principal halts the hijacked performance.

The song's lyrics, and obvious title, make it quite clear what Max is attempting. The chorus says, "...stand out above the crowd, even if I gotta shout out loud. 'Til mine is the only face you see. Gonna stand out 'til you notice me." Max tries hard throughout the film to stand out and be different so he'll be noticed and accepted. And while his reasons may be flawed, the idea of standing out is Biblical and something we should all aspire to do. We are called by God to be different and not conform to this world. We should be so unlike the rest of the world that others notice and have no choice but to wonder what makes us that way. We've already discussed others noticing our outward joy and hope in Christ, but make sure they also observe your unwillingness to conform to the sins of the world. Don't give in just to please others or "follow the crowd." Be different! Be weird even! Let people see the difference in you. I promise they'll notice which will assist in fulfilling your obligation to bring others to Christ. Stand out!

PRAYER—Lord, thank you for calling me to be different. Give me continued strength not to conform. Help others to notice my weirdness and use me to start conversations about You. Through Christ, Amen.

TODAY I WILL...stand out! I will figure out an additional obvious way I can be different from the world and noticed by others.

JANUARY 21 **Read EPHESIANS 3:14-21**

LET HIM LIVE IN THERE...ALWAYS

Disney Music – "You'll Be in My Heart"—*Tarzan*

"And you show that you are a letter from Christ delivered by us, written not with ink but with the Spirit of the living God, not on tablets of stone but on tablets of human hearts."

—2 Corinthians 3:3

Have you ever thought about how violent and slightly twisted that "Rock-a-Bye Baby" song is? I mean the cradle WITH BABY falls out of the tree, and it's supposed to be a lullaby to lull babies to sleep? No offense, but if babies understood it, I think they'd be quite terrified. In my opinion, today's song makes a much better lullaby, as it was originally intended. "You'll Be in My Heart" was written by singer/songwriter Phil Collins as a lullaby for his daughter, Lily. He was first chosen to be a part of *Tarzan* because he's a drummer by nature and the producers wanted a strong beat for the soundtrack of this jungle flick. His role was later expanded with him performing several songs on the movie's superb soundtrack.

In this delightful Disney film, today's song is also sung as a lullaby to comfort baby Tarzan while his adoptive gorilla mother holds him. She's trying to stop his crying and assure him that she will always love and protect him. At the end she sings that he'll be in her heart, and we hear the word "always" whispered, possibly the voice of Tarzan's real mother who is tragically killed near the film's beginning. This endearing lullaby scene and song title reminded me of today's reading from Ephesians. Within those verses, we learn that someone very special lives in our hearts once we follow His teachings and accept Him. Having Christ live inside us gives us a firm foundation providing us with the love and strength needed to remain faithful and follow the Lord's will throughout our lives. It's also yet another incredible gift from God for all those who truly love Him and follow His Word. I'm so honored, blessed and grateful to say to Jesus, "You'll be in my heart... always." I pray you can say the same.

PRAYER—Dear God, thank you so much for giving me Your Spirit and allowing Your Son to live within my heart. It so comforting to have Him there to guide me always. In Him, Amen.

TODAY I WILL...take the necessary steps to get Jesus inside my heart if He's not there already. I'll continue to do whatever necessary to keep Him there, forever and always!

JANUARY 22 **Read GALATIANS 6:1-10**

NEVER GIVE UP

Disney Music – "Dig a Little Deeper"— *The Princess and the Frog*

"...for the righteous falls seven times and rises again, but the wicked stumble in times of calamity."
—Proverbs 24:16

Ever feel overwhelmed in life? It's understandable. Life is hard and there are times when it may seem easier just to give up. In this film's memorable story, Tiana and Naveen refuse to give up even though they face a difficult and seemingly endless journey. Along the way, they meet Mama Odie, a voodoo priestess who sings this song, encouraging them to press on and discover who they truly are. Mama Odie was voiced by Jenifer Lewis who started on Broadway and as a backup singer for Bette Midler. If you watch carefully during this song, you can catch her character tossing a hidden Disney Easter egg...Aladdin's magic lamp.

In today's reading, Paul talks about facing difficult times in life and begins by encouraging us to help each other with those burdens. But also notice verse 9 where he says, "let us not grow weary of doing good, for in due season we will reap, if we do not give up." Being a faithful Christian is downright hard and you may feel an urge to quit at times. Facing persecution, temptation, trials and suffering makes it sometimes difficult to put forth the effort. During those times, however, it's important to "dig a little deeper" and press on. Paul also reminds us in the verse above that the righteous always get back up, even after falling many times. As a follower of God, you are promised some difficult battles and even suffering. When that happens, dig deep, get back up and keep going! Don't give up! You don't have to "find out" who you are like Mama Odie sings. You already know who you are! You are God's child with an incredible and very worthwhile reward promised to you! Never stop fighting! Dig deep!

PRAYER—Lord, life is hard! If I ever consider giving up, please help me to dig deep and press on because I know what's coming will be worth it. Thank you for that never-ending hope. Through His name, Amen.

TODAY I WILL...write down the 5 things that make life most difficult for me. I will present them to God, give Him control and vow to press on regardless while never giving up on Him.

JANUARY 23 **Read ACTS 9:1-18**

STOP AND SEE THE LIGHT

Disney Music – "I See the Light"—*Tangled*

"...God is light, and in Him is no darkness at all."
—I John 1:5

Imagine walking down a quiet, unfamiliar road at night. Zero light. Pitch dark. And then it happens...a bright, blinding light from above. This song seems like it was written in correlation with today's reading from Acts. It was of course instead written as a romantic ballad between Rapunzel and Flynn Rider and sung by their voice actors, Mandy Moore and Zachary Levi. The song was hailed by critics mainly due to the visually stunning scene in which it occurs. Over 45,000 lanterns were used to create the picturesque rowboat scene. Originally, a grand and Broadway style number had been written for the same scene, but directors didn't want to take away from the striking images and opted for this gentler and more tender song.

Can you imagine being Saul, seeing that bright light and hearing the one and only voice of Jesus? Again, this song, and especially the chorus, appears to match perfectly with this notable Bible story. Note the end of the chorus which says, "...and the world has somehow shifted. All at once everything looks different now that I see you." I think Saul, soon to be Paul, could have echoed the same about Jesus after that unforgettable night on the dark road. That bright light encounter was certainly eye-opening (pun intended) to say the least. It transformed an evil murderer into one of the most faithful examples we've ever had. Sometimes we all need to have a similar light experience. If you ever find yourself heading down a dark road spiritually, stop and see the light! Help others to see it as well. God is light, and His Son is always the answer we need to find the Way when life gets dark and dreary. The world will definitely look different once we see and know Him. And our future will shine much, much brighter!

PRAYER—God, thank You for being the light shining brightly in this dark world. Help me to see the light of Your Son if I ever wander down a dark road. In His name, Amen.

TODAY I WILL...not only make an effort to SEE the light of Jesus by reading more about Him, but I will also work hard to BE a light to those around me. I will allow the example of Christ to shine through me in all things.

JANUARY 24 **Read ECCLESIASTES 4:9-12**

TWO ARE BETTER THAN ONE

Disney Music – "Life's a Happy Song"—*The Muppets*

"A man of many companions may come to ruin, but there is a friend who sticks closer than a brother."
—Proverbs 18:24

I immediately loved *The Muppets* the first time I saw it upon its release in 2011, the first theatrical Muppet film in 12 years. I've always loved the Muppets themselves and to see them revived in film for my sons' generation was thrilling. I also fell in love with this song sung near the beginning by Gary, played by Jason Segal who co-wrote and starred in the film, and his newly-introduced, Muppet brother, Walter. I even used the song in one of our many cheesy, family Disney trip videos. Check out YouTube to see my sons singing it throughout the Orlando airport, Disney resort and parks. Yep, their dad used to love to embarrass them (and still does). The Muppets also performed this song on a 2011 episode of *Dancing with the Stars*.

"Life's a Happy Song" is a very catchy tune sung between brothers. Through the lyrics, they make it clear that life's a lot easier when you have someone to share it with, the tagline being "life's a happy song when there's someone by my side to sing along." I also love today's passage from Ecclesiastes which reiterates the same message. It's already been mentioned many times in this book how difficult life can be. It's much easier when you have someone special you can talk to, share with and lean on when needed. God gave us each other to enjoy life with but also for help during hard times. As previously mentioned, we are taught to bear each other's burdens. It may be a spouse, sibling or friend, but make sure you have someone specific you can go to and share life with, the highs and the lows. If you already have someone like that, thank God for that person and let them know they are appreciated.

PRAYER—Holy Father, thank you for giving me special people in life to share it with, in good times and bad. Help me to share the burdens of anyone in need, especially those I am close to. In His name, Amen.

TODAY I WILL...think about specific individuals in my life that fit the descriptions above. I will thank them personally and tell them how special they are.

JANUARY 25 **Read GENESIS 3:1-7**

ARE THERE STRINGS ON YOU?

Disney Music – "I've Got No Strings"—*Pinocchio*

"But I am afraid that as the serpent deceived Eve by his cunning, your thoughts will be led astray from a sincere and pure devotion to Christ."
—2 Corinthians 11:3

Ever seen *The Sound of Music*? It's not technically a Disney movie, although it's available on Disney Plus as of this writing since they bought 20th Century Fox. My favorite scene is probably the puppet show, and I remember as a child really wanting a similar stringed puppet. In Disney's classic *Pinocchio*, the former marionette himself sings today's song after losing his strings and becoming a real boy, feeling so excited to be freed. Like yesterday's song, this one was also featured on a special Disney episode of *Dancing with the Stars*. It was also used by boy band, NSYNC and has been covered by many artists including Barbra Streisand and Diana Ross.

Have you ever played with a marionette puppet? Whether or not you have, you're probably aware that the puppet on those strings is totally at the mercy of the one holding them. The puppet master controls all movements, and the puppet must do whatever he requires. Did you know that the world is full of stringed puppets? Are you one of them? In Genesis 3, we learn that the devil was more crafty and cunning than any other creature. With his schemes, he tricked Eve into taking the forbidden fruit, opening the world up to sin. Today, he still has control of so many people lost in their worldly passions and sinful ways. Even Paul was worried about those of his time telling them in the verse above that he feared they would be led astray by Satan just as Eve was. I hope and pray that he doesn't have strings on you. If he does, take immediate steps to get those strings cut. God is ready and willing to assist with that. Make sure you can echo Pinocchio and say, "I had strings, but now I'm free. There are no strings on me!"

PRAYER—Father, I never want Satan to have control of me. Cut away any strings he has attached to me and help me to always resist his attempts to get me back. In Jesus' name, Amen.

TODAY I WILL...do a self-check for any strings Satan has attached to me. I will talk to God, ask His help in getting free and refuse to allow Satan any control in my life.

JANUARY 26 **Read MATTHEW 25:1-13**

A PANICKY RABBIT

Disney Music – "I'm Late"—*Alice in Wonderland*

"You also must be ready, for the Son of Man is coming at an hour you do not expect."
—Luke 12:40

I have lots of pet peeves, but one of the biggest is being late to anything: church, work, a movie, a family function, basically anything with a set start time. And especially a Disney park! We are "rope droppers" for sure! *Alice in Wonderland* features many intriguing and unusual characters including the White Rabbit, voiced by Bill Thompson. He also voiced Mr. Smee in *Peter Pan*, King Hubert in *Sleeping Beauty* and several dogs and other characters in *Lady and the Tramp*. In this film, he sang today's song proclaiming that he was "late for a very important date." Interestingly, we see this rabbit several times throughout the film making this declaration of lateness, but we never discover what event or "date" he's actually late for?

The White Rabbit is obviously distraught and upset that he's late for... something. As mentioned, I also get a little stressed if I'm late for anything. You may be the opposite and not worry too much about a little tardiness, but in today's reading from Matthew, Jesus tells a parable to teach us about something we absolutely CAN'T be late for. He tells of ten virgins waiting to meet a bridegroom, who aren't prepared with enough oil for their lamps. When they leave to buy more, they miss the bridegroom's appearance altogether, find the door shut and are told they are not known. This is an obvious reference to Christ's return. He's the bridegroom we MUST always be ready for. All of us, even myself on occasion, are late at times to various events, appointments or activities, but the second coming of Jesus is something we simply must be on time and ready for. We have no idea when it'll happen and are even told it will occur unexpectedly. When it does happen, don't be unprepared and absent like the ten virgins or even late and panicky like that rabbit. Be there! Be ready! Be excited! But don't be late!

PRAYER—God, I can't wait for Christ's return so He can take me home. Help me to be ready at all times. I don't want to miss or even be late when He appears. In His holy name, Amen.

TODAY I WILL...do a mental checklist and make sure I am ready if Christ returns today.

JANUARY 27 **Read I CORINTHIANS 4:14-21**

WHEREVER HE MAY GO

Disney Music – "Following the Leader"—*Peter Pan*

"If anyone serves me, he must follow me; and where I am, there will my servant be also."
—John 12:26

Remember "Simon Says?" We used to play it a lot as a kid, even during P.E. at school. It seemed like such an easy game but always proved trickier than expected. "Following the Leader" is one of the many classic songs from 1953's *Peter Pan*, an iconic and memorable Disney film that was plagued with several issues. For one thing, Roy Disney disagreed with Walt about the super high price tag of $3 million that eventually rose to $4 million. Thankfully, the film did well and made that figure back many times over. Secondly, Walt was unhappy with the finished product, especially the character of Peter Pan himself whom he felt was unlikable.

"Following the Leader" is sung with a kind of "Simon Says" feel as young John leads the Lost Boys, encouraging them to shadow him. What about you? Are there others you try to follow? Is there someone at work or school you imitate to be successful? Do you follow your parents' instructions in taking care of your own household? Is there a church mentor you emulate to keep your spiritual life in line? We all need good leaders to follow in every aspect of our lives. In I Corinthians, Paul encourages the people to be like him as he follows Jesus. He also mentions sending them Timothy to demonstrate the ways of Christ, our obvious perfect example to copy. We should all strive to follow Jesus in every way possible. He even says so Himself in the verse above from John. If we want to be God's true servant, we must act, say and do as Jesus did. Like the song says, we must be "following the leader, wherever he may go." Maybe you don't play "Simon Says" anymore, but I strongly encourage you at all times to play "Jesus Says."

PRAYER—Father, thank you for giving me mentors to guide me in all aspect of life. Help me to choose Jesus as my ultimate leader and follow Him in every way possible, so I can be a dedicated servant of yours. In the name of Jesus, Amen.

TODAY I WILL... follow the leader. I will look up at least one thing Jesus said and another that He did and make an effort to imitate both today.

JANUARY 28 **Read MATTHEW 28:16-20**

SPREAD THE NEWS

Disney Music – "The World Will Know"—*Newsies*

"And he said to them, "Go into all the world and proclaim the gospel to the whole creation."
—Mark 16:15

"Extra! Extra! Read all about it!" Ever heard that? You have if you've ridden Epcot's Spaceship Earth as an animatronic newsboy shouts it out. That tagline of the past was used to sell newspapers and meant something important had happened. Today's song and film might again be unfamiliar but allow me to recommend it. The soundtrack, both catchy and memorable, includes this song the "Newsies" sing when they decide to go on strike. Loosely based on the 1899 New York newsboys strike, this film was an initial flop, but gained a cult following later and found great success as an adapted Broadway musical. It won two Tony awards including Best Original Score and was nominated for several others. During this particular song, the boys proclaim that the world will know about their cause as they band together to make a statement.

I chose this song because the title reminded me of the well-known passage above from Matthew. Called the "Great Commission," this was a pivotal moment after Christ's resurrection when He gave these important final instructions. Before He ascended into Heaven, Jesus gave this charge which is a directive to us all that includes going into the world, proclaiming the Gospel, making disciples, baptizing them into the Father, Son and Spirit and teaching them to follow His ways always. If we do this faithfully and properly, the world will know about Him. We can make a difference. I have much respect for those who take these commands literally becoming missionaries throughout the world. However, we can also follow these teachings in our own hometown. We must all do our part to spread the Gospel making sure the world will know about Jesus. So "read all about it" and spread the word...the Word of God!

PRAYER—Lord, I want all the world to know about You. Help me to do my part, follow the instructions of Jesus and spread the Gospel. Through Him, Amen.

TODAY I WILL... spread the Word! I will follow the Great Commission of Jesus and figure out a new way to spread the Gospel to others. I will also send a note of thanks to a missionary or someone who teaches Christ on a regular basis.

JANUARY 29 **Read JOHN 9:1-41**

HELP ME TO SEE

Disney Music – "I Can See Clearly Now"—*Cool Runnings*

"Open my eyes, that I may behold wondrous things out of your law."
—Psalm 119:18

Have you ever thought about what a blessing the gift of sight is? Obviously, there are some that have impaired vision or even no sight at all. For those of us still blessed with good vision, God has given us many amazing things to see, but are we truly seeing all He has to offer? Today's song was originally recorded way back in 1972 by Johnny Nash. However, another adaptation was created in 1993 when this Disney film came out. Jamaican reggae singer, Jimmy Cliff recorded a version for *Cool Runnings* that reached #18 on the Billboard top 100 chart and was even #1 in several countries. The song has also been covered by many other notable artists such as Ray Charles and Josh Groban.

Today's reading from John 9 is long, but I encourage you to read the whole story of a man born blind and miraculously healed by Jesus. It's easy to see the joy the man has after receiving sight for the first time. He is grateful and becomes a believer in Christ. Jesus uses the event to teach that He came into the world so that we can "see" His example and the proper way to follow God. Seeing the physical beauty of God's world is a blessing and one we should thank God for if we still have the ability. But there's something more important for us to see that doesn't necessarily require physical sight. We must ask God to help us see His will and purpose for our life as is requested in the psalm above. God has a plan and purpose for each of us. Ask Him to open your eyes and see what He requires of you so you can see it clearly now.

PRAYER—Father, thank you for sight. I'm grateful for the beauty of the Earth and all you've created to see. But please open my eyes to Your will and purpose for me so I can truly see what you need me to be and do. In Jesus' name, Amen.

TODAY I WILL... thank God for sight if I'm still blessed with it. I will take time to look around at His beauty, but also ask Him to open my eyes to a greater appreciation and new vision of what He wants me to be.

JANUARY 30 **Read LUKE 21:10-19**

GET OFF THE ISLAND

Disney Music – "How Far I'll Go"—*Moana*

"...fear not, for I am with you; be not dismayed, for I am your God; I will strengthen you, I will help you, I will uphold you with my righteous right hand."
—Isaiah 41:10

I recently saw a list of available jobs on Disney's private island, Castaway Cay, and I'll admit...the temptation was real. There are a few dozen people who live and work there. Due to the recent pandemic, some have been living there for over a year without any visits from ships or tourists. That would be my dream. Moana had the opposite dream singing today's song. Through the lyrics, it's obvious she was determined instead to get off her island as she felt a higher calling and purpose. If you've seen the film, you know that she does indeed play a vital role after escaping the island. This song was written by Lin-Manuel Miranda of *Hamilton* fame. It won a Grammy and was nominated for an Oscar and Golden Globe but unfortunately lost both.

Luke recorded some valuable words of Jesus warning us of difficult times ahead such as wars, disasters and pestilences, which ironically, some have speculated as the recent Covid outbreak. Christ also mentions persecution and hatred we will no doubt face for His sake. As Christians and followers of God's Word, we will be harassed and mistreated, especially when our beliefs go against the current trends of society. But notice the last two verses when Christ assures us not one hair of our head will perish, and we will succeed by our endurance. It is therefore vital we endure and stay the course! Regardless of any trials faced, we must persevere and have determination to succeed like Moana did in getting off her island. God promises protection and strength so keep fighting against the world, find determination to continue no matter what and get off your island to find God's purpose for you. You will be rewarded for how far you go!

PRAYER—Lord, thank you for preparing me for persecution I will face as Your follower. Help me not to lose faith or the determination to always keep going. I know You have a purpose for me so help me to see it through and go as far as You need me to go. In Christ I pray, Amen.

TODAY I WILL... get off any islands I'm stuck on. I will find the motivation to take any steps I've been afraid of to do something great for God. I will remember that He is always guiding me with His strength and protection.

JANUARY 31 **Read PHILIPPIANS 4:4-7**

NO INFORMATION AVAILABLE

Disney Music – "Into the Unknown"—*Frozen 2*

"...casting all your anxieties on him, because he cares for you."
—I Peter 5:7

How did we survive before the internet? If you're like me, you find yourself using it often to figure out unknown information. It's nice having the answer to most questions at your fingertips. However, there are some things in life that even Google can't answer, specifically concerning our future. Known as the "Let it Go" of *Frozen II*, this song was written by the same Lopez team from the original *Frozen*. They first presented it to Idina Menzel, the voice of Elsa, to sing while she was doing an off-Broadway play. They brought only a keyboard into her dressing room backstage and had her sing it for the first time. It is sung near the beginning of this film as Elsa is also heading towards something unknown. She's unsure of a mysterious voice she's heard and what it means for her future.

Just like Queen Elsa, we often don't know what's coming our way. Heading into the unknown can be scary. Thankfully, God brings us comfort through His Word, especially in today's passage from Philippians. We are told not to be anxious because God is always at our side, ready and waiting for our call through prayer. He can bring us unimaginable peace if we only ask for it. God cares for you as His child and creation. Whenever you face something unclear or scary, bring God into it first. You will feel much more at peace if you let Him guide you each step of the way. I have personally experienced His peace firsthand while facing uncertain and difficult times as well as tough decisions. He will give it to you as well. Just make sure to involve Him anytime you head into the unknown.

PRAYER—Heavenly Father, the unknown is scary. I don't know what the future holds for me, but I do know You hold the future. Help me feel Your presence during scary and unfamiliar times. Thank You for caring for me. Through Jesus, Amen.

TODAY I WILL... tell God about any of my fears concerning the unknown future. I will ask for His peace and feel comfort knowing He's there guiding me through every step.

FEBRUARY THEME

WALT AND THE HISTORY OF DISNEY

FEBRUARY 1 **Read I TIMOTHY 4:11-16**

GOD'S FUTURE LEADERS

Walt and the History of Disney – Walt's Young Talent

"Rejoice, O young man, in your youth, and let your heart cheer you in the days of your youth."
—Ecclesiastes 11:9

Now that we're in February, we'll be learning more about the man who started it all. Each day, we'll be discovering facts about Walt Disney's life, his work and the history of the empire he created. We begin with his childhood where Walt developed an early interest in drawing. He was actually paid as a kid to draw a horse for his neighbor and fell in love with the artform. He took art classes, became the cartoonist for his high school's newspaper and became employed as a commercial illustrator by age 18. Obviously, this talent was a huge factor leading to his success as a cartoonist, and we all know where that led. Today, Disney possesses a library full of cartoons, characters and films all streaming from Walt's original ability and passion.

Walt obviously got his start very young, finding something he was good at and working hard to develop and perfect it. It eventually led to the development of a worldwide company that has brought happiness to millions around the world. God blesses us all at all ages with talents and skills. If you're a child, pay close attention to Walt's example, but also to today's reading from I Timothy. Paul wrote this book for Timothy, a younger man he mentored and admired, but it was also written for us too. In this passage, Paul reminds Timothy not to let his youth hinder him from doing great things for God. Even children can discover talents and use them for serving others in God's name. If you're an adult and already past the point of youth, find a way to encourage children. Whether it's working with kids at church, a school or other youth program, be a mentor and example. Inspire and assist children to use their skills to glorify God. They are valuable members of His kingdom and can be great assets in spreading His Word.

PRAYER—Father, help me to use my full talent and potential to serve you at any age. Use me throughout life to inspire youth as they will be the future leaders of Your church. In Him, Amen.

TODAY I WILL... find a way to serve others even I'm young. If I'm past childhood, I will commit to finding a way to encourage children to serve the Lord and glorify Him with their gifts.

FEBRUARY 2 **Read JAMES 2:14-17**

DO IT YOURSELF

Walt and the History of Disney – Walt's Voice

"...but a doer who acts, he will be blessed in his doing."
—James 1:25

Have you ever seen video of actors in studio recording voices for various films or television? It's pretty fascinating to watch how animated some get putting full energy and movements into their various voices. Did you know Walt Disney himself did the same, providing the voice of his most famous character? From 1928 until 1947, and even periodically up until his death, he was the voice of Mickey Mouse (as well as Minnie Mouse early on.) One employee stated there were others who gave Mickey his physical appearance, but Walt provided his soul through his lively voice and dynamic energy. It's clear Walt loved Mickey and took great pride in his character that started it all. One of Walt's most famous quotes is, "I hope we never lose sight of one thing, that it was all started by a mouse." Walt cared so much for Mickey and wanted to make sure he was done right. Therefore, he took the initiative and time necessary to do the voice himself.

As Christians, we must do the same. We can't depend on others to take action for God. We must do it ourselves! In today's passage from James, we are told that faith is important, but works are just as vital. We can't just say we believe in God and His Son. We must show it openly. We can't just hope that someone serves others. We must serve outwardly. We can't just think good thoughts about God and tell others we love Him. We must actively worship and demonstrate our love through actions. Just as Walt felt it important to get involved and actively provide the voice of Mickey, we too must get involved and be active in showing our love for the Father. So how are your works? Are you being active? Are you taking initiative? Are you doing and not just hearing, thinking or hoping? Be active in your faith! Go out and do!

PRAYER—Lord, strengthen my faith, but also help me to serve You actively. Give me the determination and energy to take initiative and demonstrate my love for You through works. Through Jesus, Amen.

TODAY I WILL... do! I will demonstrate my faith through works for God. I will make sure to do something active for Him today.

FEBRUARY 3 **Read JAMES 4:1-4**

A LOOK LIKE NO OTHER

Walt and the History of Disney – Walt's Theme Park Dreams

"Do not be surprised, brothers, that the world hates you."
—I John 3:13

There is something very special kept at California's Disneyland. It's the actual park bench Walt Disney sat on while watching his two young daughters ride the merry-go-round at Griffith Park in Los Angeles. It was there while watching them ride with smiles on their faces that Walt developed a dream. He envisioned a place where parents could go and not just watch their children laugh and have fun, but actually participate with them; where families find happiness and magic together. It was on that bench that Walt dreamed up Disneyland which eventually led to multiple theme parks around the world. After forming this dream, he told a colleague he wanted his park to "look like nothing else in the world." It's safe to say he achieved that goal.

Today, all Disney parks are different in their own ways, but also similar in the fact that they look like no other theme parks in the world. They all have similar attractions, characters and theming that simply cannot be matched. Disney is one of the most globally recognized brands thanks to Walt, his dreams and goal to be like nothing else seen or experienced. Today's reading tells us in a similar way, we're supposed to look like nothing else in the world. It even says friendship with the world is basically hatred towards God and loving the world means being His enemy. We're called to be unique, to stand out and look nothing like the world. We should act, speak and look different. People should notice obvious differences because we're children of God. Make sure you stand out and refrain from following the world's ways. People should know you like they do Disney...as something unique and special like nothing they've ever seen!

PRAYER—Father, I want to be different from this world. I never want to be Your enemy by befriending or following it. Help me to never resemble anything worldly. In His name, Amen.

TODAY I WILL...take a hard look at what the world looks like and make sure I look different. I will list at least 5 ways that others see me as different from the world.

FEBRUARY 4 **Read I JOHN 3:4-10**

SECRET SINS

Walt and the History of Disney – Walt's Hidden Side

"Let not sin therefore reign in your mortal body, to make you obey its passions."
—Romans 6:12

Picture this. What if everyone had a scrolling marquee on their forehead broadcasting every single thought? Would you like that? We all have secrets...certain things from the past, or maybe present, we aren't proud of. Walt Disney himself had hidden habits he acknowledged even admitting to a type of split personality, one he used in public along with a separate private life. He once stated, "I'm not Walt Disney. I do a lot of things Walt Disney would not do. Walt Disney does not smoke. I smoke. Walt Disney does not drink. I drink." I'm not debating if Walt was sinful in taking those things too far (although he did die from lung cancer), but it's obvious from those words that he knew they were viewed negatively and didn't want the public to necessarily know about them. They were a part of his hidden side or "secret sins" if you will.

Nobody's perfect. Walt wasn't. You aren't. I'm certainly not. We've all done things we're not proud of. Obviously, God knows about these things, but in our reading today, we're told when we keep on sinning, knowing it's wrong, it's an issue with God. Verse 8 even says whoever makes a practice of sin if of the devil. Sounds harsh, but if we're true followers of God, we can't also make a regular practice of anything sinful. Sure, we mess up occasionally, but it's those repeated sins we must eliminate. We can't continue willfully sinning and also be a faithful child of God. Those two things just aren't compatible. Are there things you know are sinful you continue to be involved in? If so, don't just accept them as uncontrollable habits. Get control with God's help and abolish them. Don't lead an accepted double life like Walt admittedly did. God knows who you truly are. Be someone He's proud of inside and out!

PRAYER—God, I'm a sinner. Please forgive me of any sin in my life and especially help me not to repeat in any sin. Thank you for accepting me as imperfect as I am. Through Him, Amen.

TODAY I WILL...be honest with myself about any secret sins...anything that goes against God and His Word. I will take necessary steps to get rid of these things in my life.

FEBRUARY 5 **Read PSALM 139:1-10**

MAN IN THE FOREST

Walt and the History of Disney – Walt as a Boss

"The eyes of the Lord are in every place, keeping watch on the evil and the good."
—Proverbs 15:3

For those who work, do you like your boss? Being a teacher turned paramedic, I've had several bosses over the years, some I've really liked and some not so much. What about Walt Disney? Would you have wanted him as a boss? From what I've heard and read, he was a good one, firm in his beliefs but also kind. He was always looking for ways to improve and pushed his employees to do the same. Those under him had to work hard and take their job seriously to stay employed. In fact, there was a common phrase blurted out any time Walt Disney approached in the workplace. Someone would yell out "man in the forest!" whenever they saw him coming to let everyone know he was near. The phrase was taken from one of Walt's favorite films, *Bambi,* where the "man in the forest" was the unseen villain and hunter that shot and killed Bambi's mother. The use of the phrase proved that Walt was serious, always around watching and expected his workers to strive hard at all times, continuously seeking ways to improve.

We too have a "man in the forest" that watches us continuously? In today's psalm, David makes it clear that God knows everything about him and that he can't escape the Lord's presence no matter where he goes. He is always watching and knows our every move and thought. While that might have been scary or intimidating to some of Walt's employees, it's definitely not intended to be with God. We should be happy and feel blessed that God is omnipresent. He knows every struggle we meet, every tear we shed and every temptation we face. He's there to help us at all times and because He genuinely cares for us all. I'm eternally grateful we have a "man in the forest" to always watch over us and be there to respond whenever we call.

PRAYER—Lord, thank You for creating me, knowing everything about me and watching over me always. I'm so grateful You're ever-present in my life and listening to my every need. In Jesus' name, Amen.

TODAY I WILL...talk to God, out loud, because I know He is there, next to me, listening. I will have regular conversations with him, thanking him for being ever present in my life.

FEBRUARY 6 **Read PROVERBS 16:1-9**

MICKEY'S PREDECESSOR

Walt and the History of Disney – Oswald, the Lucky Rabbit

"Trust in the Lord with all your heart, and do not lean on your own understanding. In all your ways acknowledge him, and he will make straight your paths."
—Proverbs 3:5-6

Does life always go the way you're expecting? It's been said the only thing predictable about life is its unpredictability. A similar phrase says, "Man plans, and God laughs." Did you know Mickey Mouse was not Walt's first successful character? In 1927, Walt worked for Universal Pictures and created "Oswald, the Lucky Rabbit," who starred in several successful cartoons. When Walt left Universal a year later to create his own studio, he was unable to take Oswald with him due to contracts. Therefore, he developed Mickey Mouse instead. I'm sure there was a period of time when Walt felt Oswald wasn't so "lucky" after all, leading to disappointment and worry. Oswald was a very successful cartoon and there were no guarantees this new character would ever match that success. Obviously, we know Mickey not only matched it but surpassed it astronomically becoming the cornerstone to the Disney empire we know and love today.

Sometimes life is just like that story. We may be happy, enjoying success and feeling as if we know just where life is headed when we're thrown a huge curve ball. Those surprises can be scary and worrisome, but they often turn out better than expected, especially if God's involved. The key is to trust God and allow Him to direct our life which gives us no reason to fear. He knows what's best and often His new path is a better one as was the case with Oswald and Mickey. Today's Proverb is all about trusting God to guide us instead of relying on our own plans. The additional verses above from Proverbs 3 is one of my very favorite passages, and I repeat it often when things aren't going as expected. Don't stress over life's unexpected paths. It's most likely God leading you in a better direction. Trust Him and commit to the fact He knows best. He just may give you a Mickey Mouse instead. And who wouldn't want that!?

PRAYER—Lord, help me to always trust You, especially when life doesn't go as expected. I place my life in Your hands and have faith You know what's best. In Jesus' name, Amen.

TODAY I WILL...memorize Proverbs 3:5-6 and repeat it often, especially when life goes unexpectedly. I will not worry when that happens but simply trust God's wisdom and direction.

FEBRUARY 7 **Read JAMES 4:13-17**

THE POMPOUS MOUSE

Walt and the History of Disney – Mickey's Original Name

"Pride goes before destruction, and a haughty spirit before a fall."
—Proverbs 16:18

Have you ever realized the great responsibility parents have naming their children? They decide what that person will be called for the rest of their life. Obviously, it's possible to change a name, but most tend to stick with the one they're given. As a cartoonist, Walt Disney also had a great responsibility to invent and name many different characters. As discussed yesterday, when Oswald, the Lucky Rabbit fell through, he chose to create a new character, the famous mouse we all love. Walt Disney first named him "Mortimer." Yep, that's right. Mickey was originally known as Mortimer Mouse...thankfully for only a short time. Walt's wife convinced him to change it telling him that "Mortimer" sounded too pompous. He then chose Mickey instead.

Aren't you glad Walt's wife, Lillian spoke up? I suppose if Mortimer had stuck, we wouldn't know any better and probably wouldn't care, but I personally think Mickey is a much better name. I don't know if Mortimer is indeed a pompous sounding name, and no offense to any "Mortimers" that may be reading, but let's talk about that word. Being pompous means being arrogant, self-promoting, conceited, having too much pride or thinking way to highly of self. The Bible speaks to that attitude often, including in today's reading from James in which he warns not to boast or claim to know what's coming. This relates to yesterday's lesson of making plans without God. Only God knows what will happen tomorrow. It's not our job to boast and assume we know where life is heading. It's also wrong to be arrogant or brag about yourself in a proud way. Jesus taught and demonstrated humility. Do another self-check and confirm you are following His humble example. Don't have a pompous attitude that will turn others away. We are to bring others to Christ which we can only do by being a humble servant as He was.

PRAYER—Dear God, help me to never be pompous in my attitude, words or actions. Help me to show humility in all things and never turn others off by boasting. In His humble name, Amen.

TODAY I WILL...make sure I don't make a habit of being pompous or arrogant. I will think before I talk and demonstrate humility in the way I speak and present myself to others.

FEBRUARY 8 **Read ROMANS 15:1-7**

GIFTING YOUR GIFTS

Walt and the History of Disney – Walt's Custom Cartoons

"Therefore encourage one another and build one another up, just as you are doing."
—I Thessalonians 5:11

We've already discussed the importance of using your God-given talents to serve others. But have you ever considered there might be a way to use them you haven't thought of before? Walt Disney figured that out during World War II. That war hit shortly after the release of Dumbo, and Walt discovered a way to use his talent of filmmaking to aid and assist our military. He produced a series of short films providing instructions for soldiers. One of them, for example, was called *Four Methods of Flush Riveting and Aircraft Production Methods*. Sounds like a "riveting" picture, doesn't it? He also made short Donald Duck cartoons to promote the purchase of war bonds which also aided our military. These films didn't really make him any extra profit and basically just made enough to cover their own costs. But Walt continued to produce them to assist in the war efforts and benefit those serving.

Today's passage from Romans begins telling those who are strong they have an obligation to help those who are weak. It continues with instructions to please others and build them up. As Christians, we're called to encourage and assist others, especially in times of weakness or need. Just like Walt, we should explore our strengths and figure out how we can use them to help and support others. Not only will it provide much needed assistance, but others will see our example and have a stronger desire to pay it forward. They will also be more willing to listen to us talk about God and the importance of following Him. Take a moment today to explore your talents and figure out how you can best use them to build others up. Be creative and work hard to guide others with the help they need. You may just end up guiding them to Christ and their salvation.

PRAYER—Father, help me to encourage and help others daily. Allow me to discover what talents of mine will best benefit those in need so I can be more like Jesus. Through Him, Amen.

TODAY I WILL...explore my talents. I will note what I do well and try and figure out a creative way to use those gifts to help those in need.

FEBRUARY 9 **Read ROMANS 15:22-33**

TAKE TIME TO DECIDE

Walt and the History of Disney – Walt's Risky Plans

"The plans of the diligent lead surely to abundance, but everyone who is hasty comes only to poverty."
—Proverbs 21:5

I don't mind taking most physical risks. Skydiving is still on my bucket list. Less attractive for me would be taking a money or business risk. I don't gamble, play the lottery or dabble much in the stock market. That's actually scarier for me than jumping out of a plane. Go figure. Walt Disney certainly took some risks with his money and business at times. Walt's original studio was in Burbank, California. When he developed his theme park dreams, he first obtained a permit to build a small park there next to his studios. However, he then decided to take a risk and purchase land in the lesser known and low populated Anaheim, approximately 35 miles away. In similar fashion, when he decided to expand to the East coast, he chose the unknown Orlando, instead of a more crowded and popular city. These were both great risks met with doubt and criticism by friends and business associates, but both paid off greatly! Walt deduced correctly that placing his parks in lesser-known cities would be cheaper and give him more room to grow. Anaheim and Orlando have both absolutely thrived since Disney's expansions there.

Today we read from Romans a detailed itinerary that Paul laid out containing his future missionary plans. It's obvious from this reading that Paul was a planner, careful and detailed in where he went and how long he stayed. He took risks of course, but not without careful preparation. Like Walt, Paul thought hard about his work, making sure he made the best choices to be successful, and it paid off for him too. He was one of the most effective missionaries and teachers we have ever known. Make sure you take the right amount of time to plan any important decisions or activities in your life. Don't be too hasty in your choices. And don't forget to involve God as your guide as well. Be a smart planner! Take time and talk to God!

PRAYER—Lord, give me wisdom and patience to be careful and thorough in my planning. Help me to always involve You and take time to make good decisions. Through Jesus, Amen.

TODAY I WILL...vow to involve God in all my big decisions. I will also take the time necessary to evaluate each choice to make sure it is in line with the Word of God.

FEBRUARY 10 **Read DEUTERONOMY 11:18-25**

THE GREATEST RESPONSIBILITY

Walt and the History of Disney – Walt's Daughters

"I have no greater joy than to hear that my children are walking in the truth."
—3 John 1:4

Time flies! Ever heard that? If you're a parent, you'll probably wanna "Amen" that. Any time I talk to new parents, I advise them to enjoy every second because it will go by fast. My 2 baby boys are now 19 and 16. Walt Disney had two children of his own, daughters Diane and Sharon. It's no secret he adored his girls and spent considerable time with them. After all, he was sitting on that park bench, watching them play when he dreamed up Disneyland. It's also a fact that he drove both to school every day. He cared about them greatly and even feared for their safety given his high-profile status. He didn't allow them to be photographed and generally kept them out of the public eye.

There's no greater responsibility than being a parent. Walt Disney took that seriously and put his family before work. As Christians, parents are not only expected to care properly for their children making sure they have the basic necessities of life but are also first and foremost to raise them to know and love the Lord. In Deuteronomy 11, parents are instructed to discuss God's Word with their kids at all times. If you're a parent, ensure your children have as much knowledge as possible about God, His Son and His plan for salvation. How else will they know how to live their lives for Him? Talking about His expectations should be a daily routine like eating meals or brushing teeth. I assure you that time will fly, and your children will be gone before you know it. Make sure when they walk out the door you can confidently repeat the verse above saying that they are walking in the truth...God's truth!

PRAYER—Heavenly Father, please help me to raise my children (or teach others) to know, love and follow You as their top priority. I want nothing more than to be with You one day in Heaven with my children beside me. In Jesus' name, Amen.

TODAY I WILL...establish a daily routine to talk to my children about God. If I don't have kids, I will find a way to teach other children about Him and assist in their lifelong spiritual path.

FEBRUARY 11 **Read PSALM 121:1-8**

HE'S ALWAYS WATCHING

Walt and the History of Disney – Walt's Apartment

"The Lord your God is in your midst, a mighty one who will save..."
—Zephaniah 3:17

Today we cover a fact about Walt Disney you may be aware of. When he planned and oversaw the construction of Disneyland, he designed a special section to be built for himself and his family. He had a small apartment constructed above the fire station on Main Street. It was small, less than 500 square feet, but came fully equipped with a kitchen, bathroom with shower, patio and a desk for him to work. On opening day, he invited some of the young Mouseketeers to join him inside as the first guests poured into the park. It was later said that Walt stared out the apartment window with a huge smile on his face and a tear streaming down his cheek. He was so proud that his dream was finally realized and he could watch it all unfold from his special window above the park. Today, a lamp stays lit at all times in that window as a tribute to him.

Today's lesson is simple. Walt had that apartment built for several reasons. It allowed him to work very close to the action. It gave his family a place to relax. But most importantly, it allowed him to look out and watch over his creation with pride. Can you guess the obvious parallel here? God does the exact same thing with His creation. God made us all and is always looking down from Heaven's window proudly watching over us. Today's psalm is so reassuring showing just how much God cares for each of us. If you ever feel lost or alone, read this psalm repeatedly, and it will automatically bring you comfort. The last words are "from this time forth and forevermore." God will never stop watching over you. Forevermore. What a comforting and wonderful reality. As mentioned, there's a special light in that window even today to remind us of Walt. Similarly, when I see sunlight often beaming through the clouds, it's always a reminder of God looking down on me. And it always makes me smile. God is good!

PRAYER—God, thank you for watching over me at all times, now and forevermore. I feel such comfort knowing you're there. Thank you for loving and caring for me. In Jesus' name, Amen.

TODAY I WILL...look to my God in Heaven and thank Him for always watching, always listening and always caring.

FEBRUARY 12 **Read ACTS 4:5-12**

THE ONLY WAY

Walt and the History of Disney – The Apartment Shortcut

"Jesus said to him, "I am the way, and the truth, and the life. No one comes to the Father except through me.

—John 14:6

Speaking of Walt's apartment, which you can actually visit inside through a paid tour there, there's one more aspect I think worth mentioning. It's a fact I actually didn't know before researching this book. When the apartment was first built, Walt had a firepole installed in the closet that led to the station below. It was a shortcut from the apartment to get downstairs and into the park quickly. It's unclear if Walt or his family ever used it, but what a creative and fun addition! Apparently access between the pole and the apartment has since been removed due to an intrusion although it's unclear if that really happened or not.

In today's reading from Acts, Peter speaks to the city council following his and John's arrest after healing a crippled man in the temple. Notice Peter's words near the end of this passage. He emphasizes that the man was healed in the name of Jesus and confirms that Christ is the cornerstone of the church. Finally, he makes a very important statement saying, "there is salvation in no one else, for there is no other name under Heaven given among men by which we must be saved." Salvation is found in NO ONE ELSE! And look at the verse above where Jesus Himself says, "No one comes to the Father except through me." EXCEPT THROUGH ME! It's simple. There are NO shortcuts to God. The ONLY way to get to Him is through Jesus. We must follow His teachings, example and path clearly stated. Walt may have put a really neat shortcut in his apartment, but there are no shortcuts to salvation. Those that don't seek God through Jesus won't see God. It's a fact. Believe it. And make sure others know it so they can see God too!

PRAYER—Lord, I want only to be with You forever. Thank you for showing me the only way through Your Son. Help me to follow His path and not seek any shortcuts. In Him, Amen.

TODAY I WILL...find the Way which is Jesus. I will make sure I'm not taking any shortcuts in life and am only following the path to God laid out in Scripture. I will also commit to sharing this path with others so they too can find the proper way to eternity with Him.

FEBRUARY 13 **Read MARK 6:30-34**

JUST STOP AND LISTEN

Walt and the History of Disney – Walt's Favorite Song

"Son of man, all my words that I shall speak to you receive in your heart and hear with your ears."
—Ezekiel 3:10

Ever had a crazy, hectic day where things seem too out of control? Ever felt tired, stressed or overworked? It's easy during those times to worry, doubt, panic or become anxious, but there's a better solution I'd like to propose. Walt Disney had a favorite song. It was called "Feed the Birds" and came from *Mary Poppins*. On Friday afternoons, he would often stop by the Sherman brothers' office and simply say, "play it." They knew what he meant. Walt would sit there and listen as they played the soothing melody for him. I'm sure it provided great comfort and peace for him during the constant busyness and activity of his life.

Our lives can be demanding and stressful too. It's easy to lose control and become anxious during those times. In Mark 6, we see that Jesus has just lost a cousin and friend in John the Baptist, and many people are following Him around, pleading to see and hear from Him. I'm sure He felt some grief and stress during this demanding time. As a result, in verse 31, he invites his Apostles to find a desolate place to stop and rest. Sometimes we need to do the same. He of course has compassion on the people, teaches and feeds them just a few verses later, but for just a few moments, He needed to pause, relax and listen to God. In Joshua 1:8 we're told to mediate on the words of God day and night. Just as Walt liked to pause at the end of a stressful week and listen to his comforting song, we need to do the same by listening to our comforting Father instead. Take an occasional break from the world. Stop. Breathe. Rest. Meditate. Listen. It will be a comforting, healing medicine to your overworked body, anxious mind and weary soul.

PRAYER—Father in Heaven, help me to stop and listen to You often, especially during stressful or busy times. Thank you for always being there for me. In the name of Jesus, Amen.

TODAY I WILL... Stop! Take a break, rest and listen to God. Tell Him you are listening and allow Him to speak to you. Open up His Word and hear His voice.

FEBRUARY 14 **Read GENESIS 2:18-25**

A DISNEY LOVE STORY

Walt and the History of Disney – Walt and Lillian

"...let each one of you love his wife as himself, and let the wife see that she respects her husband."
—Ephesians 5:33

Today is Valentine's Day! A day to honor love and relationships. Therefore, we focus today on a true love story...that of Walt Disney and his wife of 41 years, Lillian. Walt first met Lillian at his own studio. She had been hired as an ink artist and actually worked on *Plane Crazy*, the first ever short film starring Mickey Mouse. Walt and Lillian fell in love, married in 1925 and remained united until his death in 1966. They were completely committed and dedicated to each other. Walt spoke very highly of Lillian, even naming his personal backyard train "Lilly Belle" in her honor. Likewise, Lillian adored her husband. Many years after his death she said, "We shared a wonderful, exciting life, and we loved every minute of it. He was a wonderful husband to me, and wonderful and joyful father and grandfather." Lillian suffered a stroke on the exact 31st anniversary of Walt's death and died the next morning in 1997.

Walt and Lillian's marriage was successful because it was based on love, devotion and loyalty. Marriage is a blessing from God and part of His plan as evidenced by our reading today from Genesis. It states that God created woman as the perfect helper for man. Verse 24 shares His plan that man and woman will leave their parents and become joined as one in marriage. Marriage is not always perfect or easy, but if you work hard at it with God at the center, it's a true blessing, bringing much joy and happiness in life. If you aren't married, you hopefully have family members you share love and devotion to. Family is another gift from God meant to help and support us through life. Thank God for love and family. Happy Valentine's Day!

PRAYER—Lord, thank you for the gift of marriage and family. Help me to work hard at my family relationships putting you always in the middle. Thank you for Your love and the compassion and devotion we share with family. In His loving name, Amen.

TODAY I WILL...(if married) tell and show my spouse how much I love them. I will rededicate my love and life to that person forever. If unmarried, I will reach out to my family members thanking them for their love. I will offer my love and care in return.

FEBRUARY 15 **Read 2 TIMOTHY 1:8-12**

SHARE WITH THE SAVIOR

Walt and the History of Disney – Disneyland's Opening Day Part 1

"And after you have suffered a little while, the God of all grace, who has called you to his eternal glory in Christ, will himself restore, confirm, strengthen, and establish you."
—I Peter 5:10

We've discussed the man behind the mouse quite a bit. Let's switch gears and talk about his first park. Disneyland opened on July 17, 1955 to anything but a successful day. It was titled an "International Press Review" and intended to be a pre-opening for the press and special guests to view the park before it opened the next day to the general public. Unfortunately, 28,000 people showed up, of which only about half had been invited. The rest had purchased counterfeit tickets or just snuck in without one. It turned into a chaotic scene with many issues and technical glitches. In the coming days, we'll examine some of the other problems they had to deal with, but it's obvious that Disneyland's first day was definitely memorable for all the wrong reasons.

We've considered suffering previously, particularly that of Paul. In 2 Timothy 1, he talks more about it making clear that suffering is not only expected for those following Christ, but necessary and in a sense, honorable. As Christians, we're expected to share in the sufferings of Christ. It's part of our calling as true disciples. Paul makes clear he has faith that God will guide and protect him through it. Additionally, in the verse above, he mentions after suffering for a short time, God will call us home where Christ will restore, confirm, strengthen and establish us. Walt and his associates certainly suffered that opening day, but they didn't give up. They pressed on, worked through difficulties and eventually triumphed. We must do the same. Suffering isn't fun or easy, but when (not if) it happens, try to see it as an honor and privilege to share with our Savior. It means we are one of His chosen, and the best is yet to be!

PRAYER—God, I know that suffering is inevitable as Your child and follower. Help me through it. Thank you for allowing me to share that with Christ knowing it will lead to eternal glory with You one day. Through His humble name, Amen.

TODAY I WILL...remember anytime I suffer that it's necessary and a privilege. If Jesus can make it through the suffering of crucifixion, I can make it through anything to be with God.

FEBRUARY 16 **Read ROMANS 14:13-19**

TRIPPING OTHERS

Walt and the History of Disney – Disneyland's Opening Day Part 2

"But take care that this right of yours does not somehow become a stumbling block to the weak."
—I Corinthians 8:9

Can you imagine being Walt Disney that first day, having planned this dream for years, only to be met with multiple unexpected issues? Things always seem to go wrong when you've prepared the most, right? Besides the flood of uninvited guests, there were many technical difficulties in the live feed being broadcast on ABC. Walt Disney was interrupted by a technician while reading the Tomorrowland plaque and had to start over, not to mention on-air reporters not being ready or losing their microphones. Finally, many guests tripped over the television camera cables which hadn't been properly covered or secured.

That particular fact reminded me of today's passage where we're told to not be a stumbling block. Paul gives the example of someone offended by what we eat or drink and how it's not worth losing someone's soul to argue over something so petty and easily altered. When someone gets offended by something we think isn't a big deal, it's not always easy to remain calm, especially if we feel strongly our way. However, consider Paul's reasoning. Is it really worth losing a friend, spiritual family member and potential saved soul over something so small? This is why I feel drinking alcohol is dangerous. It may not be sinful in small amounts, but if it influences someone else to drink which then becomes a problem for them, that's a stumbling block, and I would bear some blame. In verse 19, Paul advises to only pursue what brings peace and unity with others. Be careful of your example and find patience with those who take issue with you. Work out differences in love, learning to compromise if possible. It's not worth being a stumbling block and causing someone else to sin or lose their chance eternally with God.

PRAYER—Father, I don't want to be a stumbling block to anyone, so please let me know if I am. Give me patience to work out any differences with others and help me to always be a good example and influence for Your kingdom. In Him, Amen.

TODAY I WILL...consider my habits making sure none are bad influences on others. If someone takes issue with me, I'll be patient and work out differences in a calm, loving manner.

FEBRUARY 17 **Read PSALM 63:1-11**

I AM THIRSTY

Walt and the History of Disney – Disneyland's Opening Day Part 3

"Blessed are those who hunger and thirst for righteousness, for they shall be satisfied."
—Matthew 5:6

Think we've covered all the problems on Disneyland's opening day? Think again. As the Carpenters sang, "We've only just begun." It was extremely hot that day with the temperature around 101 degrees! Because of that, the asphalt poured that morning was still wet causing several ladies' healed shoes to sink in as they walked. Due to a plumbers' strike, Walt Disney had to choose between having working toilets or water fountains. He chose toilets. Good choice, Walt! However, on a hot day, it's not good to have dry water fountains. Many assumed it was a ploy to sell soda as Pepsi was one of the park's sponsors. Obviously, this left a lot of guests very unhappy and thirsty on a scorching, hot day.

Jesus famously cried, "I am thirsty" from the cross at His crucifixion. Perhaps you've been thirsty before, even on a similar hot day. Think about the satisfaction when you finally quenched that thirst with some cool water. In Psalm 63, David says his soul thirsts for God. In fact, the entire passage is about his longing to be with God. Are you thirsty for God? Just like an aching thirst on a blistering day, we should long for God. We should yearn to know Him, please Him, follow Him, listen to Him, talk to Him and most of all, be with Him. Why does our craving for God not match that of food, sleep, entertainment or money when He's the one who grants our eternal reward? None of those earthly things can give you what He can. Perhaps we need to rethink our priorities and what we thirst daily for. Jesus states above that those who hunger and thirst for righteousness will be satisfied. In other words, if you strongly desire, like a thirst, to be right before God, following His ways, He will satisfy you with Heaven. The feeling of refreshing water against an insatiable thirst can't even begin to compare with that!

PRAYER—Lord, I thirst for you! I want to know, please and follow You more. Most of all, I want to be with You. Help me to long for you way more than anything worldly. In Him, Amen.

TODAY I WILL...do a priority check and make sure I have a strong thirst for God. I will remember the importance of a strong faith and relationship with Him as it affects my eternity.

FEBRUARY 18 **Read JOHN 20:1-10**

SUNDAY'S COMING

Walt and the History of Disney – Disneyland's Opening Day Part 4

"For since we believe that Jesus died and rose again, even so, through Jesus, God will bring with him those who have fallen asleep."
—I Thessalonians 4:14

We've almost covered all the glitches and hitches of Disneyland's joyous opening day. And it's only taken us four devotionals! However, I haven't yet mentioned the two-hour traffic delay, the fact that several celebrities scheduled to arrive periodically throughout the day all showed up at once or that some parents literally threw their kids over crowds to get them onto rides. Quality parenting there! I also overlooked the wet paint, weeds, lack of food and drinks available, a gas leak that nearly caught the castle on fire and several rides breaking down including the Mark Twain Riverboat which sunk under the weight of too many guests. Is that enough for ya? In later years, Walt and his executives referred to that July 17th day in 1955 as "Black Sunday."

There was another Sunday nearly 2000 years earlier that looked to be disastrous. After all, the Friday before had been the saddest day in history, when our Lord and Savior suffered a cruel death on the cross of Calvary. But instead of another "Black Sunday," two days later became the greatest Sunday in history. Today's passage describes what happened early that morning. Mary and the Apostles came to Christ's tomb only to find it completely empty. Christ had risen! He had defeated death as He predicted (Mark 8:31). We celebrate the life of Jesus: His birth, His ministry, His teachings, His promises and His death. But greatest of all we celebrate His resurrection because it proves He truly was the Son of God and even death could not take away His victory. Without His resurrection, there's no faith, no church, no hope and no Christianity! Because of it, we have hope of another great day when He won't rise up but will instead come down from the clouds to collect us all. Don't give up hope! Sunday's coming! Praise God! Because this time, *we* get to rise up and meet Him!

PRAYER—Dear Lord, thank you for the resurrection of Jesus. I can't wait to meet Him in the air when He returns. Thank you for that hope. In His name, Amen.

TODAY I WILL... praise God for the hope I have because Sunday came, and He rose again. I will make sure I'm ready for His return so I too can rise up and be with Him.

FEBRUARY 19 **Read PHILIPPIANS 3:12-21**

THE GREATEST AWARD

Walt and the History of Disney – Walt's Awards

"Henceforth there is laid up for me the crown of righteousness, which the Lord, the righteous judge, will award to me on that day, and not only to me but also to all who have loved his appearing."
—2 Timothy 4:8

Ok, I've harped on Disneyland's catastrophic opening day long enough. The good news is, it only got better with each day afterwards and is today one of the most visited theme parks in the world. This is mainly because Walt Disney and his business partners, including his brother, Roy, didn't give up. They fixed all the problems and pressed on to success as was Walt's nature. As previously mentioned, he always believed things could be better whether it was the company, the parks, his films or even himself. He was always striving to accomplish a greater goal. This is evidenced by the countless awards he won during his lifetime. In fact, Walt Disney won the most Academy Awards (Oscars) of any person in history, even to this day. He received 22 of the statues on 59 nominations! He also won Emmys, Golden Globes, a Grammy and holds numerous Guinness World Records. Altogether, he secured 66 award wins along and an additional 46 separate nominations! Safe to say his trophy shelf was pretty maxed out.

In today's reading from Philippians 3, Paul discusses his greatest goal and the reward he's striving for which we should also seek. God rewards those who seek Him and follow the steps He's clearly laid out in His Word. If we walk that straight and narrow path, remaining faithful throughout our lives, He will reward us by calling us home. We will accomplish our supreme goal and receive the "upward call of God in Christ Jesus." The verse above reiterates that award, and Hebrews 11:6 says God rewards those who seek Him. Walt Disney had a right to be proud of the numerous and certainly deserved awards won during his lifetime. But none compare with the greatest award each of us can achieve. Are you giving your very best to receive it?

PRAYER—Dear God, Help me to know and follow the plan You've laid out for me. Keep my faith strong and my life free from sin so I won't do anything to jeopardize receiving the reward I want so greatly. Through Jesus, Amen.

TODAY I WILL... Read over and reaffirm my written goals in life. If I haven't written them down yet, I will do so today. I will make sure receiving God's reward is at the top of the list.

FEBRUARY 20 **Read GENESIS 28:13-22**

HE'S RIGHT HERE

Walt and the History of Disney – Walt and His Guests

"For where two or three are gathered in my name, there am I among them."
—Matthew 18:20

We've already referenced Walt Disney in his hidden apartment at Disneyland on opening day, watching out the window, looking over his guests as they entered. He also came down of course to be among them, join in the televised broadcast and witness the historical events first-hand. After getting past the first-day issues and once things were running more smoothly, Walt was known to not only watch from his apartment but come down and visit with guests. It's said he would even stand in line with them having conversations while they waited for various attractions. Most park owners and executives typically prefer to stay out of public eye and lead from a cozy office, somewhere off property. But not Walt! He enjoyed being out among his guests, seeing their reactions and listening to their comments and suggestions. He made his park the best by being there, experiencing it first-hand and watching closely over all that happened.

Today's passage is the story of Jacob when he's had to flee his family home and travel alone. He most likely felt deserted and afraid, unsure of what might happen. But God came to him in a dream reassuring him that He would be with him wherever he went. When Jacob awoke, he said, "Surely the Lord is in this place, and I did not know it." Knowing God was there with him gave Jacob the confidence and courage to keep going without fear. God promises the same to us. He's always among us, watching over us wherever we go. He makes the same promise that he won't ever leave us. Just as Walt liked being in the park, among the action, with his guests, God is right here. He doesn't just watch us from His "cozy office" up in Heaven. He's here. Among us. Right beside you anytime you need Him. What a loving, caring and nurturing God we serve!

PRAYER—Lord, thank You for Your promises to always watch over me, be here beside me and be among the church when we gather to worship You. In Jesus' name, Amen.

TODAY I WILL... realize God is always beside me, watching over me, ready to listen. I will talk to Him from now on as if he's sitting right next to me, because He is.

FEBRUARY 21 **Read ISAIAH 6:1-7**

LET THE GUILT GO

Walt and the History of Disney – Walt's Mother

"For I will be merciful toward their iniquities and I will remember their sins no more."
—Hebrews 8:12

Have you ever noticed how a lot of Disney films have absent mothers? Think about it...*Pinocchio, Bambi, Cinderella, The Jungle Book, Beauty and the Beast, Finding Nemo, Frozen*...need I go on? Some believe there's a reason for that trend related to Walt Disney himself. Yes, some of these films came out after his death, but it's believed the pattern began either consciously or subconsciously with him. When Walt finally enjoyed financial success after *Snow White*, he took some profit and bought his parents a house in North Hollywood. Less than a month later, his mother noticed a weird smell coming from the furnace. Walt himself called one of his studio repairmen, but unfortunately, they did not fix it properly. A few days later, his mother died of asphyxiation. It's said that Walt blamed himself for her death since he'd bought the house and called the repairmen. For the rest of his life, he suffered immense grief and guilt, which perhaps attributed to the lack of mothers in his films.

We've all felt guilty due to a mistake, sin, regret or even something we couldn't control. In today's reading from the prophet Isaiah, he has a vision where the Lord sends an angel to touch his lips, cleansing him from all guilt. God even tells him, "Your guilt is taken away, and your sin atoned for." If we're honest and sincere in confession of our mistakes and quest for forgiveness, the Bible's clear that God will forgive us and remember our sins no more. There's no reason to dwell on or feel guilty for past mistakes. Just admit them, give them to God, be sincere in asking for His forgiveness and forget it! He does! The tragic loss of Walt's mom was sad, and the guilt he bore was even more devastating. We don't have to agonize in guilt when we mess up with God. Once He forgives, it's gone, so that we can forget too and live in peace.

PRAYER—Father, please forgive me of any past sins. Thank you for doing that and remembering them no more. Help me to accept that and bear no guilt. Through Jesus, Amen.

TODAY I WILL... throw off any guilt I'm carrying, give it to God, accept His forgiveness and the fact that it's forgotten. I will continue to talk to Him about it until I no longer feel guilty.

FEBRUARY 22 **Read GALATIANS 3:23-29**

THE ETERNAL WALK OF FAME

Walt and the History of Disney – Walt's Star

"For just as the body is one and has many members, and all the members of the body, though many, are one body, so it is with Christ."
—I Corinthians 12:12

Have you ever been honored by having your name read aloud in recognition or posted somewhere special? It's humbling and enjoyable to see or hear your name highlighted. I'll admit the first time I saw my name on the front of a book was a special moment. Walt Disney got to see his name posted many places, and we've already mentioned how many awards his name was on. One other very special place his name was printed was in Hollywood on the infamous Walk of Fame. On February 8, 1960, Walt received his star for film and television. Not only that, but after his death, on November 18, 1978, Mickey Mouse became the first ever cartoon character to also receive a Walk of Fame star in honor of his 50th anniversary.

It's rewarding to have your name recognized, but the best place to hear it will be when it's hopefully being read out of the Book of Life, mentioned many times throughout Scripture, particularly in Revelation. You'll want to hear your name called and welcomed into eternity with God. In today's passage, we are reminded that Heaven is for everyone. It doesn't matter your background, gender, race or nationality, we are all one in Jesus and are invited to be a part of His body, the church. Just like the Walk of Fame has included many types of people and even an iconic, cartoon mouse, Heaven is available for all. Keep in mind it will be a selected few who have stayed the narrow path (Matt. 7:14), but it's clearly open to everyone. Don't be selective when you share the Gospel. Tell those you know and those you don't. Share with those you're relaxed with and those you must break out of your comfort zone to teach. Let's all work hard to spread Christ to all so that everyone has a chance to be added to Heaven's Walk of Fame!

PRAYER—Dear Lord, I want my name to be read from the Book of Life as I'm being called into Your kingdom, and I want to help many others get their name read also. Bring me souls to save. Through my Savior, Amen.

TODAY I WILL... make it known that Heaven is for everyone. I will get out of my comfort zone to figure out how to tell all kinds of people about God and His plan of salvation.

FEBRUARY 23 **Read PHILIPPIANS 2:1-11**

THE HUMBLE MS. HOWARD

Walt and the History of Disney – Walt's Housekeeper

"Clothe yourselves, all of you, with humility toward one another, for 'God opposes the proud but gives grace to the humble.'"
—I Peter 5:5

Ever seen *The Brady Bunch*? I always enjoyed that show and the family's live-in housekeeper, Alice. I kinda wished we had an "Alice" growing up. Walt Disney actually did, but her name was Thelma. Thelma Howard was the Disney family's live-in housekeeper from 1951-1981. She took care of household duties, did the cooking and was known to be an extremely caring lady. Walt's daughter, Diane, commented that the previous housekeeper banished her and her sister from the kitchen but with Thelma, they were always welcome. It was also said that before Thelma, the Disney house was just a house, but she turned it into a "warm household where people wanted to be." She gained Walt's full respect and admiration and was fully accepted as part of the family. Every year for her birthday and Christmas, Walt gave her stock in Disney. When she retired, she had over $9 million as she never sold and rarely spent her gifts. Upon her death, her will allocated money to create an arts program for underprivileged children.

It's obvious that Thelma Howard was a very kind and humble individual. She was worth millions but certainly didn't show it. She quietly did her job while looking for ways to help others, even after her death. Philippians 2 gives the perfect definition of what it means to show humility, and it's all about the humblest person who ever lived. Jesus Christ was that perfect example. The passage describes how He put others before Himself, looked to their interests first and became a servant. It also describes His ultimate act of humility when he became obedient even through death on a cross. Thelma Howard was a selfless individual whose legacy lives on through her example and foundation. We should all strive to be so caring and humble. Most of all, we should imitate the humility of Jesus and put the needs of others before our own.

PRAYER—Lord, help me to be humble. Help me to seek out the needs of others before my own and follow the example of Jesus in becoming a servant. In His name, Amen.

TODAY I WILL...list all the adjectives and descriptions of Christ in today's passage from Philippians. I will read the list often and strive to imitate as many as I can to be more like Him.

FEBRUARY 24 **Read MATTHEW 25:31-46**

ACCESS DENIED

Walt and the History of Disney – Deprived of Disneyland

"Not everyone who says to me, 'Lord, Lord,' will enter the kingdom of heaven, but the one who does the will of my Father who is in heaven."
—Matthew 7:21

How many times have you been to Disney, either World or Land? In the dozens of times I've been, the magic is never lost entering those gates. Imagine arriving at the park with all the excitement and euphoria only to be told you couldn't enter. In September 1959, the Soviet "First Secretary," Nikita Khrushchev, was visiting, the first time a Soviet leader had set foot on U.S. soil. He had two requests: to meet the western movie star, John Wayne, and visit Disneyland which had opened 4 years earlier. He got to meet Wayne but was famously denied access to Disneyland due to security concerns with his potential visit. He was supposedly outraged at having to miss Mickey, and I can't say I blame him.

Being denied entrance into Disney would be devastating, but it wouldn't compare with the unthinkable of being turned away from the gates of Heaven. Today's reading from Matthew 25 is one of the most blunt and important passages about Heaven. Jesus makes clear that we'll all be separated into two groups on Judgement Day, the goats and the sheep. The sheep will be welcomed into God's kingdom while the goats will be turned away. The goats will vastly outnumber the sheep (Matt 7:13-14). The verse above also clarifies not everyone who calls God's name at that time will enter, but only those who have followed Him throughout their lives. The day Jesus returns will be glorious, and I can't wait. Unfortunately, it will also be catastrophic for way too many who'll be denied access to eternity with God. It's not too late to obtain your ticket and become a sheep. If you already are, confirm daily your ticket is still good and you're still on the narrow path to walk through those glorious gates. You definitely don't want to hear your access has been denied. Be sure and confident in your salvation!

PRAYER—Father God, I want to be a sheep called into Your kingdom. Please don't deny my access. Help me to know and follow Your ways so I am assured entry. In Jesus' name, Amen.

TODAY I WILL...check my ticket to confirm I'm a sheep on the path to gaining entry into Heaven. I will check it daily to confirm I'm not doing anything that will get my access rejected.

FEBRUARY 25 **Read ACTS 9:10-22**

IF THEY ONLY KNEW

Walt and the History of Disney – Walt's Land Purchase

"So faith comes from hearing, and hearing through the word of Christ."
—Romans 10:17

The last four days of February will focus on Disney World. We haven't discussed it much as Walt passed before it opened and wasn't involved as much in its history. In the early 1960's, he began looking for a potential park site nearer the east coast. Research showed only 5% of Disneyland's visitors came from east of the Mississippi River which is where 75% of the U.S. population lived. Additionally, Walt didn't like all the businesses popping up around Disneyland and wanted control over a larger piece of property. He chose Orlando after a flyover in November 1963 and began purchasing land there secretly by creating fake companies so nobody would know he was the buyer. His first purchase of nearly 30,000 acres only cost around $80 per acre! Once he was revealed as the buyer, the price of land skyrocketed to $80,000 per acre!

Why did the price jump by 1000% overnight? Because of that name...Walt Disney. Once he was the known buyer, people knew what the land was really worth. Oh, the parallel to today's message! In Acts 9, Saul was completely transformed by seeing the light and hearing Jesus' voice. God called on Ananias to go to Saul, heal his blindness and baptize him, filling him with the Holy Spirit. Immediately, Saul was changed. He spent the next several days proclaiming the name of Jesus. He wanted others to know what Christ did for him, to feel what he felt and realize what accepting Christ would do for them both immediately and forevermore. Walt's name made that land priceless. If people only knew what the name of Jesus could do for their eternal future, they would be desperate to call on it. The only way they can know is by hearing it, and we must be the ones to tell them. Life only leads 2 places. Sheep and goats, remember? If people only knew how important Jesus was!

PRAYER—Father, I know Jesus' name is worth more than I can imagine. Help me to share that with others so they can know how important it is to their eternity. In His awesome name, Amen.

TODAY I WILL...go tell others about Jesus with the excitement of a changed Saul, making sure they know what He can do for them and how vital it is they know and accept Him.

FEBRUARY 26 **Read I TIMOTHY 4:6-10**

USE ALL YOUR LAND

Walt and the History of Disney – WDW Development

"I can do all things through him who strengthens me."
—Philippians 4:13

Have you ever played a simulator-type game designing something of your own? I used to enjoy playing "Roller Coaster Tycoon" where I got to create my own theme park. Maybe you've even drawn or envisioned your dream home and its layout. As mentioned yesterday, Walt Disney purchased nearly 30,000 acres of land in Florida. In the more than 50 years Disney has owned that land, they've developed only around half of it building parks, resorts, roads, etc. In other words, they own thousands of acres that haven't even been used yet. Just imagine what they could do with all that land! What would you do? Any ideas? There's so much potential there for expansion, advancement and progress. I can't wait to see where it leads in the future.

Another simple question today...are you using your full potential? God has blessed us with many gifts and talents, but are we really using them to full capacity for Him. In I Timothy 4, Paul encourages us to explore and use our full potential. He urges us to be fully trained for godliness even saying that physical exercise is of little value but training spiritually is far more important. In verse 10, he advises us to "toil and strive" because of the hope we have in Christ, meaning we should give nothing but our best for God. The well-known and inspiring verse above says with God's strength, there's no limit on what we can do. Don't make excuses or limit yourself with doubt, worry, fear or lack of confidence. Do everything you possibly can to live for Him and spread His message. If each of us would live up to our full potential in serving Him and others, there's no telling what we could do. Just like at Walt Disney World (WDW), the land is there. You have it. It's yours. See the potential. Develop it. And use it for God!

PRAYER—Lord, I know I can do anything with Your strength and guidance. Help me live up to my full potential in serving You, helping others and spreading the Gospel. In Jesus, Amen.

TODAY I WILL...make sure I'm honest with myself on how much I really can do for God. I will vow to live up to my full potential and do all I can to further His kingdom.

FEBRUARY 27 **Read PSALM 90:9-17**

JUST A MIST

Walt and the History of Disney – Walt's Death

"...you do not know what tomorrow will bring. What is your life? For you are a mist that appears for a little time and then vanishes."
—James 4:14

It was November 30, 1966, when Walt Disney decided he didn't feel well. He had just been diagnosed with lung cancer earlier that month having been a smoker since he was young. He was taken by ambulance to St. Joseph Hospital in Burbank, California. He spent his 65th birthday there on December 5 and died 10 days later, on December 15, 1966. He passed away having never seen Disney World come to life or realizing so many other dreams and visions he had, including Epcot. His remains were cremated with his ashes placed at the Forest Lawn Memorial Park in Glendale, California.

Needless to say, Walt Disney's death came as a shock. He had been healthy and active just a few days before, and nobody expected him to pass so suddenly, especially with so many plans on the horizon. His death, while sad and unexpected, is a familiar but important message to us all. Life is short, and we aren't guaranteed a single day. Today's psalm is a prayer of Moses. He mentions how brief life is and asks God to help him number his days. This is something we should all do as it's important to treat each individual day as a gift. Thank God each morning for blessing you with a new one and make a vow to use it for Him. James reemphasizes above that our life is like a mist. It's there briefly and then vanishes away. Our life is but a brief blip on the timeline compared with the eternity that is coming. Please make sure you're always prepared for this life to end and your eternal one to begin. While life is a gift we shouldn't wish away, we should always be looking forward to that day when we get to pass into forever with God.

PRAYER—Dear God, thank you for today. Help me to use it and every day You bless me with to glorify You and do Your will. Help me to always be ready for my life to end so I can begin my forever with You. Through Christ I pray, Amen.

TODAY I WILL...thank God for giving me one more day. I will do the same tomorrow and continuously for every day He blesses me with. I will be prepared at all times for my life to end.

FEBRUARY 28 **Read JOHN 13:31-35**

DO THEY KNOW YOUR NAME?

Walt and the History of Disney – Walt's Name

"Only let your manner of life be worthy of the gospel of Christ, so that whether I come and see you or am absent, I may hear of you."
—Philippians 1:27

When Walt Disney died, his brother Roy postponed his planned retirement to run the company and oversee the construction of Disney World. On October 1, 1971, nearly five years after Walt's death, the Magic Kingdom opened along with the Contemporary and Polynesian Resorts. 24 days later, Roy dedicated the park in a public ceremony. He declared that the name of the entire complex would be slightly lengthened and from then on be known as "Walt Disney World." He stated, "Everyone has heard of Ford cars. But have they all heard of Henry Ford, who started it all? Walt Disney World is in memory of the man who started it all, so people will know his name as long as Walt Disney World is here." And they do. Even today, 50 years later, the name Walt Disney is known and loved around the world and is synonymous with entertainment, family, happiness, magic and fun.

Just before His death, Jesus gave his Disciples a message intended for us all. He said, "A new commandment I give to you, that you love one another: just as I have loved you, you also are to love one another. By this all people will know that you are my disciples, if you have love for one another." Millions around the world know Walt's name, but even more know the name of Jesus Christ because of who He was, what He did and how He loved. Now the question remains: do they know your name too? Christ said others would know we are His by our love. So do they? Do they know you believe and have accepted Him as your Savior? They should know without a doubt you belong to God because of your outward showing of His love. They should know your name is synonymous with Christ and the love and service He showed to others. Have people heard of you? Do they know your name?

PRAYER—Lord, I want the world to know my name because of my example, service and the love I show to all. I want my name to reflect the name of Jesus in every way. In Him, Amen.

TODAY I WILL...make my name known. I will make sure I'm a good example and demonstrate love in all things, so others know my name parallels the name of Jesus.

MARCH THEME

DISNEY RIDES

MARCH 1 **Read EPHESIANS 1:3-14**

BACKSTAGE PASSES

Disney Rides – Rock 'n' Roller Coaster Starring Aerosmith

"But you are a chosen race, a royal priesthood, a holy nation, a people for his own possession, that you may proclaim the excellencies of him who called you out of darkness into his marvelous light."
—I Peter 2:9

New month. New theme. During March, we'll be discussing some of your favorite Disney park ride experiences. We begin with one of my favorites, the adrenaline-pumping, thrilling adventure that is the Rock 'n' Roller Coaster Starring Aerosmith. This attraction opened in Hollywood Studios (then called Disney-MGM Studios) in late July 1999. On opening day, there was a special, invitation-only experience hosted by Aerosmith themselves. Those invited got a free meal, limousine ride to the park and the chance to ride the attraction with a member of the band. This exhilarating roller coaster is over half a mile long, goes from 0 to 57 mph in 2.8 seconds and plays Aerosmith music throughout, thanks to five speakers surrounding each rider.

If you've experienced this exciting ride, you may remember it begins with a pre-show where the band is shown. During the video, a cast member is supposed to suggest some back-stage passes for all those riding. Sometimes the cast member forgets or is absent leading to a slightly awkward exchange by lead singer, Steven Tyler offering the passes unprompted. I've always enjoyed the music of Aerosmith and wouldn't mind an actual backstage pass to meet them. While I may never get that, I do have another backstage pass that's way more important, and it's offered to you too. In Ephesians 1, it's made clear that we were chosen before the world was even formed and predestined to be adopted by God. The verse above also states that we're a chosen people in God's possession. If you've accepted Christ, are following Him and remain faithful, it comes with a backstage pass to meet Him in Heaven. The end of today's passage says we receive the Holy Spirit as a guarantee of our eternal inheritance. Can you believe that? We are guaranteed those passes to meet God and His Son. Make sure you score a pass and hold on tight to it. They are limited and absolutely priceless!

PRAYER—Father, thank you for giving me Your Word so I know I'm chosen and adopted by You. Help me to remain faithful so I can keep my backstage pass to You. In His name, Amen.

TODAY I WILL...secure my backstage pass to God and help others find theirs too.

MARCH 2 **Read PSALM 42:1-11**

WATCH OUT FOR WATERFALLS

Disney Rides – Radiator Springs Racers

"Why are you cast down, O my soul, and why are you in turmoil within me? Hope in God; for I shall again praise him, my salvation and my God."
—Psalm 42:11

Have you ever seen a large and powerful waterfall? I'll never forget seeing Niagara Falls the first time. I was stunned by the sheer magnitude, force and beauty of it. Today's ride has just a small taste of that. We're going to travel all the way across the country to Disneyland's Radiator Springs Racers. This is definitely my personal favorite ride there. It opened in June 2012 and immediately had wait times up to six hours! It cost over $200 million to build, nearly 1/5 of the entire $1.1 billion dollar budget for the Cars Land expansion. This unique attraction features a race at the end between your ride vehicle and another with the winner always randomized.

There is one particular scene during this ride I want to focus on. Right as it begins, you travel leisurely around some curves and up into the "mountains" of Radiator Springs. There's one special moment when you come around the corner, the music blares from speakers around you and you see the most beautiful waterfall just above you. It's a spectacular moment where the physical beauty and music combine to give you that breathtaking feeling. It reminds me of today's reading where the psalmist states he's overwhelmed with life and his soul is downcast. He compares it to a great waterfall crashing over him. Life can become burdensome, and it may feel like a great waterfall is crashing upon you as well. But God is always there surrounding you with His love, ready to pull you out from underneath and into a peace only He can provide. At the end of the psalm, he asks himself why he's so dejected when he has hope in God and salvation promised. We can rest assured in the same. Don't let the waterfalls of life make you forget His love and care. He's there ready for your call. He will dry you off and give you everlasting love and unimaginable peace.

PRAYER—Father, thank you for being there when I feel overwhelmed and defeated. Give me Your peace and love and help me to feel You most in difficult times. In Jesus' name, Amen.

TODAY I WILL...hope in Him. I will tell God about any overpowering struggles I am dealing with and ask for a calm only He can provide.

MARCH 3 **Read ISAIAH 53:1-12**

OUR KEY CHARACTER

Disney Rides – Soarin' Around the World

"And there is salvation in no one else, for there is no other name by under heaven given among men by which we must be saved."
—Acts 4:12

In August, all devotionals will focus on various characters, but let me ask who's the most prominent or viewed Disney character? You might think Mickey Mouse, but I'd argue there's another possibility. Today we're riding an attraction featured on both coasts called Soarin' Around the World. Did you know while waiting in line for this ride there are clouds that pass overhead? The lights will even dim when the cloud is above you and then brighten when it passes. The tracks that hold the ride vehicles are one million pounds of solid steel! Not only that but each ride vehicle holds up to 30 people and weighs 37 tons a piece. This is one heavy ride!

If you've experienced both the original and current versions of this ride, you'll notice they are quite different, with one notable exception. At the end of both, Tinkerbell appears to wave her magic wand over the Disney Park. When you think about it, Tinkerbell emerges in a lot of Disney features, logos, promos and advertisements. She often opens or closes a film and is featured flying across the Magic Kingdom during their fireworks show. One could argue she has become their key character. In relation, I ask who is your key character? If you had to advertise yourself, who would you want others to see illustrating who you are? I hope the answer is obvious. Today's reading from Isaiah is a prophecy all about Jesus indicating who He will become and what He will endure for us. It's a significant passage that should be read often. We've already discussed how Jesus, as stated above, is the only path to our salvation. He should be our key character representing the goals we're all striving for and who others see in us. The most important person to ever live should be the one we base our entire lives around. Jesus is the key to our purpose, our mission and our eternal happiness.

PRAYER—Lord, I want to center my life around Jesus' teachings and example and for others to see Him in me. Help me to know Him better and strive to be like Him. In His name, Amen.

TODAY I WILL...list every burden or difficulty of Jesus listed in Isaiah 53. I will then thank God for each one and praise God for the sacrifice of His Son.

MARCH 4 **Read MARK 4:35-41**

GIMME A BREAK

Disney Rides – Avatar Flight of Passage

"Now may the Lord of peace himself give you peace at all times in every way."
—2 Thessalonians 3:16

Let's move to Animal Kingdom to ride Avatar Flight of Passage. We've certainly started March off with a bang, riding some of the best Disney has to offer. This one's no exception. It includes the sights, the smells and the exhilaration of flying through the air while riding on the back of a banshee that you can actually feel breathing. *Avatar* was a 2009 blockbuster that currently tops the list in worldwide box office revenue at $2.8 billion. This related attraction opened in May 2017 and the lines haven't subsided since. There is one exit from this attraction where you can see three red handprints on the wall with initials under them. They belong to *Avatar* director, James Cameron, producer, Jon Landau and Disney Imagineer, Joe Rohde.

This is one of my favorite rides in all of Disney World. Every part is exciting, but I actually enjoy most a scene in the middle when your banshee enters a cave, stopping to rest. The beauty of the cave along with the scent makes it extremely tranquil and enjoyable. It's just nice to have a peaceful, quiet moment graciously placed within an action-packed, heart-pumping journey. At the end of Mark 4, we read an incredible story of a rough storm at sea. Jesus' disciples are fearful they might perish while He's asleep. Talk about a heavy sleeper! But He simply awakes and says, "Peace! Be still!" And it is. He rebukes the storm and then his disciples, questioning their lack of faith. This teaches us to have a stronger faith that God will give us peace during the noise of life if we only ask for it. When He gives you those quiet moments, make sure to focus on Him, thank Him and use the calmness to restore your faith in Him. Just like that special cave scene in this ride, God will provide peace if you just ask. Don't forget to seek Him in all things, especially when you just need a break.

PRAYER—God, thank You for peace. Please grant me periodic moments of quiet, especially when I'm too busy or stressed. Help me to remember you during those times. In Christ, Amen.

TODAY I WILL... find a moment of peace. I will take a break from life today, find a quiet place, breathe and talk to God without any interruptions from the world.

MARCH 5 **Read I JOHN 5:1-5**

DOES HE RULE YOUR WORLD?

Disney Rides – Mr. Toad's Wild Ride

"We know that we are from God, and the whole world lies in the power of the evil one."
—I John 5:19

I love living where we have two great choices when it comes to vacationing at Disney. We typically choose World because it's much closer to home, but we also love heading to Land every few years. The parks share similarities of course, but there are also many differences historically and in the many unique ride experiences. Today's choice is one of those rare ones that makes an occasional trip west well worth it. Mr. Toad's Wild Ride is one of the few 1955 opening day attractions still around in Disneyland. It's a simple, dark ride that used to reside on both coasts. The Disney World version had two separate tracks providing two unique ride experiences. Die-hard fans were not happy when the WDW version closed and staged in-park protests called "toad-ins" to show their displeasure.

This ride is exciting of course, but it's also dark and a bit spooky throughout, especially with the final room being a depiction of hell! It's a scene not found in either the film or the book the ride is based on, but it's certainly a memorable one as you enter a heated room full of bouncing devils, see a large, judicial demon and then nearly get scorched by an enormous, fire-breathing dragon. Sound fun? In I John 5, we are told as long as we believe in Christ and love the Father, we will overcome this world. Sad but true, our world is run by Satan, as evidenced by the verse above, and can be a scary place like that final "wild ride" room. But we need not fear as long as we are holding steadfast to God's love and showing Him constant love in return which will help us to overcome the world and be saved in the end. Satan's control on this world is evident all around us, but don't let him rule your life. Keep your faith strong and your love everlasting, and you'll make it through any dark ride heading your way.

PRAYER—Holy Father, help me to maintain my faith in You and Your Son at all times. Keep Satan from ruling my life so I can escape the evils of this world. Through Jesus, Amen.

TODAY I WILL...not let the devil control any part of me. I will firmly tell him "No!" when tempted with anything worldly.

MARCH 6 **Read MATTHEW 14:22-33**

WHAT ARE YOU LOOKING AT?

Disney Rides – Finding Nemo Submarine Voyage

"When he saw the wind, he was afraid, and beginning to sink he cried out, 'Lord, save me.'"
—*Matthew 14:30*

Since we're here, let's stay for a few more unique attractions Disneyland has to offer. Today we're going below the surface to an attraction that once had a similar experience at WDW before it closed in 1994. Thankfully, you can still enjoy this rare submarine ride in the Tomorrowland area of Disneyland. When it originally opened in 1959, it was based on the *USS Nautilus*, the first nuclear-powered submarine to journey to the North Pole. The original version shut down in 1998 and stayed closed until 2007 when it finally reopened to its current Pixar-hit theming. More than 30 tons of recycled crushed glass was used to create the appearance of colorful rockwork and coral. The ride still uses the original fleet of 8 subs which were inspected in 2001 by a naval engineering firm who discovered they each have 40-50 years of life remaining.

Experiencing this attraction represents the only times I've ever gotten to ride in a submarine which is probably the case of many park guests. It's slightly unnerving and a bit claustrophobic but also very exhilarating to sink below the surface for the nearly 14-minute ride. In Matthew 14, we read a familiar story of Jesus walking on the water towards his disciples. When Peter asks to join him, Jesus tells him to come. Peter steps out of the boat and begins walking on the water too, but when he takes his eyes off Jesus focusing on the wind and waves instead, he begins to sink. What an obvious, relatable lesson! In the NIV version, Hebrews 12:2 tells us to "fix our eyes on Jesus." If we do that at all times, we won't sink into the storms of life like Peter or slip below the surface like those impressive Disney submarines. We must keep focus on Christ, who He was and what He did and then mirror Him. As long as we do that always, we too can stay above water and survive in this tumultuous world.

PRAYER—Dear God, I want to step out of the boat and walk towards you throughout my life. Help me to always keep my eyes fixed on Jesus so I don't sink. Because of Christ, Amen.

TODAY I WILL...stay afloat. I will look to Jesus by reading about Him, learning more about Him and imitating Him in every aspect of my life.

MARCH 7 **Read 2 PETER 3:7-13**

LET HIM IN

Disney Rides – Monsters, Inc. Mike and Sully to the Rescue

"Behold, I stand at the door and knock. If anyone hears my voice and opens the door, I will come in to him and eat with him, and he with me."

—Revelation 3:20

Pop quiz! What do you do when someone knocks on your door? It may be an unwanted visitor, making you reluctant to open it. Today's Disneyland ride features a memorable scene of multiple doors mirroring the film it's based on. Monsters, Inc. Mike and Sully to the Rescue is another one our family really enjoys, although we've noticed it's a little hard to find, tucked away at Disney's California Adventure (DCA). The dark ride transports you through several scenes from the original *Monsters, Inc.* film. A fun task while riding is trying to find "Boo" in each scene. When you see her on top of Randall, banging him on the head, one of the colors he changes to is the wallpaper from the Haunted Mansion ride.

As mentioned, a pivotal scene near the end of both the film and ride is when Mike and Sully are desperately looking for Boo's door. In both cases, you see hundreds of doors all around you. In the verse above from Revelation, Jesus Himself states He is knocking at our door, waiting for us to answer and invite Him in. He's asking you to let Him into your life and your heart. In today's reading from 2 Peter, we are warned that the final day will come when we least expect it and like a thief in the night. Normally, a thief is someone you definitely wouldn't want coming to your door. However, if it means the promised second coming of Christ, I'm ready to see Him at my doorstep. We're told in verse 11 to be ready at all times and to live lives of holiness and godliness, waiting in haste for His return. You can ignore an unwanted salesman, visitor or thief at your door, but don't snub the knocking Savior. He's trying to enter and become a part of your life before it's too late. Let Him in!

PRAYER—Dear God, I'm so grateful that Jesus is knocking at my door. Help me to let Him in and never let Him go. Help my life to reflect Him at all times. In Jesus' name, Amen.

TODAY I WILL...let Jesus in. Open your door and let Him into your life, your thoughts, your heart and your soul. Don't ever let Him leave and don't wait until it's too late!

MARCH 8 **Read MATTHEW 7:24-29**

A FIRM FOUNDATION

Disney Rides – Pixar Pal-A-Round

"...on this rock I will build my church, and the gates of hell shall not prevail against it."
—Matthew 16:18

I've ridden several Ferris wheels over the years with only one unpleasant experience. Also found at DCA, the Pixar Pal-A-Round was originally known as the Sun Wheel and then Mickey's Fun Wheel until it was rethemed to feature various Pixar characters in 2018. It originally opened in February 2001, is 160 feet tall and lit by 1400 LED computer-controlled lights. It was inspired by the famous Wonder Wheel from Coney Island, NY that was built in 1920 and still runs to this day. There are two types of gondolas riders can choose. Most remain fixed and stable, but there are a few on this particular attraction that slide in and out of the wheel as it revolves. As they slide and catch, they swing back and forth giving the riders a thrilling experience. Or in my case, a nauseous one. The first time I rode, I thought it would be fun to swing. I was quite wrong. I've ridden it since, but always make sure to choose a fixed gondola. No fixed = No feel good = No fun.

Today's reading is a familiar analogy from Jesus comparing a wise and foolish man. The wise man builds his house on sturdy rocks creating a firm foundation, while the foolish man builds on sand causing his house to collapse during the first storm. Similarly, Jesus teaches our foundation must be firmly rooted in His words. We can't be weak or wishy-washy in our faith. We can't just choose the parts of the Bible we want to follow. We must be fixed and secure, determined to follow Christ and all Scripture as closely as possible. Otherwise, like those unstable gondolas, we'll slide right out of God's favor becoming sick with sin under Satan's control. If you want to try a swinging gondola at DCA, go for it. Good luck! But don't let life's storms knock down your house. Choose to be firm in your faith and your following of Jesus.

PRAYER—Lord, help me to have a strong foundation and be firm in my faith. Help me follow all the words of Christ and Your Word and not waver. In His name, Amen.

TODAY I WILL...check my foundation confirming it's deeply rooted in a strong, Godly faith. Right and wrong won't be determined by me, but only what comes from Christ and the Word.

MARCH 9 **Read PSALM 49:5-12**

THE OLDEST RIDE

Disney Rides – Prince Charming Regal Carousel

"For the living know they will die; but the dead know nothing."
—Ecclesiastes 9:5

Back across the map we go to board Prince Charming Regal Carousel at the Magic Kingdom in the middle of Fantasyland at WDW. Speaking of middle, when originally placed, Walt's brother, Roy, noticed the carousel was slightly off-center looking through the castle breezeway, so the entire structure was moved just eight inches. Talk about detail! It was formerly called Cinderella's Golden Carousel, but there is debate on whether she has her own horse. Many Disney enthusiasts, cast members and even some publications have claimed her horse is in the 2nd layer with a golden bow on its tail. However, other experts have debunked that myth stating her horse would never be on an inner row but instead prominently displayed and decorated.

I chose this classic ride simply because it's the oldest in all WDW. Originally built in 1917 and placed in Detroit, MI, it was purchased by Walt Disney in 1967. Its sister ride in Disneyland, the King Arthur Carrousel (yes, spelled with an extra "R"), is almost as old having been built in 1922. In Genesis 5:25-27, we read of the oldest man to ever live, Methuselah at 969 years old! Obviously, we don't live quite that long anymore. In today's psalm, we read about death's inevitability with the above verse stating the same. Death is an obvious and certain truth unless Christ returns first, but how much do we think about and plan for it? That's not stated to be disturbing or gloomy but in fact should be something we look forward to as we pass into eternity with God. It's fine to want to live a long and full life, but we must also always be prepared for the end. Life is short and will pass quickly. We won't outlive Methuselah or probably even today's iconic carousel, so make sure you're comfortable, confident and excited for what's to come when God decides to call you home.

PRAYER—Father, I'm grateful for life, but I also want to be always ready for your call home. Help me to realize death is certain and be prepared and sure of my eternity. In Jesus, Amen.

TODAY I WILL...meditate on my undeniable fate making sure I'm 100% confident in what will come next when that day comes and be excited about my eternal future.

MARCH 10 **Read LUKE 14:12-14**

LESSONS FROM A TOAD

Disney Rides – The Many Adventures of Winnie the Pooh

"Show hospitality to one another without grumbling."
—I Peter 4:9

We recently discussed Mr. Toad's Wild Ride at Disneyland and the fact it was also formerly a WDW attraction. It was shut down there in 1998 to make way for a honey-seeking, pooh bear and his bouncing friend. The turnaround time between Mr. Toad's closure and this ride's opening was only 9 months! As mentioned, there were some minor protests with the change, but Imagineers felt justified as Walt himself had always been a big fan of Winnie the Pooh ever since his daughter, Diane, fell in love with him at a young age. Nevertheless, they placed a couple of tributes to remember Mr. Toad and his friends. Early on in this ride, you enter a room with several portraits. One shows Mr. Toad handing over the deed to Pooh's friend, Owl, while another displays Pooh himself standing with Moley, one of Mr. Toad's best friends.

In true Disney fashion, these special images attempt to convey the message of no hard feelings from the attraction switch. These characters, who aren't normally seen together, are shown smiling, happy and welcoming to their new friends. In today's reading from Luke, Jesus shares a brief but important parable teaching us to also be welcoming, and not just to friends or the wealthy, but to all types of people, especially those in need. Hebrews 13:2 trains us to show brotherly love and hospitality to strangers with the above verse saying to do so without grumbling. As Christians, we are to be friendly to everyone, not just those we're comfortable with. There are many different people in the world, some needing desperately to hear about Jesus. We must be willing to share that good news with everyone, even those we wouldn't normally associate with. Take a lesson from the hospitality of a toad and his friends. Be open and welcoming to all, especially strangers. They might just be a soul God needs you to save.

PRAYER—Father, help me to show hospitality to everyone, especially strangers or those in need. Give me courage and knowledge to talk to them about You. Through Jesus, Amen.

TODAY I WILL...make sure to always be welcoming and friendly to all people. I will smile and speak to anyone I come in contact with knowing I might be the one to help them find Jesus.

MARCH 11 **Read 2 TIMOTHY 4:1-5**

REACHING ALL NATIONS

Disney Rides – It's a Small World

"Go therefore and make disciples of all nations..."
—Matthew 28:19

"There is just one moon and one golden sun, and a smile means friendship to everyone." Those lyrics are from a song you've probably heard way too often if you're a Disney regular. In correlation to that lyric, there's an actual sun and moon to search for in each room of the "Small World" ride. Did you know there's not a single minute of the day this song is not playing? Since the ride is found in 5 of the 6 Disney parks throughout the world, it's playing at all times and well over 1000 times per day per park. When it opened in Disneyland in 1966, Walt invited children globally to dress in their native garb, bring water from their nearest sea and pour it into the ride's river symbolizing the uniting of the waters as well as people of all cultures.

The message of the ride and song are pretty evident as is the lesson from today's reading. In it, we are charged to be always ready to teach the Word of God. Additionally, we're warned of a time when people won't want to hear the truth but only listen to what suits them. My friends, that time is now! There's so much taught in our world today that goes against Scripture and God's desires. We're commanded to teach His truth no matter the cost to "all nations" according to the verse above. Referring back to yesterday's message, we can't just teach those we know or see daily. We must make efforts to reach those all over the globe. If we're unable to physically travel, we should support those who do aiding any way possible. You may get tired of this ride's song, but you can't deny the importance of its message. It is a small world, and we must learn to appreciate and unite with all cultures. More importantly, we must spread His message all over so that many come to know His truth and how to be with Him forever.

PRAYER—Heavenly Father, I ask for peace and unity around the world. Most of all, I pray that every culture will come to know the truth about You. Help me to assist in spreading Your message to many different cultures and locations. In Jesus' name, Amen.

TODAY I WILL...make plans to do mission work or at least aid or encourage a missionary.

MARCH 12 **Read 2 THESSALONIANS 3:6-15**

GET TO WORK

Disney Rides – Seven Dwarfs Mine Train

"Whatever you do, work heartily, as for the Lord and not for men..."
—Colossians 3:23

If you currently hold a job, what are some words you'd use to describe it? Strenuous? Exciting? Tiring? Challenging? Stressful? Fun? There are probably times you could use all those words. I enjoy my job, but there are certainly moments when it's difficult. During those times, I'll admit I typically don't break into a happy song while working. But Disney characters sometimes do! Seven Dwarfs Mine Train opened in May 2014 and is one of only two rides currently on property that sends you a video of your experience. (Tower of Terror is the other.) It's also one of hopefully very few rides that have caught fire. In November 2014, some embers from the "Wishes" fireworks show landed on the exterior causing a brief blaze. Thankfully, nobody was hurt, the fire was extinguished quickly and the ride reopened the next afternoon.

I especially enjoy entering the mine on this ride and getting to view some amazing and advanced animatronics of all seven dwarfs. In line with the film, they are laboring happily while singing the well-known "Heigh-Ho" song. Perhaps their on-the-job, outward joy and chipper attitudes can assist today's lesson. In 2 Thessalonians 3, Paul warns against not working and being too idle. He even states if someone is unwilling to work, that person should not eat. Many other passages, including the verse above, command us to work energetically and positively. The good Lord blessed most of us with the capacity to labor, make a living and provide for our families. We must take that role seriously. It's not always easy, but we can use trying times to lean on God, use His strength and realize what a blessing it is having the ability in the first place. Understand the importance and find the motivation to do your job effectively with contentment. Please God with your work ethic and attitude which may be a needed encouragement to others.

PRAYER—Lord, if I'm able, thank you for my health and ability to work. Help me do my job with joy and a positive attitude, so I may be pleasing in Your sight. In Jesus, Amen.

TODAY I WILL...vow to work hard for God at whatever job(s) He has blessed me with. I will realize what a gift it is to be healthy and able to work.

MARCH 13 **Read ROMANS 3:9-23**

SOAKED WITH SIN

Disney Rides – Splash Mountain

"Are we to continue in sin that grace may abound? By no means!"
—Romans 6:1-2

Think quick! Which park at Walt Disney World does NOT have a water ride? (Answer at the end.) The other three parks have at least one. Some might get you wet, but others are a sure thing. Welcome to Splash Mountain! This iconic attraction exists in Florida, California and Tokyo. It was originally going to be named "Zip-a-Dee River Run" after the classic song. However, then CEO, Michael Eisner, really wanted to use the attraction to promote 1984's *Splash,* the first film Disney produced under the "Touchstone Pictures" label. Most of his suggestions were ignored, but he was able to rename it to market the film.

Some Disney planners suggest sitting in the back on this ride to avoid getting wet, but I can tell you from experience, it's gonna happen to some extent no matter where you sit. Most likely to a great extent! In Romans 3, Paul emphasizes something else that's gonna happen, teaching that every single person sins even adding in verse 23, "all have sinned and fall short of the glory of God." I John 1:8 echoes saying, "if we say we have no sin, we deceive ourselves, and the truth is not in us." We all go against God's instructions. Thankfully, He offers immeasurable grace to cover us if we're sincere asking for forgiveness. However, as the important verse above states, His grace doesn't give us permission to sin freely. We can't be complacent in sin expecting God to constantly forgive. We must strive to be perfect like Christ. We'll never get there, of course, but it should still be a goal. Getting wet on Splash Mountain is inevitable, just like our sin and God's grace to cover a repentant heart. But don't let that be a free pass. Strive for perfection. Stay dry and pure before God. Become more like Christ each day. (Hollywood Studios has no water ride, although you might get wet at Fantasmic if you sit close enough.)

PRAYER—Lord, I don't want to sin against you, but I do. I repent and will strive to be sin free and perfect like Jesus. Thank You for Your grace helping me to get me there. In Him, Amen.

TODAY I WILL...confess my sins to God and make sure I don't have the attitude that I can sin freely due to God's abundant and generous grace.

MARCH 14 **Read EXODUS 19:16-20**

A MIGHTY VOICE

Disney Rides – Big Thunder Mountain Railroad

"Our God is in the heavens; He does all that He pleases."
—Psalm 115:3

Let's stay in Frontierland, or "Westernland" if we're in Tokyo, and ride another well-loved attraction nearby. Big Thunder Mountain Railroad is located in the same three parks as Splash Mountain but can additionally be found in Paris as well. This mine train, roller coaster includes a creative back story and many special details, including a hidden Tinker Bell near the exit of the WDW version. It's a little hard to find so ask a cast member to help. Did you know this ride can help cure kidney stones!? A medical doctor actually asked Disney and received permission to do a study while riding this attraction. Several of his patients had been cured of kidney stones while riding, so he took a 3D kidney model and rode several times finding that 70% of the time, the stones passed. Good to know as I've had them twice. Next time it'll be Disney to the rescue!

Speaking of thunder...Exodus 19 contains the story of Moses being called up to Mount Sinai to speak with the Lord. He will receive the Ten Commandments in the next chapter. In these verses, it says that God spoke to Moses "in thunder." In John 12:28-29, God again speaks from Heaven, and the people who hear it think it's thunder. God's voice, at least in these cases, has a powerful, thunder-like sound. Our God is obviously mighty and authoritative. His voice is like thunder, and we know He can do all things. Take comfort in the fact that He's your Father, is on your side and uses His power and strength to protect and save you. Remember this whenever you hear a thunderstorm. Such storms can be unsettling and scary, but maybe thinking of it as God's voice will make it less so. Thank God for his awesome power and mighty voice. He will speak to you too if you only take the time to listen.

PRAYER—Heavenly Father, thank You for Your mighty power. I'm so grateful You are on my side. Help me to listen to You. Guide me and let me hear Your voice. In Jesus' name, Amen.

TODAY I WILL...listen to God by reading His Word and letting His Spirit speak to me. Next time I hear thunder, I will make a point to listen to God and thank Him.

MARCH 15 **Read I PETER 4:12-19**

HAPPILY HAUNTED

Disney Rides – Haunted Mansion

"Count it all joy, my brothers, when you meet trials of various kinds..."
—James 1:2

Dim the lights. Cue the creepy music. And let's get a little ominous fog flowing in here as we visit a spooky manor full of "999 happy haunts." The Haunted Mansion is found in five of the six Disney parks around the world. It first opened at Disneyland in 1969, although the building that houses it had been sitting empty since 1963. In California and Paris, the "stretching room" is actually an elevator moving downward. However, in the other parks, the ceiling moves upward making it appear you are dropping. When first planned, this was going to be a walk-through attraction. A boat ride was also proposed. There was also a time when Disneyland used live actors in knights' armor to jump out and scare riders. However, they quit this a short time later due to guests jumping out of their seats and attacking the unlucky cast members.

Do you find joy in being scared? I know some don't, but I enjoy a good scare occasionally. In a similar way, Peter talks in today's reading about suffering as a Christian, instructing us to actually find joy in it knowing it means we are God's chosen. James says the same above. Additionally, take a look at Acts 5. In verse 40, we read the apostles were beaten for talking about Christ. But look at the very next verse when it says they left "rejoicing that they were counted worthy to suffer dishonor for the name." They rejoiced for getting beaten! They found joy in suffering for Christ. Hopefully, we won't suffer to that extent, but we should consider it an honor and blessing if persecuted in any way for our Christian beliefs. You may not enjoy being frightened at the Haunted Mansion or something even more terrifying but try to rejoice when you suffer for Christ. It's a privilege and means you're doing it right!

PRAYER—Father God, I know I will suffer trials throughout my life because of my belief and faith in You. Help me to see it as honorable and find joy in it. Through Jesus, Amen.

TODAY I WILL...consider any trials or suffering I'm currently facing. If it is due to my faith in God or belief in Jesus Christ, I will see it as a blessing and badge of honor.

MARCH 16 **Read 2 TIMOTHY 3:10-17**

TURN ON THE LIGHT

Disney Rides – Space Mountain

"Your word is a lamp to my feet and a light to my path."
—Psalm 119:105

We just had a scare, so let's keep our hearts pumpin' with one of the original adrenaline boosters. Space Mountain opened first at Disney World in 1975 and two years later in Disneyland. Like Thunder Mountain, it is now in five of six Disney parks around the world, although in Hong Kong and Paris, it's called "Hyperspace Mountain" and includes a Star Wars overlay. This was the first ever roller coaster to be both indoors and controlled by a computer. One of the most bizarre incidents ever at WDW occurred when a couple tried to smuggle their baby onto this attraction stuffed in a duffel bag. Thankfully, cast members noticed the bag moving, asked that it be opened and discovered the child. Parents of the year right there, folks!

I used to love this ride, but my excitement has unfortunately diminished over time, mostly because it takes place completely in darkness. While I thought that was super cool as a kid, my adult body disagrees, needing to see what's coming. In 2 Timothy 3, Paul stresses the importance of the written Word making clear it's straight from God and vital for believers to use to guide their lives. The psalm above states it's like a light guiding our lifelong path. God's Word is the very foundation showing us how to live. If we don't use it, it's like riding Space Mountain. We're in the dark and can't see where we're going which, in my case, can cause some queasy feelings. Life without the Word will do the same, leading us down the wrong path and making us sick with sin. We need the light of God's Word to luminate each step of our path. It's an essential tool to avoid ending up in eternal darkness. Focus daily on God's Word which will light the way to the everlasting brightness of an eternity with Him.

PRAYER—Father, thank you for Your Word. I know it's vital to my survival as Your faithful follower. Keep me from the darkness of the world by keeping me focused on the light of Your Word. In His name, Amen.

TODAY I WILL...see the light. I will continue to give focus daily for the rest of my life to God's Word knowing it's the only guide to keep me moving forward spiritually and eternally.

MARCH 17 **Read LUKE 4:1-13**

A TASTE OF TEMPTATION

Disney Rides – Tomorrowland Transit Authority PeopleMover

"Watch and pray that you may not enter into temptation. The spirit indeed is willing, but the flesh is weak."
—Matthew 26:41

Time for a break! We've had several consecutive thrills with a scare thrown in to boot, so let's hop on something a bit more calming. Today's ride opened at WDW in 1975, the same year as Space Mountain. It had opened 8 years earlier in Disneyland but sadly closed there permanently in 1995, although the track has remained for over two decades since. WDW's version was originally called the WEDway PeopleMover using Walt's initials. The name has since been lengthened twice, although most today just call it the PeopleMover or TTA for short. Guests seem to enjoy this attraction for many reasons. It's long (10 min.), holds a lot of people, rarely has a long line and best of all, is super relaxing and peaceful. In addition, it includes a sampling of all Tomorrowland offers as you travel over, around and even through many of its attractions, shops and eateries as well as a gigantic model displaying Walt's vision of Epcot.

In Luke 4, we read the story of Jesus being tempted by Satan with food (He hadn't eaten in 40 days), power and authority. Jesus, of course, doesn't fall into the devil's evil traps and uses the Word, as discussed yesterday, each time to combat him. Like Christ, we will all face temptation throughout life. As the TTA gives you a taste of all Tomorrowland offers, we will be enticed to explore and sample all the pleasures of the world. As previously mentioned, our world is full of evil, dressed up to look like entertainment and fun. Jesus spoke the verse above to His disciples the night before His death, and it holds true for us today. We may desire to serve God in spirit, but our bodies are weak often desiring to just taste what the world offers. Take the advice of Jesus by watching closely and praying diligently that temptation doesn't ever get the best of you.

PRAYER—Lord, please help me to recognize and resist the temptation to sample anything of this world that goes against You or Your Word. In Jesus' name, Amen.

TODAY I WILL...make sure I'm not falling into the temptations of Satan to do anything going against God. I will continually pray for the strength to resist.

MARCH 18 **Read I PETER 2:21-25**

SYNCHRONIZE YOUR STEPS

Disney Rides – Mickey & Minnie's Runaway Railway

"...whoever says he abides in him ought to walk in the same way in which he walked."
—I John 2:6

Ever seen synchronized swimming? Check it out on YouTube. It's fascinating how perfectly the teams are matched step-for-step. It reminds me of one portion of this long overdue tribute to Mickey and Minnie that debuted recently. It opened in 2020 in WDW and is under construction in California's Disneyland as of this writing. It is bathed in history and hidden tributes to the past. I'll share just a couple in that it uses several sound effects created by Disney legend, Jimmy Macdonald, who passed away in 1991. He was not only a "sound effects wizard" who had a 48-year history with Disney, but he also took over for Walt voicing Mickey for a brief period. This was also the final job for another legend, Russi Taylor, who had voiced Minnie since 1986. She passed away in 2019, just a short time after recording for this attraction.

I've really enjoyed this the few times now I've gotten to ride. There's so much to see and take in, plus the fact that it provides such a variety of different ride sequences. One of the unique rooms during the journey is a dance studio where Daisy Duck leads the ride vehicles in a waltz followed by a conga. During this sequence, you can see your ride vehicle and all others in large mirrors surrounding the room. Each one dances and moves perfectly in sync to the music reminding me of those synchronized swimmers. It also parallels today's reading from I Peter where Christ is highlighted, and we're told to follow His direct steps and example. The verse above repeats telling us to walk the same way He did. Like those synced up swimmers and ride vehicles, we should be perfectly aligned with everything Christ did. His words. His works. His ways. Reading and learning more about Him should provide us a perfect pattern. When you look in a mirror, do you see a reflection of Jesus and do your steps perfectly match His?

PRAYER—Lord, I want to be perfectly aligned to the steps of my Savior. I'm so grateful for His example. Help me know Him better so I can imitate everything about Him. In Him, Amen.

TODAY I WILL...decide if I see Jesus in the mirror or if my steps need to be altered and realigned to His.

MARCH 19 **Read 2 PETER 1:5-11**

BUILDING A CHRISTIAN

Disney Rides – Test Track

"...be all the more diligent to confirm your calling and election, for if you practice these qualities you will never fall."
—2 Peter 1:10

Back in February, I asked if you'd ever designed your own house or park on a simulator-type game. Let's take it a step further. What if you could design a person? What qualities would they need to have? Think about that while we experience another extreme thrill. Test Track opened in Epcot in 1999 and has continually been a favorite but also a ride that tends to break down quite often. It holds the current record for being both the fastest (65mph) and longest (5,246 feet, just short of a mile!) ride at WDW. It was originally planned to go 95mph but was lowered for safety. The attraction uses 25 cars at a time and can transport up to 1200 guests per hour. Each car travels 50,000 miles per year and is designed to last up to a million miles!

When this ride debuted, guests rode along as each vehicle faced several road and environmental tests. In 2012, after a major refurbishment, the experience changed to each guest designing their own vehicle to be rated in various categories along the way. Personally, I like the new experience better. It's fun to create your own car and see how it ranks. Today's Bible passage focuses on designing not a perfect car, but the perfect Christian. Peter teaches they should have the following qualities: faith, virtue, knowledge, self-control, steadfastness, godliness, brotherly affection and love. Do any of those match what you would've included in your person design? Better question... do they match your own qualities? We're told if we add these assets to our lives, we will not fall. More importantly, verse 11 says we will be granted entrance in God's kingdom. Seems like these qualities are pretty important! Make sure you include them when building yourself. They are vital in creating an effective Christian heading in the right direction towards the gates of Heaven.

PRAYER—Father God, help me to evaluate myself often adding all the qualities from today's passage to my life so I may be worthy of Your eternal kingdom. In His name, Amen.

TODAY I WILL... write down all of the qualities listed above and how I am demonstrating each in my life. I will make it a goal to exude them both openly and within.

MARCH 20 **Read MATTHEW 4:18-22**

GRAB YOUR ROD AND REEL

Disney Rides – Living with the Land

"And he said to them, "Follow me, and I will make you fishers of men."
—Matthew 4:19

We just zoomed outside on WDW's fastest. Our hearts are pounding, and our hair is likely unmanageable. Back to some calm. Trying to provide a nice balance here. Living with the Land, also at Epcot, offers a long, pleasant, tranquil voyage through an agricultural focus. When it opened with the park in 1982, it was called "Listen to the Land." In 1993, it got its only major refurbishment to date which included the name change, along with a new song, opening and final scene. At one time, it featured live narrators who rode along in your boat as opposed to the current recorded narration. The dog in the farmhouse scene might look familiar as he's also used in the Pirates of the Caribbean jail scene and the Carousel of Progress.

I enjoy this ride but also loved walking through it during the "Behind the Seeds" tour which allows guests to tour the greenhouse, hear fascinating information and even do a little taste test. (The cucumbers were the absolute best I've ever tasted!) My favorite part was the aquarium area where we got to see and feed the hundreds of fish housed there. I also got to fulfill a lifelong dream and touch the famous hidden Mickey hose. (Yes, I'm a Disney geek!) Seeing the surplus of fish in those tanks reminds me of several New Testament stories. In addition to the passage above, read John 6:1-14 and 21:1-14, both well-known fish stories. In Matthew, Jesus calls His first disciples who are fishing, telling them they will now fish for believers instead. The other passages include Jesus multiplying 2 small fish to feed over 5000, as well as Him telling his disciples to recast their nets leading to an enormous catch. In all 3 stories, the goal is to multiply the fish. We are all fish before being called and multiplied into Christ's church. Once we know and accept Him, we are disciples with a new calling to multiply the catch by fishing for others. Take that calling seriously and see just how many fish you can reel in for our Father.

PRAYER—Dear God, I want to be Your fisherman. Give me the ability and courage to catch many fish for Your kingdom. Help me multiply them as Jesus so often did. In His name, Amen.

TODAY I WILL...catch fish for God.

MARCH 21 **Read JEREMIAH 29:10-14**

WHAT'S MY FUTURE?

Disney Rides – Spaceship Earth

"Commit your work to the Lord, and your plans will be established."
—Proverbs 16:3

Ever been to a fortune-teller? It would be fun to try even though I don't personally believe they can see the future. Spaceship Earth, which opened with Epcot, also attempts to give you a glimpse of the future as you complete your ride around the enormous, geodesic sphere that took 26 months alone to build. It weighs 16 million pounds and is covered with 11,324 triangular facets. Riders experience a leisurely, 15-minute journey through the history of our world with narration throughout. Vic Perrin, Walter Cronkite, Jeremy Irons ("Scar") and Judi Dench have all served as narrators. When it first opened, there were some mechanical issues particularly when the vehicles rotate to travel backwards. As that didn't always work, a cast member was often stationed at the top to manually rotate and lock the vehicles into place before descent.

As a former World History teacher, I covered nearly everything seen during this ride and always dreamed of somehow transporting my students to Epcot for a phenomenal object lesson. Therefore, I love the history involved here, but also enjoy the end during your descent "back to Earth" when you are asked questions to determine your future. You are then shown animated figures, with your actual face (always a highlight), experiencing several possible futuristic technologies that are fun to dream about possibly someday coming true. What does your future hold? Today's reading is God telling Jeremiah He knows and holds his future. Sure, it'd be nice if God told us the same directly, but He doesn't have to. Proverbs assures us if we simply give everything to Him, He will guide our future. Knowing God is in and holds our future is enough. Don't fear what's coming down the road. If you're doing everything possible to follow God and keep His commands, your future rests with Him. He's got it, and it'll be incredible!

PRAYER—Lord, I commit to you my body, my work, my future and my soul. It's all Yours to do what you will. I'm so glad You hold and will be in my future. Through Christ, Amen.

TODAY I WILL...close my eyes and picture what my future will look like making sure to see God in every part of it.

MARCH 22 **Read EPHESIANS 1:15-23**

ONE LITTLE SPARK TO SERVE

Disney Rides – Journey into Imagination with Figment

"Now there are varieties of gifts, but the same Spirit; and there are varieties of service, but the same Lord."
—I Corinthians 12:4-5

We've been stuck in Epcot for several days here, but why stop a good thing? We'll do one more before moving on to a different park. Today's ride opened in 1983 as "Journey into Imagination." It's had two name changes and several refurbishments since. The original and current version of this ride within the Imagination Pavilion feature the lovable Figment, a purple dragon with a hefty imagination. He's one of Disney's only characters to be created exclusively for a park. The attraction used to also include Dreamfinder, another beloved character who could sometimes even be found wandering throughout the park with his dragon sidekick. Many Disney diehards are still aching to bring him back. The featured song, "One Little Spark," was written by the infamous Sherman brothers, who wrote many Disney attraction theme songs.

The entire theme of this ride is an encouragement by the playful dragon to use our imaginations. God has blessed us with very complex and capable minds that have the ability to be creative in doing so many things, including how we serve Him. In today's reading, Paul reminds the Ephesians that God has blessed their minds with wisdom and knowledge of Him. Unlike any other creatures God created, we have the capacity to understand His purpose, greatness and immeasurable power. We also have the capability to serve Him in many unique ways. Paul echoes this above reminding us there are a variety of God-given gifts and methods to serve. I encourage you to explore your abilities and try to discover new ways of service in your everyday life. There are so many ways for us to make this world better, bring people together and spread Christ. Never limit or doubt what you can do. Everyone can do something for Him. Use your imagination. Explore your creativity. Share ideas. And serve any chance you get.

PRAYER—Lord, I want to serve You by helping others. Give me the wisdom to know how to do that. Help me to be creative and serve in a new and imaginative way. Through Christ, Amen.

TODAY I WILL...use my imagination. I will meditate, explore my talents and research a new way I can serve God in my daily life.

MARCH 23 **Read MATTHEW 11:25-30**

TAKE A BREAK

Disney Rides – Slinky Dog Dash

"So God blessed the seventh day and made it holy, because on it God rested from all his work that he had done in creation."
—Genesis 2:3

We're finally leaving Epcot and heading to Hollywood Studios which is quickly becoming my favorite park due to its addition of so many immersive lands, attractions and experiences the last few years. Slinky Dog Dash is one of those and opened with the new Toy Story Land in June 2018. Stepping into this land, you become a toy seeing everything on a much larger scale including Andy's giant shoe prints seen on the ground throughout. This ride's backstory is that it was built by Andy which you can see evidence of during the queue. Look for his drawings showing plans for different parts of the ride. In the same queue, you can find the original boxes for some of his famed toys such as Rex and Wheezy. Make sure to also ride this at night. The special lighting throughout makes it a totally different experience.

This is Disney's only double-launched coaster with a takeoff at the beginning and in the middle after your coaster stops momentarily for a break. It's that central pause I want to focus on because sometimes we all need the same. We often become overworked, overwhelmed and overcome with the pressures and trials of life, and it's important we find time on a regular basis to just stop and rest. In Matthew 11, Jesus offers that needed rest saying, "Come to me, all who labor and are heavy laden, and I will give you rest." He also says even our souls can find rest in Him. Taking a pause from life's stresses is not only healthy and smart, it's Biblical and essential for our spiritual growth. Even God Himself rested after taking six days to create the world. It's during those crucial breaks we can recharge and refocus, making sure our priorities are in order with God on top. Take a time out every once in a while and find rest with Jesus.

PRAYER—Father, I need a break. Help me plan some periodic, regular rest time and use that time to better my relationship with You. Thank you that Jesus offers Himself as a respite for the weary. In Him, Amen.

TODAY I WILL...rest. I will find some extended time today or soon to simply rest in the arms of Jesus. I will use that time to renew my faith and restore my spirit.

MARCH 24 **Read EPHESIANS 6:10-20**

ALL PARTS REQUIRED

Disney Rides – Toy Story Midway Mania

"...present your bodies as a living sacrifice, holy and acceptable to God, which is your spiritual worship."
—Romans 12:1

Let's just stay in Toy Story Land and take on another terrific attraction nearby. I remember many years of racing to this ride first due to super long lines. However, the addition of a third track here, along with the park's recent expansions providing so many new attractions, have greatly lowered this ride's wait times. At least that's true at WDW. It also exists in California and Tokyo. The California version opened less than three weeks after WDW's making it the first time Disney created an attraction at two parks simultaneously. This is a 3D (actually 4D), interactive experience where riders try their skills on six arcade-style shooting games plus a bonus screen. The artists who created the unique designs wore 3D glasses while painting.

This has always been a favorite because I like the competition and scoring aspects. I typically give my all, pulling that firing mechanism like a madman, trying to better my previous score. One thing is certain, my arm is always extremely sore from overuse when this ride is complete. Ephesians 6 contains a familiar and important passage with instructions to defeat the devil. We're told to put on the "whole armor" of God which includes a belt of truth, breastplate of righteousness, shoes for readiness, shield of faith, helmet of salvation and sword of the Spirit. We must have all parts and subsequent qualities to defeat Satan's schemes. Similarly, the verse above says to give our whole bodies as a sacrifice to God. This ride really only requires your arm, and you pay the price in pain if you go all out. However, with God, we must use all our parts, giving our entire body and taking up His full armor to withstand temptation and remain on the narrow path to salvation. Give God your full attention, strength and self as a sacrifice of service. It's what He asks for and what's required to withstand Satan's power and evil.

PRAYER—Father, I give You my full body as a sacrifice. Use all of me in service and help me to add Your full armor of qualities to stand up to the devil's tricks. In Jesus' name, Amen.

TODAY I WILL...give God my complete self. I will write down each part of His armor making sure I have all the attributes covered.

MARCH 25 **Read LUKE 13:22-30**

GOING UP?

Disney Rides – Tower of Terror

"I press on toward the goal for the prize of the upward call of God in Christ Jesus."
—Philippians 3:14

As a paramedic, there's one transportation method I use almost as much as an ambulance. Taking patients to and from rooms in multi-storied hospitals, I thank God for the invention of elevators. Stretchers on stairs would not be a pretty picture! I don't mind elevators. I know some aren't comfortable on them, especially a particular one found in four Disney parks around the world, although California's has been completely overlaid with *Guardians of the Galaxy* theming. At 199 feet, it is WDW's second tallest structure (Everest is 6 inches higher.) In the planning stages, there were several unique proposals for this ride including one based on Stephen King novels, a ghost tour, a murder mystery and even a real hotel with haunted theming? Otis Elevators, the premier in the industry, assisted in building this version, their most expensive ever.

So you know how this one works. You go up multiple times, each time falling several stories, right? Wrong. You're never actually falling. You're actually being pulled down at a controlled speed apart from gravity. Regardless, it still provides a terrifying, heart-in-your-throat experience. So what about your personal elevator? Is it moving steadily up or falling towards the ground? In Luke 13, someone asks Jesus how many will enter Heaven. He is blunt telling them it will be few and that many will be denied entry despite their pleas. We've discussed this devastating truth before. Heaven is reserved for those who truly follow God, enter through Jesus and remain humble ("the last will be first."—v 30). Paul makes it clear above that he's always striving for the prize of the UPWARD call of God. So I ask again...is your elevator traveling upward? Or is it violently plummeting like this ride and like so many others unfortunately will, according to Christ. Tower of Terror offers you no choice, but thankfully in life, you get to control your own elevator. Make sure it's always going up!

PRAYER—God, I want to be among the few called into Heaven. Like Paul, help me to always be striving for Your upward call. Don't let me plunge into eternal punishment. In Him, Amen.

TODAY I WILL...keep constant control of my elevator making sure it's always traveling up.

MARCH 26 **Read ACTS 20:17-35**

THE FULL EXPERIENCE

Disney Rides – Star Wars: Rise of the Resistance

"If anyone would come after me, let him deny himself and take up his cross daily and follow me."
—Luke 9:23

Hollywood Studios' most prominent ride, Rise of the Resistance (ROTR), is actually so much more than that. It's a full-on experience! It's found on both coasts in the fully engaging Star Wars-based land called Galaxy's Edge. The attraction's timeline takes place between the 8th and final films in the Star Wars canon. At 18 minutes, it's one of the longest rides at WDW. (Only AK's Kilimanjaro Safari is slightly longer.) ROTR involves elements of show, hologram, walk-through, simulation, trackless movement, a Tower of Terror-like drop and so much more. It's an event like no other you must experience in its entirety to fully appreciate. Coincidentally, "Star Wars: Galactic Starcruiser" is an forthcoming resort where participants will be "launched into space" and completely immersed in a Star Wars environment throughout their stay.

Today's reading is lengthy but important as Paul discusses what all he's been through to spread Christ. He talks of sufferings already faced and knows there will be more. Regardless, he is fully committed, knowing his calling and mission will be a complete experience full of ups and downs. If done right, our lives as Christians will also involve many emotions and experiences. Some will be exciting and joyful while others will be difficult and distressing. Being God-focused and Christ-centered means being willing to accept the total and complete experience of Christianity and all it brings. It takes dedication, prayer and focus, but we must take up His cross daily and do whatever God asks. Give your life to the full-on Christian experience. It won't always be easy, but the final scene will be well worth it!

PRAYER—Lord, I know that serving You faithfully will bring many good times and bad. Help me to prepare for the full experience of being a proper Christian. In Jesus' name, Amen.

TODAY I WILL...prepare for the complete experience. I will be ready for both joy and suffering as a Christian realizing I must endure all things to carry the cross of Christ.

MARCH 27 **Read PSALM 27:1-14**

THE PILOT POSITION

Disney Rides – Star Wars: Millennium Falcon-Smugglers Run

"It is the Lord who goes before you. He will be with you; he will never leave you or forsake you. Do not fear or be dismayed."
—Deuteronomy 31:8

We've now been at Hollywood Studios for a good while. Just one more here before we move on. Smugglers Run, as we'll call it for short, is the other headliner in Galaxy's Edge on both coasts. It's not nearly as complex as Rise of the Resistance but is a technologically advanced simulator based on the Millennium Falcon from the Star Wars series. Guests begin by entering just beneath the full-size replica of the famed ship. The queue itself is interactive and full of hidden tributes for die-hard fans. While in line, you might hear Disney legend, Jim Cummings, who lent his voice for Hondo, one of the most highly advanced audio animatronics on property. If his voice sounds familiar, it's because he's also the voice of Winnie the Pooh.

For this attraction, you are assigned one of three possible roles during your mission: pilot, gunner or engineer. Each is full of heart-pumping, constant action and exciting responsibility. If you're a pilot, you obviously get to steer the Falcon during your interactive "smuggling" assignment. Psalm 27 is a comforting work of David where he affirms the power and importance of God. He makes clear that God is his stronghold in life, as well as his light, protection and salvation. He boasts confidence due to the Lord's strength and security. At the end, he even proclaims he will wait for the Lord and allow Him to lead his life. In other words, David knew it was best for God to be his pilot. You may be chosen to steer the notorious Millennium Falcon on this attraction, but I hope God pilots your life. The verse above says it is God who "goes before you." Don't try going before Him by driving your own ship. Sit behind and let Him guide the way. Choose to maybe be the gunner fighting off Satan or the engineer repairing any mistakes made or issues you face. But let Him pilot. His guidance will never fail.

PRAYER—Lord, I don't want to be my own pilot or even co-pilot. I want You to be my only guide with total control. Lead me in the direction of Your choosing. Through Jesus, Amen.

TODAY I WILL...take a backseat. I will tell God He has total control to pilot me in whichever way He deems best and accept His directions.

MARCH 28 **Read PROVERBS 4:20-27**

GNIOG SDRAWKCAB

Disney Rides – Expedition Everest

"...one thing I do: forgetting what lies behind and straining forward to what lies ahead."
—Philippians 3:13

What type rides are your favorite? Roller coasters? Simulators? Dark rides? Can you handle them all? Going backwards? Upside down? Spinning? No thanks for me on the spins...those devil-sent teacups! If you can do it all, enjoy it, because it probably won't last forever. You'll notice you don't see a lot of older folks on these thrill rides. We're heading to Animal Kingdom for the last four rides of March starting with its greatest thrill. Expedition Everest opened in 2006 becoming WDW's tallest and fastest roller coaster as well as the world's most expensive at the time. Did you know this ride is a giant hidden Mickey? Take a look on Google Earth. The mountain itself is the head with the curve of the tracks forming the two ears. This was also Disney's first ride to go forward and backward. If you're near the front or back of the train, you can actually see the tracks flip over to accomplish this feat.

I mentioned spinning rides get to me, but I'm also at the age where I can't take the backwards either. One Everest ride per visit is enough for me. Proverbs 4 ends by advising us to always keep our eyes looking forward. We're also told to watch our steps, stay on the path and not swerve. Similarly, in the verse above, Paul proclaims his one goal is to forget what's behind and strain forward to what lies ahead. You may enjoy going backwards on Everest and be able to handle it much better than me. But don't go backwards when it comes to your spiritual path. Don't focus on the past or get involved in something that's going to damage your relationship with God. That will only push you backwards. Instead, look to your eternal future and always be moving forward towards Him. Like Paul, that should be the "one thing" we do above all else.

PRAYER—Dear God, help me to always be moving forward towards You. Keep me from falling backwards with guilt, sin or anything that pushes me away from my ultimate goal of being with You one day. Through His name, Amen.

TODAY I WILL... make small daily goals and large lifetime goals that always keep me moving forward towards God. I will get rid of anything forcing me backwards away from Him.

MARCH 29 **Read PSALM 143:7-12**

SURPRISE! IT'S LIFE.

Disney Rides – Dinosaur

"Many are the plans in the mind of a man, but it is the purpose of the Lord that will stand."
—Proverbs 19:21

When my youngest son was in 7th grade, his class trip was to Disney World. Lucky kid! My 7th grade trip was to Chattanooga, TN (insert eye roll). Anyways, as part of his "physics lesson," they got to ride Space Mountain with the lights on. Lucky kid again! I've never done that, but I did once get to experience today's ride with the lights on. Dinosaur was originally called "Countdown to Extinction" when it opened with the park in 1998. You can see a nod to the former name on the loading area wall. It's probably overstated, but I love that the formulas for ketchup, mustard and mayonnaise are on the red, yellow and white pipes in the same area due to McDonalds original sponsorship. Restaurantosaurus nearby used to serve McDonalds' food too!

Seeing Dinosaur with the lights on due to "technical difficulties" was pretty fascinating, but it removed so many of the ride illusions. We could clearly view the ride track, hidden screens showing projections of dinosaurs and walls cleverly hidden by strategically placed brush. Suddenly, it was just a warehouse-type building with decorations and visible technology instead of an immersive and electrifying journey through the Cretaceous period. It certainly wasn't what it appeared to be. Sometimes life's the same. In Psalm 143, David declares where his trust lies and even tells God, "Make me know the way I should go." David certainly had some unexpected and difficult turns in life but remained faithful trusting God's direction. Our lives won't always go as we plan or how we picture it going, but according to the verse above, it's God's purpose that will stand. Don't be surprised when you're surprised by life, even if it's scary or troublesome. Trust in God's purpose and direction. He has plans for you, but they may include some unanticipated means to the end.

PRAYER—Father, help me to put my full trust in you, especially when life surprises me. You know what's best so take full control, lead me and help me accept it. In Him, Amen.

TODAY I WILL... write down where I see myself in 5, 10 and 20 years. I will then give those expectation to God and accept if His plans look different.

MARCH 30 **Read LUKE 14:28-32**

PLAN AND GO

Disney Rides – Spinning Rides

"Prepare your work outside; get everything ready for yourself in the field, and after that build your house."
—Proverbs 24:27

Exiting Dinosaur at AK, the nearest ride is TriceraTop Spin. I've decided to lump it in with several similar rides found at MK such as Dumbo, the Magic Carpets and Astro Orbiter. Did you know Dumbo is the only ride found at all six Disney parks around the world? The Astro Orbiter used to be at all of them, but the Tokyo version closed in 2017. All four of these spinning rides are similar in that they last 90 seconds and have some form of controller inside to adjust the height. They're also alike in one other obvious way...they don't go anywhere. It's estimated that each Astro Orbiter vehicle travels 1.2 million miles every year spinning 11 times per minute. The other three are likely comparable. But the fact is that no matter how many times you ride these attractions, you just go around and around and typically end up at the same spot you started. Don't misunderstand, these are fun in their own way, and I know kids love them, but there's a spiritual application to be found in the fact that you don't really get anywhere.

In our reading today, Jesus stresses the importance of planning and being prepared so you can accomplish important tasks. He uses the examples of building a tower as well as a king preparing for war. We mentioned yesterday how God may surprise you and change your plans to accomplish His goals for you, but that doesn't mean you shouldn't plan and be prepared. To be successful, achieve duties and go places in life, we must be good stewards and work hard using the talents and skills God gives us. The verse above stresses the importance of preparation and hard work also. It's important to avoid idleness (Prov. 19:15), remaining too stale or stable. Make sure you are preparing your goals, working hard to accomplish important tasks and going somewhere in life that will make a difference for other and for God.

PRAYER—Lord, I want to accomplish great things in life for others and You. I know You will lead me, but help me to work hard and prepare for all life has to offer. Through Christ, Amen.

TODAY I WILL... make sure I'm going somewhere and not just spinning around ending up in the same spot. I will get up, get going and get my goals accomplished.

MARCH 31 **Read GENESIS 1:24-31**

CARING FOR HIS CREATURES

Disney Rides – Kilimanjaro Safari

"The righteous care for the needs of their animals."
—Proverbs 12:10 (NIV)

I can recall many animal encounters I've had over the years such as receiving a kitten, our first family pet and being surprised a few years later with my own puppy. I have memories of riding a horse, elephant and camel, feeding a sting ray, petting a kangaroo and the list goes on. Each encounter has been a blessing met with fascination. I love animals and would've enjoyed becoming a veterinarian. If you love animals too, there's no better experience than Kilimanjaro Safari at AK. This immersive attraction is the largest at WDW, so large in fact that all of the Magic Kingdom could fit inside it. It also fulfills a dream of Walt Disney himself as he originally envisioned Jungle Cruise with live animals. Of the 34 possible species seen during your "African savannah safari ride," all are contained using camouflaged barriers.

We see examples of animals throughout Scripture, many of them used to teach us or give direction. In the first book of the Bible, we read how God made every living creature and even allowed Adam to name the animals (Gen. 2:20) and have dominion over them. After creating and providing nourishment and habitats for them all, God saw that it was good (Gen. 1:31). Animals are one of God's greatest gifts we are still blessed to look after and take care of. I'm grateful to places like Disney that take care of so many animals, allowing us to safely view and appreciate them in a large habitat like Kilimanjaro Safari. Show God you appreciate this gift by taking time to learn about and appreciate them. If you have a pet, take care of it. If you have the means, give back to zoos or other animals charities that tend to their needs. God has given us so many wonderful things, but animals are one we can appreciate and cherish on such a large scale. Thank God for His many animals and do your part to fulfill his instructions to care for them.

PRAYER—Lord, thank you for the gift of animals and our ability to care for them. Help me to appreciate and treat them appropriately doing my part to aid in their care. In Jesus' name, Amen.

TODAY I WILL...take time to value God's gift of animals by visiting a zoo or similar park or even just going outside to watch, appreciate and thank God for them.

APRIL THEME

RESTAURANTS, RETAIL AND REFRESHMENTS

APRIL 1 **Read PROVERBS 1:1-7**

DON'T PLAY THE FOOL

Restaurants, Retail and Refreshments – Goofy Candy Company

"A fool takes no pleasure in understanding, but only in expressing his opinion."
—Proverbs 18:2

This book is a total joke. It's all false information. Get rid of it. April Fools!! Good one, huh? This book is brilliant of course, all factual, and you should continue reading it and all the author's other books. Just my opinion. New theme starting today!! Hope you're ready to spend some money, because during this beautiful, Spring month of April, it's the best of Disney eats, drinks and shops. We start with a place I've certainly visited but have never made a purchase. Not sure why because I've certainly been tempted with the whole place always looking so colorful, edible and delicious! Selling candy in hundreds of varieties, Goofy Candy Company is located at Disney Springs but also has products scattered abroad in various park and resort shops. A float in the "Mickey's Boo-to-You Halloween Parade" at the MK party each year is also inspired by the store, being covered in candy, with Goofy as the driver.

Speaking of Goofy, I used his appetizing candy shop today for good reason. Here on April Fool's Day, if any character could be named a fool, I would think Goofy is the prime candidate. Based on his cartoons, he often does foolish things, makes poor decisions and gets himself into trouble, however oblivious he may be. In the first chapter of Proverbs, Solomon stresses the importance of wisdom and gaining instruction. He says the best way to that knowledge is by fearing or respecting the Lord. He also teaches that those who avoid wisdom and instruction are fools. Nobody, not even Goofy, wants to be labeled a fool. As Christians, it's our responsibility to avoid foolishness by learning as much about God and His Word as possible. The more we know, the better equipped we'll be to handle life's trials and assist others. Don't be foolish like Goofy, even if it is celebrated today. Fear, respect and know God so you can gain the wisdom needed to remain in His favor and be fully prepared to be called home one day.

PRAYER—Lord, I don't want to be a fool. I want to know as much as possible about You. Help me to study, listen and learn so I can be armed for this world. Through Jesus, Amen.

TODAY I WILL...develop a plan to gain as much knowledge as I can about God's Word.

APRIL 2 **Read I SAMUEL 16:1-12**

GET TO THE HEART OF THE MATTER

Restaurants, Retail and Refreshments – Mickey Bar

"Do not let your adorning be external...but let your adorning be the hidden person of the heart with the imperishable beauty of a gentle and quiet spirit, which in God's sight is very precious."
—I Peter 3:3-4

As I age, I'm realizing I enjoy Disney trips for new reasons. It used to be all about the attractions, but now it's more the full experience, relaxation, meals and snacks. Oh, the snacks! So many to discuss, so little space. But we can't leave this one out! The Mickey Bar is about as classic and iconic as the mouse himself. Disney estimates annual sales of over 3 million of the delicious Mickey-shaped treats with creamy ice cream on the inside and a delicious, milk chocolate outside, melting in your mouth with each scrumptious bite. Is your mouth watering yet? You might be able to find these now available in your local grocery stores.

If you've had one of these delectable treats, you know the best part. It's that tasty chocolate outer coating. At the same time, it's also thin, fragile and certainly doesn't last near as long as the thick ice cream inside that helps the bar keep its form and shape. Basically, without the inside, the outside would collapse. It's the inside that really matters. Can the lesson here be any more obvious? In I Samuel 16, we see a familiar story of Samuel choosing the next king. God advises him to choose the boy, David, telling him to ignore his outward appearance and lack of height. Instead, God makes clear He sees David's heart inside. That's what really matters and makes David one of the greatest Godly leaders ever known. He was even called a "man after God's own heart" (Acts 13:22). Sure, David made mistakes, but he always came back to God and served Him faithfully. If David can be a man after God's heart, what about you? Only God knows your inside and where your heart is. If it's not in the right place, change it! It's what matters most to God. Keep your heart pure and strong so it keeps your outer form in the shape it should be, a true Godly servant.

PRAYER—Father, I want to have a pure heart inside You are proud of. Help me to be like David and keep my heart always focused on You. In Jesus' name, Amen.

TODAY I WILL...focus more on my inside than my outside. I will remember that God knows where my heart truly lies and make sure it's in a place He is proud of.

APRIL 3 Read GENESIS 8:20-22 & 2 CORINTHIANS 2:14-17

TAKE A WHIFF

Restaurants, Retail and Refreshments – Disney Popcorn

"...let us continually offer up a sacrifice of praise to God...the fruit of lips that acknowledge his name. Do not neglect to do good and to share what you have, for such sacrifices are pleasing to God"

—Hebrews 13:15-16

Yesterday, I mentioned enjoying Disney now as an adult for a variety of reasons, so I'll add another...so many incredible smells! Think about your favorites. It may be piped in during a ride like Soarin', the natural scent of a particular resort or one you can detect simply walking through the park. I love Disney smells and have even purchased several for my car, like the Polynesian Resort fragrance currently dangling from my rear-view mirror. I love driving these days! One of those memorable and abundant fragrances received while strolling park streets is Disney's delicious popcorn. Whether it's caramel flavored, the maple version found near Epcot's Canadian Pavilion (have got to try that!) or just good ole' buttered and original, it's estimated that Disney guests eat enough popcorn annually to fill the Tower of Terror! Wow!

How can you not love that popcorn smell? I'm grateful to God for the gift of smell to enjoy so many wonderful Disney scents. The two short passages today were both related to smell. In Genesis 8, Noah offered a sacrifice after the flood, and God was so pleased with its aroma, that He made a covenant with Noah and all mankind. In a related passage, 2 Corinthians 2 takes sacrifice a step further saying we are now the pleasing sacrifice to God and the fragrance of Christ spread everywhere, even to Him. Our acceptance of Jesus and the spreading of His example and message are like a delightful aroma to God making its way through those we influence. Our service to others also pleases Him according to the verse above. Take a moment today and imagine your favorite Disney smells. Now picture God sniffing what you've offered through your own self-sacrifice. Are you providing Him a pleasing aroma? Does He smell the beauty of Christ through you? Are you continually offering sacrifices that delight Him?

PRAYER—Father, thank you for the blessing of smell. I want to give my whole self as a pleasing sacrifice and pray You can smell Christ through me. In Him, Amen.

TODAY I WILL...close my eyes, take a deep breath, enjoy a pleasant smell and thank God for the gift. I will imagine God doing the same over me, making sure He's pleased with the scent.

APRIL 4 **Read PSALM 139:13-16**

GOD'S BLOCKS

Restaurants, Retail and Refreshments – The Lego Store

"So God created man in his own image..."
—Genesis 1:27

We've had candy, chocolate and popcorn so far this month. Tummy ache alert! We'd better pause on the snacks to visit a beloved store you simply must see to believe. The Lego Store is found at four Disney sites including WDW, Anaheim, Paris and Shanghai. The stores are owned by "The Lego Group," a private, Danish company technically competing with Disney in the film and theme park industry. However, they also produce a large variety of Disney related building sets using the famed blocks. Each Disney-affiliated store contains several large, impressive Lego structures, mostly Disney characters, providing great photo spots. The company has been making the interlocking blocks for over 70 years producing well over 600 billion of them.

I was never much into Legos. However, I am big into Disney of course and would love to own the Cinderella Castle set. It looks incredible! The imaginative Lego blocks come in so many different shapes and sizes providing endless building possibilities. In today's psalm, David praises God for His building of something very important...us! Like crafting a careful and detailed Lego structure, David says God "knitted" us together, "formed" our parts and that we were "intricately woven." It's obvious God was very meticulous, detailed and thorough in creating our bodies and making us just right. David even notes we were "fearfully and wonderfully made." If that weren't blessing enough, the verse above says we were made in God's own image. What an honor that God cared so much in carefully fashioning us together. How anyone can look at the human body, it's intricacy and complexity and not believe in God is unfathomable. Focus on the huge blessing of being formed by God. Praise His name, thanking Him that His little construction project gave you life along with the chance of eternal happiness.

PRAYER—Father, I'm so grateful to be one of Your creations. Thank you for taking the time to build me perfectly and wonderfully and in Your own image. In Jesus' name, Amen.

TODAY I WILL...wear with honor the fact that I was created in the very image of God. I will take that name seriously and make Him proud to have molded me.

APRIL 5 **Read REVELATION 21:9-27**

A STUNNING SIGHT

Restaurants, Retail and Refreshments – World of Disney

"But as it is, they desire a better country, that is, a heavenly one. Therefore, God is not ashamed to be called their God, for he has prepared for them a city."
—Hebrews 11:16

Have you ever seen something so beautiful or awesome that it made you gasp or stare in wonderment? Perhaps it was a majestic sky or stunning landscape that momentarily took your breath away. While it can't compare with the beauty of God's creation, as a Disney enthusiast and collector, I remember being completely stunned and overwhelmed the first time I set foot in the World of Disney. Finding home in the same four locations as The Lego Store, this retailer has the world's largest supply of Disney merchandise and first opened in WDW's Disney Springs in 1996. There used to be an additional site in New York City occupying a three-story building on Manhattan's famed Fifth Avenue, but it unfortunately closed after just five years.

I don't love shopping, but I could spend all day at this place. I try to go each trip as I enjoy browsing, seeing what's new and possibly picking up an addition to my collection; although I have to keep a tight rein on my wallet as I could easily spend my annual salary in a single visit. As mentioned, the first time I entered, I was like a kid at Goofy's Candy Company, wide-eyed and filled with awe. I can only imagine a similar reaction, only greatly magnified when taking that first step into Heaven one day. Revelation 21 attempts to give a description of Heaven's beauty, although I'm guessing our human minds can't even fathom how truly picturesque and magnificent it will be. If our saved souls have a breath, the first sight of our eternal home will most certainly take it away. God has prepared for us a better place, a city of incredible and unconceivable beauty that will be greater than anything we've ever seen including His gorgeous, naturistic beauty or even an overabundance of Disney merchandise. We often hear "you have to see it to believe it." But for Heaven you must believe it first and then do whatever necessary to see it. You for sure don't want to miss it!

PRAYER—Father, there's so much beauty in this world, but I know it doesn't compare with what You've prepared for me up there. I must see it. Please bring me home! In Him, Amen.

TODAY I WILL...do whatever necessary to know I'll get to see the beauty of Heaven one day.

APRIL 6 **Read PHILIPPIANS 2:4-8**

PUT YOUR SERVICE TO THE TEST

Restaurants, Retail and Refreshments – Be Our Guest

"For even the Son of Man came not to be served but to serve..."
—Mark 10:45

We've now indulged in some tasty snacks and done a bit of shopping, so it's finally time to sit and enjoy a meal. Disney is famous for an amazing food selection found in a wide variety of sit-down and counter-service restaurants. Our family attempts to try a new place each trip, and we never run out of options. Be Our Guest opened in 2012 as part of WDW's New Fantasyland expansion and quickly became a favorite place to feast. Themed around Beast's castle, the enormous dining room is divided into three sections: The Grand Ballroom with high-domed ceilings and chandeliers, the Castle Gallery housing large figures of Belle and Beast dancing and the Beast's mysterious hidden lair, the West Wing, complete with his enchanted rose.

You probably know the song that named this restaurant, right? It's famously sung in the film when all the castle's enchanted inhabitants welcome Belle for the first time, fix her an extravagant meal and vow to serve her in every way possible. The lyrics are all about serving with one of the lines being, "we only live to serve." This leads to an obvious Biblical parallel. Philippians 2 gives the definition of a servant as it describes Christ's main purpose. It says He took the form of a servant, and the verse above echoes saying He came here to serve. As we strive to follow in His footsteps, serving others also becomes our purpose. When Belle enters the castle, her new friends openly demonstrate their strong desire to serve her every need. We must imitate that, showing God we accept our calling to serve by doing so with enthusiasm. Another lyric says, "Life is so unnerving for a servant who's not serving." If we don't serve, our life's purpose is lost. Find the drive to serve openly in the name of Jesus. Spread His message through your example as you "live to serve" others' needs, both physical and especially spiritual.

PRAYER—Dear Lord, I know my purpose is serving others any way I can, especially in finding and knowing You. Help me to be a strong servant like Jesus. In His name, Amen.

TODAY I WILL...realize my role as a servant of others. I will do so with enthusiasm, happiness and a good attitude, being a good example of Christ as I spread His message.

APRIL 7 **Read LUKE 14:15-24**

A ROYAL INVITATION

Restaurants, Retail and Refreshments – Cinderella's Royal Table

"You prepare a table before me in the presence of my enemies..."
—Psalm 23:5

Have you ever met a celebrity? Possibly. What about this...have you ever dined with royalty? Less likely. At today's famed restaurant, the goal is to make you feel special as you dine amongst royalty inside the legendary castle we all know and love. This restaurant originally opened with the park in 1971 as "King Stefan's Banquet Hall." That may seem an odd name to be found inside Cinderella Castle as King Stefan was Sleeping Beauty's father! Imagineers so named it because they wanted a regal title. Cinderella had no named father, and so Sleeping Beauty's dad was their best option. It was finally changed in 1997 ending years of confusion.

I've never actually experienced this classic Disney meal set among royal princesses, and I've definitely never dined with any other royalty I can recall. However, I've certainly been invited to a royal table, and you have too! In Luke 14, Jesus tells a parable with some very real symbolism. He talks of a man giving a great banquet. All those invited make excuses and don't show, so the man then invites some uncommon guests such as the lame, blind, poor and crippled. Those that originally received invitations are taken off the guest list due to their excuses. They had their chance. So which group are you in? Make no mistake, you've been invited to sit around God's banquet table. If that's not a royal invitation, I don't know what is. Will you accept His invitation or make excuses and be denied? I know my choice. I've accepted. No excuses. After all, my Father will be there and He's certainly royalty... the King of the Universe! What about you? There's a seat open. Hope to see you there!

PRAYER—Holy Father, thank You for preparing a table for me and inviting me to Your royal banquet. I accept, plan to attend and pray nothing stands in my way. In His name, Amen.

TODAY I WILL...secure my invitation to His royal table and make plans to attend without excuse.

APRIL 8 **Read GALATIANS 5:16-24**

THE BEST FRUIT

Restaurants, Retail and Refreshments – Dole Whip

"But the fruit of the Spirit is love, joy, peace, patience, kindness, goodness, faithfulness, gentleness, self-control; against such things there is no law."
—Galatians 5:22-23

Do you have a favorite fruit? Mine is probably strawberries. Especially dipped in chocolate. Does that count? I also like bananas...when they're in pudding with whipped cream and Vanilla Wafers. And of course peaches, you know, in a cobbler with ice cream. Are you seeing a pattern here? Today's snack, probably Disney's most famous, is technically a fruit too. But like the above creations, I'm unsure of its nutritional value. In 1968, the Disneyland Tiki Bar opened outside the Enchanted Tiki Room attraction. At that time, they served pineapple spears and pineapple juice. When the Dole Company took over in 1986, they began serving the notorious Dole Whip, a pineapple flavored soft serve. Today, it's found on both coasts at several locations with multiple flavors offered periodically. It can even be turned into a float or other creation. There's even one with bacon! There is also abundant Dole Whip merchandise available.

Ok, so maybe the Dole Whip isn't pure fruit, but it certainly tastes like it. That delicious pineapple flavor reminds me of Galatians 5. In it, Paul discusses the desires of the flesh versus the Fruits of the Spirit. If we don't have God's Spirit within us, we tend to give in to the desires of the flesh which Paul lists as things like drunkenness, sexual immorality, envy, jealousy and anger, among many others. However, if we live by the power of the Spirit, we focus instead on the nine qualities listed above. Those are the pure fruit attributes we need to add both inside and outwardly. Paul ends this passage by saying those who belong to Jesus have crucified the passions and desires of the flesh. Being one with Christ means being different. It means not giving in to worldly temptations which include fleshly desires. It means instead relying on the Spirit inside and demonstrating the positive fruits on a regular basis.

PRAYER—God, help me to focus on the Spirit's good fruits showing them outwardly to others. Help me to get rid of any bodily desires that are not of the Spirit. In Jesus' name, Amen.

TODAY I WILL...write down all nine fruits and list at least one new or better way I can demonstrate each in my life.

APRIL 9 **Read EPHESIANS 2:1-10**

CHOSEN

Restaurants, Retail and Refreshments – Windtraders

"...he chose us in him before the foundation of the world... In love he predestined us for adoption to himself as sons through Jesus Christ, according to the purpose of his will..."
—Ephesians 1:4-5

When we first visited the Harry Potter section of Universal Studios, our oldest was picked for the popular ceremony where a certain wand "chose" him and allowed him to "perform magic." As expected, said son begged to keep the wand meaning his dad had to fork over some serious cash, much to Universal's delight. Disney has found a similar way to capitalize at a popular Animal Kingdom shop. Exiting the top tier, Flight of Passage ride in the park's Pandora section, leads you through Windtraders, a gift shop filled with *Avatar*-themed merchandise. It also contains a special corner where guests are paired with a personal "Ikran" (the native Na'vi name) or "Banshee" (human name), the flying creatures used for travel in both the film and ride. They come in 10 varying styles, each with a remote leash controlling a wide range of movements.

In the *Avatar* film, the main character is told "you must choose an Ikran, and he must choose you." A memorable scene follows where he selects and tames his own "Banshee" after it decides to choose him back. In the verse above, we're told we were chosen by God and adopted by Him as a son of Christ. Reading on in Ephesians 2, we see that despite our being dead in sin, God rescued us and made us alive in Christ because of His great love for us. He has chosen us to save through His grace if we have a committed faith in Him. Being selected by a flying Banshee or even a wizarding wand can't compare with being chosen by the God of the Universe. Praise God for choosing you to know Him and be called to live for Him. Live up to that calling and make Him proud to have saved you from the depths of sin. Be worthy of your adoption in Christ, for it's an honor some will never know or choose to accept.

PRAYER—Father, I'm so grateful You chose me to hear Your Word, know what is right, accept Your plan and receive salvation through Your grace and the sacrifice of Jesus. Thank You that I'm chosen. In His holy name, Amen.

TODAY I WILL...live a life worthy of being chosen. I will also do more to spread His Word to others so they can be chosen too.

APRIL 10 **Read PSALM 24:1-6**

WASH YOUR HANDS

Restaurants, Retail and Refreshments – Basin

"Cleanse your hands you sinners and purify your hearts, you double-minded."

—James 4:8

Sing the "Happy Birthday" song. All the way through at a normal pace. Twice. That's the recommendation. We're talking hand washing, and it's advised you do so for a full 20 seconds which is about how long it takes to sing that song twice. I've got the perfect place for you to practice. It's free. It's wonderful. And you'll want to stay a lot longer than 20 seconds. Have you ever visited Basin? Our family visits every trip simply for the hand washing alone. You won't believe how clean and smooth your hands feel afterwards. We've also made some wonderful purchases as they have all kinds of salts, soaps, bombs, butters and much more to make your personal bath time just as magical as your Disney experience. Basin opened first in Minnesota's Mall of America in 1997. They now offer products in numerous drug stores around the country, but a trip to Disney World includes two chances to visit an actual store with locations in Disney Springs and at the Grand Floridian Resort.

In Psalm 24, David clarifies who will be allowed to "ascend the holy hill" and join God in Heaven saying it will be those who have "clean hands and a pure heart." James teaches the same above. Obviously, this doesn't literally mean we must wash our hands to enter Heaven. Instead, we're being told to not get involved in anything dirty or worldly. We must keep our hands clean, not touching anything that will pull us away from God. This would include physical temptations or anything that could harm our bodies, minds or souls. Visit Basin on your next trip. You won't be disappointed. Take 20 seconds (or longer!) to wash your hands, trying out the many flavors of free soaps. While there, or anytime you wash your hands, make sure they are also pure before God. Don't touch anything that will damage that relationship or future with Him!

PRAYER—Lord, I want to be totally pure before you. Help me to wash my hands of all sin and cleanse me from my errant past. In Jesus' name, Amen.

TODAY I WILL...wash my hands while meditating on God and His desires for me. I will make sure to purify my life of anything that gets my hands dirty with sin.

APRIL 11 **Read 2 CORINTHIANS 4:7-12**

THE CLAY ARTIST

Restaurants, Retail and Refreshments – The Art of Disney

"But now, O Lord, you are our Father; we are the clay, and you are our potter; we are all the work of your hand."
—Isaiah 64:8

I'm not a big art connoisseur, unless it's Disney related. I would decorate my whole house in Disney if I could, but my lovely wife has her limits. She's allowed me a Disney bedroom, hallway and basement display. It's a start. I'm secretly working my way toward the whole house, one section at a time. That being said, I absolutely love visiting today's store at Disney Springs as well as the smaller version in Epcot. I love the wall art, but I even more enjoy the large figurines and Disney sculptures. This is yet another store in which I could easily empty my bank account. It often features renowned Disney artists in person to meet with guests, demonstrate their abilities and sign their works.

In the verse above, Isaiah teaches we are God's artwork. He's the potter, and we are His clay. He created and formed us, the work of His hands. Today's reading takes it further with Paul telling the Corinthians God keeps His treasure inside us as "jars of clay." In ancient times, clay jars were common in every household to hold items for safe keeping. The Dead Sea Scrolls, for example, were found in these jars. While good for storage, they were fragile and not as durable as those made of metal or glass. In other words, God's treasure of Himself, His plan and the knowledge of Jesus is living and active inside us. We are the jars holding that information, but our bodies are imperfect and breakable, and God's treasure is too immense and great to contain anyway. Therefore, we can't simply hold this treasure indefinitely. We must let it out and share it. That's why God molded us in the first place, as clay jars to both carry His treasure and spread it. Thank God today for being His artwork. Live for the day when, just like at this store, you can meet your personal artist, the One who designed and fashioned you for His purpose.

PRAYER—God, I'm honored to be Your artwork. Thank you for creating and shaping me to do whatever You need. Help me to share the knowledge You've entrusted unto me. In Him, Amen.

TODAY I WILL...realize I'm a fragile clay jar holding immense treasure. I will let it out and share the incredible knowledge I have of God as well as His desires and promises.

APRIL 12 **Read GENESIS 25:29-34**

DANGEROUS TRADING

Restaurants, Retail and Refreshments – Disney Pin Traders

"But seek first the kingdom of God and his righteousness, and all these things will be added to you."
—Matthew 6:33

As a kid, I briefly collected and traded baseball cards but wasn't very good at it. I remember my friend being shocked to discover an early Jose' Canseco card of some value in my stash. I had no idea of its worth. Disney has also discovered and capitalized on a profitable way for guests to trade. Pin trading can be done most anywhere, even internationally, but there are shops set up like this one on both coasts. Disney had sold pins for many years but trading them really kicked off with the millennium celebration in late 1999. Today, Disney produces thousands of pins based on characters, rides, resorts, parks and anything else Disney-related you can think of. Most cast members wear them and will trade any of theirs for one of yours. This new tradition has boomed with many Disney regulars collecting their favorites and becoming avid pin traders.

Today's reading from Genesis contains what is arguably the Bible's most famous trade. Esau trades away his birthright to his twin brother, Jacob for some food due to extreme exhaustion and hunger. His birthright was an important inheritance promised to him due to his position as oldest son. This trade led to confusion, deception, anger and ultimately a breakup of the entire family. Esau's moment of weakness and poor trading decision cost him greatly. Similarly, we all have times in life when we may be tempted to trade away something important to try something unimportant or even dangerous. It's vital we firmly set our priorities in order keeping them properly placed, and it all starts with the verse above. As long as God is first and at the top of our list, everything else will fall into place. If we instead trade away our good standing or relationship with Him, we risk our lives, both earthly and eternally. Don't trade away what you have with God. Nothing is worth it, and it may, like Esau, end of costing you greatly.

PRAYER—Heavenly Father, I am putting You first above all else. Help me in moments of weakness not to trade You away for something sinful and less important. Through Christ, Amen.

TODAY I WILL...make a list of blessings I have due to my relationship with God. I will vow to never trade these things away knowing they are priceless and cannot be bought.

APRIL 13 **Read PSALM 68:1-3**

THE MELTING ENEMIES

Restaurants, Retail and Refreshments – M&M's Store

"...in which the heavens shall pass away with a great noise, and the elements shall melt with fervent heat, the earth also and the works that are therein shall be burned up."
—2 Peter 3:10 (KJV)

Imagine this. You haven't eaten in days and are in pain from hunger. In a weird twist, you're graciously allowed one item from the candy display by the cash register. What's your choice? I'd probably go for my favorite Cookies and Cream Hershey Bar or perhaps a Reese's, Snickers or Kit-Kat. Love all those. But you also can't go wrong with a pack of M&M's, right? Those famed, little candy-shelled chocolates were invented in 1941 and now even have specialty stores at 7 locations around the world including Shanghai, London, Berlin and four U.S. sites. I attempted to visit the newest on a recent trip to WDW's Disney Springs, but the line to enter was staggering. Needless to say, this store, with life-size character photo ops, merchandise, apparel and a huge chocolate wall containing every M&M color imaginable, is doing quite well.

Over the years, there has been a lot of marketing for M&M's including added colors, flavors and even beloved characters. Their most famous slogan dating back to 1949 is "Melts in your mouth, not in your hand." The Bible also paints a vivid picture of melting to come. The verse above is one of many predicting the end of times saying the Earth will eventually burn up and everything in it will melt. Psalm 68 also prophecies the end stating that God will rise to power victorious, after which His enemies will scatter and perish as wax melts in fire. Finally, it contrasts the righteous, saying they will be joyful before God. The end is coming. It may not be tomorrow, next year or even during your lifetime, but it will come. We simply don't know when. It's vital to be ready at all times and avoid being one of God's scattered enemies left to burn for all eternity. That may be blunt and graphic, but it's God's truth. Don't put yourself in danger of melting as an enemy of God. Choose to stay on His side, the side of right.

PRAYER—Lord, I don't want to be Your enemy. I desire more than anything to be with You on the last day. Keep me far from anything leading to my destruction. In His name, Amen.

TODAY I WILL...choose to be righteous and never an enemy of God, knowing my salvation is too important.

APRIL 14 **Read 2 CORINTHIANS 5:6-10**

ROLLING TOWARD PERFECTION

Restaurants, Retail and Refreshments – Splitsville Luxury Lanes

"Not that I have already obtained this or am already perfect, but I press on to make it my own, because Christ Jesus has made me his own."
—Philippians 3:12

The entire place fell silent. Every previous roll had been a perfect strike. He lined himself up, stepped toward the lane and let it go. Everyone exhaled, someone yelled at the ball and we all stood wide-eyed and hopeful. All ten pins fell. A perfect game of 300. My son was on the high school bowling team, and no that wasn't him. That was a kid on the opposing team, but it didn't matter. We were all jumping up and down. It was something special to witness a perfect game. I'm sure Disney has had its fair share of perfection at its own bowling venue in Disney Springs. Splitsville Luxury Lanes, built in 2012, is a 50,000 square foot facility, the largest Splitsville ever built, with 2 levels, 30 lanes, 60 TV's, an outdoor patio, live music and a menu about the size of the facility. Splitsville has 2 other locations in Florida as well as Texas and Virginia.

The game of bowling can be paralleled to our spiritual life if you think about it. In bowling, you strive for perfection, but it's extremely challenging to obtain a perfect score of 300, even for the most skilled. Similarly, we should strive for perfection with God. We won't succeed, but we still make it our goal as Paul did based on the verse above. Jesus also told us in Matthew 5:48 to be perfect as God is perfect. In 2 Corinthians, it says we should aim to please God for we will all appear before Him in judgement. In bowling, you always aim to knock down all the pins. Sometimes you miss a few or even get a gutter ball. We all make mistakes. But you don't stop aiming and striving for a perfect strike. Aim to please God in all things. Go for that perfect game. Don't give up because of one bad roll. You may not achieve perfection in life, but if you keep striving for it while aiming towards God, you will achieve a perfect eternal home.

PRAYER—Father, I want to be perfect before you. That is my goal. I will mess up and I'm sorry. Thank you for Your grace when I miss what I'm aiming for. In Jesus' name, Amen.

TODAY I WILL...strive for a perfect game every day regardless of any bad rolls I make. I will aim towards God in everything I do.

APRIL 15 **Read JOHN 8:39-47**

THE MAGIC OF DECEPTION

Restaurants, Retail and Refreshments – Blue Bayou

"Or do you not know that the unrighteous will not inherit the kingdom of God? Do not be deceived..."
—I Corinthians 6:9

We've been shopping for several days along with a quick bowling stop, so it's time to eat again. Let's travel to Disneyland in California for a unique and historical restaurant there. Blue Bayou opened in 1967 after some criticism of the food quality at the park. Walt Disney himself said about this restaurant, "the food is going to be the show, along with the atmosphere." It's found in the same building as the Pirates of the Caribbean ride with boats traveling around and even under the dining room. This cajun-style restaurant is also found in Tokyo Disneyland and Disneyland Paris, although the theme in Paris is Caribbean-style.

I've never eaten here, but I've certainly seen it riding Pirates. The most fascinating part of its theming is how Disney magic makes diners feel as though they are outside beneath the stars despite being inside the ride's building. This is accomplished with a high ceiling, projections that imitate the night's sky and special lighting including the glow of fireflies along with sounds of crickets and frogs. In other words, diners are delightfully deceived into thinking they are somewhere else. This is fine for Disney magic. It's why we keep going back. But we can also be deceived in a way that's not fine. In John 8, Jesus rebuked the people for being deceived by the devil telling them they claimed to be the sons of Abraham and serve God, but that's not how they were acting. Their actions did not match up with their words. The devil is good at what he does. He deceives us into thinking sin is acceptable. We may think we are following God, but our words or actions prove otherwise. Make sure Satan isn't deceiving you with his own magic schemes. Be firm in your dedication to God making sure your words, actions and even thoughts prove it. Jesus said nobody can serve two masters (Matt. 6:24). Which one are you serving?

PRAYER—Lord, I am weak at times, especially when the devil is coming full force against me. Please help me in these times of weakness that I may serve You only. Through Christ, Amen.

TODAY I WILL...not be deceived. I will make sure my thoughts, words and actions match those of Jesus Christ and not give in to any of the devil's tricks.

APRIL 16 **Read TITUS 2:1-7**

A PROPER PATTERN

Restaurants, Retail and Refreshments – Mickey Waffles

"For to this you have been called, because Christ also suffered for you, leaving you an example, so that you might follow in his steps."
—I Peter 2:21

I'm not sure how popular Play-Doh is these days, but I used to love that stuff as a kid. I had a barber shop I used a lot as well as many other different tools and molds to make numerous shapes and patterns with the iconic, colorful clay. Disney is known for another pattern used to form multiple creations. Not so much with clay, but with food. They have Mickey-shaped cookies, ice-cream bars, pretzels, candy apples, cucumbers and many others, but possibly none so famous as the Mickey waffle. That classic, breakfast favorite is a staple on a Disney vacation, especially for children. It's estimated that guests on both coasts enjoy nearly 8 million of the famed waffles annually. The first Mickey shaped food was actually pancakes premiering in Disneyland early on which can actually still be found in a few select restaurants on property.

Mickey waffles are fairly simply to make. All you need is a waffle maker with the proper pattern which can actually be bought for your home. Using a pattern like that to form something important reminded me of Titus 2 where Paul stresses the importance of us being a pattern by setting a good example, especially for the younger generation. He even breaks it down for males and females, both old and young, teaching what is best to demonstrate in their lives that will lead to successful households and relationships with God. In verse 7, he says to basically be a model of all good things with the KJV version actually using the word "pattern." Like that classic Mickey waffle mold, we must be the Godly pattern others use for their own lives. And what pattern do we use? Look above. There are many verses telling us to use Jesus Christ as our perfect pattern. What kind of example are you setting, especially for the youth, because they will look up to you and follow your pattern of service to God. Make sure it's one worth copying!

PRAYER—Dear Father, I want to be a pattern of Godliness for others as Jesus was. Help me to set a good example, especially for the younger that I can help mold into faithful servants of Yours. In His name, Amen.

TODAY I WILL...define my pattern. Do others see me as a Godly pattern worth following?

APRIL 17 **Read I CORINTHIANS 1:10-13**

TOO MANY FLAVORS

Restaurants, Retail and Refreshments – Churros

"...watch out for those who cause divisions and create obstacles contrary to the doctrine that you have been taught; avoid them."
—Romans 16:17

Flavors. There are so many these days! Whether it's ice cream, coffee, milkshakes, soda, potato chips or even water. And now the churros! This is yet another Disney staple you tend to find more often at Disneyland, who estimates they sell nearly 4.5 million per year! I actually recall tasting my first churro and being astonished by how delicious it was. Of course, I only had to deal with one flavor back then. Today Disney guests must grapple with the choice of multiple, appetizing options such as: salted caramel, Oreo, apple cinnamon, strawberry cheesecake, spicy and sugar cookie among many others. Not to mention the specialty options such as churro fondue or light saber churros. Too...many...choices!! I'll just stick with the original.

Flavors aren't just for foods, you know. Paul warns about different flavors of something else...Christians. He pleads with the Corinthians to eliminate divisions and arguments between them caused by too many spiritual leaders. Unfortunately, that's still a big problem today. Within Christianity alone are numerous denominations, ideas, beliefs and interpretations. Talk about division! As stated above, we must be watchful for those who cause division by misconstruing what God says. Many interpret the Bible how they want instead of learning what it actually means. In John 17:21, Jesus prayed all believers would unite as one. We must try to eliminate all the flavors by using Him alone as our example and following only God's Word. Flavors may be good for food, even churros, to satisfy various palates and cravings, but they are dangerous when it comes to our faith. Make sure you're not just a flavor of Christian. Instead, stick with being an original, Bible-believing, Christ-following, God-loving, servant of faith.

PRAYER—Lord, I don't want to be an unauthorized Christian flavor but instead only what you have asked of me in Your Word. Help me to recognize and refuse any false doctrine that comes my way. In His name, Amen.

TODAY I WILL...be unflavored when it comes to my Christian beliefs and test any new teachings against the Bible, following only what it says.

APRIL 18 **Read ROMANS 14:1-12**

TO EAT OR NOT TO EAT

Restaurants, Retail and Refreshments – Turkey Legs

"Have nothing to do with foolish, ignorant controversies; you know that they breed quarrels."
—2 Timothy 2:23

Thanksgiving is my favorite. Not holiday, but eating day! That traditional meal of turkey along with multiple, delicious sides...Yum! I really don't eat much turkey otherwise, although I certainly can at Disney if I want to pay handsomely for it. Turkey legs began selling at Disney in the late 1980's. A traditional snack of Renaissance fairs, Disney has capitalized selling the 1.5-pound legs with nearly 2 million sold annually between both coasts. Disney confirms they are in fact turkey meat and not ham or even emu (say what!?) as some have speculated. The reason for the rumors is that each is cured in salt which is more typical of ham over turkey.

I don't typically eat Disney turkey legs strictly because of size and price. However, I'm sure I'd like it as I enjoy most types of meat. On the other hand, I know many choose to be vegetarian or vegan. Sometimes these eating preferences, particularly with meat, can breed controversy and disputes. Some will say God gave us animals to eat (Gen. 9:3) while others may choose not to or even think it wrong. We touched on these disputes that divide us yesterday and Paul continues to address the subject today. In Romans 14, he begins with the very topic of eating disagreements also mentioning clashes over observing holidays. His whole message is avoiding hostility and petty arguments over such things which don't affect salvation. Paul makes clear God is our only judge, and we are not to pass judgement for minor issues we may disagree with. If you want to enjoy a Disney turkey leg, go for it. If you want to stick to vegetables, no problem. Make sure you aren't breeding aggression or anger towards someone for something that really doesn't matter in the long run. Avoid foolish controversies and focus instead on uniting for the common cause of spreading God's love and message.

PRAYER—Lord, help me to avoid judging others on petty differences and only focus on their salvation. I ask fervently for more unity among believers. Through Jesus, Amen.

TODAY I WILL...evaluate any disputes to determine if they are Biblically-based and important. I will work towards compromise so I am more effective in bringing others to God.

APRIL 19 **Read PSALM 78:1-7**

PASS IT ON

Restaurants, Retail and Refreshments – Café Orleans

"Remember the days of old; consider the years of many generations..."
—Deuteronomy 32:7

It's time to get off our feet and sit down to eat...yet again. In fact, loosen your belts because we're going to be eating for the next eight days! There are just too many beloved, Disney restaurants we can't leave out. We'll start with a significant and historical one that debuted in 1966 with New Orleans Square, Disneyland's first new park section since opening in 1955. Walt Disney was heavily involved in the creation and design of this new land which included this Cajun-style eatery. The restaurant is still popular today with nostalgic and treasured menu items along with character displays from *The Princess and the Frog*. The café also includes an outdoor patio with gorgeous views of the Mark Twain Riverboat sailing around the Rivers of America. One super cool fact is that you can still find the same espresso machine inside that provided Walt his favorite brew. If you look online, there's even a photograph of him standing beside this antique and favorited machine. It still sits as an awesome tribute to Walt and his continued influence passing along happiness and magic to millions of Disney fanatics every year.

When I asked my future father-in-law's permission to marry his daughter, he obviously knew my plans and had prepared a gift. He gave me a framed, printed copy of Psalm 78 that I treasure to this day. This psalm emphasizes the importance of one generation passing on God's Word and teachings to the next. I so appreciated my father-in-law sharing this psalm and realized the importance of what he was saying. It's our Christian duty to teach the next generation, making sure they are well-equipped to handle the world and live faithful lives in Christ. Just as Walt passed along his wisdom and creativity forming this legendary restaurant, we must teach the next generation so they can be spiritually prepared to receive their salvation.

PRAYER—Father, I want to keep Your ways, words and wisdom alive for as long as there are souls to save. Help me do my part in teaching the next generation. Through Christ, Amen.

TODAY I WILL...pass it on. I will figure out one new way to share what I know about God with the next generation.

APRIL 20 **Read TITUS 3:1-8**

MIND THOSE MANNERS

Restaurants, Retail and Refreshments – 50's Prime Time Café

"Do to others as you would have them do to you."
—Luke 6:31 (NIV)

Eat those vegetables! Elbows off the table! Finish your dinner! These are just some of the phrases you might hear at our next fine dining establishment. The 50's Prime Time Café, at Hollywood Studios since 1989, has become a park favorite serving many American classics such as fried chicken, meatloaf, pot roast and milk shakes. Speaking of shakes, theirs constantly rank among the highest at Disney in quality and taste. They even offer a peanut butter and jelly flavored shake. I've tried it, and it's actually really good...much better than it probably sounds. The theming here is obviously the 50's complete with Formica tables, vinyl chairs and waitresses dressed in old-fashioned attire serving you "mom-style" like you were seated in your own kitchen. Each table is complete with a retro TV showing 50's sitcoms and blurbs as well.

As mentioned, once seated here, you'll feel as though you're being served by your own mother, complete with scolding and plenty of reminders of good manners. It's all done in good fun of course, but good manners are actually important, even as Christians. Paul lists several important instructions throughout today's passage, but specifically notice his teachings "to show perfect courtesy toward all people" and to be "careful to devote yourselves to good works." When it comes to manners and how we treat others, it's important to show common courtesy and general kindness. The Bible's basic rule of thumb here is the infamous "Golden Rule" found above which essentially says treat others the way you want to be treated. We love this place and don't mind getting razzed a bit to mind our manners. We all need the same in our daily lives. Show good manners when dealing with others. Treat them with kindness, in the same way you want them to treat you. We can then honor the wishes of Christ in unifying with others.

PRAYER—Dear God, help me to show courtesy and good manners towards others. Above all, help me to follow the Golden Rule any time I am around others. Through Jesus Christ, Amen.

TODAY I WILL...mind my manners. I will make a true effort at all times to treat others exactly how I want to be treated.

APRIL 21 **Read PSALM 51:1-7**

A SINK FULL OF SALVATION

Restaurants, Retail and Refreshments – Beaches and Cream

"But you were washed, you were sanctified, you were justified in the name of the Lord Jesus Christ and by the Spirit of our God."
—*I Corinthians 6:11*

Yesterday I mentioned 50's Prime Time Café ranking among Disney's best in milkshakes, but today's restaurant may win the prize! Beaches and Cream is found between the Yacht and Beach Club resorts just outside Epcot's entrance along the boardwalk. It was recently expanded to accommodate its ever-increasing popularity. Themed around a classic soda shop, complete with a retro jukebox, this hip house of hamburgers has a famed menu selection full of high-calorie creations to satisfy any sweet tooth. Their most famous dessert is the "kitchen sink," literally served in a metal sink with eight scoops of various flavored ice cream, every topping they own and an entire can of whipped cream! It currently costs $35 and feeds four (at least!).

I've eaten here once, and it was wonderful. No, I didn't go for the full sink, although I was tempted. They do have a plastic, mini-sink dessert you can keep which I did buy...and eat...by myself. Yes, I was a bit ashamed...but also very happy. Thinking about the kitchen sink made me realize how much we use water: for handwashing, bathing, drinking, cleaning food, dishes and clothes and so much more. It can also be used for something else very important, saving our souls. Today's psalm shows David asking God to wash him clean from sin. God offers us the same chance, to be washed clean through baptism. Jesus demonstrated this example despite being sin-free. The waters of baptism don't just cleanse sin, but also demonstrate acceptance of Christ by symbolizing His death, burial and resurrection. Acts 2:38 commands us to be baptized to wash away sins and receive the Holy Spirit. I Peter 3:21 literally says water saves us. Praise God today for sinks...full of ice cream certainly, but also full of life-sustaining water that saves us eternally through the cleansing of sin and power of baptism in Christ.

PRAYER—Lord, thank you for the abundance of water, serving so many of our basic needs including the cleansing of our sins through baptism and the sacrifice of Jesus. In Him, Amen.

TODAY I WILL...list everything I use water for, thanking God for each as His blessing. I will also consider following Christ in baptism if I haven't already.

APRIL 22 **Read PSALM 96:1-13**

LOOKIN' DOWN ON CREATION

Restaurants, Retail and Refreshments – California Grill

"For his invisible attributes, namely, his eternal power and divine nature, have been clearly perceived, ever since the creation of the world, in the things that have been made."
—Romans 1:20

In 1972, the Carpenters had a chart-topping hit called "Top of the World." The chorus began with, "I'm on top of the world lookin' down on creation." Just a year earlier, Walt Disney World had opened, along with the spectacular Contemporary Resort. Located on the 15th and top floor was a restaurant coincidentally named "Top of the World." It featured Broadway-style shows, top entertainment acts, comedy groups, dinner, dancing and Sunday brunches. In 1993, the name was changed to California Grill, and to this day, it's one of the top dining establishments in all WDW. "Top of the World" is now the name of a lounge exclusively for Disney Vacation Club members on top of Bay Lake Tower, next door to the Contemporary. Whether you're relaxing there or dining at the California Grill itself, you can still look "down on creation" to see the most stunning and picturesque views of Bay Lake, the Seven Seas Lagoon and the Magic Kingdom.

Happy Earth Day! It's also Animal Kingdom's birthday by the way. My wife and I traveled to Disney last year, and she surprised me with a resort upgrade. I thought we were staying at Pop Century, but we ended up at the Contemporary with a room facing the Magic Kingdom. It was my favorite resort stay of all time, simply because of our balcony view. I could've spent hours out there just taking it all in. The California Grill is known for high quality, delicious food, but it's also famous for its panoramic views of gorgeous scenery, landscapes, water and fireworks. Psalm 96 is a worship and praise to God for the beauty and glory of all He's created on this majestic Earth. Never forget He made it all, piece by piece, for our benefit and enjoyment. The world may be scary and difficult at times, but you can't deny its beauty. On this Earth Day, take some time to look around and appreciate the world we've been given. Take care of it as thanks and appreciation to the One who created it all.

PRAYER—Lord, Your Earth is beautiful. Thank you for blessing us all with its splendor and majesty. Help me to take time to appreciate and take care of it. Through Jesus' name, Amen.

TODAY I WILL...find a beautiful view, spend some time taking it in and thank God.

APRIL 23 **Read LUKE 22:14-20**

AN ELITE FEAST

Restaurants, Retail and Refreshments – Victoria & Albert's

"...and I assign to you, as my Father assigned to me, a kingdom, that you may eat and drink at my table in my kingdom..."
—Luke 22:29-30

If you thought yesterday's restaurant was elite and superior, you ain't seen nothin' yet! The California Grill may be rated high among Disney guests, but today's location has won several national awards. Victoria and Albert's opened in 1988 inside the Grand Floridian Resort. It has won AAA's five diamond award for excellence in dining every year since 2000, only one of three restaurants in Florida to receive the accolade. Trip Advisor even ranked it #2 in the entire United States when it comes to fine dining. Named after Queen Victoria (and her husband, Prince Albert) who ruled Britain for 63 years in the late 1800's, it features three possible settings. There is the main dining room, the Queen Victoria room which is a more intimate setting for up to 8 guests and the Chef's Table. The final option is an exclusive, unmatched experience with a table right in the kitchen. The chef personally converses with guests as they are served an 11-course feast. The current cost of this elite event is $250 per person.

I've never eaten here, but it's definitely on the bucket list. Enjoying an 11-course feast of the highest quality food at a multiple award-winning restaurant sounds like a dream. Thankfully, I've been invited to share in another feast. Much smaller, but way more important. In Luke 22, Jesus reclined at a table with His apostles and initiated a very important and symbolic meal. He instituted the Lord's Supper, a remembrance of His body, broken on the cross and His blood, shed as a sacrifice for us. At the end of the chapter, He invited His apostles to a table in His kingdom forever. He extends us the same invitation. Observing the Lord's Supper or communion is still a part of our worship to remember Christ, His life and sacrifice. It also helps keep us spiritually guided towards a future where we too can sit around His table for all eternity. A Chef's Table, 11-course feast at Florida's most elite restaurant can't even compare with that!

PRAYER—Holy Lord, I want to sit at the table of Christ in Your kingdom for all eternity. Thank You for the invitation and what an amazing experience that will be! In Him, Amen.

TODAY I WILL...realize the importance of communion and participate to remember Him.

APRIL 24 **Read 2 CORINTHIANS 5:1-5**

I'M GOING HOME

Restaurants, Retail and Refreshments – Chef Art Smith's Homecomin'

"He who has prepared us for this very thing is God, who has given us the Spirit as a guarantee."
—*2 Corinthians 5:5*

My church has hosted a summer camp for 35 years. I've been attending since age 9 and have only missed four years either as camper or counselor. Six years ago, our dining hall tragically burned to the ground. For 3 years after, we used a large tent and were then unable to go for two years due to construction and Covid. In 2021, we finally got to "go home" with a magnificent, brand-new, dining hall in place. This theme was "Home," and we were so excited to be back.Art Smith is a professional chef who worked for two Florida governors as well as being Oprah Winfrey's personal chef. In 2016, he opened Homecomin' at Disney Springs. The specialty is homegrown, comfort food with a Southern flair. As Smith explained, "it's where Florida heritage meets new Southern cuisine." We've eaten here once, and it was delicious! "Homecomin'" is a perfect name. Not only is the food farm-fresh and homemade, but diners are made to feel as though they're back home, enjoying a meal around the family dinner table.

There's nothing like going home, especially when you've been away for a while. In 2 Corinthians 5, Paul compares our earthly home to a tent. It's temporary and won't last. He even says we groan in our tent longing for our permanent home of Heaven. One of my favorite Bible verses is found in this passage and above saying that God has not only prepared a permanent home for us but has given us His Spirit as a guarantee we're going. A guarantee! No need to worry or doubt! If we follow His instructions and the footsteps of Christ, we're going home. After 3 years, our camp dining tent was looking pretty worn, and we were glad to see it finally come down for a more permanent replacement. Even better is the eternal home God has prepared for us all that will never need replaced. That will be the ultimate in homecomin'! I can't wait to be at home with God. And I have a guarantee! I know I'm going! Do you?

PRAYER—Father, I can't wait for my homecoming! Thank You for preparing me a permanent home and giving me Your Spirit so I can know. I can't wait to see You and Jesus. Amen.

TODAY I WILL... follow His Word to assure His Spirit as my guarantee of home.

APRIL 25 **Read 2 TIMOTHY 3:1-5**

SPINNING OUT OF CONTROL

Restaurants, Retail and Refreshments – Garden Grill

"And Jesus answered them, 'See that no one leads you astray.'"
—Matthew 24:4

There are 37 revolving restaurants in the U.S., although many have closed or no longer spin due to high maintenance costs. We used to enjoy one here in downtown Nashville, but it closed in 2000. Thankfully, we can still visit our favorite one in Epcot. The Garden Grill, previously known as "The Good Turn Restaurant" and "The Land Grille Room," serves delicious food, much of it grown there within the Land Pavilion. The character meal is served as guests sit atop a slowly, rotating platform, giving them a 360-degree view of the Pavilion including the boat ride below. I'm grateful it still spins, and at a nice, leisurely pace. I'd hate to imagine if it began spinning too fast or out of control...not a pretty picture for those enjoying the family-style meals.

On a double date in college, we decided it would be fun to roll down an extremely steep, grassy hill (yes, we were weird). That night, I learned my body couldn't handle that spinning out of control. Apparently, I pinched a nerve or something because on the car ride back, I became nauseous and lost all feeling in my hands, unable to move them. Needless to say, that date was a one and done. In today's passage, Paul warns of turbulent times ahead listing multiple sins people will unfortunately fall into. He cautions they might have the appearance of good and godliness but will ultimately deny God. He ends by saying, "avoid such people." As I've previously mentioned, those "turbulent times" are now. The world is currently soaked with sin as many are involved in practices accepted in society that blatantly go against God. The Bible is basically ignored on many issues today as instead, what makes people feel good becomes the accepted way of life. The world is spinning out of control and it's causing irreparable harm to so many and their relationships with God. Avoid such people! Don't get caught up in the spinning!

PRAYER—Lord, help me to be strong when others try to lead me away from You. Keep me from spinning out of control in sin. Through Jesus, Amen.

TODAY I WILL... stay grounded and not get caught up in the "sin spin" just because it looks fun or is accepted.

APRIL 26 **Read JEREMIAH 1:4-5**

FORMED FOR A PURPOSE

Restaurants, Retail and Refreshments – Mickey Pretzels

"For we are his workmanship, created in Christ Jesus for good works, which God prepared beforehand, that we should walk in them."
—Ephesians 2:10

Now this is weird! I enjoy irony and coincidences, but this one's a bit bizarre! Not only am I writing April 26th's devotional on April 26th, but in doing pretzel research for this one, I discovered there's actually a National Pretzel Day...on April 26th!! It's true! Look it up! Is that freaky or what? We talked previously about all the Mickey-shaped food offered throughout all Disney parks. Mickey pretzels are certainly a popular choice with various flavors and versions sold depending on the season. Stuffed pretzels and those with dipping sauces tend to also be very well-received. Pretzels were invented as early as 7th century and even have religious significance in both ingredients and shape. 80% of pretzels are produced in Pennsylvania which was also where National Pretzel Day got its start when the governor there declared it in 2003.

Pretzels are made with a fairly simple recipe using few ingredients. The only requirement to officially call them pretzels is to form them into their classic shape, or in this case, that classic Mickey shape. Today's reading was short but powerful as God told Jeremiah that He knew him long before he formed him in the womb. Additionally, the verse above states that we are God's workmanship created by God to do good works as Christ did. Just like that pretzel, carefully formed into the shape of Mickey's head, God has designed, molded and shaped us just the way He wants us. We were each perfectly made in the image of God Himself, created to do good things for Him. Figure out your purpose, live up to it and carry out the plans God has for you.

PRAYER—Dear Father, thank You for knowing me, forming me and giving me life. I know I was created for a special purpose, so help me to discover it and live up to my full potential for You. Through Jesus, Amen.

TODAY I WILL...realize I am made perfect by God in Christ. I will work hard to discover God's purpose for which I was created.

APRIL 27 **Read JOB 38:1-11**

THE TRUE DEFINITION OF SCI-FI

Restaurants, Retail and Refreshments – Sci-Fi Dine-in Theater

"And he is before all things, and in him all things hold together."
—Colossians 1:17

In high school, my friends and I were told that *Plan 9 from Outer Space* was the worst movie ever made, so of course we rented a copy simply to make fun. That's just one of many films used at a well-known Disney restaurant dedicated to the fictional part of Science. The Sci-Fi Dine-in Theater is a truly unique experience with most guests being seated in booths resembling 1950's convertibles. While enjoying an appetizing menu of traditional American cuisine, diners view a large screen with classic Sci-fi movie clips from the same time period. The restaurant, a favorite for our family, opened in 1991 along with 19 other new attractions to celebrate WDW's 20th anniversary. It also offers complimentary popcorn and yummy milkshakes.

I appreciate Science Fiction but have also always enjoyed the actual subject of Science. I've had some great teachers and can recall constructing and launching rockets, assembling a radio, riding a homemade hovercraft and figuring a way to drop an egg off a building without breaking it. Discovering how things work is fascinating but can also be a controversial topic when mixed with religion. Many use Science to explain away God saying there must be a logical explanation for everything instead of believing a higher power was involved. In Job 38, God explains that He's the one that laid the foundation of the Earth, determined its measurements and planned everything we see in nature. God created Science! If you look at the complexity of Earth, our bodies and how everything works, there's no way you could logically explain it just happening by chance. The "big bang" is a big joke. Proverbs 14:15 says "the simple believes everything, but the prudent gives thought to his steps." It's obvious that Science requires a designer that can only be explained as God. It's okay to enjoy and believe in Science, as long as there's no denying God is the one behind it. Science without God is just another form of Science Fiction.

PRAYER—Lord, thank You for Science allowing us to discover how things work. I know You carefully designed all we see and learn. Help others to realize the same. In His name, Amen.

TODAY I WILL...discover something new in Science while thanking God for creating it.

APRIL 28 **Read JOHN 6:25-51**

THE BEST OF BREADS

Restaurants, Retail and Refreshments – Disney Bakeries

"I am the bread of life."
—John 6:48

Imagine entering the Magic Kingdom. You spot the magnificent castle and begin your stroll down Main Street, U.S.A. Can you smell it? As you get close to the Main Street Bakery, it becomes even stronger. All six Disney parks around the world have a Main Street, and most include a bakery of sorts. WDW's now includes a Starbucks, but still offers multiple, delicious baked goodies. In California, not only do you have a bakery on Main Street at Disneyland Park, but Disney California Adventure park offers a self-guided, bakery tour where each guest receives two complimentary pieces of sourdough bread as they learn how it was made.

Read today's passage from John 6 carefully. What is Jesus teaching? He had just multiplied five small pieces of bread into enough to feed well over 5000 people. He tells his disciples not to seek that type of bread that will perish, but to instead strive for bread that will last eternally. He refers to the Old Testament when God dropped manna, a type of bread, from Heaven to feed His wandering people and compares that to a new and more important type of bread God has also sent from Heaven. That bread is Christ Himself as He calls Himself the "bread of life" multiple times. In the final verse, He says anyone who eats of this "living bread" will live forever. Forever! Try to imagine that! Just a few days ago, we referenced the Lord's Supper that Jesus instituted. Sharing in that communion is so important as we are symbolically consuming this "living bread" that gives us a forever life with Him. Disney bread and baked treats may be among the best on Earth, but they are no match for the bread of life that assures our eternal future. Make sure to get your fill of this extremely, essential bread. Understand its meaning and power, take it with seriousness and sincerity and praise God that He has offered it to you.

PRAYER—Father God, thank You for providing me with delicious bread to enjoy. More importantly, thank You for sending the living bread of Jesus to ensure my place with You. Help me to understand its significance and share it boldly. In the name of the Bread Himself, Amen.

TODAY I WILL... enjoy some form of bread while thanking God for the living bread of Christ.

APRIL 29 **Read JOHN 14:1-6 & 21:9-13**

WHAT HAS HE PREPARED FOR YOU?

Restaurants, Retail and Refreshments – Chef Mickey's

"Behold, I am with you and will keep you wherever you go and will bring you back to this land."
—Genesis 28:15

Get those napkins ready! We're almost through April, but we can't leave without visiting what is arguably the most iconic restaurant on WDW's property. It may not have the best food, but you can't deny the unforgettable nostalgia and environment. Set as a buffet within the Contemporary Resort, the magical atmosphere is made complete by the monorail traveling right above the dining room. If that weren't enough, you also get the Fab 5 of characters with Mickey, Minnie, Donald, Goofy and Pluto traveling around while you dine and dancing to the music as you twirl your napkins in the air. Chef Mickey's was originally the name of a restaurant at Disney Village Marketplace (Disney Springs today). It was open there for just 5 years before being replaced with the Rainforest Café and moving to the Contemporary.

Eating at Chef Mickey's is a rite of passage at WDW. You gotta do it at least once! Seeing the most classic of characters in their chef's outfits is reason enough. Did you know that Jesus also displayed some chef qualities? In John 21, He prepared breakfast for His Apostles to talk and prepare them for His upcoming departure and ascension along with their charge to begin His church. Jesus may not be around to prepare our breakfast, but He has prepared something way more important for us. Earlier, in John 14, He said He was going home to prepare a place for us within His Father's house. In addition, He said He would come back and take us there with Him. He has made us that promise. Our place with God is prepared. The question is...are *you* prepared to accept it? Are you on the right path and entering Heaven through Jesus which is the only Way to get there? Let Chef Mickey prepare your meal next time at Disney but allow Christ to prepare your place of eternal bliss and do whatever necessary to make sure you receive it!

PRAYER—Lord, I am so excited that Christ has prepared a place for me within Your kingdom. Help me to be worthy to receive such a gift and do all You require. Through Christ, Amen.

TODAY I WILL...prepare breakfast while meditating on Christ preparing a place for me, making sure I'm worthy to receive it.

APRIL 30 **Read GENESIS 1:28-31**

LET'S EAT!

Restaurants, Retail and Refreshments – Earl of Sandwich

"...whether you eat or drink, or whatever you do, do all to the glory of God"
—I Corinthians 10:31

In 1992, Vanessa Williams had a hit single called "Save the Best for Last." I realize there may be some disagreement over my final choice here in April, but in my mind, that's exactly what I've done. This is my absolute favorite Disney restaurant, and it's not even technically Disney-owned! But it's simple, has easy access and tastes so good! As the story goes, in 1762, the 4th Earl of Sandwich, John Montagu didn't want to leave his beloved gaming table and therefore requested his roast beef be brought between two pieces of bread so he could eat it with his hands while playing cards. Thus the sandwich was invented and so named. To honor the fame of his ancestor, the 11th Earl of Sandwich, also named John Montagu, founded the Earl of Sandwich restaurant chain in 2004 in Orlando. He partnered with Planet Hollywood founder Robert Earl (Earl...seriously?) along with his son, Orlando (this just keeps getting better). The chain has since spread to 36 locations throughout the U.S., as well as Canada, France and the Philippines.

I always choose "The Original," which is roast beef, cheddar and horseradish (the best part) between two delicious slices of toasted bread. For me, it's the absolute perfect sandwich, but they have many other appetizing choices. There's nothing like good food, which has consumed a majority of our April devotionals. At the end of Genesis 1, we read that God is the provider of food for all his creatures including us, His most beloved. He has given us so many delicious food choices, so today's reminder is quite simple. Don't take for granted the daily blessing of food. Many of us pray before meals, but do we do it with sincerity or does it become rote and without thought? God constantly provides our basic needs, and we must genuinely acknowledge and praise Him daily. Our Father is most loving and generous. Don't forget to thank Him for something as simple as a perfect sandwich.

PRAYER—Lord, thank You for providing me with food and drink regularly. Help me to remember You every time I am blessed to consume it. In Jesus' name, Amen.

TODAY I WILL...spend more time in prayer before meals and savor every bite as a gift.

MAY THEME

PIXAR

MAY 1 **Read MATTHEW 12:33-37**

HOLD YOUR TONGUE

Pixar – Finding Nemo

"Keep your tongue from evil..."
—Psalm 34:13

Welcome to May! Hopefully the weather is warming up and you are seeing some beautiful, sunny days. This month, we're focusing on a division of Disney that has become an empire all its own. Pixar began in 1979 as simply the computer division of Lucasfilm before becoming its own company in 1986. Twenty years later, after having worked together for years, Disney purchased them outright for $7.4 billion! As of this writing, Pixar has produced 25 films and won 23 Oscars for their high-quality, computer-animated, family films. *Finding Nemo*, their 5th film, was released in 2003 and quickly became the highest grossing animated picture of its time. It has since been surpassed but remains the best-selling DVD ever. Today we focus on one of its lesser known and underrated characters. Nigel, voiced by Australian actor, Geoffrey Rush, is a clumsy pelican that doesn't get the credit deserved for saving Marlin and Dory from a flock of seagulls. During that scene when he has the fish and a good bit of seawater scooped up in his gullet, Rush held his tongue while speaking his lines to give a more authentic performance.

Have you ever held your tongue while trying to talk? It makes clear speech a bit difficult. James 1:26 basically says we can't be right with God if we don't hold our tongues. Working in the secular world, this is by far the most common sin I witness. I love my coworkers, but the language I often hear is anything but righteous. In Matthew, Jesus says we are either justified or condemned by our words which can have so much influence over others, good or bad. As Christians, we must remember to have pure speech before others and "hold our tongues" from any filth. Those words may be commonplace, but God is always listening. Each impure, offensive or coarse word is another nail through His Son's body on the cross.

PRAYER—Lord, help me to watch my language and only speak positive words that build others up and provide a good influence to lead them closer to You. Through Jesus, Amen.

TODAY I WILL...hold my tongue when tempted to say anything that might condemn me due to improper or ungodly speech.

MAY 2 **Read ROMANS 8:18-25**

PREPARE TO BE LAUNCHED

Pixar – *Brave*

"Let us not grow weary of doing good, for in due season we will reap, if we do not give up."
—Galatians 6:9

Have you ever tried archery? It's harder than it looks! As a new teacher during a Medieval unit, I foolishly allowed two students to try firing a homemade bow and arrow at a classroom knight poster. Big and dangerous mistake! The boy, as I expected for both, was unable to fire it properly, and the arrow harmlessly fell to the ground. The girl, however, let loose like she was hunting buffalo, giving me a slight stroke and creating a permanent hole through both the knight's heart and my office door on which it was hanging. Princess Merida, from 2012's *Brave*, was also highly a highly skilled archer. This was a Pixar film full of firsts: first female lead, first Disney princess with brothers, first one without a love interest, first to not sing and finally, the first princess not based on a preexisting historical or literary character.

I'm sure you know to fire the arrow you must first pull back on the bow's string causing tension to launch the arrow forward. Therefore, to go forward, you must first move backward. Similarly, it's been said when life is dragging you backwards, it simply means it's getting ready to launch you forward into something great. In Romans 8, Paul talks about this saying the present sufferings don't compare with the future glory to be revealed. He says we must have hope while waiting patiently for what we can't see. It often takes time to move forward. When it feels like we're being pulled backward too much, we must remember to have patience, faith and trust in God because we're on His time, and it simply means He's launching us forward even further. Romans 12:12 tells us to be patient in tribulation and the verse above advises not to give up, for we will eventually reap a reward. Don't give up on God. You are His arrow. Give Him time to pull back and aim because He's got big plans to launch you further than you can imagine.

PRAYER—Father, help me to trust in Your plans for me. Give me patience when life pulls me backwards knowing it means I will be launched even further in due time. In Jesus, Amen.

TODAY I WILL...give God the bow and all the time He needs to launch me wherever and as far as He wants.

MAY 3 **Read PHILIPPIANS 2:19-24**

HONORING OUR MENTORS

Pixar – *Coco*

"One generation shall commend your works to another..."
—Psalm 145:4

Steven Spielberg is one of the greatest directors in cinema history. His 1982 film, *E.T.*, was one of the biggest blockbusters of my childhood. That same year, a talented 16-year-old kid was asked to repair some of Spielberg's old 8mm films. He took the job, got to know Spielberg and collaborated with him on several projects. Spielberg became his mentor. Since then, J.J. Abrams has become one of the greatest filmmakers himself, some even calling him "the next Spielberg." *Coco*, my favorite Pixar film, inspires a similar message with the importance of remembering the contributions of past mentors and passing along their heritage, words and influence. The film, while successful in the U.S., did even better in China and was Mexico's highest grossing movie in history. Its title was changed in Brazil due to an unfortunate Portuguese meaning. (I'll let you look that one up.) *Coco* took six years to complete with the first shot of the Land of the Dead taking a year itself due to over 7 million animated lights.

In Acts 16, Paul chooses a young disciple named Timothy to accompany him on his journey. He ends up mentoring him into a strong, Christian leader. In Philippians 2, Paul tells the people he's sending Timothy to them while complimenting his qualities, progress and hard work. Timothy is sent to continue the work of his mentor, Paul and pass along his wisdom. It's important to remember our past mentors and pass on their legacy to the next generation as the psalm above mentions. Sharing what they gave us is a way to pay tribute to them. Hopefully the cycle will continue, and our guidance will be passed on in mentoring others. Remember those who have influenced you in your walk with God. Honor them by keeping their influence alive!

PRAYER—Dear Lord, help me to honor my spiritual mentors by passing along what they've taught me from Your Word. Help me to mentor others so Your message can continue to pass through generations. Through Christ I pray, Amen.

TODAY I WILL...remember my mentors and make record of their wisdom so I may pass it down to others.

MAY 4 **Read NUMBERS 6:22-27**

MAY THE LORD BE WITH YOU

Star Wars Day

"May the Lord be with you."
—Ruth 2:4 (NASB)

I originally had another topic planned here but realized what a mistake it would be to let today's holiday go by without recognition. Today is unofficially "Star Wars Day!" It supposedly began on May 4, 1979 when Margaret Thatcher had been elected as Prime Minister of the United Kingdom. Her political party placed a congratulatory message in the newspaper that read, "May the Fourth Be with You, Maggie. Congratulations." And the holiday was born. I realize we're doing Pixar this month, so it's a little difficult to relate the two. But there are actually several Star Wars references throughout Pixar films. The most notable takes place in *Toy Story 2* when the evil, emperor Zurg, who is based on Darth Vadar to begin with, tells Buzz Lightyear he is his father, an obvious reference to the famous scene from *The Empire Strikes Back.*

The play on words between today's date and the iconic Star Wars line is uncanny. "May the force be with you" is said numerous times throughout the series. However, I ask that you consider an alternate phrase, changed ever so slightly. In Ruth 2, Boaz greets Ruth by saying, "May the Lord be with you." He then praises her for all she has done in kindness to her mother-in-law. The Lord was with Ruth and blessed her greatly for her hard work, generosity and unselfishness. Today's reading from Numbers 6 contains a similar and familiar blessing from God that has been turned into a well-known hymn. The Lord blesses and keeps those who remain faithful to Him. He rewards them for good works. He is gracious and brings peace to those who follow His Word and proclaim His name. So Happy Star Wars Day! May the Lord be with you! As you celebrate today, consider sharing this new phrase with others regularly. God loves all His children, but especially blesses those who are faithful and remain in Him.

PRAYER—Lord, thank you for being with me. Help me to always remain faithful so I may keep favor with You and feel Your constant presence. In the name of Christ, Amen.

TODAY I WILL...find a recording of "The Lord Bless You and Keep You", listen and possibly sing along. Tell someone, "may the Lord be with you," and thank God for His goodness.

MAY 5 **Read I CORINTHIANS 6:12-20**

OUR INCREDIBLE BODIES

Pixar – The Incredibles

"Do you not know that you are God's temple and that God's Spirit dwells in you? If anyone destroys God's temple, God will destroy him. For God's temple is holy, and you are that temple."
—I Corinthians 3:16-17

Guess which of the following facts is true: 1) your nose can detect up to one trillion different smells, 2) your body produces 25 million cells per second, 3) your bones are stronger than steel, 4) the entire surface of your skin is replaced monthly. You may have figured it out. They're all true! The human body is incredible, and the stars of today's film also have incredible bodies that do incredible things. See what I did there? *The Incredibles* released in 2004, but Brad Bird, who wrote and directed both *Incredibles* films, first had the idea in 1993. He held it for seven years before pitching it to Pixar execs in 2000. He also voiced the Edna Mode character in the film, although it was first offered to famed actress, Lily Tomlin. When she heard Bird's attempt, she supposedly said, "What do you need me for? You got it already."

The Incredibles' family, a.k.a. the Parrs, each have their own superpower which include: Mr. Incredible's strength, his wife, Elastigirl's stretching ability, daughter Violet's invisibility and shielding powers and finally son, Dash with his super speed. (Baby Jack-Jack also has powers in the sequel.) While it's fun to watch superhero films and dream of having superhuman bodies, it's a fact that we do have an incredible bodies created by God. He gifted them to us, and it's up to us how we care for them. God has some reminders like the verse above and in I Corinthians 6 where it says our bodies are temples for the Holy Spirit inside us and shouldn't be used for immoral or improper acts. Additionally, we are told to glorify God with our bodies. We must treat our bodies with respect, take care of them and realize their importance and blessing. They may not have special powers, but the fact they are a gift from God is pretty powerful. You only get one body and one shot to take care of it. Take that "incredible" responsibility seriously.

PRAYER—Lord, thank You for my body and the incredible things it can do. I know You created it as a temple for Your Spirit. Help me to take care of it always. In Jesus, Amen.

TODAY I WILL...take care of my body. I will create a plan to keep it healthy and do nothing that will cause it harm realizing what an important gift it is.

MAY 6 **Read I TIMOTHY 6:6-10**

LIVE EVERY MINUTE

Pixar – *Soul*

"...for I have learned in whatever situation I am to be content."
—Philippians 4:11

Have you ever heard the statistic that says most lottery winners go broke? Some resources put it as high as 70%, although that's an exaggeration with the real figure being closer to 1/3 that file for bankruptcy within 5 years. But why? The message from today's film may explain it. *Soul* never came into theaters due to 2020's viral pandemic but released direct to Disney Plus on Christmas day. This was the first Pixar film not to feature the voice of John Ratzenberger, although his likeness was used for a subway character. The film does show the famed Pizza Planet Truck, visible in all Pixar films except one...yesterday's film, *The Incredibles*.

Soul is a charming story with a phenomenal message easily relatable to today's Scriptures. The main character, Joe, dreams of playing in a Jazz band. When he finally gets the chance, he doesn't feel fulfilled which is what tends to happen with many lottery winners also. They expect joyful and dramatic life changes, but simply don't find it with more money. Like Joe, they must learn to be content with what they've been given. In I Timothy 6, Paul reminds us we brought nothing into the world and can take nothing out. He also addresses directly those who desire to be rich saying they will fall into temptation and never be satisfied. Understand there's nothing wrong with seeking more money or fulfillment of life goals, but we must be content if it doesn't work out the way we expect. At the end of *Soul*, Joe makes a profound statement with the very last line when asked how he'll spend his new life. He replies, "I'm not sure. But I do know I'm going to live every minute of it." We must learn to simply appreciate life itself and the numerous, often unrealized blessings that come with it, both great or small. Learning to be content is the key to satisfaction, happiness and the salvation of our soul.

PRAYER—Father, help me realize how much I'm blessed and be content in all things, realizing I can take nothing with me into Your kingdom. Thank You for it all. Through Christ, Amen.

TODAY I WILL...count my blessings and realize how much I really have. I will also promise God to be content with what He's given knowing it's enough.

MAY 7 **Read ROMANS 12:9-21**

YOU MAY HAVE A FRIEND IN THEM

Pixar – Toy Story

"Strive for peace with everyone..."
—Hebrews 12:14

As a teacher, I was the only male on a five-teacher team for many years. When one of the ladies retired, we were included on the new-hire committee. The most qualified applicant was another male, and I'll admit I initially had mixed feelings. Part of me worried having another male on the team would diminish my unique position and distinction. Those feelings were selfish at best, but I couldn't help considering them. I'm proud to say it worked out for the best. He was a fantastic addition to the team, and I gained a lifelong friend. Today's imaginative and unprecedented film contains a similar story. *Toy Story* was the first completely computer-animated film and began an epic collection of timeless Pixar films. When it released in 1995, Disney wanted a company to produce a line of toys from the film, but the big names such as Hasbro and Mattel declined, fearing the short time frame. The job instead went to Thinkway Toys, a small, Canadian-based company which has now grown astronomically. Disney also asked them to produce Sid's mutant toys from the film, but they politely declined. Wonder why?

As you probably know, this first film's story involves Andy's toys and his original Woody being worried about his place due to a new, advanced toy named Buzz Lightyear. Woody's no longer the favorite causing fear and doubt. Romans 12 is a powerful passage teaching us to love one another, live in harmony, show hospitality and contribute to others' needs. We are taught above all to seek peace with everyone providing an easier path toward Christian unity. We are all different people, and it's not always easy to see eye to eye with everyone. But we must try, like Christ, to be a friend to all. We must love everyone knowing each is God's child. And who knows? Giving each person a chance may just gain you a lasting friendship. It did for me.

PRAYER—Dear God, help me to see every person as Your child and strive for peace with each one showing them proper love and hospitality as Jesus did. In His name, Amen.

TODAY I WILL...get out of my comfort zone to speak to and get along with one person whom I see as different. I will strive to make peace and work towards a friendship.

MAY 8 **Read ACTS 5:1-11**

A MONSTER CHEATER

Pixar – Monsters University

"Whoever walks in integrity walks securely, but he who makes his ways crooked will be found out."
—Proverbs 10:9

In 1980, Rosie Ruiz was declared the winner of the 84th Boston Marathon...for only eight days. An investigation determined she jumped onto the course just a half mile from the finish line and claimed victory, having only run a very small portion of the race. The passion of competition and the thrill of victory unfortunately tempts many to consider cheating. The athletic world in particular is full of similar stories. The Pixar world also contains a cheating story in this *Monsters, Inc.* sequel. *Monsters University* released in 2013, twelve years after the original. Disney had wanted a sequel since 2005, but disagreements with Pixar led them to task another company with making the film. However, when Disney purchased Pixar a year later, conflicts were resolved, and plans resumed for the sequel, which actually became a prequel.

The film showcases Mike and Sulley's introduction in college and their attempts to win the "Scare Games," a fierce club competition. They start out slow but gradually improve and are close to victory, only to have Sulley cheat in desperation. As a former teacher, I dealt with cheating quite often. We even had an honestly pledge and privacy folders for testing to curb the issue. Acts 5 contains an eye-opening story of Ananias and Sapphira cheating the apostles out of pledged money. They claim to have brought all proceeds from a property sale but have actually kept a portion for themselves. They both pay the ultimate price for their dishonesty. Cheating is one of Satan's greatest temptations as it can often be done so easily. Sometimes he even causes us to justify it to lessen our guilty feelings. Fair play and integrity are Godly qualities we must strive for. Cheating, just another form of lying, is an abomination God hates (Prov. 12:22). Strive to serve Him with integrity and righteousness. Don't sink to cheating in any aspect of life. It may provide a temporary victory, but the long-term effect will be a loss with God.

PRAYER—Heavenly Father, I want to be a person of integrity and honesty. Help me to resist any temptation to lie or cheat to get ahead in life. In Your Son's holy name, Amen.

TODAY I WILL...become a person of integrity vowing to always be honest and fair in life.

MAY 9 **Read HABAKKUK 3:1-4**

WHERE'S GOD?

Pixar – Pizza Planet Truck

"Rejoice always, pray without ceasing, give thanks in all circumstances; for this is the will of God in Christ Jesus for you.
—I Thessalonians 5:16-18

Where's Waldo? Remember those books? I used to love searching for Waldo amongst the many colorful pictures full of various characters and events. Pixar has developed their own version by hiding the same item in each of their films. A few days ago, I mentioned *The Incredibles* as the only film thus far that doesn't show the famous Pizza Planet Truck somewhere within the movie, although it does appear in the video game based on that film. The original truck is an important plot point in *Toy Story*, the first Pixar film. The renowned yellow pickup with "YO" on the rear, strongly suggesting it's a Toyota, is driven recklessly as Buzz and Woody stowaway to try and make their way back to Andy. In the sequel, it's the toys themselves that drive it quite wildly. *Toy Story 4* doesn't show the actual truck, but it does appear as a leg tattoo.

Finding that legendary truck in each film might be difficult but finding God in all parts of our lives is not, if we only stop to look for Him. In today's reading, Habakkuk tells God he can see Him in all things saying His splendor covers the heavens and the earth is full of His praise. He also mentions God's brightness like rays of sunlight. My favorite view of God has always been rays of light beaming down between clouds. It has always made me think of God, even before finding this Scripture. If we truly look, God's handiwork is so evident throughout all creation. The verses above say to rejoice always and pray without ceasing. This doesn't mean a constant solemn prayer. Instead, it's reminding us to look for God in all things and be in a continuous acknowledgement of Him, praising and thanking Him when we see, hear or feel Him. Do a hunt for the Pizza Planet Truck next time you watch a Pixar classic. More importantly, do a hunt for God in what you see daily. It'll be a lot easier than finding that truck because He's everywhere!

PRAYER—God, help me to take the time to look for you in all I see. I want to have continuous conversation with you praising Your name for being all around me. In Christ's name, Amen.

TODAY I WILL...look for God! I will pray without ceasing by acknowledging Him often while thanking Him for being present in all I see.

MAY 10 **Read JOHN 20:24-29**

OUR HIDDEN GUIDE

Pixar – Ratatouille

"...and behold, I am with you always, to the end of the age."
—Matthew 28:20

SpaghettiOs and grilled cheese. That's about the extent of my culinary skills. I enjoy cooking, have tried some recipes over the years and generally do okay, but I've never been much of a chef. In *Ratatouille*, a young, garbage boy becomes a surprise sensation in food preparation, but only with the help of a hidden, furry friend directing his work. 2007's *Ratatouille* was Pixar's 8th film. It was also written and directed by Brad Bird, whom we mentioned a few days ago being responsible for both *Incredibles* films. He and some of the film's crew visited Paris, France for inspiration and consulted multiple French and American chefs to make the film's animated food look authentic. Bird actually replaced the original director, who left Pixar during production for unclear reasons, although he was recognized in the credits and received an Oscar nomination.

Alfredo Linguini is the name of the unexpected chef who gets unexpected cooking assistance from an unexpected source...a rat. Remy the rat is the true expert and hides under Linguini's hat watching and advising his every move. He even guides his movements like a marionette puppet, pulling on Linguini's hair to steer his hands in the right direction. In John 20, Jesus reappears to the disciples, the first time they see Him after His death. Thomas is not there the first time and says he won't believe unless he actually sees Jesus with his own eyes and feels His crucifixion wounds. Later, when Thomas does see Jesus and believes, Christ makes an important statement saying, "Blessed are those who have not seen and yet believe." He's talking about us. Do you believe in Him without seeing? Do you truly believe the verse above that Jesus is always with us now and forever? Do you believe Matthew 18:20 when Jesus said He's among us? Christ is here! Like Remy, He's always within you, guiding you like a puppet. You only have to accept Him, listen to Him, follow Him and allow Him to be your guide, giving Him full control.

PRAYER—Father, I believe in Jesus. I believe He's here with me right now, inside me, guiding my every move. Help me to submit to Him always giving Him full control. In His name, Amen.

TODAY I WILL...submit to the will of Christ giving Him full control over my every move.

MAY 11 **Read PROVERBS 24:30-34**

WORKIN' FOR A LIVIN'

Pixar – *WALL-E*

"If anyone is not willing to work, let him not eat."
—2 Thessalonians 3:10

Albert, trash! I must've heard that exclamation 17 jillion times growing up. Thankfully, the two words weren't being yelled as synonyms but as a directive. Taking out the trash was my chore. And not just the large, kitchen trashcan, but all the little wastebaskets throughout the house. I think there were nine! That's a whole lotta trash I eradicated over the years. WALL-E is a lovable, little robot tasked with the same chore, although his coverage area was a lot greater than mine. *WALL-E* is unique in that it has no dialogue for the first 22 minutes and no human dialogue until 39 minutes in. It's also the only Pixar film with live-action scenes and the one with the most Oscar nominations (6). While the name WALL-E officially stands for "Waste Allocation Load Lifter: Earth Class," some speculate it's also a nod to Walter Elias Disney.

Some viewers felt this film was too political with hidden agendas. The message of Earth's care and conservation is pretty evident. Set in the 29th century, it predicts the Earth as fully trashed while humans are all overweight blobs having vacated the planet on giant, luxury, space cruisers. It may be a bit farfetched, but the message is worth considering. Laziness and being unwilling to work is a real issue. Proverbs 24 speaks to this describing a sluggard unwilling to work his field which becomes overgrown and useless. The proverb states that laziness leads to poverty, a sentiment echoed in the blunt verse above. God created us most of us with the capability to work. He expects us to earn the food on our plate and avoid laziness. Work to the best of your ability, and don't let idleness creep into your life. Keep healthy and strong so you can work hard always. Most importantly, work in service to God daily to further His kingdom.

PRAYER—Lord, help me to avoid laziness and work hard with the strength and health You've given me. Give me the motivation and determination to maintain a strong work ethic throughout my life. In Christ's name, Amen.

TODAY I WILL...avoid laziness by getting up and doing some work, whether around the house, at my job or in service to others.

MAY 12 **Read PSALM 34:17-22**

KEEP FIGHTING

Pixar – *Onward*

"Fight the good fight of the faith. Take hold of the eternal life to which you were called..."
—I Timothy 6:12

2020 was a difficult year...to say the least. When I think back to all that we dealt with, it's quite overwhelming. For us, it began with horrific tornadoes in March, but we also faced an extended power outage, job instability, multiple cancelled events, political unrest and racial tension, not to mention the dreadful Corona Virus that plagued every part of our lives. Dealing with one problem after another is a common theme in many films, including *Onward*. This film was itself a victim of the Corona Virus having to close in theaters just 2 weeks after opening. For that reason, it and *Soul,* which followed, have by far the lowest revenue totals for Pixar. The director used personal experiences in this story, even utilizing an old family photo of himself leaning on his older brother as inspiration for a similar photo near the end of the film.

It's a shame this movie bombed due to the pandemic, because it's really good. I thoroughly enjoyed this story of two brothers' journey to meet their father. They too face multiple problems and even danger along the way. Giving up in the face of these trials would be understandable, but they press onward (hence the title) and keep fighting for their goal. Psalm 34 admits our trials will also be plentiful if we are righteous before God. Giving up may seem much easier in those situations. However, the psalm encourages us to call on the Lord's name, promising He will be near us, hear us and redeem us. In fact, the final verse says, "none of those who take refuge in Him will be condemned." Isn't that comforting? As long as we lean on God and keep fighting the good fight as the above verse directs, we will be greatly rewarded. Life is hard no doubt. But God is here, ready for your call, especially during the most difficult of times. Keep fighting and pressing onward. The goal you're striving for is way too important to give up on.

PRAYER—Thank You Lord for always listening for my call. Help me to lean on you in hard times and not give up. Give me the strength and resilience to press onward for my goal of Heaven. In the name of Jesus, Amen.

TODAY I WILL...press onward, never give up and call on God's name in hard times.

MAY 13 **Read I JOHN 3:1-3**

UP WHERE WE BELONG

Pixar – Toy Story 2

"...whether we live or whether we die, we are the Lord's."
—Romans 14:8

Its name was Honey, and it was my doll. Yes, I had a doll! I'm not embarrassed. Much. It's not like I was a teenager. I was under 5. But I carried that thing everywhere. Wonder if my parents still have it. One thing I know...it was mine. Honey was special because it belonged to me. That's the same message in *Toy Story 2*, Pixar's 3rd film which had triple the budget of the first and brought in 33% more in revenue. The entire story was developed in a single weekend and was originally going to be released direct to video. The entire film was nearly lost after two years of work when one of the animators accidently began deleting everything when doing some routine computer file cleaning. When the error was realized, the servers were quickly shut down, but 90% of the movie was gone. Thankfully, one of the technical directors had been working from home to take care of a newborn and had backups of everything on her home computer.

The plot of this one revolves around Woody discovering he's a rare and valuable toy meaning he must decide whether to go home or leave Andy and take a place of honor in a museum. In the end, after a talk with Buzz, he realizes he is Andy's toy and needs to stay where he belongs. Woody belonged to Andy. Honey belonged to me. We belong to God. I John 3 assures us we belong to God and are His children. It says the world doesn't know us and we are different because we belong to Him. Psalm 100:3 reads, "Know that the Lord, He is God! It is He who made us, and we are His; we are His people, and the sheep of His pasture." Woody could've chosen to leave but knew he belonged at home with Andy. We can also choose to leave God. But it's a poor choice because we belong to Him and always will. He will never leave us. Don't ever leave God. You're His child. Choose to stay with Him now and eternally.

PRAYER—Holy Father, I'm so grateful I'm Your child and belong to You. I never, never want to leave You. Help the world to see me as different because I'm Yours. In Christ, Amen.

TODAY I WILL...let it be known that I belong to God and will never, ever leave Him.

MAY 14 **Read 2 CORINTHIANS 7:8-11**

GOOD REGRETS

Pixar – Monsters, Inc.

"For godly grief produces a repentance that leads to salvation without regret, whereas worldly grief produces death."
—*2 Corinthians 7:10*

Do you have any regrets? I have a few. I wish I'd learned Spanish in high school instead of Latin, which I never use and don't even remember. (Sorry, Latin lovers). I wish I'd attempted to hike the Appalachian Trail when I was younger. Now I'm old and fragile. And I love my job, but there are others I wish I had tried such as a pilot, veterinarian or working my way up at Disney (of course!). One of the stars of today's Pixar classic had a major regret. *Monsters, Inc.* was Pixar's 4th film and the directorial debut for Pete Doctor, who also directed *Up, Inside Out* and *Soul*. His original idea for this one was to have an adult haunted by the monsters he drew as a kid. Billy Crystal and John Goodman who voiced Mike Wazowski and Sulley respectively actually recorded their lines together in the same room, a rarity in animation.

Billy Crystal fits perfectly as Mike Wazowski, but it wasn't the first Pixar role he was offered. He was originally chosen as Buzz Lightyear in *Toy Story* but turned it down. To this day, he admits it's one of his biggest regrets. We all have regrets, some of which are sins against God. I have some of those too which I won't mention. In 2 Corinthians 7, Paul talks about godly grief, which is regret we feel for sin. He says that's actually a good thing because it leads to repentance or turning back to God to maintain our proper salvation course. He discusses a difference between godly and worldly grief. Those not of God may have worldly grief for mistakes, but it only leads to death without salvation. If we are one with God, we should feel godly grief when we sin or a guilt for disappointing Him. This leads to a desire to do better for Him. If you feel guilty when you let God down, see it as a blessing. You have godly grief! Use it to do and be better. Take comfort that you want to please Him, and don't let Him down again.

PRAYER—Lord, I'm sorry for my sin against You. I want to be right with you and not let You down. Help me to turn my guilt and regrets into repentance and a stronger faith. In Him, Amen.

TODAY I WILL...make sure I have godly grief when I sin and use it to repent back to God.

MAY 15 **Read MATTHEW 7:15-20**

LEAVE YOUR MARK

Pixar – The Good Dinosaur

"You will recognize them by their fruits."
—Matthew 7:16

From 1999-2007, Epcot guests had an opportunity to leave a permanent mark behind. The "Leave a Legacy" program invited guests to pay for a self-photo to be placed on giant monoliths just inside the entrance. In 2020, the pictures were moved during a major Epcot entrance refurb to a new home on giant, colorful walls outside the entrance. Speaking of regrets from yesterday, I wish I'd taken part. It would be neat to have a permanent mark at Disney. Leaving a mark is also the goal of Arlo, the youngest dinosaur from *The Good Dinosaur,* which premiered in Paris in 2015 and subsequently became Pixar's first bomb; that is before Covid greatly diminished revenue for films like *Onward* and *Soul.* This film grossed just $332 million worldwide, which is actually low for Pixar standards. It went through multiple revisions, interruptions and cast choices. At one time, big names like John Lithgow, Neil Patrick Harris and Bill Hader were attached to the film, but they were all removed due to budget cuts and delays.

Some critics believed this film just wasn't up to Pixar storytelling standards. It's certainly not my Pixar favorite, but I definitely enjoyed it. The story of young Arlo trying to earn his mark of success on the family silo is both heart-warming and entertaining. It also begs a question...have you left your mark yet? It's fairly easy to leave a mark with money, such as with the "Leave a Legacy" walls, but that doesn't do much to fulfill our spiritual duty. In Matthew 7, Jesus says healthy trees bear good fruit while diseased trees leave bad fruit. Evil will leave its mark on our society too if we don't overpower it with good fruit. In John 13:35, Jesus said others will know us by our love. If we truly do the work of Christ by going out into the world and showing His love to others, they will know us and desire to follow. That will be our mark! Mark sure you're leaving your mark behind so others have no doubt what, or actually Who, you stand for.

PRAYER—Father, I want to leave my mark behind, make a difference for Your cause and bear much good fruit. Help others to be influenced by my love to follow You. In Christ, Amen.

TODAY I WILL...leave my mark! I will show Christ's love to all so I can bear fruit for God.

MAY 16 **Read GENESIS 18:1-14**

THAT'S IMPOSSIBLE

Pixar – The Incredibles

"Is anything too hard for the Lord?"
—Genesis 18:14

Have you ever heard someone say, "That's impossible!" That was actually the title of a short-lived TV show on the History Channel in 2009 which looked at seemingly impossible theories and technologies such as invisibility cloaks, terminators, mind control and even eternal life and discussed what would be needed to make them reality. (One of those is already reality, of course.) We return to *The Incredibles* today where nothing is impossible for this superhuman family where each member's personality is reflected in their superpower: Mr. Incredible's strength with being the strong family head, Elastigirl's stretchability shown in her flexibility juggling all the family duties, Violet's invisibility reflected in her typical teenager persona of isolation and Dash's super speed paralleling his short attention span and fast talking.

The reason we returned to this "incredible" family is to discuss that word which is only found once within the Bible's most common translations. In Acts 26:8, Paul is giving his defense and asks, "Why is it thought incredible by any of you that God raises the dead?" In Genesis today, we read a familiar story of Abraham and Sarah being told they will have a baby at a very old age. Both are shocked with disbelief, and Sarah even laughs at the notion. God then speaks to them asking the question above, "Is anything too hard for the Lord?" That's an obvious rhetorical question. If God wants to raise the dead, He can. If God wants to make an old woman pregnant, He can. The Incredibles may be a fictional, computer-animated family, but God most certainly is not. He is real, He is incredible and nothing is impossible for Him (Luke 1:37, Matt. 19:26). Don't ever think your problems are too big for God. He can bring you out of the direst of situations that you deem too impossible. He is the only incredible superhero you will ever need and will come to your rescue if you just call on His name.

PRAYER—You are incredible, Lord, and I know You can do all things. Help me to remember this in my darkest times and always lean on You. In the name of Jesus, Amen.

TODAY I WILL...make a list of 5 incredible things God did both in the Bible and for me.

MAY 17 **Read PSALM 71:12-18**

SHARE MORE THAN TOYS

Pixar – Toy Story 3

"Do not neglect to do good and to share what you have, for such sacrifices are pleasing to God."
—Hebrews 13:16

As a kid, I never cried in movies. I only remember crying out of pain or sadness. When my first son was born, I cried tears of joy for the first time ever, and I think that must have expanded my tear ducts or something because I'm more emotional now and find myself crying in certain films. And I can't turn it off! *Toy Story 3* was definitely one that brought tears to my eyes. This 2010 film received 5 Oscar nominations including Best Picture. It won for Best Animated Picture and Best Original Song. It was the first ever animated film to receive over $1 billion in sales as well as the first to have a $200 million dollar budget, more than six times that of *Toy Story* and the highest ever for a Pixar film to date, although several since have had the exact same budget.

Speaking of tears...the end of this movie. Oh, the end! It's super emotional when Andy has grown up, is heading off to college and decides to share his toys by giving them to Bonnie. When the toys watch Andy driving off in the final scene, wow! Ok, I gotta stop. Here come the tears again. Giving those toys away is a big sacrifice and you can see Andy's hesitation when he realizes he'll never see them again. We can also share something way more important than toys, but it's joyful and should occur without hesitation. Psalm 71 contains a promise we should repeat to share the wondrous works of God with others. From His "mighty deeds" to his "righteous acts," verse 18 encourages us to proclaim His name to the next generation. The verse above also urges us to share what we have. What we have is the Gospel of Christ. What we have is knowledge of the amazing sacrifice of Jesus. What we have is the hope and promise of eternal life with God. Everything He offers must be shared with the next generation, and it's up to us to pass it on. Don't hesitate! Understand the importance of the gift you have and share!

PRAYER—Dear God, I'm so grateful for all You've given me, especially the hope and promise of eternity through Your Son. Help me to share it often and boldly. In His name, Amen.

TODAY I WILL...share what I have. I will tell the next generation of my blessings and knowledge of what God has done, is continuing to do and will do for my eternal future.

MAY 18 **Read ROMANS 15:14-21**

REMEMBER WHO YOU ARE

Pixar – Finding Dory

"Now I commend you because you remember me in everything and maintain the traditions even as I delivered them to you."
—I Corinthians 11:2

Working regularly with the elderly as a paramedic, I encounter many dementia patients. I also have several friends who have had a family member go through the same. Not being able to remember the events of your life is a very difficult diagnosis I don't wish on anyone. Pixar's Dory suffers the same trials, although hers is caused by short-term memory loss. *Finding Dory*, the sequel to *Finding Nemo*, released in 2016 to immediate popularity and enormous revenue. This was the second animated film in history to make over $1 billion. (Yesterday's film, as you'll recall, was the first.) For this film, animators actually studied Psychology, particularly with adoption, to better understand how Dory would adjust to her new family of Nemo and Marlin while still wondering about her past. Bonus *Finding Dory* fun fact: The tentacles for Hank the Octopus were created separately and when animators tried attaching them to his body, 8 wouldn't fit. They instead left him with 7 and created a backstory for the missing limb.

If you've seen this film or the original, you know that Dory's memory loss provides some comic relief but is also the basis for this sequel's story. Dory begins to have flashbacks of her parents and wants to find them, but her memory loss creates a huge obstacle. There's an elder at our church who has a famous line, well, famous among our church members at least. He tells everyone young and old "remember who you are." Paul is essentially telling the Romans the same in today's reading. He first commends them on a job well done but then notes he is writing to them as a reminder of his ministry and teachings. He's basically saying, "remember who you are." In the verse above, he commends the Corinthians for the same. I encourage you to not only remember WHO you are, but also WHOSE you are. You are a child of God, called to be His servant who will deliver His message to the world. And don't you forget it!

PRAYER—God, I'm grateful for my memories and ask comfort for all who struggle with theirs. Help me to always remember I'm Yours and have a job to do as Your servant. In Christ, Amen.

TODAY I WILL...remember who and whose I am.

MAY 19 **Read MATTHEW 6:25-34**

DEALING WITH DOUBT

Pixar – Inside Out

"Do not be anxious about anything, but in everything by prayer and supplication with thanksgiving let your requests be made known to God."
—Philippians 4:6

What's your most common sin? Thought I'd start out pretty blunt today. You certainly don't have to advertise it, but at least consider the question. I'll share mine because it happens to be what Riley deals with in one of Pixar's best. *Inside Out* was another directed by Pete Docter who began developing it after noticing changes in his own daughter's personality. Each of the five emotions presented originally had names, but it was ultimately decided to just name them after the emotion they represented. Joy was originally called "Optimism" until it was decided that wasn't an emotion. Kaitlyn Dias, who voiced Riley in the film, admitted to imagining her cat dying in order to trigger an emotional response and make herself cry when needed.

Speaking of crying, the end scene where Riley breaks down in front of her parents...wow again! So powerful and emotional. Riley has to deal with some tough situations: moving, a new house, leaving friends and other changes which all culminate causing understandable sadness, worry, anxiety and depression. I often struggle with the same allowing worry and doubt to creep into my life causing stress and anxiety when I should be giving it all to God. Today's passage is one I use often, finding it very helpful to read the words of Christ. He speaks directly to us concerning doubt and anxiety promising God will take care of us as long as we seek Him first. Worrying does nothing to help our situation and only shows a lack of faith and trust. When you have doubts or anxiety about your situation, work hard to give those to God and trust. I know worry is natural and it's easier said than done, but keep this passage handy and read it often. As Paul says above, don't be anxious about anything. Simply give it to God and let Him handle it.

PRAYER—Father, I'm sorry when I worry and doubt showing a lack of trust in You. Help me to remember You in my trials and seek You first in all things. In Christ's name, Amen.

TODAY I WILL...make a habit of seeking God first and giving my worries and fears to Him, trusting in His promise to take care of me.

MAY 20 **Read PSALM 81:10-16**

A "CHANGE" OF ATTITUDE

Pixar – *Up*

"...they should not be like their fathers, a stubborn and rebellious generation..."
—Psalm 78:8

Working for a private ambulance, I transport a lot of elderly people both to and from hospitals. I enjoy it and have found a vast majority of them don't fit the typical senior stereotype of being ornery and stubborn. Sure, I've had to deal with a few stinkers, but most are pleasant if given proper attention and conversation. Today's classic Pixar film demonstrates the same transition as Carl Fredricksen starts out an irritable, grouchy old man (with good reason) but changes after his adventure with a young boy. *Up* was released in 2009 as the 10th Pixar film. It won Oscars for Best Animated Picture and Music, although it was also nominated for overall Best Picture, the first Pixar film to receive that honor. In early February, we talked about Walt Disney losing his first character, Oswald the Lucky Rabbit, to Universal whose executive at the time was Charles Mintz. The villain in *Up* is Charles Muntz, an obvious nod to the "stolen" character.

The storyboard alone for the first 8 minutes of *Up* brought some of the production staff to tears. It is during those memorable and heart-warming scenes that we see why Carl is so obstinate and grumpy. He has lost his lifelong love and isn't interested in dealing with change, which can lead any of us to poor attitudes. I know I certainly don't like change. In today's reading from Psalm 81, we are reminded of God's chosen people, freed from Egypt by Moses. They too rebelled against change and became stubborn due to their unfamiliarity and fear of new surroundings. They didn't trust God's promise to care for and lead them to the Promised Land. Remember that God does things on His time, and just because we want something done faster doesn't mean we can rebel or become stubborn. Changes are inevitable and may be leading us to greater things and growth in our relationship with God. Don't let stubbornness lead you away from Him and His plans. Choose to see change as opportunity and find patience throughout.

PRAYER—Father, help me to accept change as part of Your plan for me. Help me to grow through them and accept them with patience. In Jesus' name, Amen.

TODAY I WILL...not be stubborn and rebellious against God, despite any changes in my life.

MAY 21 **Read I KINGS 12:1-16**

HELP WANTED

Pixar – A Bug's Life

"Without counsel plans fail, but with many advisers they succeed."
—Proverbs 15:22

Did you know the book of Proverbs praises bugs? Twice! Specifically, ants are commended in chapters 6 and 30 for their hard work ethic. That's certainly seen in today's film, Pixar's 2nd ever whose budget was twice that of *Toy Story*, yet it brought in less revenue. It was directed by former head of Pixar, John Lasseter, who also directed the first two films in both the *Toy Story* and *Cars* series. Speaking of ants, there was a feud during production over stolen material between Pixar and DreamWorks as they were also working on a bug film called *Antz*. It was released a month and a half before this one but only brought it half the profits. This was the first Pixar film to have outtakes, a popular feature that has now appeared in several of their movies.

Speaking of ants (again), the story here revolves around Flik trying to save his ant colony from the evil Hopper and his grasshopper minions. Flik decides to seek help as they can't defend themselves alone. It ends up being a wise move as they win by teaming up with a group of circus bugs. In I Kings 12, King Rehoboam sought help as well. As a new king, his people asked him to make their work easier. Not knowing what to do, Rehoboam asked his father's advisers as well as his friends. He ended up listening to the wrong group and making a poor choice, but at least he sought help. Not only does Proverbs praise bugs, but it also advises us above to seek counsel in our decisions. In life, we no doubt face difficult choices where the best course of action will be talking to those who have been through the same situations. God doesn't expect you to figure everything out alone which is why He blesses you with family, friends, mentors and spiritual leaders to guide you. Seek God and Scripture first, but don't be afraid to ask others. God will always guide you, but perhaps by leading you to someone who can help.

PRAYER—God, help me when I face big life decisions to swallow my pride and seek help from individuals you put before me. Thank You for their guidance and Yours. Through Jesus, Amen.

TODAY I WILL...seek help for any tough decisions I am facing. First and foremost, I will talk to God and allow Him control of the situation.

MAY 22 **Read GENESIS 50:15-21**

NOT MY PLANS

Pixar – *Cars*

"For I know the plans I have for you, declares the Lord...to give you a future and a hope."
—Jeremiah 29:11

This is not right! Why is this happening to me? I didn't want this! This is not what was supposed to happen! Ever felt, thought or actually said those things because your life was going in an unexpected direction? Lightning McQueen's life certainly takes an unplanned turn in a 2006 Pixar film. *Cars* premiered at the Lowe's Motor Speedway (now the Charlotte Motor Speedway) in Concord, NC. Animators drew over 43,000 different car sketches in preparation for the film's visual development. This was the final and highest grossing film for both Paul Newman and George Carlin, two famed actors. This film is dedicated to its co-writer and co-director, Joe Ranft, who ironically died in a car accident during production.

Lightning McQueen begins this story as a lean, mean, racing machine, but he ends up stuck in Radiator Springs after a series of unfortunate events completely alters his plans. At the end, however, he actually decides to remain there and accept his unexpected future even declining a big sponsorship he was seeking. Similarly, we may think we know where we are going, only to find ourselves heading in a complete opposite direction. I love the story of Joseph. It's lengthy, covering Genesis chapters 37-50, but it's worth a read. Like Lightning McQueen, Joseph's life is completely upended with multiple, unexpected outcomes, but he makes an incredible statement near the end of the story when his brothers are afraid for their lives having sold him into slavery. He says, "Do not fear, for I am in the place of God... you meant evil against me, but God meant it for good." Joseph understood his crazy life was all part of God's plan to elevate him to help the people of Egypt. We don't always know where our lives are headed, but God does! He knows His plans for us which may be completely different than what we're expecting. Trust Him. He has a purpose for you and will lead you in whatever direction needed to fulfill it.

PRAYER—Father, help me to trust in Your plans and not my own. I give you complete control of my life. Lead me where you want me to go and use me however You see fit. In Him, Amen.

TODAY I WILL...give God control and trust in His plans for my life.

MAY 23 **Read HEBREWS 9:23-28**

IT'S COMING

Pixar – Toy Story 3

"...the dust returns to the earth as it was, and the spirit returns to God who gave it."
—Ecclesiastes 12:7

It's coming. There's nothing they can do. They can't stop it. "What do we do?" she asks. But he knows there's no answer. He simply takes her hand so they can face it together. She understands and grabs another hand. Joined in unity, hand in hand, they stand together, ready to accept their fate. It's a powerful and gut-wrenching scene from *Toy Story 3*. The majority of the film's story involves the toys trying to get away the Sunny Side Day Care and the conniving villain, Lotso. Animators actually studied prison films to prepare and formulate escape ideas. Speaking of Lotso, short for Lots-o'-Huggin' Bear, Disney actually got sued by another company that already had a product called "Lots of Hugs" stuffed bears.

You no doubt remember the scene described above when our favorite toys are trapped on a conveyer belt headed for a garbage incinerator. Despite their best efforts, their escape attempts prove futile, and they are slowly forced toward a fiery demise. The panicked look on their faces slowly turns to one of sadness mixed with acceptance as they join hands, ready to accept the end. The first time I saw the film, I doubt I was alone in thinking it might really be the end. After all, this was supposed to be the series finale, so it seemed a plausible (yet cruel) ending. But alas, it's Disney. It certainly wouldn't have been a popular choice, so the toys do receive a miraculous rescue from their green buddies just in time. But the fact remains, they had accepted death and were ready to face it together. Hebrews 9 makes perfectly clear we will all eventually face death. It may sound grim and be a subject you avoid talking or thinking about. But it's certain. Ecclesiastes states the same. Today's question is therefore a simple one: are you ready? Can you, like the toys, accept your inevitable fate? Hopefully, you'll be given a long, full life. But death will ultimately come and you don't know when. So I ask once more, are you ready?

PRAYER—Dear God, I know my life will end one day. I pray for a full life of service if it be Your will, but help me to always be prepared for death as well. In the name of Christ, Amen.

TODAY I WILL...accept my fate and be always prepared for the end.

MAY 24 **Read 2 CORINTHIANS 4:1-6**

YOU'RE GETTING VERY SLEEPY

Pixar – Incredibles 2

"Whoever makes a practice of sinning is of the devil, for the devil has been sinning from the beginning."
—I John 3:8

I'm sorry, but I'm skeptical. It's hard for me to believe. Maybe because I've never seen it in person and certainly never had it "done" to me. But I've seen videos where it apparently occurs, and it certainly happens to our favorite, animated, super family in *Incredibles 2* which holds the distinct honor as Pixar's highest grossing film with $1.2 billion worldwide. While there were 14 years between the original and this sequel, the story picks up right where it left off. Fans had been calling for a sequel for years, but writer and director, Brad Bird noted all along he wouldn't produce one until he found a better story than the first. While 14 years is a lot, it's surprisingly not the longest between Disney sequels. That honor belongs to *Mary Poppins* with a whopping 54 years between original and sequel, the most for any film series in movie history.

A major plot point of this story is the use of hypnotism to control the Parr family, almost allowing the villains a victory. I've always been a hypnotism skeptic, but maybe I'm like the apostle Thomas and must see it (or experience it) to believe it. I do believe in one master hypnotist that has controlled all of us at times. 2 Corinthians 4 warns that Satan is essentially a hypnotist saying he has the power to "blind" the minds of believers to keep them from seeing the light of the Gospel. The devil is malicious and desires all to follow him making evil and sin look desirable. He can get into our minds causing us to forget God and the importance of remaining faithful. He tempts us making us think a little sin won't hurt, and we can always come back to God. But the verse above warns that making a practice of sin plays right into his hands and can even cause us to forfeit our soul to him. If you want to try hypnotism and cluck like a chicken, be my guest. I'm not looking to try it anytime soon. Just don't let Satan hypnotize you. He's sneaky and will try it when you least expect it. Be watchful! Resist his mind controlling powers.

PRAYER—Lord, I hate Satan and reject him wholly from my life. Help me to withstand his temptations and hypnotism of my mind. Keep me firmly focused on You. In Christ, Amen.

TODAY I WILL...make sure the devil doesn't have me hypnotized to sin.

MAY 25 **Read COLOSSIANS 3:1-8**

AMERICAN IDOLS

Pixar – *Up*

"You shall have no other gods before me."
—Exodus 20:3

Did you ever have a hero? A famous athlete, movie star, singer or other celebrity you idolized? Did they ever let you down? We return to *Up* to revisit Carl Fredricksen who also has an idol that turns into a disappointment, and even a danger. Did you know there was a real-life "Carl" named Edith Macefield? In 2006, she refused a $1 million dollar offer on her tiny Seattle home. A five-story, commercial development was built all around her house in an eerie similarity to the story of *Up*, which ironically was already in production when this occurred. Macefield died in 2008, but a year later, Disney attached a bunch of balloons to her house to promote this film. To this day, the house stands, has a Facebook page and has become somewhat of a tourist attraction.

At the beginning of *Up*, a young Carl Fredricksen idolizes the legendary explorer, Charles Muntz. Carl grows up, longing to be an explorer just like him which leads to him turning his home into a balloon-hoisted, flying airship. During the journey, the old Carl actually runs into Muntz, discovering he's not the heroic idol he always thought, but instead a ruthless villain he must risk his life to defeat. We're encouraged in Colossians to set our minds on things above and not earthly things, which can become idols. This includes not putting our faith in others. It's okay to admire a celebrity, but we should never idolize them or long so much to be like them that we contradict God's Word. Celebrities will probably let you down anyway as their faults often become public. Some of my biggest sports heroes as a kid have turned into poor examples when it came to their personal lives, marriages and choices. Nobody's perfect and my sin is no better than theirs, of course, but just be careful about putting too much adoration or admiration in the direction of earthly heroes. Instead, set your minds on things above and the only idol ever needed. Jesus Christ never sinned. He was perfect. Follow, admire and idolize Him alone.

PRAYER—Lord, help me to idolize no thing or person here on Earth. Help me to only set my sights on Christ and give all my adoration to Him alone. In His holy name, Amen.

TODAY I WILL...make sure I have no earthly idols I glorify, but only Jesus Christ.

MAY 26 **Read ACTS 7:54-60**

ONE CHOICE

Pixar – *Luca*

"So everyone who acknowledges me before men, I also will acknowledge before my Father who is in heaven."
—Matthew 10:32

"It was a test we could all hope to pass, but none of us would want to take. Faced with the choice to deny God and live, for her there was one choice to make." Those are lyrics to a Michael W. Smith song called "This is Your Time." He co-wrote it as tribute to Cassie Bernall, one of 13 victims of the 1999 Columbine shooting who was known to have an open and outward faith which many feel led to her being targeted and killed. In Pixar's 24th film, Luca, a young sea creature trying to conceal his true identity by staying dry, must choose whether or not to reveal himself to save his friend. Conquering his fear and risking his life in a dramatic and pivotal moment, Luca rides into a rainstorm, acknowledging who he truly is to save his friend. This film is brand new as of this writing. I watched it yesterday and thoroughly enjoyed it. The end of the credits read, "Produced in our slippers around the bay area," indicating that a majority of the film was created from home due to the pandemic. Many of the voice actors recorded lines from their own houses, and the film released straight to Disney Plus instead of theaters as originally scheduled.

In Acts 7, we read the story of Stephen who also revealed his true identity at great risk. He saw the people shouting. He saw them grinding their teeth in anger. He knew what was coming. He could've denied Christ to possibly save himself, but instead, he said in paraphrase, "I see Heaven open and Jesus standing next to God." He knew those words would mean his life, but he was prepared to acknowledge Jesus no matter the cost. Jesus Himself said above if we stand up for and acknowledge Him, He will in turn acknowledge us to God. It's not always easy to stand up for Jesus in a world that so often goes against Him, but we must find the courage to do so and never deny His existence. Are you prepared to admit your belief in Christ no matter the cost?

PRAYER—Father, I acknowledge Jesus Christ as Your Son and Savior of the world. Give me the boldness to tell anyone the same, regardless of what it may cost me. In His name, Amen.

TODAY I WILL...make my choice about Jesus and be prepared to defend it no matter what.

MAY 27 **Read LUKE 18:9-14**

IT'S GOOD FOR THE SOUL

Pixar – *Brave*

"...confess your sins to one another and pray for one another..."
—James 5:16

"You've made your wagers. Here is your final question." The Jeopardy competition in the 4th grade Sunday school class was getting intense. Both teams submitted identical answers, and being the prepared, intelligent host that I was, I told them they were both wrong. Nope! I was wrong! I had to come back the next week and admit my error, resulting in the opposite team as victors. We all make mistakes. Some are relatively harmless like my example, but some can cause real sorrows, setbacks and separation from God when sinful. We return to *Brave* to see Princess Merida figuring out that confession leads to the solution she's been searching for. Did you know that the *Brave* logo has a hidden Merida and Elinor? Check out the "B" and the "E" to find them. Merida is also the first Disney princess with curly hair. Animators wanted curls in prior films but hadn't figured out the breakthrough technology to animate them until this one.

Brave features an entertaining story when Merida accidently turns her mother, Queen Elinor, into a bear and then must figure out how to change her back. At the end, all hope seems lost until Merida admits her mistakes fulfilling the curse's wish which had said she must "mend the bond torn by pride." By confessing, Merida gives up her pride while realizing and admitting fault. In Luke 18, Jesus tells a parable of two men: a proud and boastful Pharisee and a humble tax collector that openly confesses sins to God. Jesus commends the tax collector for humility and confession. In addition to the verse above, we are told in I John 1:9, Proverbs 28:13, Numbers 5:6-7 and so many others, that confession is an important part of our walk with God. Mistakes are inevitable, but we must be honest with God and admit sin. It's also wise to confess them to someone you trust who can offer prayer for you. You might have heard "confession is good for the soul." What a true statement! It may just be vital for the salvation of our soul!

PRAYER—Lord, I confess sin to you. Please forgive me. Through the name of Jesus, Amen.

TODAY I WILL...confess each individual sin to God and consider doing the same to a trusted family member, friend or mentor.

MAY 28 **Read LUKE 1:26-38**

LET IT BE

Pixar – Monsters, Inc.

"...Your kingdom come, Your will be done..."
—Matthew 6:10

Can you imagine it? You're at home, minding your own business when you see a sudden, bright light. An angel appears and tells you not only is God pleased with you, but you will have an exceedingly, special child. He will be great, reign forever and be the Son of God. What's your reaction? Fear? Skepticism? Shock? Doubt? All expected and understandable. But not her. Not Mary. Let's move to another Mary. Did you know that Boo's real name is Mary? In *Monsters, Inc.*, there's a brief glimpse of her drawing with the name "Mary" clearly printed at the top. Coincidentally, Boo's voice was actually recorded by a Mary. Mary Gibbs was the daughter of one of the film's story artists. Just 2 years old at the time of recording, the crew found it quite difficult to keep her still. Therefore, they simply followed her around with a microphone, recorded her while she played and then pieced Boo's lines together from whatever she said. To get her to laugh, director Pete Docter would entertain her with sock puppets.

Back to the original Mary. In Luke 1, the angel, Gabriel, appears to Mary telling her she will bear the Son of God. It would've been very easy for Mary to show disbelief or doubt, but look at her statement once she understands. She says, "Behold, I am the servant of the Lord; let it be to me according to your word." Wow! What a powerful and bold acceptance of God's will and an important lesson to us all. A portion of the Lord's prayer that Jesus instituted says, "Your kingdom come, Your will be done." We may pray that, but do we really mean it? Being a God-focused, Biblically-centered, Christ-following servant means giving complete and total control to God. Whatever happens is accepted because it's His will. Work hard to give God everything including full management of your life. Be like Mary and simply say to Him, "Let it be!"

PRAYER—Father God, I am but your humble servant. I give You complete and total control of my life. Let it be to me according to Your will and Your word. In Christ's name, Amen.

TODAY I WILL...give God complete control. If something unexpected happens, I will accept it as part of His plan.

MAY 29 **Read COLOSSIANS 3:12-16**

STRAIN TO TRAIN

Pixar – *Cars 3*

"Until I come, devote yourself to the public reading of Scripture, to exhortation, to teaching."
—I Timothy 4:13

I was asked to run HiSTEP at our church over 20 years ago. HiSTEP stands for High School Taught Elementary Program and is basically a class for high schoolers, training them how to be children's Bible class teachers. It's very similar to student teaching for college education majors. As a former teacher, it's an honor and privilege to train others to be teachers. It's also similar to the storyline of *Cars 3*, the final chapter in the Pixar racing series. Cars 3 was the directorial debut for Brian Fee, who had worked on many other Pixar films in various roles. According to Fee, the production team did a lot of research to prepare, even speaking to sports psychoanalysts to get into the mind of racers. They were told a lot of car racers can't picture themselves doing anything else in life, which not only led to the plot of *Cars 3*, but also directs our thoughts today.

Cars 3 shows our hero, Lightning McQueen a bit older and finding it tough to race against the newer, next generation of vehicles. Throughout the film, he discovers he can be more of service in the area of training by passing on his expertise and directing a new racer to victory. We are also called to be trainers for the next generation. Colossians 3 contains a list of directives meant for those who have become new creatures in Christ specifically mentioning we are to "teach and admonish one another in all wisdom." The verse above also encourages us to share Scripture, encourage others and teach. With age, we may lose the ability to be as active, but like Lightning, we can always train and share knowledge so that others can gain what they need to become strong followers of Christ. That's the goal of the HiSTEP program, training the next generation to become teachers themselves so the cycle never ends. Strive to be a trainer, especially as you find more free time with age. Pass along your knowledge and all the Lord has done for you!

PRAYER—Father in Heaven, help me to find the time, courage and drive to train others in service to You. I want to encourage and motivate others to be as excited about Your Word and plan of salvation as I am. Give me the opportunity to share Your message. In His name, Amen.

TODAY I WILL...become a trainer. I will seek out a group or someone to mentor in Christ.

MAY 30 **Read ISAIAH 43:1-7**

YOU ARE NOT TRASH

Pixar – Toy Story 4

"I praise You, for I am fearfully and wonderfully made."
—Psalm 139:14

She actually made me feel bad...about a stick! As a child, walking on the beach during a family vacation, I found a random stick and chucked it into the waves. My mom, attempting humor, made comments about the "poor stick" and how I had "hurt its feelings." I continued to retrieve it and throw it back, but she kept making me feel bad. Eventually, she won out and that stick lived on my bedroom shelf for my entire childhood. I think my parents still have it! A stick! It had no feelings! Of course, you wouldn't think a plastic fork would have feelings either, but Forky felt he was trash. *Toy Story 4,* the 2nd highest grossing Pixar film after *Incredibles 2*, released in 2019 with multiple new characters including Forky. Animators used incredible detail with 17,000 carnival lights, six billion tree leaves, and over a trillion individual pine needles. They also wanted to keep the legendary Don Rickles who had passed as Mr. Potato Head so they pieced together lines from past recordings to the delight of Rickles' family.

In my humble opinion, *Toy Story 3* was the perfect series ending, and this film, while great, was unnecessary. I would've at least liked to see Andy return. Forky, arguably the most prominent of the memorable new characters, is certain he is trash, and Woody must convince him he is instead an important possession for Bonnie. Similarly, Isaiah 43, along with the verse above, assures us we are God's possession, carefully formed by Him. We're additionally told God loves us as His precious creation. In short, we are not trash, so don't ever feel that you are. God loves you no matter what. He created you, released you to life but longs for you to return. You may have heard the old proverb "one man's trash is another man's treasure." If you are ever down on yourself or feel like trash, remember you are indeed God's treasure. Like Forky, and that dumb stick apparently, you are needed, valued and belong to someone very important.

PRAYER—Father, thank You for creating me and seeing me as Your precious possession. Help me to realize I am treasured and strive to return to You one day. In Jesus' name, Amen.

TODAY I WILL...realize I am special to God, and He longs for me to return to Him.

MAY 31 **Read I KINGS 19:1-9**

NOWHERE TO RUN

Pixar – Inside Out

"And no creature is hidden from his sight, but all are naked and exposed to the eyes of him to whom we must give account."
—Hebrews 4:13

Did you ever run away from home? I never did, although I sometimes wished my sisters would. Kidding! (ish) It's estimated nearly 2 million children run away annually. As a teacher, we once had a student run away. I'll never forget searching the school grounds desperately while search helicopters flew overhead. Thankfully, he was found several hours later in a city park 5 miles away. Our final Pixar choice of the month takes us back to *Inside Out* for one more lesson from Riley and her emotions. She also chooses to run away when Sadness takes over, causing her to give in to worry and doubt as previously discussed. The original antagonist to break Riley was to be Fear, but after 3 years in development, that idea was scrapped when director, Pete Docter stated he realized that sadness was a more profound choice, especially from an adult perspective.

The lesson of this film teaches that sadness is a necessary emotion we must all deal with. Riley initially chooses to cope by running away. Sometimes we all feel like running from our problems, whether sadness, fear, doubt, worry or even a struggle of sin. In I Kings 19, even the great Elijah chose to run away from his problems, even begging God to take his life in fear of Queen Jezebel's wrath. If you continue reading, God basically tells him he can't run away and must rise and face his trials head on. We can't escape life's problems simply by running away. We should instead remember the above verse reminding us we can't escape God's sight. We must boldly face emotions and struggles using His help. Thankfully, Riley realized that running away from her problems wouldn't work, and she returned home to the arms of her loving parents who helped her deal with her sadness. We also have a loving father with open arms waiting at home, always ready to help. Your problems may seem too huge to handle, but nothing is too big for God. Don't run away. Run to Him. Run into His arms! He's the only answer you need.

PRAYER—Father, my struggles, worries and fears are often too difficult to handle. Help me not to run away, but to face them head on with Your help and guidance. In Christ, Amen.

TODAY I WILL...promise God to never run away from problems but go to Him instead.

JUNE THEME

DISNEY QUOTES

JUNE 1 **Read PSALM 40:1-4**

TRUST AND FALL

Disney Quotes – Peter Pan

"Now faith is the assurance of things hoped for, the conviction of things not seen."
—Hebrews 11:1

Ever tried a trust fall? As a teacher, we would annually take students to a nature camp where they participated in several team building activities including the trust fall. I always enjoyed watching them learn to fall back and trust their peers to catch them, some with minor hesitation and fear. Of course, I also enjoy the YouTube video where the kid accidently chooses to fall forward. Oops! Peter Pan tells the Darling children, "**all it takes is faith and trust**," along with a bit of pixie dust, when teaching them to fly. *Peter Pan* was originally a play Walt Disney saw and even acted in as a child. He always loved it and planned on making it his 2nd film after *Snow White* but was delayed due to World War 2 and his ability to get the rights. Disney actually gave Peter his traditional green color. The original play had the flying boy clad in brown and tan.

Obviously a bit more dangerous than a trust fall, it certainly would take a good bit of faith and trust to be willing to soar above the streets of London as the Darling children did. We likely won't have to worry about finding the faith and trust to fly, but we will certainly need a good bit in our spiritual walk. The trials of life call for a sizeable amount of faith and trust in God. David states in Psalm 40 that those who put their trust in God are blessed. You want an ultimate story of Godly trust? Read Daniel 3, starting in verse 8, to remind yourself of Shadrach, Meshach and Abednego. Would you be able to continue worshipping God knowing you would be bound and thrown into a fiery furnace? Talk about faith and trust! Hebrews tells us faith is being sure of what we hope for and convicted of things unseen. That's the very definition of God. We must put our hope in Him, despite not being able to see Him, and have faith and trust that He exists, is in control and will guide us every step of the way, even in the toughest times. All it takes is faith and trust for us to one day soar into His kingdom. And we won't even need the pixie dust.

PRAYER—Lord, help me to always have strong trust and devout faith in You. In Christ, Amen.

TODAY I WILL...trust fall into the arms of God knowing He will always catch me.

JUNE 2 **Read ISAIAH 40:28-31**

GIVE HIM TIME

Disney Quotes – Fairy Godmother (*Cinderella*)

"...with the Lord one day is as a thousand years, and a thousand years as one day. The Lord is not slow to fulfill his promise as some count slowness..."
—2 Peter 3:8-9

I'll never forget her excitement telling me the doctor had agreed to induce her the next day. "You're going to be a father tomorrow!" she said. Boy was she wrong! Due to complications, my incredible wife went through 22 hours of labor, delivering our first son early the following day. "**Even miracles take a little time.**" That same line is said in *Cinderella* as her surprise Fairy Godmother prepares her for the royal ball. Cinderella is actually a very, old tale dating back as early as the 1st century B.C. It's been retold numerous times with the details ever changing, but always the "rags to riches" story. In older versions, Cinderella's glass slippers are made of gold or fur. The Brothers Grimm version takes a dark turn with the wicked stepsisters slicing off parts of their feet to fit into the glass slipper. Yikes! I'll stick to Disney, thanks!

Do you believe in miracles? I certainly do. I've witnessed at least two being born firsthand, although as mentioned above, the first one took way longer than expected. At one point, I went into the tiny bathroom we had, fell to my knees and prayed, begging God that my son would be born safe and healthy. He was. God took care of him. Seeing him born was an absolute miracle. It just took some time. Sometimes God's work in our lives, miracle or not, takes time. The end of Isaiah 40 assures us that God is our almighty creator, never tiring as we do. It also states that if we wait patiently on Him, He will come through for us while renewing our strength, making us soar like eagles and run without fatigue or fainting. When you feel overwhelmed or weary, remember to depend on God first and then wait on Him. He's not slow to fulfill His promises as the above verse states. He just does it on His time, when He thinks best which in the long run is always the perfect plan. Give God some time. His plan may take years longer than you're hoping or expecting, but He will come through for you, even miraculously if needed.

PRAYER—Lord, help me to put full trust in Your plans for me, waiting on Your perfect timing. I want to do great things for You and know You'll guide me when I am ready. In Christ, Amen.

TODAY I WILL...wait on God, never doubting the miraculous things He can do, even for me.

JUNE 3 **Read MARK 4:21-25**

OPEN THEM EARS

Disney Quotes – Timothy Mouse (*Dumbo*)

"Whoever is of God hears the words of God."
—John 8:47

A fork scraping a plate, an electric drill, someone retching, a baby crying and of course the classic, nails on a chalkboard. Know what those are? They are 5 of the top 10 most unpleasant sounds to the human ear according to a recent University study. I agree but would add my top choice...wipers scraping a dry windshield. Can't stand that sound! Turn them off people! Did you know the ear contains not only the human body's smallest bone but also the strongest? We're talking ear facts today since we're focusing on a quote from the classic *Dumbo*, a film based on a book like so many early iconic Disney films. "Dumbo the Flying Elephant" was a "roll-a-book," a series of illustrations readers would view by turning a little wheel. This film had to be made on a very low budget due to the war and cost only $812,000 to make, a bit less than recent Pixar films with a budget of $200 million! Time magazine planned to put Dumbo on its cover as "Mammal of the Year" until Pearl Harbor happened demanding a more serious story.

Timothy Mouse, Dumbo's sidekick and coach, yells at Dumbo when he's plummeting towards the ground after losing his "magic feather" and says, **"Dumbo! C'mon Fly! Open them ears!"** Thankfully, Dumbo listens at the last second and doesn't go splat into the ground. That would've been a definite downer. We should also take Timothy's advice, not for flight, but to open our ears to listen. In Mark 4, Jesus encourages the people to pay attention to what they hear. In John 8, He says those of God will hear His words. Basically, Jesus is telling us to "open them ears!" There's a reason God gave us two ears and only one mouth. We need to listen twice as much as we speak. God has some valuable and frankly vital information to tell us which we may hear through a minister, Bible class teacher, friend or even self-study, but we must be willing to listen. So open them ears! Hear His words, seek to understand and live by them.

PRAYER—Father God, help me to open my ears to all You have to say, seeking as much of Your instruction as possible throughout my life. In the name of Jesus, Amen.

TODAY I WILL... find an audio Bible reading or devotional, close my eyes and listen to God.

JUNE 4 **Read MATTHEW 6:19-24**

NO TREASURE HERE

Disney Quotes – Walt Disney

"I have stored up your word in my heart..."
—Psalm 119:11

In 2013, a California couple was walking their dog on their own property when they spotted a rusty can sticking out of the ground. Digging it up, they discovered 1,427 gold coins inside dating back to the 1800's. They would later discover the coins had an estimated value of over $10 million! What a treasure! Today's quote, also about treasure, is from Walt Disney himself. Walt had many famous quotes we will sporadically focus on during this month. He once said, "**there is more treasure in books than in all the pirates' loot on Treasure Island.**" Incidentally, *Treasure Island* was Disney's first ever live-action film from 1950. It was also the first color adaptation of Robert Louis Stevenson's 1881 classic novel. It starred Robert Newton in a memorable performance as the pirate, Long John Silver. It's believed that Newton was the first to use "Arr" in his pirate speech which has become a common label used even to this day.

In Walt Disney's opinion, books are an invaluable treasure. I would tend to agree, at least for one in particular. The Bible is the literal written Word of God. You can't put a price on that treasure. In addition, it talks about additional treasure we should all be seeking and where it's located. In Matthew 6, Jesus stated our treasure is found in Heaven and that we shouldn't be searching for or storing treasures here on Earth. He also said any treasures we do have here will only fall prey to thieves or the elements in nature. He advised seeking only eternal treasure which will also lead our hearts in the right direction. The verse above echoes, reemphasizing the importance of God's Word and how it is the true treasure to be stored within our hearts. Sure, it would be nice to discover $10 million in your backyard, but it ain't gonna happen. Don't focus much on building up earthly treasures. Instead, look to Scripture for your true treasure. It will direct your focus to Heaven where our greatest, eternal and priceless treasure lies.

PRAYER—Holy Lord, help me not to focus on earthly treasures, but direct my thoughts, time and efforts on obtaining Heaven by following the treasure of Your Word. In His name, Amen.

TODAY I WILL...seek treasure from above by finding and reading 5 passages about Heaven.

JUNE 5 **Read PHILIPPIANS 4:10-20**

BLOOM THROUGH ADVERSITY

Disney Quotes – The Emperor (*Mulan*)

"If you faint in the day of adversity, your strength is small."
—Proverbs 24:10

"The unluckiest man in the world." That's the nickname of Frane Selak, a 91-year-old Croatian. It began in 1962 when his train flew off the tracks and landed in a river. He survived, only to later face: falling out of a crashing airplane, a bus crash (also into a river), his own car catching fire twice, being hit by a bus and crashing into a guard rail after a near head-on collision with a large truck. (Amazingly, he won over a million dollars in the lottery at age 73, so maybe he's not so unlucky after all.) Talk about adversity! Today we look at a quote from *Mulan* who also faced much adversity. This story was based on the Chinese legend of Hua Mulan dating all the way back to the 6th century. To this day, it's unknown if the legend is true. In the original story, Mulan had a younger brother which may be why her dog in the movie is named "Little Brother."

In this extraordinary story, the Chinese Emperor refers to Mulan saying, "**The flower that blooms in adversity is the most rare and beautiful of all.**" Mulan not only faced adversity hiding her true identity as a female soldier, but she also had to train, fight and find the self-confidence to be successful. In Philippians 4, Paul talks about his adversities while sharing the secret to his success. He says in all his difficulties, he learned to be content knowing he could do anything through God's gift of strength. Also look at 2 Corinthians 4:8-9 where Paul says he was afflicted but not crushed, perplexed but not driven to despair, persecuted but not forsaken and struck down but not destroyed. Despite all his adversities, Paul kept striving, never gave up and knew God would ultimately take care of him. We'll all face some level of adversity in life, hopefully not as bad as Mr. Selak! But when it happens, try to find the strength and attitude of Paul, or even Mulan. Face it with contentment and courage, using God's strength and support.

PRAYER—Lord, bless me with strength and courage, especially when I face adversity. Help me, like Paul, to press on to my goals to fully fulfill Your purpose for me. In Jesus name, Amen.

TODAY I WILL...make a list of any adversities I'm currently facing and give them to God while vowing to fight through with His strength.

JUNE 6 **Read JEREMIAH 17:5-10**

PURIFY YOUR HEART

Disney Quotes – Zeus (*Hercules*)

"Blessed are the pure in heart for they shall see God."
—Matthew 5:8

100,000 beats daily, which is 2.5 billion in a normal lifespan. 2,000 gallons of blood daily through 60,000 miles of blood vessels, just within your body. Yet only the size of a fist. The heart is a pretty amazing muscle. Did you know that laughing is good for your heart, sneezing doesn't stop it, as many believe, and it works twice as hard as the leg muscles of a sprinter?! Your heart is the very life source of your body, and you certainly can't live without it. In Disney's Hercules, his father Zeus tells him "**a true hero isn't measured by the size of his strength, but by the strength of his heart.**" This film was derived from a Greek myth as opposed to a fairy tale or story like most Disney movies. Did you know that Hercules and Ariel are technically cousins, as his father Zeus has a brother, Poseidon, who is the father of Triton, Ariel's father. Did you get all that? Not sure they see each other at family parties. Finally, as of this writing, there is a live-action remake planned that will feature songs from the original film.

When Zeus says this, he's trying to convey to his son it's not how strong he is that matters, but what's in his heart that's important. The same could certainly be said of us. In fact, God does say it several times. Remember when David is chosen as a boy to be king in I Samuel 16? God says he chose him because of what's in his heart. In today's reading from Jeremiah, the Lord curses the heart that turns from God while saying He searches man's heart to know who he truly is. One of Christ's Beatitudes from his Sermon on the Mount is written above. "Blessed are the pure in heart, for they shall see God." They get to see God! Don't you want to see Him? Isn't that reward important enough to keep your heart pure and righteous before God? Like Hercules, you will be measured based on what's inside your heart. God gave us strong, enduring hearts to keep our bodies thriving. Give it right back to Him by keeping it clean and just before Him.

PRAYER—Father in Heaven, thank you for my strong heart. Help me to make it right before You. Keep it pure and worthy of Your eternal reward. In His holy name, Amen.

TODAY I WILL...purify my heart before God so that I can be assured of seeing God one day.

JUNE 7 **Read JONAH 3:1-5**

LEARN OR RUN

Disney Quotes – Rafiki (*The Lion King)*

"Return to me, says the Lord of hosts, and I will return to you..."
—Zechariah 1:3

I laid on the floor for two hours, trying so hard to avoid the ER, but eventually I couldn't stand the pain any longer. Kidney stones. Twice now. The first time I passed out from the pain and nausea, but the second time was even worse cause I stayed conscious. I now drown myself in water to avoid the trifecta. So far, so good. Knock on wood. Have you ever had intense pain? I know the mothers are yelling at me. Ok, you win. I'll keep my kidney stones. Nobody likes to hurt. According to Rafiki from *The Lion King,* the past can hurt also. Not physically per se, but it can hurt our emotions, feelings and the drive to keep going. Did you know "Rafiki" means friend in Swahili? In fact, many character names are Swahili words. Rafiki is the only character without an American or English accent, using instead one more native to the African setting. His name is said only by himself. No other characters say it, instead calling him monkey or baboon.

Rafiki's quote contains valuable advice for Simba and us. He says, "**Oh yes, the past can hurt. But the way I see it, you can either run from it or learn from it.**" It's human nature to remember our past and feel guilty for mistakes or to become anxious due to past situations that were difficult. But Rafiki's right. We have 2 choices when we're hurt by the past. You're probably familiar with Jonah's story. We'll look at the familiar part later but look at chapter 3 today. It says God spoke to Jonah a *second* time. God gave Jonah another chance after he ran away the first time. Jonah learned from his past, went to the city of Ninevah as commanded and helped the people there believe in God. Jonah may have messed up and been hurt by it, but he learned from it, changed his ways and it paid off. Don't dwell on or run from the past, especially your sins. God has forgiven those. Instead, simply return to Him, for He's waiting and promises above to return to you. Learn from the past and move forward! You can't change it anyway.

PRAYER—Lord, I'm sorry for my past. I wish I could change mistakes and hard times, but I know I can't. Help me to learn from them and move forward towards You. In Him, Amen.

TODAY I WILL...learn from my past, stop running from it if I am and head in God's direction.

JUNE 8 **Read I TIMOTHY 1:3-7**

LISTEN TO THE VOICE

Disney Quotes – Blue Fairy/Jiminy Cricket (*Pinocchio*)

"But the Helper, the Holy Spirit, whom the Father will send in my name, he will teach you all things and bring to your remembrance all that I have said to you."
—John 14:26

It's not one of the more popular Disney songs, but some of the lyrics are: "**When you get in trouble and you don't know right from wrong... when you meet temptation, and the urge is very strong...take the straight and narrow path and if you start to slide...always let your conscience be your guide.**" I can't prove it, but it appears that song from *Pinocchio* came straight from Scripture. Right and wrong, temptation, the straight and narrow path! It's like a sermon in a song! Today's quote is said by both the Blue Fairy, who turns Pinocchio into a real boy, and by his appointed "conscience," Jiminy Cricket. If you think this Disney film is a bit dark, you should check out the book it's based on. In "The Adventures of Pinocchio," published in 1883, the puppet is stabbed and hanged only to be rescued and changed into a boy. And not by a blue fairy, but by a "child with blue hair." Not sure that all would've gotten the standard "G" rating.

We all have a conscience or little voice telling us right from wrong and guiding our decisions. For those in Christ, it's clear Who that voice belongs to. In I Timothy, Paul says a good conscience is a goal for all Christians along with sincere faith and a pure heart (as discussed two days ago). In the verse above, Jesus Himself said that once He was gone, the Holy Spirit would be left behind to "bring to (our) remembrance" all Christ had said. If we follow the proper steps and accept Christ, we are given the Holy Spirit inside to guide us, be our conscience and remind us of Christ's teachings. In that case, we need to, without a doubt, always let our conscience, or Christ inside, be our guide. What a special gift from God! Pinocchio sometimes failed to listen to his conscience (Jiminy), causing trouble. Make sure you are listening to yours if you have the Spirit within. If not, become one with Christ so you too can hear Jesus guiding you home!

PRAYER—Dear God, thank You for offering me the gift of Your Spirit as my conscience and guide knowing You are speaking the words of Christ right to me. In His name, Amen.

TODAY I WILL...receive the free gift of the Holy Spirit inside and allow it to be my internal guide for every decision I make and step I take.

JUNE 9 **Read LUKE 18:1-8**

PERSISTENT SWIMMING

Disney Quotes – Dory (*Finding Nemo)*

"Blessed is the man who remains steadfast under trial, for when he has stood the test, he will receive the crown of life, which God has promised to those who love him."

—James 1:12

Between the Great Barrier Reef and Sydney, Australia, it's estimated that Marlin trekked nearly 1500 miles to find his son, Nemo. And being that clownfish are 200 times smaller than the average adult, he journeyed the equivalent of 300,000 miles or 12 times around the Earth. That's true love and dedication right there, folks! *Finding Nemo* was co-written and directed by Andrew Stanton who admits the story came from "a very personal place." While writing it, he was a new father, struggling with the challenges of being overprotective. Did you know it really took just one word to sell this film? Stanton gave an elongated and exhaustive pitch to get it green-lit. When finished, Pixar's chief creative officer simply said, "You had me at 'fish.'"

As indicated above, the journey to finding Nemo was extensive and plagued with multiple challenges. Along the way, the concerned Marlin gets understandably frustrated and is given good advice from none other than the inadvertently, absent-minded Dory. Her full quote is, "**When life gets you down, you know what you gotta do? Just keep swimming.**" It may sound simple, but that's good advice for us too. There will be many times when our spiritual journey will be difficult and may seem like 300,000 miles, but we must always find the drive to press on. In Luke 18, Jesus tells a parable of a persistent widow, refusing to give up in a court case. The judge even admits he doesn't want to give her justice but does only because she keeps bothering him. Jesus is teaching us to persist to our eternal goal no matter what burdens we face, even beginning the parable telling the people to keep praying and not lose heart. In similar fashion, James says we're blessed when we remain steadfast during life's trials, and that we'll receive God's eternal reward if we withstand the test. Life is hard, and we will be tempted to lose faith, but the reward is too important to give up. God won't give up on you so just keep swimming!

PRAYER—Father, help me to look to You when life is hard, and I'm tempted to quit. Give me strength, persistence and a reward reminder so I will just keep swimming. In His name, Amen.

TODAY I WILL...just keep swimming no matter what comes my way.

JUNE 10 **Read GENESIS 39:1-6**

DARE TO DREAM

Disney Quotes – Walt Disney(?)

"He said to them, "Hear this dream that I have dreamed."
—Genesis 37:6

Do you remember Susan Boyle? She was a Scottish singer who rose to fame after appearing on "Britain's Got Talent" in 2009. Her first impression gave the audience and judges some serious doubt of her singing ability. But they were all proven wrong once they heard her amazing voice. The song she chose was "I Dreamed a Dream." Probably the most famous quote attributed to Walt Disney is, "**If you can dream it, you can do it.**" But did he really say it? Many resources say he did, and even the Walt Disney company agrees. But others say while it sounds like something Walt would've said, he never actually spoke those words. In 1999, an Epcot dark ride closed in the spot where "Mission: SPACE" now sits. Apparently, this quote was originally a part of that ride and can even be heard within the ride's theme song available on YouTube.

Regardless of who said it, it's a valuable and timeless quote attributed somewhere within the Disney company. And it's certainly befitting of Walt and his life story. I don't think anyone would argue he was a dreamer who worked tirelessly to see his dreams realized. Similarly, anyone with Bible knowledge knows who best fits the definition of "dreamer." In the verse above, Joseph tells his family, "hear this dream that I have dreamed." He then predicts the outcome of his amazing story where he will eventually rule over not only his family but all of Egypt. In Genesis 39, we read of Joseph's success and rise to power after a rocky start to say the least. Joseph was a dreamer in many ways who never gave up and never doubted God would eventually lead him to success. We also have the ability to dream and do anything with the God's strength. (Phil. 4:13) Never underestimate what you can do for Him. Make big goals, involve God every step of the way and you will get them accomplished. Dream big and do it!

PRAYER—Heavenly Father, thank You for offering Your strength, giving me the ability to accomplish anything I dream to do. Give me the knowledge to create big goals that will benefit Your kingdom along with the drive and determination to get them done. In Jesus' name, Amen.

TODAY I WILL...come up with a new and significant, spiritual goal, involve God and do it!

JUNE 11 **Read EPHESIANS 4:29-32**

THE GOLDEN RULE OF THUMPER

Disney Quotes – Thumper (*Bambi*)

"A soft answer turns away wrath, but a harsh word stirs up anger."
—Proverbs 15:1

As a wee lad of 7 or so, my older sister and I would often throw insults at each other as siblings often do. At one point we got in the habit of calling each other "fool" and made the mistake of saying it in front of my grandmother. Big no-no! She sat us both down, had us read Matthew 5:22 aloud and then listen to a lengthy, granny sermon. I still can't use that word without thinking of her and being afraid for my soul. She always urged us to only talk nice to each other. She was obviously very special, and I can't wait to see her again. Today's quote apparently originated right here with Thumper in the classic *Bambi*. In fact, the phrase is sometimes called the "Thumperian principle." Thumper wasn't in the original book that the film is based on, but there was a "friend hare" that influenced Disney's creation of Thumper. Six-year-old, Peter Behn was chosen to voice Thumper after animators were won over by his soft sounding voice.

Of all the quotes this month, this one would probably be the most well-known. You've no doubt heard "**if you can't say somethin' nice, don't say nothin' at all**," but maybe you weren't aware it was a foot-stompin', adorable bunny rabbit that said it. This snippet of guidance from ole' Thumper is not only good advice to just be a decent, moral person, but it's also Biblical. The end of Ephesians 4 commands that we only speak words that will build others up and say nothing that corrupts. The final verse reminds us to simply be kind, compassionate and forgiving to one another. Wouldn't this world be such a better place if everyone followed that instruction? Before you open your mouth to speak to someone harshly, in anger or to put them down, stop and consider if it's really necessary. Try to be the bigger person and hold yourself to a higher standard. As always, reflect on what Christ would say and try to imitate His example. Use your words for good and encouragement only. Otherwise, just don't say nothin' at all.

PRAYER—Father God, help me to think before I speak, especially when I am planning harsh words against someone else. Keep my speech pure, kind and helpful for others. In Him, Amen.

TODAY I WILL...compliment or say something kind to at least five different people.

JUNE 12 **Read MATTHEW 14:26-29**

TAKE THE STEP

Disney Quotes – Merlin (The Sword in the Stone)

"...for you know the testing of your faith produces steadfastness."
—James 1:3

My 7th grade, P.E. coach saw something I didn't. He apparently noticed a bit of "runner" in me, pulling me aside one day and telling me I ought to run. It didn't appeal at first, but a couple years later, I decided to try it and fell in love. I ran Cross Country and Track three years and have continued into adulthood with 7 half and 4 full marathons, including Disney, my favorite! At first glance, today's quote may look like one from *Moana* based on the hit song. However, it was actually said in a classic from 1963 called *The Sword in the Stone* about a boy and his adventures with a whimsical wizard. Walt Disney actually acquired the rights for this film in 1939, but it took over two decades to produce it. This was the first animated Disney picture the infamous Sherman Brothers created music for and the last, completed animated film for Walt Disney. He was involved with *The Jungle Book* as well but died during its production.

Merlin's complete, creative and rhyming quote to young Arthur is, **"It's up to you how far you'll go. If you don't try, you'll never know."** We've looked at the story of Jesus walking on the water before but pay attention to today's specific portion. When the disciples realize it's Jesus walking towards them, Peter makes a bold move asking to join Jesus and walk on the water too. Most tend to focus on what happens next when Peter takes his eyes off Jesus and begins to sink. However, let's not forget what he did first. He took that first step. He tried. Like Merlin said, if we don't try, we'll never know if we could've been successful or not. I'm so grateful my P.E. teacher pushed me to try something new. I found something I was good at and a lifelong hobby as well. If he hadn't encouraged me, I most likely never would've tried. Try something new, especially if it will enhance and improve your spiritual life and relationship with God. It's up to you. Don't sit and wonder if you could have. Give it a shot. You may surprise yourself.

PRAYER—Father, give me courage like Peter to take the first step and try. I want to always be improving my relationship with You, so help me to discover ways to do that. In Christ, Amen.

TODAY I WILL... Brainstorm new things I can do to grow closer to God and try at least one.

JUNE 13 **Read PSALM 139:17-24**

TAKE A LOOK INSIDE

Disney Quotes – Merchant (*Aladdin*)

"Do not judge by appearances, but judge with right judgement."
—John 7:24

You've no doubt heard, "you can't judge a book by its cover." The same was true of that plain, old, lamp in *Aladdin*. Didn't look like much, but as the merchant said in the first scene, "**Like so many things, it is not what's outside, but what is inside that counts.**" The late, great and hilarious Robin Williams is famous for voicing the well-known Genie, but did you know he was the merchant too? In fact, when they shot this scene, they simply gave him a table full of items he had never seen before and let him go. The entire dialogue was made up on the spot. Much of it was unsurprisingly inappropriate for a Disney film, but what they did use was both memorable and comical. In fact, Williams would often go off script and ad-lib many of his Genie lines too. When all was finished, they had nearly 16 hours of his material to work with and edit down.

The whole plot of *Aladdin* revolves around what was inside that old lamp. A true treasure for whoever found it and controlled the genie within. In Psalm 139, David begs God to search inside him, within his heart and mind, to see who he truly is. We've already discussed that's how God operates, as he coincidentally did with David when chosen king (I Sam. 16:7). We are told to do the same, judging others not by appearance, but by who they truly are inside. We tend to base opinions of others on first impressions without really getting to know the person inside. In doing that we may be blinded and distracted by what we see and not notice a soul in need. Take time to really get to know others, especially those who don't know Christ. Move past appearances, get to know the person inside and assist with whatever needs they have. You may be their only chance to hear about Christ. You can't judge a person by their cover either.

PRAYER—Dear Lord, help me to look past appearances and premature judgements to see others for who they truly are. Lead me to a soul in need. In Jesus' name, Amen.

TODAY I WILL...take another look at someone I may have misjudged based on appearance or first impression to see if they have a spiritual need I can assist with.

JUNE 14 **Read JAMES 1:22-27**

START DOING

Disney Quotes -Walt Disney

"But be doers of the word, and not hearers only..."
James 1:22

I've mentioned skydiving still being on my bucket list, but I actually checked off another item recently...eating at Whataburger. While on vacation, I waited nearly an hour in line just for the satisfaction of crossing it off my list. Worth it? No. But tasty nonetheless. We probably all have bucket-list things we'd like to do, but how many will just stay on there simply because we never find the drive to get up and do them. Walt Disney had some advice about that when he said, "**The way to get started is to quit talking and begin doing.**" He was certainly known to quit talking and do when it came to his dreams and visions, even before creating our favorite theme parks. I'm sure you're aware of his fascination and love of trains since childhood as his father and uncle had worked on them. He later constructed his own elaborate model train, the "Carolwood Pacific Railroad" on a half-mile track in his backyard. He would dress as an engineer and give free rides to neighborhood guests. There are trains in 5 of the 6 (silly Shanghai!) worldwide Disney parks due to his passion and resolve to do something about it.

In James 1 we're told to be doers and not just hearers of the Word. In our Christian walk, knowledge of the Bible is certainly vital, but there's another important component. We must be active in taking that knowledge and physically serving others to spread His message. What if Walt had only talked about trains or theme park ideas but never pursued them? This book wouldn't exist for one, and we most likely wouldn't know much about who Walt even was. Because he chose to actually "begin doing" as he preached, we have all the wonderful films, parks and characters the Disney name has provided. If one man can do all that, think of what you can do for God's plan. Actually, do more than think about it. Do it! Stop wishing you were more active or could make a difference, get up and just do it! (Sorry, Nike, I'm using it today.)

PRAYER—Father, give me the passion and drive to actively serve You with physical works in Your name. Help me to be a doer of Your Word and not a hearer only. In His name, Amen.

TODAY I WILL...be a doer and become physically active in my service to God and others.

JUNE 15 **Read PROVERBS 6:6-11**

WAKE UP AND WORK

Disney Quotes -Tiana (The Princess and the Frog)

"Whatever you do, work heartily, as for the Lord and not for men..."
Colossians 3:23

In the U.S., it's just over 34. Japan's jumps to between 60 and 70. The lowest is the Netherlands at 29 while the highest is in North Korean labor camps where some log over 110. When it comes to average weekly work hours, there's certainly a large variety. I once tried 120 as a paramedic. Never again! I'm all about hard work, and the money was nice, but that was a bit on the crazy side. Most Disney princesses deal with the stereotypical difficulties of huge royal expectations, negative treatment and loss of family. But then there's Tiana who is quite different from cthe others when it comes to work. She was the first Disney princess to work a proper job due to a dream she simply couldn't afford and her decision to work hard to achieve it. This led to her quote, "**The only way to get what you want in this world is through hard work.**"

If you've seen *The Princess and the Frog*, you know Tiana's dream is to open her own New Orleans restaurant. It takes a wild adventure and a little frog kissin' to get there, but she achieves it thanks to her hard work. In Proverbs 6, we are encouraged to work hard and warned if we instead choose to "sleep and slumber," we will find ourselves in poverty. Proverbs 13:4 additionally says, "The soul of the sluggard craves and gets nothing, while the soul of the diligent is richly supplied." The Lord expects us to use His gift of our bodies and the energy within to work hard to provide for our families as well as for His kingdom per the verse above. It's easy to find ourselves basking in laziness, especially when blessed with material wealth. Make sure that regardless of how much you've been given, you are following His command to work. It's part of His purpose for you, so don't ever lose that working drive, especially when it comes to your eternal reward. That takes hard work too, so find the motivation and work for it!

PRAYER—Father, help me to find the proper balance of rest and hard work. Help me to avoid idleness so I may fulfill my purpose of hard work for You and others. In His name, Amen.

TODAY I WILL...resolve to work hard while always looking for new opportunities to serve God through my labor.

JUNE 16 **Read PSALM 55:16-23**

NO WORRIES!

Disney Quotes – Timon and Pumbaa (*The Lion King*)

"Anxiety in a man's heart weighs him down, but a good word makes him glad."
—Proverbs 12:25

Back on May 14th I revealed a regret about not learning Spanish in high school, yet another item on my current bucket list mentioned a couple days ago. I'm proud to say I've actually started doing something about this one. Every heard of Duolingo? It's a free app that can teach you most any language. It's kinda fun to be honest. I've been slowly making my way through Spanish, but there are many others available including Swahili. I don't have plans to learn that one, but I do know a little already, at least a two-word phrase I'm sure you're also familiar with. Timon and Pumbaa said (or sang) it best in *The Lion King* when they told Simba, "**Hakuna, Matata!**" You know what it means! You're probably singing it in your head right now! Did you know there's a hidden mickey on one of the bugs during that song? See if you can find it.

It means "no worries." For the rest of your days. It's our problem free... ok, I'll stop. But it's no doubt a familiar quote we too can live by. No worries. No anxiety. No fears. Wouldn't that be nice? We've touched on this a bit, but it bears repeating as worry tends to creep back into our life often and without warning. Thankfully, God knows this and offers many comforting words about this very topic. Psalm 55 is one of those passages telling us to cast all problems on Him, and He will hold us up. It also reminds us that God hears our calls regardless of when or where. The verse above advises that a good word can cheer us up when we find ourselves doused in worry. That good word can certainly come from God, but also may be an encouragement from a friend. You may be called on to be that friend to help someone else through their anxiety. That's what Timon and Pumbaa were trying to do...cheer Simba up with a good word (actually 2). It's easier said than done of course, but give your anxiety to God and offer kindness and reassurance to those going through the same. Hakuna Matata! No worries!

PRAYER—Dear Heavenly Father, thank You so much for bearing my burdens and letting me cast all my cares on You. Thank You also for always being there when I call. In Christ, Amen.

TODAY I WILL...submit to Hakuna Matata by giving any worries I have to God immediately.

JUNE 17 **Read GALATIANS 1:6-10**

YOU GOTTA BE YOU

Disney Quotes – Wreck-It Ralph

"For everything created by God is good, and nothing is to be rejected..."
—I Timothy 4:4

Ever heard of a Broadway musical entitled *Golden Rainbow*? Probably not since it was only open from 1968-1969. The only reason it might be remembered is due to one hit song that came out of it. The great Sammy Davis, Jr. recorded his own version of the song that same year causing it to reach number 11 on the Billboard chart. It's called "I've Gotta Be Me" and would certainly make a good theme song for the speaker of today's quote. *Wreck-it Ralph* was released in 2012 as the story of a Ralph, a muscular villain and video game character, trying to find his purpose. It featured many classic and nostalgic arcade games and characters. In the early stages of development, Ralph was brainstormed as a bulldozer, ogre, monster, gorilla, caveman and even a Sasquatch before settling on his current form. For a time, there was an actual arcade game, Fix-it Felix, Jr., just like in the film near Disneyland's Space Mountain for guests to play.

As mentioned, the plot of this delightful story revolves around Ralph trying to find his place. He's tired of being the villain and causes a good bit of chaos in his attempt to change and earn the respect of the other characters. In the end, he discovers he's needed just the way he is as his game wouldn't work without a villain. Figuring this out, he says, "**There's no one I'd rather be than me.**" Sometimes we too will do anything in seeking the approval of others, even feeling we must change to please them. Galatians 1 speaks to that saying we should only be seeking the approval of God and if we are trying to please other people, we are not true servants of Christ. God made you just how he wants you. The verse above affirms everything made by God is good and should never be rejected. Don't try and change simply to please others. Be true to who you are and find your value within. I promise it's there. Ralph eventually found his and was proud of who he was. God has a purpose for you too and has made you just the way He wants.

PRAYER—Lord, help me to find my purpose and see value in myself as Your child and creation. Help me to seek only Your approval and not change for that of others. In Him, Amen.

TODAY I WILL...look inside to find value within realizing God made me just how He wanted.

JUNE 18 **Read MATTHEW 7:13-14**

STAY ON THE PATH

Disney Quotes – Grandmother Willow (*Pocahontas)*

"I have said these things to you, that in me you may have peace. In the world you will have tribulation. But take heart; I have overcome the world."
—John 16:33

I said it every day for 16 years. Every school day that is. I told my students each year that "stay on the path" meant three things: they were dismissed to go home for the day, I love you and STAY ON THE PATH!! Grandmother Willow has a similar quote in *Pocahontas*, a Disney classic released in 1995, exactly 400 years after the assumed birth year of its subject. This film was made simultaneously with *The Lion King* with many animators choosing this project over the latter, assuming it would be the bigger hit. Wrong! Grandmother Willow is an important character guiding Pocahontas with important advice. Originally, it was to be a male named Old Man River, and actor, Gregory Peck, was offered the role. However, he painstakingly declined because he felt Pocahontas needed a motherly figure instead. The filmmakers eventually agreed.

One of the many words of guidance from Grandmother Willow is when she tells Pocahontas, "**Sometimes the right path is not the easiest one.**" It was certainly true for Pocahontas and her goal of uniting the settlers with her people. It's also very true for us and our spiritual path. Today's short but crucial reading from Matthew makes very clear the road to hell is wide and heavily followed while the path to Heaven is narrow and much-less traveled. The right path for us is definitely not the easiest. Jesus told us above we will face trials if we continue to follow it. But like I told my students repeatedly, we must stay on that path no matter what. I explained they were entering an important time in life where they would make vital decisions about their life's path. I begged them to choose the narrow path, clarifying it wasn't a one-time choice. It's an everyday decision. You too must choose daily which path to travel. The large one is much easier to follow, and you'll find many traveling with you. But it's the wrong choice. Choose the narrow and unpopular one. I promise it'll be worth it. The best is yet to be. Stay on the path!

PRAYER—Father, help me to be one of the few that stays on the difficult path to eternal life with You. I want more than anything to find You alone at the end of it. In Christ's name, Amen.

TODAY (and everyday) I WILL...stay on the path!

JUNE 19 **Read LUKE 2:41-52**

KEEP GROWING

Disney Quotes – Walt Disney

"But grow in the grace and knowledge of our Lord and Savior Jesus Christ."
—2 Peter 3:18

Ever heard of Robert Wadlow. Born in Illinois in 1918. Lived a mere 22 years. Officially known as the tallest man to ever live. At death, his height was 8 feet, 11 inches! His extreme height was due to the abnormal enlargement of his pituitary gland. Even at death, there was no indication he had stopped growing. Who knows how tall he might have grown? In similar fashion, Walt Disney said, "**Disneyland will never be completed. It will continue to grow as long as there is imagination left in the world.**" That principle lives on, long after Walt's death in Disney parks around the world that are forever changing, expanding and refurbishing. This is Disney's secret to bringing people back. The constant growth, addition of new experiences or improvement of old ones leads to curiosity and a desire to return. This is why Walt wanted to expand to Florida. He felt space was severely limited at Disneyland and wanted a new site with potentially endless growth possibilities. WDW still has thousands of acres of undeveloped land meaning growth potential for many years to come, long after our park days are done.

In Luke 2, we read an impressive story of 12-year-old Jesus. Separated from his parents, He is found in Jerusalem's temple, sitting among the teachers, listening, questioning and learning. The last verse states Jesus grew in wisdom, stature and in favor with God and man. Even the Son of God desired to grow in His knowledge of the Father. What a great example to us all at such a young age! We can never stop growing with God. There's no such thing as being too close or knowing too much about Him. Like Christ, we should continue to grow in wisdom and favor with God. Peter advises the same above. Take Walt's philosophy and Christ's example of growth and apply it to your spiritual life. Don't ever think you are completed with God. Continue to grow and gain valuable knowledge that will fully equip you to be what He desires.

PRAYER—Lord, help me, like Christ, to never stop growing in my knowledge, relationship and favor with You. I want to grow closer to You daily until I get to be with You. In Christ, Amen.

TODAY I WILL...find a new passage or story in Scripture and study it to learn something new.

JUNE 20 **Read PSALM 103:8-14**

OUR ETERNAL DAD

Disney Quotes – Ian Lightfoot (*Onward*)

"(There is) one God and Father of all, who is over all and through all and in all."
—Ephesians 4:6

Wow! Another amazing coincidence! When I planned today's quote, which just so happens to be about fathers, I had no idea it would fall on Father's Day! Father's Day is always the 3rd Sunday of June so it rotates, but in the year I'm writing this, it falls on today, June 20th!! It was first proposed in 1909, but it wasn't an official holiday until 1972 when President Nixon signed it into law. It's estimated there are 75 million fathers in the U.S. alone. The Pixar film, *Onward*, is a heartwarming story about two brothers on a quest to meet their father who they've basically never known. I won't spoil the ending because it's too good. Have tissues ready! But throughout the journey, the brothers grow closer and come to realize the value in their relationship with each other, fulfilling the role their dad couldn't. When Ian, the younger brother realizes this, he tells his brother, Barley, "**I never had a dad, but I always had you.**"

Some of you, like myself, may have a wonderful relationship with your dad. On the other hand, you may have lost yours or your relationship isn't the best. We all have different types of bonds with our dads but we're all exactly alike when it comes to our Father. Psalm 103 praises God for being a Father of mercy, grace, who is slow to anger and abounding in love. It compares him to a loving dad with compassion for his children. Family relationships aren't always easy. They take work from both sides and sometimes individuals are unwilling to give what's required. But you don't have to do anything special to receive God's love. He gives it no matter what. On the night before He died, while praying in the garden, Jesus cried out, "Abba, Father." "Abba" is an Aramaic word for father but with a more personal touch. Jesus was basically crying out "Daddy." We can cry the same and tell God, like Ian, "I always had You." He is always there, listening and ready to shower you with compassion, more so than any earthly dad ever could.

PRAYER—Most loving Father, I am so grateful to call you my Father and am so blessed by Your love and compassion. I cannot wait to see You and be with You forever. In Jesus, Amen.

TODAY I WILL...get on my knees, call out to my caring Father and thank Him for loving me.

JUNE 21 **Read LUKE 9:57-62**

EYES ON THE PRIZE

Disney Quotes – Edna Mode (*The Incredibles)*

"Therefore, if anyone is in Christ, he is a new creation. The old has passed away; behold, the new has come."
—2 Corinthians 5:17

Try this experiment in a large open space, maybe a field or yard to avoid obstacles. Pick a point several yards away and time yourself walking to it keeping your eyes focused straight ahead. Now, time yourself again while looking to the side or backwards. My guess is it will take longer. Edna Mode is half-German, half-Japanese and full-on entertaining in both *Incredibles* films. She is the fashion-savvy, costume creator for the super family but serves as their babysitter in the sequel as well. At the 2005 Academy Awards, Edna presented the Oscar for Costume Design alongside Pierce Brosnan. This was the 2nd Pixar film in which a male voiced a major female role, with the first being Roz from *Monsters, Inc.* This was also the 2nd time a director voiced a major role after Andrew Stanton of *Finding Nemo*, voiced Crush. One of Edna's many memorable quotes is, "**I never look back, darling! It distracts from the now.**"

Near the end of Luke 9, Jesus teaches a blunt, but important lesson. Two different individuals agree to follow Him, but one wants to first bury his father and the other simply wants to say goodbye to his family. Jesus rebukes them both telling them they should follow Him without hesitation or looking back. It may sound harsh, but Jesus is trying to demonstrate how important it is for us to put Him first. When we accept Christ, we become a new creature according to the verse above. At that point, we must put following Him above all else. We can't walk through life looking backwards, or even to the side. We must look straight ahead with our eyes on the prize of eternal life. Edna Mode definitely could have been talking about Jesus with this quote. We can't be distracted by anything, even family, that might get in the way of our Heavenly calling. Christ is our gateway into Heaven, so we must keep our focus straight ahead, on Him without distractions. That's the cost of following Him. And it's definitely worth the price.

PRAYER—Dear Lord, help me to not be distracted by anything trying to take my focus away from Jesus. I know He is my goal, and I must enter Heaven through Him. In His name, Amen.

TODAY I WILL...get rid of any distractions threatening to take my focus off Jesus.

JUNE 22 **Read EPHESIANS 5:11-17**

TODAY'S THE DAY

Disney Quotes – Quasimodo (The Hunchback of Notre Dame)

"This is the day that the Lord has made; let us rejoice and be glad in it."
—Psalm 118:24

Procrastination. Are you guilty? I used to struggle with it, but now I can't stand having something hanging over my head. It's more common among students with one study reporting 70% admitting to procrastinating assignments. I can certainly vouch for that being the father of two school-age boys. What about in your spiritual life? Have you put off any spiritual goals or quality time with God? Quasimodo, a.k.a. the Hunchback of Notre Dame, has advice about that in the 1996 Disney classic based on the 1831 novel of the same name. The character designer who created Quasimodo also created Belle which is probably why she makes a flash appearance in this film. If you've seen the movie, you know it has some pretty dark themes. For that reason, Disney was actually surprised to receive a "G" rating, fully expecting a "PG." Jason Alexander, the famed actor who voiced a gargoyle, wouldn't even let his 4-year-old son see it.

Quasimodo's kind demeanor doesn't match his rugged appearance which is one of the main plot lines when he's seen as a stereotypical monster and not for the gentle giant he is. In an early scene with some resident birds at the cathedral he calls home, he calmly encourages a young one to take its first flight asking it, "**Will today be the day, you ready to fly? You sure? Good day to try.**" In Ephesians 5, we're encouraged to make the best use of our time and seek to understand God's will for our lives. We often procrastinate important tasks, even those that bring us closer to God. Daily time with Him to grow and gain knowledge are a vital part of our spiritual walk. Job 14 reminds us our days are numbered. We aren't guaranteed tomorrow so we should take advantage of each day as a gift. Start each one in praise, repeating the psalm above. Don't delay your goals, especially ones that will bring you closer to God. Make today the day you fly and find your purpose from the One who created you and is waiting to show it to you.

PRAYER—Father, thank you for today. Help me to take advantage of it and get my tasks done promptly, especially time spent with You. In the name of Your Son, Amen.

TODAY I WILL...make a habit of starting each day in praise and thanksgiving to God.

JUNE 23 **Read MATTHEW 19:16-29**

FAITH AND FAMILY FIRST

Disney Quotes – Walt Disney

"For the love of money is a root of all kinds of evils. It is through this craving that some have wandered away from the faith..."
—I Timothy 6:10

In addition to today's Bible reading, take time to listen to the 1974 folk song by Harry Chapin entitled "Cats in the Cradle," or at least read through the lyrics. It tells a compelling story about a father who finds himself too busy with work to give proper attention to his son. When the father retires and finally longs to spend time with his son, the boy is grown up and too busy with his own job, having become just like his dad. Powerful message. Walt Disney once said, "**A man should never neglect his family for business.**" We discussed already how Walt lived by that principle. Despite creating one of the biggest and most influential companies in the world, he always worked hard to put family first. When his daughter, Diane, was interviewed in the latter years of her life, she stated that he never brought his work home. She even quoted him saying, "I live with (work) all day. I want my home apart from this." She said he wouldn't even talk to the family about work or ask for ideas. He drove his daughters to school daily and had "Daddy's Day" every weekend which was spent with his girls, taking them somewhere special.

In Matthew 19, we read another powerful story of a young man who longs for Heaven, but when he's told he must sell all his possessions, he walks away sad, unable to part with his riches. Work and making money are not evil but putting more effort and love into them than God, or even family, certainly, is. Read the verse above very carefully. We must be diligent to not get too caught up in our work and the building of wealth. Our first responsibility is to God and then family right behind. We must be present for our children throughout their lives, to give them a foundation in God's Word and teach them the proper way to live. Otherwise, the cycle will continue like the song says, and our children will become like us, putting work ahead of their own families. Check your priorities. Are you giving proper time and effort to your family?

PRAYER—Father, I'm so grateful for my relationship with You and for my family. Help me to consciously put these things ahead of any work and get my priorities straight. In Jesus, Amen.

TODAY I WILL...do something special with my kids (or family) and make a habit of it.

JUNE 24 **Read I JOHN 4:7-12**

THE DEFINITION OF LOVE

Disney Quotes – Olaf (*Frozen*)

"Let each of you look not only to his own interests, but also to the interests of others."
—Philippians 2:4

There's a true story of a drawbridge operator who took his son to work, allowing the 5-year-old to pull the switch that raised the bridge so boats could pass and then lower it again for the train to cross overhead. Later in the day, while raising the bridge for a passing ship, the father lost track of the boy. Stepping out of the booth, he was horrified to see his son caught in the large gears of the bridge mechanism. Running to free the boy, he heard the whistle of an approaching train and faced an impossible choice: free his son which would mean the train crashing, no doubt killing many or run inside and lower the bridge just in time meaning the sacrifice of his son. With gut-wrenching pain, he made the choice. He ran inside, fell to his knees with a loud cry and pulled the switch. So maybe it's not an actual true story, but isn't that exactly what God did for us?

Who doesn't love Olaf? When Josh Gad, the voice of the adorable snowman, took his four-year-old daughter to see *Monsters University,* there was a trailer for *Frozen*. Hearing Olaf's voice, she said, "That's Dada, more Dada" bringing Gad to tears right in the theater. Olaf has a very important quote near the end of the story when he says, "**Love is putting someone else's needs before yours**," a quote very similar to the verse above. The previous verse (Php. 2:3) instructs us to be humble and see others as more important than ourselves. In I John 4, we're given the example of God sacrificing His own Son for us as the true example of love and told that if God loved us enough to allow that, we ought to at least love one another. If we do, it says God will abide in us, His love will be perfected, and we will know Him. Seek to love everyone and put their needs ahead of yours. Spread God's love by sharing what He sacrificed for us. Show love to others by giving them quality time and helping with whatever their needs may be.

PRAYER—Most loving Father, thank You for the supreme sacrifice of Your Son for me and for demonstrating through that what love truly is. Help me to demonstrate that type of love to everyone by putting their needs ahead of mine. In the name of Your loving Son, Amen.

TODAY I WILL...actively seek to put others' needs ahead of my own.

JUNE 25 **Read ECCLESIASTES 9:11-18**

WHAT'S THE WEATHER LIKE?

Disney Quotes – Remy (*Ratatouille*)

"Do not boast about tomorrow, for you do not know what a day may bring."
—Proverbs 27:1

My boy, the weatherman! My oldest son began his first year of college this year majoring in Multimedia Journalism. Through his practicum, he auditioned and won the role of meteorologist on the University's daily news program. We got a kick out of watching him a couple nights a week. He had to come in early each time and do research to find out what the weather was going to be, learning quickly that it was impossible to be accurate all the time. Like the weather, our lives are also fairly unpredictable. Remy, our favorite Disney rat from Pixar's *Ratatouille* would agree as he said, "**The only thing predictable about life is its unpredictability.**" Did you know that pet rats were kept at the studio during production of *Ratatouille* so animators could study their movements? Also, to save time, all human characters were created without toes.

The writer of Ecclesiastes notes in chapter 9 that things aren't always as expected. He gives examples like a race not won by the fastest, a battle not gained by the strongest and riches not going to the smartest. He then tells of a poor, wise man saving a whole city from being taken over by a great army. He's making the point of the importance of wisdom but at the same time, stating how unpredictable life can be. The proverb above warns of boasting about tomorrow as we don't really know what's going to happen. Only God truly knows what's coming our way. We can plan, but there are no guarantees of our expectations. As suggested recently, live for today, remembering each day is a gift. Take life one day at a time and remember that God's plan for you may be completely different from what you are anticipating. Expect the unexpected. Foresee unpredictability in life. That's the only forecast that will most likely come true.

PRAYER—Lord, I know You alone control my life and future and only You know what is to come. Help me to put full trust in You, accepting wherever You lead me. In Christ, Amen.

TODAY I WILL...live for today without expectations of tomorrow, giving my future to God.

JUNE 26 **Read JOHN 17:1-5**

TIME ALONE WITH GOD

Disney Quotes – Rhino (*Bolt*)

"But when you pray, go into your room and shut the door and pray to your Father who is in secret. And your Father who sees in secret will reward you."
—Matthew 6:6

A traditional part of our church's youth retreats is something called "Time Alone with God," where each teenager is given time to find a solitary place to sit, reflect, pray and spend quality, undistracted time with God. A few years ago, a typo on the schedule listed it as "Tim Alone with God." As our youth minister's name was Tim, there was expected confusion with the kids wondering if our fearless leader was going to head off into the wilderness to privately converse with the Father. Have you seen *Bolt*? It's not as well-known as many other Disney films, but it's an entertaining story. The original director had completed the film and titled it "American Dog," but when the heads of Disney animation asked him to make some changes, he refused and was removed from the project. The new directors reworked the story and title to the current version which made over $300 million worldwide and earned several award nominations.

"Rhino" is an oversized hamster in a ball that is mesmerized by Bolt and the famous, super dog he thinks he is. At one point, Rhino tells Bolt, "**Every minute spent in your company becomes the new greatest minute of my life.**" In John 17, Jesus prays telling God He knows His earthly life is about to end, and He is excited to be approaching the presence of God once again. Getting to see God should be goal #1 for us all. In the meantime, we can spend alone time in his presence at any point. Time alone with God is vital to our spiritual survival. In Mark 6:30-32, Jesus calls the Apostles away to a desolate place to rest and do just that. In the verse above, when teaching us how to pray, He recommends doing so in a quiet location to provide undisturbed time in His presence. Make sure you take time, daily if possible, to be alone with God. Like the hamster said, every minute spent in His company will become the greatest minute of your life, especially when it leads you closer to Your eternal life in His physical presence.

PRAYER—Lord God, I want to grow closer to You each day. Help me to find and make time to be alone with You so that I may one day be in Your actual presence. In Jesus' name, Amen.

TODAY I WILL...spend quality and uninterrupted time alone with God.

JUNE 27 **Read ROMANS 1:8-17**

SPREAD SOME SUNSHINE

Disney Quotes – Snow White

"...that we may be mutually encouraged by each other's faith, both yours and mine."
—Romans 1:12

Some of my favorite YouTube videos are when people tell family a baby is on the way. It's fun to watch reactions typically consisting of shock, excitement, screaming and joy, although sometimes there are tears, either happy ones or sad in the case of some older siblings. Those are fun to watch too. I remember the enjoyment of surprising our family when our boys were on the way. It's fun to give good news and brighten someone's day. Disney's original princess, Snow White, had something to say about that. One of her lines is, "**Remember you're the one who can fill the world with sunshine.**" She certainly tried to do the same with her cheery attitude, continual singing and care for all creatures. There are several memorable songs in this film, but there were also a couple that never got animated including one called "Music in Your Soup." This was also one of Adolf Hitler's favorite films. Not sure if that's a compliment or not.

I don't watch the news anymore, and I cancelled the newspaper a year ago. It just seemed to always be bad news. Why can't there be more good news reported? The truth is there can be, if we, like Snow White, are the ones to "fill the world with sunshine." In today's passage, Paul shares excitement with the Romans that their faith is being proclaimed throughout the world. He tells them how he longs to see them again so he can be "mutually encouraged by each other's faith" as noted above. He ends these verses saying he is eager to share more good news with them and is not ashamed of the Gospel because of the power and salvation it brings. The word "gospel" means "good news." When we imitate Paul's eagerness and share the Gospel of Christ, we are spreading good news to all who hear. In a world full of bad news and sin, the good news and power of the Gospel is desperately needed. You can be the one to fill the world with sunshine. And people will enjoy hearing it because it's good news that can change their life.

PRAYER—Holy Father, thank You for the good news of the Gospel of Christ. Help me to spread it far and wide. Give me opportunities daily to tell others. In the name of Christ, Amen.

TODAY I WILL...spread the sunshine of the Gospel to someone who needs good news in life.

JUNE 28 **Read PHILIPPIANS 2:12-18**

BE PRACTICALLY PERFECT

Disney Quotes – Mary Poppins

"Therefore, leaving the discussion of the elementary principles of Christ, let us go on to perfection..."
—Hebrews 6:1 (KJV)

What's the longest you've gone without food, water or sleep? I once fasted for 48 hours. Wasn't easy. Don't know why anyone would purposely go without water, but I've certainly been super thirsty and without it before. And I can't go much over 24 hours without sleep before nodding off. How about this...what's the longest you've gone without sinning? Personally, I'm not exactly sure, but I wish my answer was longer than it probably is. Hopefully, we're striving to be like Jesus, but it's difficult to be "**practically perfect in every way**," as Mary Poppins said. The Disney classic starring Julie Andrews as the "practically perfect" nanny, was the highest grossing film of 1964. It won 5 Oscars including Best Actress along with Best Song ("Chim Chim Cher-ee"), Musical Score, Film Editing and Visual Effects. Julie Andrews' husband at the time, Tony Walton, was the film's costume designer and was also nominated for an Oscar.

Mary Poppins may have been the perfect singing nanny, but I doubt she was without sin. The truth is all have sinned and fallen short of God's glory (Rom. 3:23). But does that mean we give up the goal of perfection? In Philippians 2, Paul encourages us to be blameless, innocent and "without blemish" in the sight of God. One chapter later in Philippians 3:12, he claims he's not *yet* perfect but is striving to make it his goal. Jesus said to be perfect in Matthew 5:48, and the verse above tells us to "go on to perfection." Is perfection even possible? No, only Christ achieved that. But it should still be what we strive for daily. Make a concentrated and conscious effort to go without sin. Try a whole day. Then go for 2. Identify the sins you struggle with most and work hard to eliminate them. Don't settle on "a little sin" because "everyone does it" or "I'm human" or "God will forgive." Why not truly do your best to imitate Christ's perfection. Think how much better you'll feel and how much better your relationship with God will be!

PRAYER—Lord, I don't like it when I sin against You. Help me to be perfect like Jesus. Help me to be aware of my sins and have the courage and restraint to avoid them. In Christ, Amen.

TODAY I WILL...truly strive to be perfect without sin. Tomorrow, I'll try for day two.

JUNE 29 **Read PSALM 127:3-5**

OUR GREATEST RESOURCE

Disney Quotes – Walt Disney

"Train up a child in the way he should go; even when he is old he will not depart from it."
—Proverbs 22:6

What do you picture when you hear "natural resources?" You may know they are materials that appear naturally on our planet...God-made of course. Our most important and abundant natural resource is water, covering 75% of the Earth, but sunlight, air, oil, coal, iron and trees are also important ones. What if I said there was another natural resource that is most important, even more so than water? On the wall of the American Pavilion at Epcot, I noticed a Walt Disney quote on our most recent trip and snapped a picture so I could include it here. He said, "**Our greatest natural resource is the minds of our children.**" Think about that. Do you agree?

I love the American Pavilion. Originally intended to be the host pavilion and at the front of World Showcase, it was designed as a traditional and beautiful, Colonial-style building. On the inside walls are quotes from famous Americans including Walt, who loved children and believed in them as the leaders of the future. The Bible teaches the same. Today's reading is short, but Psalm 127 assures us that children are a heritage of the Lord meaning an important possession of God's, given as our inheritance. There are many Scriptures that praise the importance of children, and even Jesus Himself called children unto Him as an example of how we should be. In the proverb above, we are told to train children in the ways of the Lord. They are not only the business and political leaders of tomorrow, but they will also guide the future church. In that regard, they definitely are our greatest natural resource. They will have the power to lead future generations either closer or further away from God. Therefore it is vital we train them to follow His Word and the Gospel of Christ. Don't neglect our greatest resource. Do your part to train children in the right direction so the future of the Lord's church is secure and Biblically sound.

PRAYER—God, thank You for the gift of children to raise and train in Your service. I pray for them as the future leaders of Your church. Help them to always follow Your Word. Help me to do my part in training them to be strong, Godly leaders of the future. In Christ's name, Amen.

TODAY I WILL...see value in children as the future and assist in training them properly.

JUNE 30 **Read ROMANS 6:15-23**

TO ETERNAL INFINITY

Disney Quotes – Buzz and Woody (*Toy Story*)

"I am the living bread that came down from heaven. If anyone eats of this bread, he will live forever."
—John 6:51

Can you picture it? Just try. Take a moment to try and imagine living forever. Forever! Never ending! Can you even comprehend it? If you're like me, you have a hard time wrapping your mind around that. Our brains, while complex and perfectly designed by God, want to give everything a beginning and end. That's why it's hard for us to imagine God as having always been. We want to give Him a beginning date, but it doesn't exist. Our final quote is arguably the greatest line in the four *Toy Story* films. It's said multiple times in each including being the last line of the whole series when it's shared by Buzz and Woody, a very emotional moment. As they recorded separately, Tim Allen (Buzz) went first and warned Tom Hanks (Woody) via text about the emotional toll the last few pages brought. Hanks admitted having to turn his back to the crew while saying those final lines to avoid breaking down. You can still almost hear a crack in his voice as he finishes the timeless line that Buzz starts, "**To infinity and beyond!**"

The end of Romans 6 talks about sin and how some are slaves to it. It makes clear that those of us in Christ still deserve eternal death because of our sin, but because of His sacrifice on the Cross, God gifts us eternal life instead. ETERNAL LIFE! Jesus confirms this above telling us that if we accept and follow Him, partaking of Him as the living bread, then we will live forever. FOREVER! It will never end. Bliss, happiness, joy and praise for eternity in Paradise. It's real. It will happen. But not for everyone. Are you on Heaven's guest list? Is your name in that Book of Life? You can't afford for it not to be. Why would we do anything to jeopardize that? Make sure you never fall off the path to receive your infinity and beyond with God. INFINITY!!

PRAYER—Most generous and loving Father, thank You for the gift and hope of life forever with You. I want and have to be there in Heaven. Please help me to stay on the path and not fall astray so I can experience forever with You and Your Son. In His perfect name, Amen.

TODAY I WILL...close my eyes and picture infinity and forever with God. I will get there!

JULY THEME

DISNEY SHOWS

JULY 1 **Read LUKE 15:11-24**

FINDING YOU

Disney Shows – Finding Nemo—The Musical

"And he arose and came to his father. But while he was still a long way off, his father saw him and felt compassion, and ran and embraced him and kissed him."
—Luke 15:20

Can you believe the year is halfway done? How has it gone for you so far? Regardless, vow right now to make the second half even better. Rededicate your life to God and promise to give Him even more of your time, service and love. This month's we'll be discussing the many wonderful shows throughout the parks, and we begin with my personal favorite, at least of the daytime shows. I began another devotional book saying, "There's nothing more motivating that a good story," and it's so true! That's why Disney is and continues to be so successful. They tell great stories. Jesus also told great stories, called parables. As a master teacher, it's how He captured his audiences' attention. Today's passage is my favorite of His stories. It's called the lost or "prodigal" son, and you may see some similarities between it and a certain Pixar film?

Finding Nemo appears to be a rough adaptation of this parable. Not only is it a great story and film, but it was also turned into an outstanding show. Finding Nemo – The Musical debuted in AK in 2006 and has been thriving ever since. Since the film wasn't a musical to begin with, the spousal team of Robert and Kristen Lopez, who would go on to write the award-winning *Frozen* soundtrack, were brought in specifically for this attraction. Together, they came up with several catchy, memorable songs and combined them with many of the actual film lines to create a 40-minute, unforgettable and emotional stage version of the film. And it gets me every time, especially when Nemo and dad are reunited. Just like in Jesus' version, there's no anger from his father, only sincere and profound relief the boy has come home. Jesus' story even says the father saw him coming from a long way off and ran to meet him. Clearly, this represents God, always watching and waiting for us to return if we wander off. It doesn't matter how far away we get or for how long, He is always there with His loving arms open to welcome us back home.

PRAYER—Loving Father, thank You for always being there, waiting for my return if I stray. Help me to never be too lost to find my way back to You. I love you, Lord. In Christ, Amen.

TODAY I WILL...make sure I'm not lost, but home, wrapped in the arms of my Father.

JULY 2 **Read 2 SAMUEL 12:15-23**

I WILL GO TO HIM

Disney Shows – Festival of the Lion King

"Blessed are those who mourn, for they shall be comforted."
—Matthew 5:4

A parent should never have to bury a child. Losing a son was the hardest burden I've ever had to bear. Any loss of family, whether expected or not, is difficult and can be a real test of our faith. Many Disney stories include emotional scenes of death, and *The Lion King*, on which today's show is based, is no different. There have actually been several park shows based on this hit film. This one began in AK in 1998 and has been running ever since with a few refurbishments along the way. There is also a version in Hong Kong. The show contains many of the film's notable characters and whimsical, familiar songs, but thankfully doesn't contain what may be the "king" of Disney's sad scenes, when poor Simba loses his father, Mufasa. James Earl Jones, the voice of Mufasa in the original film and modern remake, also voiced another famous father in a film series and sequels. He was the voice of Darth Vadar in the *Star Wars* franchise.

As stated many times before, suffering is part of life, and facing the death of loved ones is perhaps the most difficult type of suffering we must endure. In today's reading, David faces the same when his newborn son is taken as punishment for sin, but read carefully his impressive reaction. Not only does he go to church and worship in verse 20, but in verse 23, he makes a statement that brought me the most comfort when we experienced the same. He said, "Can I bring him back again? I will go to him, but he will not return to me." Death is painful and very difficult, but it's NOT the end. We can still be with our loved ones again on that glorious day of Christ's return. Praise God! I have a son and many other family members waiting, and I can't wait to see them. I'm sure you can say the same. It's okay to mourn their loss. It says above we are blessed and will be comforted when we do. But always remember that if we are in Christ, death is just a step leading us to our ultimate goal and eternal reward.

PRAYER—Father God, I miss my loved ones, but I'm so grateful I can see them again. Please grant me passage into your kingdom so I can. I can't wait for that day. In Jesus' name, Amen.

TODAY I WILL...assure my own and my family's reward so we can all be reunited one day.

JULY 3 **Read PSALM 95:1-7**

COME, LET US SING

Disney Shows – Frozen Sing-Along

"Praise the Lord! For it is good to sing praises to our God; for it is pleasant, and a song of praise is fitting."
—Psalm 147:1

Whether listening, playing or even singing, music is one of my favorite hobbies. Have you seen Pixar's *Soul* where the characters "get in the zone" while playing music? That's me! I can totally block out the world and its stresses by playing a little piano or belting out a tune in my car. I typically do those things alone, but I don't mind occasionally singing aloud, you know with hundreds of happy, Disney guests. Today's show is technically called "For the First Time in Forever: A Frozen Sing-Along Celebration." In 2014, the *Frozen* soundtrack sold over 10 million copies making it the year's best-selling album worldwide. With so many incredible songs, it's no surprise that a quarter, or 24 minutes of *Frozen* is dedicated to musical sequences.

Do you like to sing? Whether you do or not, singing is something we're all commanded to do. In Psalm 95, we are told to sing and make a joyful noise before God. And why should we? The psalm gives several reasons: Because He's great! Because He created the Earth. Because He controls the mountains. Because He made the seas. Because He formed the land. Because we are His people and sheep under His care. Do you need any more reasons to sing His praises? God created singing as a way to show Him gratitude (Col. 3:16) and a way for our hearts to express love to Him (Eph. 5:19). Even if you don't enjoy or can't sing well, you can't deny that He deserves it as just a tiny way we can give back and thank Him for all He's done and created for us. The Frozen Sing-Along show is not only funny, but I enjoy singing the songs, and the music makes me feel good. Singing praise to God should do the same on a much greater level. More importantly, it's commanded to show Him our dedication and complete submission to His will and power. Finally, according to Revelation, it's what we'll be doing in Heaven, so you better get used to it. I for one can't wait to sing there for the first time...and forever!

PRAYER—Most Holy God, I praise Your wonderful name! Thank you for music and the ability to sing praises to You. I can't wait to do it forever in Your presence. In Christ, Amen.

TODAY I WILL...sing a song of praise to God even if I'm by myself.

JULY 4 **Read GALATIANS 5:1, 13-15**

FREEDOM TO CHOOSE

Disney Shows – The American Adventure

"...and you will know the truth, and the truth will set you free."
—John 8:32

Happy 4th of July! And happy birthday, U.S.A.!! Did you know that America technically didn't declare independence on the 4th? That was done by vote on July 2nd. However, on the 4th, the declaration was actually published and so that date was chosen to celebrate. It wasn't until 1870, nearly a century later, however, that it was made an official federal holiday. It's only fitting that today we travel to the American Pavilion at Epcot and view the spectacular show found there. The American Adventure opened with Epcot in 1982 and is considered to be one of its greatest technological achievements. If you've seen the show, you know that it's done in a massive, sloped auditorium capable of holding over a thousand guests. The nearly 30-minute show contains multiple, massive sets cleverly hidden both above and below the stages and audience. The speeches within the show are real with many being word-for-word reenactments. Others are paraphrases and one by FDR is even an actual recording from his inaugural address.

The U.S.A. isn't perfect, but there are still many great things about it. One of its greatest blessings is freedom. Many other countries simply don't share the same freedoms and rights that Americans enjoy. Today's passage from Galatians also talks about freedom saying Christ has set us free. It goes on to advise us to use our freedom in Christ to serve one another in love. The well-known verse above tells us that the truth of God's Word has also provided freedom. Since we have been given God's Word and know His plan, along with the fact that Christ gave His life in place of ours, we now have the gift of freedom. God has given us our bodies, our minds and our lives to do as we please. We can choose to indulge in worldly pleasures as today's reading warns against or fulfill our purpose of using our freedom to serve others and bring as many as possible to know Christ. What will you do with your spiritual freedom? Choose wisely.

PRAYER—Lord, thank You for my freedom, politically and especially spiritually. Help me to make wise decisions with it and choose to serve others in love. In the name of Christ, Amen.

TODAY I WILL...celebrate my spiritual freedom in Christ by providing service to others.

JULY 5 **Read PHILIPPIANS 3:17-21**

WHERE ARE YOU REALLY FROM?

Disney Shows – The Voices of Liberty

"So then you are no longer strangers and aliens, but you are fellow citizens with the saints and members of the household of God."
—Ephesians 2:19

We're gonna keep the patriotic theme going for the next couple days because...well, why not? Since we're here in Epcot's American Pavilion, why not stick around for another highly rated show? Speaking of freedom (a.k.a. liberty) from yesterday, let's listen to the beautiful and harmonized Voices of Liberty singers that often perform right inside the pavilion's inner rotunda. The talented group, typically composed of 4 men and 4 women, perform a 12-15 minute show which includes patriotic songs with an occasional Disney, Broadway or other fun song thrown in.

I'll never forget visiting Mount Rushmore with my family in high school. It was breath-taking to finally see the famous monument I had only seen in pictures. While there, we got to witness a special, patriotic, nighttime program, and I remember distinctly singing "God Bless America" with many other families. We certainly didn't sound like the Voices of Liberty singers, but it was a memorable moment, nonetheless. Singing those songs, viewing historical monuments and hearing about your country's past can feel you with patriotism and devotion to your country, but take a close look at today's reading from Philippians. Being a citizen of your home nation is only temporary as Paul tells us where our real citizenship belongs. In verse 20, he says we are natives and future residents of Heaven. We were envisioned, conceived, formed and created by God there and sent here just temporarily to fulfill life's purpose. But our home is there, and we should be striving each day to return. Feel free to be patriotic towards your native citizenship. Just be sure to take more pride in your actual and permanent home of Heaven.

PRAYER—Lord, I'm so thankful to have a native citizenship and I pray for my country to thrive and be united under You. However, I'm most grateful that I am an eternal citizen of Heaven. I long to return home to be with You and Jesus. In His precious name, Amen.

TODAY I WILL...take pride in my country and strive to be a good citizen while remembering where my permanent and eternal citizenship lies.

JULY 6 **Read I PETER 2:13-17**

RESPECT THE POSITION

Disney Shows – The Hall of Presidents

"Let every person be subject to the governing authorities. For there is no authority except from God, and those that exist have been instituted by God."
—Romans 13:1

To complete our patriotic trilogy, we're traveling to the highest office in the land...that of the President of the United States. Did you know that on the 50th anniversary of the Declaration of Independence, July 4, 1826, both John Adams and Thomas Jefferson died within 5 hours of each other? And James Monroe died five years later, also on July 4th! That means 3 of the first 5 presidents died on July 4th. Weird, right? Traveling back to the MK today, we can see audio animatronics of all 46 U.S. Presidents. This attraction, which opened with the park in 1971, resembles Philadelphia's Independence Hall outside and has a rare "Great Seal of the United States" inside. It took an act of Congress to get approval to put it there. This attraction is special because it's something that Walt really wanted. He originally planned to put it in Disneyland and call it "One Nation Under God," but the technology wasn't quite advanced enough yet.

So what do you think of our current President? That topic of conversation seems to cause quite the stir these days. It seems no matter who is elected, there's controversy and political unrest that basically divides the country in half. Here's the deal: you don't have to agree with the President or even like him. However, we must remember what God says in today's readings. I Peter tells us it's God's will for us to honor political leaders, submit to their authority and respect the position. Unless we're told to do something that directly goes against Scripture, we should respect and obey the laws of the land. The verse above is similar saying it's God Himself that institutes our governing authorities. So while you may not like or agree with the President, realize it's God's will and trust in His ultimate power and control. We're also most certainly expected to pray for the President and all leaders. Make sure to have a proper Christian attitude when discussing our country's leader. He's God's child too and needs our prayers.

PRAYER—Dear God, please bless all political leaders, especially our President. Help me to have the proper attitude to always respect and honor that position. In Jesus I pray, Amen.

TODAY I WILL...pray for all political leaders, by name if possible, regardless of my feelings.

JULY 7 **Read MATTHEW 23:25-28**

BEAUTY IS FOUND WITHIN

Disney Shows – Beauty and the Beast – Live on Stage

"For the Lord sees not as man sees: man looks on the outward appearance, but the Lord looks on the heart."
—I Samuel 16:7

"Once upon a time, in a faraway land, a young prince lived in a shining castle. Although he had everything his heart desired, the prince was spoiled, selfish, and unkind. But then, one winter's night, an old beggar woman came to the castle and offered him a single rose in return for shelter from the bitter cold. Repulsed by her haggard appearance, the prince sneered at the gift and turned the old woman away, but she warned him not to be deceived by appearances, for beauty is found within." That's the familiar beginning of both the film and stage versions of the "tale as old as time." This live show has been performed for as long as the film has been in existence. In fact, it began at HS the exact same day the film debuted. Most of the show is pre-recorded with lines and songs lip-synced except for Belle and Gaston who sing live with microphones.

Beauty and the Beast is one of Disney's most successful and beloved films due to its lovable characters and memorable music, although you can't deny its wonderful story. When the spoiled prince turns away the old, unsightly woman, he is ironically transformed into something hideous masking his true inner self. It takes nearly the entire film and someone as kind as Belle to realize he too has true beauty within. In Matthew 23, Jesus rebukes the people for appearing righteous on the outside but being repulsive and unclean inside. Quite the opposite of the Beast. Humans (and movie characters) are very different from God. We tend to judge others and even ourselves based on the outside. But Jesus and the verse above teach that God looks at our hearts and who we truly are inside. Belle was good enough to see it, and the Beast learned his lesson and saw it. We must learn the same. Focus on your inner self making sure it's pure and right, and then learn the true heart of those around you before judging them based only on what you see.

PRAYER—Help me Lord, like You, to look within to see true beauty. Help me to focus on my own self and get to know the true character of others before making judgments. In Him, Amen.

TODAY I WILL...no longer judge others based only on appearances but make efforts to get to know them for who they truly are.

JULY 8 **Read I JOHN 4:13-21**

CONQUERING THE OCEAN

Disney Shows – Disney & Pixar Short Film Festival

"...for God gave us a spirit not of fear but of power and love and self-control."
—2 Timothy 1:7

When I was young, my grandmother used to love to tell me the story of when we all went on a beach vacation when I was just a baby. She had a fond memory of carrying me far out into the ocean and holding me, allowing my baby feet to feel the water and waves. Each time she told the story, she reminded me that while it was a wonderful moment, she also had some fear. As I obviously couldn't swim at that time, she worried in that moment about being hit by a big wave and accidently losing me. The ocean can be a scary place, especially if you are unskilled at swimming or staying afloat. Pixar has made great films, but they also have many wonderful short films. I'm sure you've seen a few. You can always catch a couple at the Magic Eye Theater in Epcot's Imagination Pavilion. This theater has also housed many notable film-based attractions such as Michael Jackson's "Captain EO" and "Honey, I Shrunk the Audience."

The current attraction typically shows three, 3D short films. They tend to rotate from time to time, but I'd like to discuss one in particular that has been a part of the lineup for many months. It's called "Piper" and you can watch it on YouTube. In the film, a newborn bird must conquer his own fear of the ocean so that he can feed off the tiny mollusks buried in the sand. He unfortunately learns firsthand the power and terror of the mighty waves leading to some justified hesitation and fear. Today's passage is a beautifully written reminder of God's love. It says if we confess Jesus Christ as Lord and love God with all our hearts, God and His love abide in us. His love is so powerful and strong that it can remove any fears we may have. The verse above is also compelling, demonstrating that God did not create us to be fearful creatures. Instead, He gave us the ability to overcome our fears with His love and power. We can't use the fear excuse with God, especially when it comes to speaking out for Him and boldly proclaiming our faith.

PRAYER—Lord, thank You for giving me Your love and power which are stronger than any fears I may have. Give me confidence and boldness to proclaim Your name. In Jesus, Amen.

TODAY I WILL...admit any fears and realize the power God has given me to overcome them.

JULY 9 **Read PROVERBS 24:1-7**

PREPARE FOR DANGER

Disney Shows – Indiana Jones Stunt Spectacular

"Where there is no counsel, the people fall; But in the multitude of counselors there is safety."
—Proverbs 11:14 (NKJV)

Do you know what's even better than watching a Disney show? Being in one! I'm happy to say I've been chosen twice to be a part of today's show. But that's nothing compared to my wife who's participated at least 5 times. She knows the secret, which I will graciously share. The key is to wear a bright color, sit near the stage and be ready to jump up, wave your arms and scream as soon as volunteers are asked for. It works every time! I did find it fascinating how cautious they were with us. Not only did we have to sign a release in case of injury, but they warned us several times to do exactly as we were told. The Indiana Jones Stunt Spectacular is a 25-minute, visually engaging performance full of stunts mainly from the first film, *Raiders of the Lost Ark*. It's a fun, exciting show, but it's also very dangerous with actual, hazardous stunts going on. One performer even died in 2009 after a head injury suffered during rehearsal. The entire show takes careful planning and no doubt many hours of practice. Any time a stunt is performed either live or on film, those involved must take careful precautions to avoid serious injury or death.

Proverbs 24 strongly advises careful planning, knowledge and wisdom before taking on a serious project. Verse 6 also instructs pursuing guidance in the face of war or danger. Like this stunt show, life can be dangerous. Satan is out there trying to wage war on our souls, and unfortunately, he's often victorious. If we want to defeat him and keep our souls securely on track for Heaven, it's a good idea to seek counsel and carefully plan our steps. We don't want to walk into temptation or trials that will test our faith or damage our relationship with God. Seek counsel with God or others who can help you as you strategically plan your walk of faith so that you'll know how to face danger and make it through without spiritual injury or eternal death.

PRAYER—Dear God, help me to plan, be mindful and cautious of all situations I get involved in. Help me to seek counsel and guidance so I can avoid Satan's attempt on my soul. Help me follow in the footsteps of Christ knowing it will be the best path for success. In Jesus, Amen.

TODAY I WILL...be strategic and take the time to plan my life to avoid spiritual dangers.

JULY 10 **Read DEUTERONOMY 32:9-12**

THE GREAT EAGLE

Disney Shows – Feathered Friends in Flight

"You yourselves have seen what I did to the Egyptians, and how I bore you on eagles' wings and brought you to myself."
—Exodus 19:4

A few months ago, while out on our back deck, I noticed a nest on the gutter underneath the soffit of our house. I had seen this nest before, but this time it was different because three tiny heads were sticking out of it. In the next few seconds, I observed mama bird fly up to the nest and drop food into the three little mouths, their necks now outstretched and begging. It was fascinating to watch that process happen repeatedly within just a few minutes. Birds are amazing creatures which is very evident at today's unique, captivating and generally underrated Animal Kingdom show. Feathered Friends in Flight has gone through some refurbishments and name changes over time, but it's always intriguing to see what several different varieties of birds can do. The 25-minute show takes place at the covered Caravan Theater in the Asia section of AK.

I've seen multiple versions of this show, but it's always ended the same way. They bring out a majestic and beautiful bald eagle and talk about the incredible things it can do. Did you know eagles can dive at 100mph? They are also no longer endangered, a point always celebrated during this show. Eagles also take great care and are very protective of their young, being very watchful for predators. Deuteronomy 32 compares the way God cared for Jacob to an eagle caring for its young. The verse above is God reminding the Israelites how He "bore (them) on eagles' wings" and brought them out of Egypt, saving them from bondage and misery. God is similar to an eagle in the way He cares for us too. He provides for our basic needs, protects us from harm and watches out for us, giving us ample warnings and tools to fight off predators like Satan. We should feel warm and protected, as if in a nest, surrounded by God's love and care. Isn't it wonderful to have such a compassionate Father who genuinely cares about each of our lives and longs for us to be safe from Satan and saved from sin? Praise God!

PRAYER—Holy Father, thank You for your love, care and compassion on me. I don't deserve it, but I'm so grateful. Please continue to protect and provide for me. In Christ's name, Amen.

TODAY I WILL...do some bird watching, remembering the similarities to God's care for me.

JULY 11 **Read GENESIS 4:1-12**

THE FINAL COMMANDMENT

Disney Shows – Voyage of the Little Mermaid

"For where jealousy and selfish ambition exist, there will be disorder and every vile practice."
—James 3:16

How many of the Bible's 10 Commandments can you name? Do you know the last one? It's probably the least remembered but ironically may be the one most often broken. It says, "Thou shalt not covet." Do you know what that means? Coveting is wanting what someone else has, so much so that you think negative thoughts or have improper feelings towards that person. It's your basic jealousy. Today we visit another show in Hollywood Studios with an abbreviated version of a Disney classic. Voyage of the Little Mermaid is a 17-minute rendition containing three of the film's beloved songs. It features only two live actors, Ariel and Prince Eric. The rest of the cast is portrayed as puppets, some rather large in the case of Ursula who is 12 feet tall and 10 feet wide. In the "Under the Sea" song alone, there are over 100 puppets used.

The Little Mermaid is a story based on jealousy. The evil Ursula is jealous of King Triton's power and wants it all to herself. But she's not alone. Even sweet Ariel is jealous of humans and longs to be just like them, leading to her predicament. If you think about it, most Disney films are built around stories of jealousy. But jealousy is not just found in animated films. It's rampant in our world today. It was also one of the very first sins we read about in the Bible. In Genesis 4, Cain was jealous because of God being more pleased with his brother, Abel's sacrifice. His jealousy led to rage, hatred and the violent killing of Abel. It's okay to wish for what someone else has. But if that turns into jealousy, negative feelings or improper thoughts, it becomes a problem and a sin. In the verse above, James tells us that jealousy leads to disorder and evil practices. Make sure your desires aren't leading you to improper feelings of jealousy. Be content with the blessings you've been given by God and be happy for others in theirs.

PRAYER—Dear Lord, help me both be content with the many blessings You've given me and control any feelings of jealousy I ever have toward others and what they have. In Christ, Amen.

TODAY I WILL...be genuinely happy for others and their blessings and tell them so.

JULY 12 **Read 2 KINGS 6:15-23**

OPEN YOUR EYES

Disney Shows – Canada Far and Wide

"All things were made through him, and without him was not anything made that was made."
—John 1:3

I love traveling. To Disney of course, but anywhere with exciting things to see. The great thing about Epcot is you can essentially travel through 11 different countries by simply walking a 1.2-mile loop around World Showcase. Let's head that way today, turn right and visit the first country we come to. Canada contains more than half the world's lakes, has the world's longest coastline and is the 2nd largest country in size behind Russia. When this Pavilion was built along with Epcot, Disney sought financial help from the Canadian government, but they refused due to worry about stereotypes being portrayed there. Disney threatened to cancel the Pavilion but thankfully decided not to. This is arguably the most beautiful Pavilion with a huge waterfall and gorgeous gardens displayed. I've been to actual Canada but have only really seen the urban side. According to the 360° film inside this Pavilion, there are many beautiful landscapes to be found throughout the country. I'd love to see it in person one day. I didn't think I'd enjoy this film, but it's actually pretty good. The scenery displayed is nothing short of incredible and stunning.

2 Kings 6 contains an amazing story of the prophet Elisha and his servant, who panics after seeing a large army surrounding them. Elisha knows that God is with them and prays the servant's eyes will be opened. When the servant goes out a second time, he also sees the Lord's army, much greater and more powerful. Sometimes we too need to just open our eyes to see God surrounding us. Traveling to Canada, or maybe your own backyard, and taking the time to just open your eyes and look around, you can't help but see God's power and creation everywhere. This film shows great evidence of that. Everything we see was made by God. We just need to dedicate the time to appreciate it all and see it for the gift and blessing from Him that it is.

PRAYER—Almighty Father, as You did for Elisha's servant, please open my eyes to see Your beauty and power displayed throughout this world. Thank You for all You've created and given me to see. I can only imagine how much more beautiful Heaven will be. In Jesus' name, Amen.

TODAY I WILL...open my eyes and look around to appreciate the beauty God has provided.

JULY 13 **Read MATTHEW 21:1-11**

THE ONE FLOAT PARADE

Disney Shows – Disney Parades

"This Jesus, who was taken up from you into heaven, will come in the same way as you saw him go into heaven."
—Acts 1:11

One of the neatest things I've ever gotten to do at Disney World was when my wife and I took the "Keys to the Kingdom" tour. We heard so many interesting facts and secrets and got to see many "backstage" areas including the warehouse where the parade floats are kept. Seeing these ginormous floats just parked while we heard tons of information about them was fascinating. Did you know that each float has hidden buttons on either side? Cast members always walk beside the floats and can press these buttons to immediately stop them in an emergency. We were also taken to the spot where the floats enter the parade route. There is a line painted on the ground backstage. The cast members on board know that once the floats touch this line, they must be in constant "show mode" because they can potentially be seen by the public. There's another line backstage at the exit point letting them know they can stop performing.

I love parades. Disney has had so many good ones over the years, and I have fond memories of them. There's another parade I wish I could've seen though. It wasn't put on by Disney. In fact, it was pretty short. Only one "float." It took place almost exactly 2000 years ago, and we can read about it in all four Gospels. It is called the "Triumphal Entry" and is the account of Jesus riding into Jerusalem on a donkey just a few days before His arrest, trial and crucifixion. As he rides, the people put their cloaks and palm branches on the road in front of Him and shout, "Hosanna to the Son of David! Blessed is He who comes in the name of the Lord! Hosanna in the highest!" It was a short, simple parade, but it was so important. Jesus knew He was riding into town for the last time. He knew He was facing death. He knew He was the sacrifice for every one of us. He knew. We may not have gotten to witness that parade, but He's coming back. As the verse above says, this time it'll be a parade in the sky. I can't wait to see that one.

PRAYER—Lord, thank You for the Triumphal Entry of Jesus leading to His crucifixion to atone for my sins. Please send Him back quickly. In His blessed name, Amen.

TODAY I WILL...say, sing or even shout the same thing said to Jesus during his "parade."

JULY 14 **Read JOB 37:1-13**

THE POWER OF GOD

Disney Shows – Frozen-Live at the Hyperion

"Behold, I am the Lord, the God of all flesh. Is anything too hard for me?"
—Jeremiah 32:27

Have you ever seen a movie so good you wanted to immediately see it again? I mentioned back in January that when *The Lion King* came out in 1994, I saw it twice the first week because I loved it so much. I did the same with *The Greatest Showman*. (I know that's not Disney, but it is on Disney Plus!) I know we did a *Frozen* show recently, but that's a sing-along that basically focuses on the music. It's great, of course, but doesn't compare with this elaborate, 55-minute, production at Disneyland's Hyperion Theater. The first time I saw this show, I knew I had to see it again, and so I went back the next day. It began in 2016 replacing an Aladdin show that had been around since 2003. A version of this show also appears on the Disney Wonder cruise ship.

During this show's most popular song, "Let it Go," Queen Elsa appears on a spectacular, giant staircase that actually rotates out over the audience. Combined with unique lighting, sounds and special effects, it's a powerful scene you must see to appreciate. It's during that song in this show and even in the film that you see her true powers come alive as she builds an entire palace out of ice in a matter of minutes. In today's reading, Job describes the power of God and there are a couple of coincidental and downright eerie similarities. Verse 3 says under the heavens God "lets it go" (it really says that!), and verse 10 says by His breath "ice is given." How about that? The whole passage describes what God can do through His awesome power. The truth is God has the power to do anything. His own rhetorical question in the verse above proves that. He has parted seas, flooded the Earth and sent fire from Heaven, not to mention creating the world to begin with. Rejoice that His almighty power is on your side and He wants to use it for little ole you. He longs to know you, help you and save you with it. Will you allow Him?

PRAYER—Almighty and most powerful Father, I'm go grateful You are willing and longing to use Your mighty powers for my benefit. Help me to accept them. Change my life with them. Bring me to You eternally with them. In the name of Jesus, Amen.

TODAY I WILL...submit to God's power and let it to change me to who I need to be for Him.

JULY 15 **Read I CORINTHIANS 9:19-23**

MANY DIFFERENT BEARS

Disney Shows – Country Bear Jamboree

"And this gospel of the kingdom will be proclaimed throughout the whole world as a testimony to all nations..."
—Matthew 24:14

Did you know bears have many similarities to humans? Like human children, bear cubs are very playful, and if they get too rough, mama bears will make them stop to avoid injury. That sounds pretty human too. Bears are also very intelligent. Their navigation skills are even superior to humans as they have excellent sight, smell and hearing. We're talking bears today because we're going to see the most famous bear show in the world. Well, at least in Disney World. The Country Bear Jamboree can be seen in Tokyo too. It was in California's Disneyland but closed in 2001 to make way for Winnie the Pooh. In fact, there used to be a whole area of Disneyland called "Bear Country." It was changed to "Critter Country" in 1989 when Splash Mountain opened. Walt Disney originally envisioned this bear show as part of a planned ski resort.

This show is certainly not Disney's most innovative attraction, but I'm glad it's there. It's nostalgic and you can't help but enjoy the music. During the show you meet nearly 20 different bears of all shapes, sizes and personalities and even get to see them all during the exciting finale. In I Corinthians 9, Paul admits an interesting strategy in converting souls. For the Jews, he says he became a Jew. For the weak, he became weak. And so on. Basically, he met people where they were. Just like the many bear varieties, there are also many different types of people. You will meet those who know the Bible well and others who haven't heard a single verse. You will find some very receptive to your teaching while others don't care. You can't use the same methods with everyone. We are to proclaim God's Word to all people throughout the world, and it will take many different strategies to do so. Meet people where they are to better understand them. Put yourself in their shoes and approach them with patience, kindness and love.

PRAYER—Dear Lord, please continue to give me boldness to proclaim Your Gospel. Help me to meet others where they are to better understand their situations and needs. In Christ, Amen.

TODAY I WILL...imagine being someone I know that needs to hear God's Word so I know how best to approach and talk to them. How would I want to hear it if I was in their shoes?

JULY 16 **Read PSALM 23:1-6**

HIS CARING IS FOR THE BIRDS

Disney Shows – Enchanted Tiki Room

"Consider the ravens: they neither sow nor reap, they have neither storehouse nor barn, and yet God feeds them. Of how much more value are you than the birds!"
—Luke 12:24

It just flew right in, and the room went silent. I'll never forget that day in the cafeteria, sitting at the teachers' table while monitoring over 100 students eating lunch. They were loud, as usual, but certainly got quiet when the pigeon flew in. But only for a second. What followed were screams, laughs and the erupting sounds of an overly excited bunch of 6th graders. 'What do we do now?' I remember thinking. It had landed on a low windowsill and was freaking out half the students. While I was contemplating a strategy, my co-teacher calmly walked over to the fairly large bird, grabbed it with two hands and released it outside. She got a much deserved, standing ovation for calmly and humanely taking care of that bird. God does the same, you know.

Yesterday it was bear facts, today birds. There are over 10,000 species of birds worldwide with the chicken the most common. Hummingbirds weight less than a nickel and can fly backwards. Most have hollow bones to aid in flying. The Enchanted Tiki Room is a celebration of birds that has been around since 1963 in Disneyland and since day one at WDW. It was also in Tokyo at one time. This attraction is famous for having the first ever audio-animatronics, which Walt was quite proud of. It was originally to be a restaurant with the birds serenading guests as they ate. There are many stories and passages in Scripture about birds. They are an important part of the stories of Noah, Elijah, Peter and others. Even Jesus used birds to say if God takes care of them as He does, then surely He's going to care for each of us as well. We are His most valued creation, created us in His own image. He loves and cares for us more than any creature He made. Today's reading is the most familiar psalm. Read it carefully and remember the words I, me and my are talking about you. Sure, David wrote it, but God inspired it because He wanted you to hear it and know it's meant to bring you comfort and peace. God takes care of His birds. He takes even better care of His sheep. Let that pacify you today and bring you joy.

PRAYER—Read Psalm 23 again as a prayer to God replacing the word "He" with "You".

TODAY I WILL...memorize Psalm 23 so I can repeat it daily and hear God saying it to me.

JULY 17 **Read HEBREWS 5:11-14**

MILK OR FOOD?

Disney Shows – Mickey's Philharmagic

"Rather train yourself for godliness; for while bodily training is of some value, godliness is of value in every way..."
—I Timothy 4:7-8

It was an honor to be chosen, but I was a bit terrified. I was in chorus for three years in high school and the week before graduation, I was asked to direct them during the ceremony. I had never conducted a 60-member chorus, especially one of my peers! But it was a special moment as they sang "The Lord Bless You and Keep You" to my direction. Needless to say, I practiced many times to ensure I was fully prepared. That's more than I can say for the surprise conductor of Mickey's Philharmagic Orchestra in this enjoyable, Fantasyland, 4D film found in five Disney parks with Shanghai the lone exception. The film has the largest amount of Disney characters to ever appear in the same film transitioning through songs and scenes from several different classics. The screen it is shown on is the largest, seamless, projection screen in the world!

If you've seen this film, you know the story in that Donald Duck mischievously takes over Mickey's orchestra trying to direct and control them. However, he is unprepared causing all kinds of chaos and transporting himself through the various scenes. His lack of experience and training may be humorous, but it also teaches a good lesson. The writer of Hebrews reprimands the people telling them they ought to be teachers but instead need more instruction themselves to re-learn God's basic principles. He compares it to them needing an infant's milk instead of solid food. 2 Timothy 3:16-17 says the Bible was given so we might be "complete" and "equipped." If we don't study it regularly, we can't be as prepared as God expects and needs us to be. If Donald had been properly equipped to conduct, he would've been successful, but because he wasn't, it caused confusion. We can cause the same if we aren't careful. We don't want to teach false doctrine or answer questions improperly. Make sure you are properly trained for godliness like the verse above suggests. Study His Word to be fully prepared when called upon to share it.

PRAYER—Father, help me to be properly trained and prepared to teach Your Word, answer questions about You properly and equip myself with righteousness. In Christ's name, Amen.

TODAY I WILL...make sure I have a regular training routine so I am thoroughly equipped.

JULY 18 **Read MATTHEW 5:10-12**

TOUGHER THAN BEING A BUG

Disney Shows – It's Tough to be a Bug

"Indeed, all who desire to live a godly life in Christ Jesus will be persecuted..."
—I Timothy 3:12

1.5 million different species in the world. Over 91,000 of those in the U.S. alone. One type can lay 40,000 eggs per day. Another was the first living creatures sent into space. Some beat their wings 190 times per second while others can drag over 1000 times their weight. Some taste with their feet or fight with their necks, and still others breathe through their bottoms. What an incredible phenomenon is the world of bugs as we visit a related 4D film experience within Animal Kingdom's Tree of Life. This attraction based on the 2nd Pixar movie actually opened at WDW a full 7 months before the film released. Imagineers knew they wanted something inside the giant tree but struggled with ideas. Then CEO, Michael Eisner, suggested a tie-in with the upcoming Pixar film and the team went to work creating this enjoyable yet slightly scary film.

The premise of this show involves Flik, the famed ant and star of *A Bug's Life*, teaching the audience about various insects and their abilities, but another message shines through echoing the attraction's title. It's tough to be a bug! Bugs. often seen as enemies by humans, get stepped on, sprayed, attacked and destroyed. I agree it's tough to be a bug, but I would argue in today's world it's even tougher to be a Christian! They get "stepped on" too. Matthew 5 contains the Beatitudes of Christ with the last one saying we are blessed when we're persecuted, reviled and falsely accused of evil, as expected for followers of Christ. Paul agrees telling us above that living a Godly life will bring persecution. Living properly as Christians will not be easy and will mean suffering and rejection by the world. We must be prepared, remembering that Matthew 5:10 goes on to say we will be given the kingdom of Heaven as a reward for facing it. Don't let persecution deter you from living a Christian life to the best of your ability. Fight through the hard times, stick to your beliefs and be proud of your faith. Your reward is coming!

PRAYER—Lord, You tell me to expect suffering, and I know it will be tough to be a Christian. Give me Your strength to stay on the path regardless and face persecution. In His name, Amen.

TODAY I WILL...vow to always wear the Christian name proudly despite how tough it is.

JULY 19 **Read EPHESIANS 4:11-16**

A PART IN PROGRESS

Disney Shows – Carousel of Progress

"The righteous flourish like the palm tree and grow like a cedar in Lebanon."
—Psalm 92:12

As a paramedic, I encounter a lot of dialysis patients who have lost a limb due to their kidney disease. It has caused me to consider an uncomfortable question. If you had to live without one part of your body, what would you choose? It's not easy as each part proves useful at times. There's another body that can't afford to lose any of its parts, and you and your progress play a pivotal role. The Carousel of Progress at WDW is the oldest show on property as it has been around even longer than the park itself! It was created for the 1964 New York World's Fair. After that, it was moved to Disneyland until 1973 when it was relocated across the country to WDW. This was known to be Walt's favorite attraction, a fact even his family confirmed. It is therefore probably the only attraction at Walt Disney World actually touched by Walt himself.

The whole idea behind this "longest running stage show in the history of American theater," as you'll hear when the show begins, is a visual of progress made throughout the last century. The final scene is supposedly a look into the future of progress, although it probably needs to be updated as many of the projected developments have already come to fruition. In Ephesians 4, Paul advises us to continue growing in Christ. Verse 15 states that we are to "grow up in every way" into Jesus, who is the head of the church, or body of Christ. Verse 16 says the church will only grow when every part is working properly. You are one of those parts! Each of us must continue to progress and grow as an integral part of Christ's church. When we fail to do so, we make it more difficult for that body to grow and thrive. The whole church can suffer without our growing in knowledge and service. I'm sure you don't want to live without any part of your body. Why would the body of Christ be any different? It needs all its parts. It needs you!

PRAYER—Lord, I realize I'm an important part of the church and body of Christ. Help me to continue to grow and progress in my faith so I give my full potential to the church and help it to also grow. Thank You for making me a part of Your body of believers. In Christ, Amen.

TODAY I WILL...do my part to be a vital part of the church, always progressing in faith.

JULY 20 **Read JOHN 10:7-18**

HE KNOWS YOUR NAME

Disney Shows – Muppet Vision 3D

"...for you have found favor in my sight, and I know you by name."
—Exodus 33:17

An essential lesson I learned as a teacher is that it's important to treat children as individuals and give attention to each one. All children are created different and therefore don't all learn the same. An effective teacher gets to know each child so they can cater to their specific needs. During today's show, there's a point where it feels like a character is talking to you specifically as well. Muppet Vision 3D opened back in 1991 at Hollywood Studios and was directed by Muppet creator, Jim Henson. In fact, his name used to appear in the title of this attraction until Disney purchased the Muppets in 2004. It also operated at Disney California Adventure from 2001-2014. Despite this film being several years old, some of the 3D effects are pretty clever. During one portion, a character begins to whisper and says something to the effect of, "all these other people think I'm talking to them, but I'm really only talking to you." He then points his nose right in your direction and it really does look and feel like he's talking just to you. While it's a pretty amazing and funny part of the film, it's an important lesson, not only for teachers as mentioned above, but from God as well.

In John 10, Jesus says He is the Good Shepherd for His sheep, also stating He knows his sheep as His own and would lay down His life for them. We know that not only are we those sheep but that He already gave His life for us. In Exodus 33 above, God tells Moses He knows him by name. Guess what? He knows yours too. Just as Christ knows each of us as His sheep, God knows us as individuals. He hears our individual prayers, knows our individual needs and loves each of us individually. During this classic Muppet film, you know deep down that the character is not really looking just at you. But you can rest assured that God truly is. He's watching over you as His sheep. Just make sure not to wander away from His flock or His loving care.

PRAYER—Holy Lord, thank You for knowing my name and treating me as an individual. I'm so blessed that You call me Your own. Help me to remain safe in Your flock. In Jesus, Amen.

TODAY I WILL...call upon God by name and thank Him for knowing mine.

JULY 21 **Read ACTS 17:10-14**

PUT YOUR BELIEFS TO THE TEST

Disney Shows – Beauty and the Beast Sing-Along

"All Scripture is breathed out by God and profitable for teaching, for reproof, for correction, and for training in righteousness..."
—2 Timothy 3:16

I remember being in college and for some reason the question just hit me... why do I believe what I believe? Is it just because my parents told me so? Or do I really know it's true? How do I know I was taught the right way? What if I'm wrong about God and the Bible? After all, I was apparently wrong about *Beauty and the Beast*. Well, at least about one character. Have you seen this Sing-Along show within Epcot's French Pavilion? It opened in January of 2020 and currently shares the theater with the original *Impressions de France* film. It's narrated by Angela Lansbury, the voice of Mrs. Potts herself. Not only does it offer most of the film's memorable songs to sing along with, but it also suggests a twist for Gaston's short and silly sidekick, LeFou. He is shown actually working behind the scenes the whole time, trying to get Belle and the Beast together. Therefore, it suggests we as the viewers were wrong all along about his evil intentions.

Was LeFou really noble and righteous the whole time? Were we wrong about him? What about your spiritual beliefs? Could you be wrong about those too? In Acts 17, the Bereans are commended for studying the Scriptures daily to see if what they were told was true. They didn't just take Paul's word for it when he spoke to them. They listened and then confirmed it to make sure, which is the proper way to use the Bible. We should know why we believe what we do. We can't just believe it because someone says it's so. Humans aren't flawless. Some will make mistakes in their teachings, either accidently or on purpose. The Bible even warns about false teachers. (I John 4:1) We must have a standard to test what we hear, and the Bible is the perfect choice. The verse above says the Bible has several purposes including to correct any false information. Be sure to what you hear and confirm that your beliefs can be backed up by Scripture. For best results, just follow the words of Christ and you'll never go wrong.

PRAYER—God, give me the dedication and desire to test what I hear using Your Word. Help me discover any false teachers that attempt to lead me astray and follow Christ above all. Amen.

TODAY I WILL...question my beliefs and make sure they are backed by Scripture.

JULY 22 **Read JEREMIAH 8:4-7**

A PRESIDENTIAL FAILURE

Disney Shows – Great Moments with Mr. Lincoln

"For the sake of Christ, then, I am content with weaknesses, insults, hardships, persecutions, and calamities. For when I am weak, then I am strong."
—2 Corinthians 12:10

His mother died when he was nine. He was demoted while serving in the military. He was broke and failed in a business deal. His sweetheart died unexpectedly. He lost bids for state legislature, speaker of the House and Vice-President. All these failures and disappointments, and yet he became one of the greatest Presidents this country has known. Great Moments with Mr. Lincoln has been a stage show at Disneyland since 1965. It's gone through many changes over the years but still features Walt's childhood hero, Abraham Lincoln, as an audio-animatronic. It was originally part of the 1964 World's Fair in New York just like the Carousel of Progress. The original Lincoln used there was lost for decades until it was found, tucked away in a shipping crate. It is currently on display at the One Man's Dream attraction at Hollywood Studios.

Lincoln's life was full of failure, but he was generally undeterred, continuing to strive for greatness and the chance to become an influential leader. Jeremiah 8 tells of God's expectations for us to rise again when we fall, as well as His frustration with those who refuse to do so. God did not create us to quit and dwell in failure, but instead endowed us with strength and resilience to overcome difficulties and push past our trials. The Apostle Paul admitted to many weaknesses and hardships, including in the passage above, but also said he was content because they made him stronger. My guess is Lincoln would've said the same. Figuring out how to persevere through trials grants us the knowledge to do better and overcome in the future. Work hard to view your trials the same way. When I coached Cross Country, I often told my runners to use the downhills for speed and to gain energy to use when going back up. When life is tough and forcing you downhill, learn from it and use it to push yourself back up. Above all, keep your focus on God and He will guide you through your trials and lead you to your next success.

PRAYER—Lord, thank You for difficulties and failures. Though not easy, I know they make me stronger and wiser. Help me to continue to get back up when I fall. In Him, Amen.

TODAY I WILL...use the downhills. I will see trials as a means to get stronger and persevere.

JULY 23 **Read PSALM 37:1-24**

BACK TO SCHOOL

Disney Shows – The Animation Academy

"The steps of a man are established by the Lord, when he delights in his way..."
—Proverbs 37:23

I'm done with school! After 4 years of pre-school, 12 in grade school, 4 in college, 3 with graduate school and 3 in a vocational school to become a paramedic, I feel like I've been a student most of my life, so I have little desire to return. However, last time I was at Disneyland, I did go back to school or at least it felt that way. We were ushered into a classroom, given our own workspace, paper and pencil and then sat quietly, waiting for our teacher to arrive. I realize it may be a stretch to call The Animation Academy a show, but I figured it's more of a show than a ride. Plus I hated to pass it over because I ended up attending that "class" three times that day. This attraction also appears at WDW, Paris and Hong Kong. In Shanghai, they have a Marvel Comic Academy where you learn to draw Marvel characters. There is also a planned version for Epcot where Edna Mode from *The Incredibles* will teach guests to draw various characters.

I'm not a talented artist by any means, but by patiently following the "teacher" step by step, I was able to produce some pretty decent character drawings. In today's psalm, David encourages us to have patience with the Lord and trust in His plan. Verse 23 also reminds us that God establishes our steps. After attending the Animation Academy several times, I daresay even the least talented of artists could produce a Disney character by simply following the master one step at a time. In a similar way, we must have patience with God, follow the steps He's laid out for us and allow Him to guide ours. David makes it clear throughout this psalm that evil will always be present, but he also confirms that God is always in control, even saying God laughs at the wicked. Be patient with God. Tell Him you trust Him, that your steps are under His control and that your life is in His hands. He is the master Artist, so let Him guide you step by step.

PRAYER—Father, I trust You with my life. Please take control and guide my steps. Give me patience in dealing with evil knowing that You will give me victory in the end. In Christ, Amen.

TODAY I WILL...attempt to draw a Disney character by following the step by step instructions on YouTube (type "Disney Animation Academy"), while thanking God for controlling my steps.

JULY 24 **Read ROMANS 1:18-23**

FACT OR FANTASY

Disney Shows – Fantasyland Theatre

"For you formed my inward parts; you knitted me together in my mother's womb."
—Psalm 139:13

Bulls get angry when they see red. Sharks can smell blood a mile away. Swimming right after eating is dangerous. A coin thrown from the top of a skyscraper can kill someone. It takes 7 years for gum to digest. Know what those "facts" have in common? They aren't facts at all. They are commonly accepted as truth but are actually just fiction or fantasy. With Fantasyland, the Festival of Fantasy parade, the Fantasy cruise ship and today's attraction, "fantasy" is a theme Disney knows all too well. The Fantasyland Theatre is a 5000-square-foot facility at Disneyland and was first called "Videopolis" when opened in 1985. It has hosted various shows over time, including the current "Mickey and the Magical Map." The original Fantasyland Theater (different spelling) opened soon after the park in 1956 and featured cartoons and short films. It closed in 1981 and was replaced by the Pinocchio ride during a Fantasyland overhaul.

Sometimes it's hard to tell truth from fantasy. My mom always said I would have arthritis from cracking my knuckles. Not true! I was taught the Great Wall of China was visible from space, a "fact" I even found in a History book. Also, not true! It often takes time and clear evidence to prove something as fact. Romans 1 tells us God's wrath is on those who try and suppress His truth. It also makes clear that God is real and has shown evidence to all, even those who doubt, saying His power and divinity should be obvious in all that has been made. I'll say again...how anyone can look at the complexity of the human body or the creation of the world and not believe in a higher power is simply perplexing. God is fact and anyone who believes otherwise is called foolish in today's reading. Fantasy and made-up stories are fun at Disney. But there's nothing fantasy about our Father. He is real and the evidence is all around us. Rest assured in your faith and do your part to help make "fantasy" become fact to those in doubt.

PRAYER—Holy Father, I know You are real and I'm so grateful You are. Help others to see the clear evidence and use me to convince those who are skeptical or lack faith. In Him, Amen.

TODAY I WILL...look for proof of God's existence all around me and share it with others.

JULY 25 **Read PSALM 126:1-6**

THE GIFT OF LAUGHTER

Disney Shows – Monsters, Inc. Laugh Floor

"He will yet fill your mouth with laughter, and your lips with shouting."
—Job 8:21

Two hunters are out in the woods when one collapses. He doesn't seem to be breathing and his eyes are glazed. The other guy whips out his phone and calls 911. He gasps, "My friend is dead! What can I do?" The dispatcher says, "Calm down. I can help. First, let's make sure he's dead." There is a silence; then a gunshot is heard. Back on the phone, the guy says, "OK, now what?" Did you laugh? Even a little? Come on! Now that was funny! In fact, that was judged by several sources to be the funniest joke in the world. Maybe you've heard one you think is funnier, perhaps even during the show we're discussing today. The Monsters, Inc. Laugh Floor is a WDW Magic Kingdom attraction that opened in 2007. It features the characters from the Pixar hit telling jokes and interacting with audience members, meaning no two shows are ever the same. The show uses digital puppet technology and live voice actors backstage who can see and talk to the audience with hidden cameras and microphones.

Do you like to laugh? Who doesn't? It's no fantasy that laughter is good for you and can have genuinely positive effects on your body. Laughter is also a Biblical quality. Today's reading is a short psalm that praises God for good fortune causing laughter and joy. The verse above from Job also says God fills our mouths with laughter. Laughter is one of God's gifts to bring joy to our hearts and minds. It can make us feel good and drive away fears, worries and stress. Luke 6:21 calls those "blessed" who weep now, saying they will eventually be full of laughter. I imagine Heaven full of joy, shouts of praise, feelings of happiness and loads of laughter. Think about how much you enjoy laughing with family, friends or even yourself and multiply that feeling exponentially to picture what Heaven will be like. Strive to make it there and experience that joy. In the meantime, enjoy the laughter we have here and thank God for it.

PRAYER—Heavenly Father, thank You for the joy and good feelings laughter brings. Help me to continue striving for Heaven and the happiness and laughter it will bring. In Christ, Amen.

TODAY I WILL...work hard to make someone laugh, especially one who need joy in their life.

JULY 26 **Read MATTHEW 6:5-14**

HE CAN HEAR YOU

Disney Shows – Turtle Talk with Crush

"For the eyes of the Lord are on the righteous, and his ears are open to their prayer."
—I Peter 3:12

When we took our first Disney cruise several years ago, we sat down to dinner one night only to have Crush suddenly appear on a screen next to our table. He immediately started conversing with our boys, and I remember thinking it was a recording until he began to actually respond to what they were saying. I couldn't believe the ingenuity and technology. The boys, however, just conversed with him as if was perfectly normal. The cruise version, found on the Dream and Fantasy ships, is a mini adaptation of this interactive show that opened at Epcot in 2004 and soon spread to Disneyland, Tokyo and even a Children's Hospital in California. It also formerly appeared in Hong Kong. Similar to yesterday's attraction, this one uses hidden cameras and live actors to voice the famous turtle so he can talk to and hear the children who typically sit up front.

With Siri, Alexa and the like so common these days, it's no wonder kids of today perhaps aren't as impressed as I am with technology that can hear, understand and respond, something I never had as a kid. However, I've always had something similar that was even better, used no technology and still works today. I had (and still have) a Father, ready to listen anytime I spoke. And like Crush, He responds! In Matthew 6, Jesus gave an example of how to pray making it clear that God rewards us when we do and even knows what we need before we ask. Despite that, God wants us to talk to Him often. I Thessalonians 5:17 tells us to pray without ceasing. Isaiah 65:24 says God hears us and answers even before we ask. The verse above echoes saying His ears are open to our prayers. There's no doubt God is listening when we speak to Him, and it's equally certain He answers back. You may not hear His immediate reply, but He'll always listen and do what's best for you. What a blessing to have our own version of Turtle Talk with Crush called prayer time with God, available 24/7. Take advantage and talk to your Father.

PRAYER—God, thank You for hearing and responding to me when I talk to You. I don't always get the answer I want, but I know You respond with what's best. In His Name, Amen.

TODAY I WILL...spend private time talking to God, perhaps aloud, and listen for His answer.

JULY 27 **Read 2 TIMOTHY 1:3-7**

PROUD TO BE A JUNIOR

Disney Shows – Disney Junior Play and Dance

"Honor your father and mother."
—Ephesians 6:2

Has anyone ever said that you look or act just like one of your parents? Or have you ever found yourself sounding or doing something just like them? We tend to become our parents in one way or another. I can't count the number of times people have told me I look like my dad. Plus, I'm a junior, meaning I not only share the look and mannerisms of my father, but also his name. Disney Junior Play and Dance is a show definitely geared towards kids, showcasing their favorite characters from the TV shows found on the Disney channel. This show opened in 2001 at Hollywood Studios and has gone through several refurbishments and name changes over the years. There have been similar shows at California's Disneyland as well as Disneyland in Paris.

I haven't seen this show in years as my boys are now grown, but I remember sitting in the back with the other parents on many occasions when they were young. That mental image is a reminder of how parents will sit through anything, especially at Disney, to bring happiness to their children. In 2 Timothy 1, Paul commends not only Timothy, but his grandmother and mother from which he received His example and faith. While not all parent relationships are perfect, many of us would admit our beliefs and most of who we are came from our parents. I'm happy to be a junior as I admire my parents who endowed me with a solid, spiritual foundation and demonstrated how to live a proper, Godly life. Parents are another significant blessing from God to aid us in knowing how to navigate through life and its challenges. Ephesians 6 instructs us to obey and honor our parents, which is also one of the Ten Commandments. Take time today, and routinely, to follow that command. If you're still blessed with your parents, tell them how much you appreciate all they sacrificed for you. If they have passed, reflect on the gifts and words they left behind and honor their memory by passing those on to others.

PRAYER—Dear Lord, thank You for the gift of parents. Help me to honor them often either with words or by demonstrating the good lessons they taught me. In the name of Jesus, Amen.

TODAY I WILL... honor my parents, either personally or through reflection of their memory.

JULY 28 **Read I JOHN 1:5-8**

FOLLOW THE LIGHT

Disney Shows – World of Color

"The people who walked in darkness have seen a great light; those who dwelt in a land of deep darkness, on them has light shone."
—Isaiah 9:2

My wife recently got a call from a friend who told her there was a rainbow around the sun. We both jumped up, ran outside and looked up, only to be immediately blinded. We had forgotten to put on sunglasses which later allowed us to indeed see a gorgeous rainbow, perfectly encircling the sun. The beautiful colors along with the bright light reminded me of today's spectacular nighttime show. World of Color takes place at Disney California Adventure on the Paradise Bay Lagoon. It includes 1200 fountains along with multiple lights and lasers bathed in color. The show premiered in 2011 after 15 months of construction and a cost of $75 million. It has seen several changes and alternate versions since, sometimes coinciding with the various holidays.

As you know, and as I should've remembered, the sun is extremely bright and powerful. Not only does it immerse our world in light, but it regulates the proper temperature we need to survive, helps all things grow and provides some of the most beautiful scenery we can imagine including rainbows, sunsets and the magnificent colors of our ever-changing sky. I John 1 tells us God is also light and we are to walk in it to avoid the darkness of sin. The power of God's light brings us out of the darkness and cleanses our sin through the shed blood of Jesus Christ. Don't forget the story of Saul in Acts 9, a prime example of one being brought out of the darkness of sin. He had spent his life performing horrible acts including the murder of numerous Christians. But once he saw that bright light of God while traveling the road, he repented and became Paul, one of the greatest teachers of the Gospel in history. We too can be changed by seeing the light of God. If you catch this fantastic show at Disneyland, let the bright lights and constant colors remind you of the power and beauty of God. His light changes us and leads us out of darkness so that we can one day see His light in person.

PRAYER—Lord, I'm grateful for the physical light of the sun, but also the fact that You are my light, rescuing me from sin and providing the way to be with You eternally. In Christ, Amen.

TODAY I WILL...go outside and enjoy the sunshine while reflecting on the light of God.

JULY 29 **Read HEBREWS 10:19-25**

PURE HARMONY WITH ALL

Disney Shows – Harmonius

"May the God of endurance and encouragement grant you to live in such harmony with one another, in accord with Christ Jesus."
—Romans 15:5

Pure Harmony. Four of my high school chorus friends and I decided that would be our name about 10 minutes before our debut performance in the school's talent show. Afterwards, we kept it going and ended up performing a few times at various venues. We weren't the best a capella group ever, but we tried to harmonize our voices and entertain those who would graciously listen. Harmonius is scheduled to open on WDW's 50th birthday, October 1, 2021 as Epcot's newest nighttime show. Therefore it should be open when you read this, but not as I'm writing. The Disney website describes it as "fireworks, fountains, magnificent lighting, visual effects and multimedia magic" that will "send your spirit soaring." It also claims the audience will be transported around the globe as favorite Disney tunes will be reimagined in over a dozen languages by a diverse ensemble of over 200 musical artists. It's clear based on the name and description the goal will be to "harmonize" and bring people together from around the world.

While creating harmony through music and the collaboration of cultures is both enjoyable and valuable, the concept is also important spiritually. In Hebrews, we're told to "stir up one another to love and good works" through meeting together and encouragement. The verse above advises us to live in harmony with others while Psalm 34:3 urges us to exalt the Lord's name together. Psalm 133:1 adds that it's good when we dwell in unity. Clearly God desires that we live in harmony, meet regularly and come together in unity to praise His name and build each other up. Learning about and uniting cultures in harmony has always been a goal of Epcot, but make sure your goal is to learn about your Christian family and how you can best help and encourage them. Live in harmony with all, attend church regularly and work hard to establish unity while there.

PRAYER—Heavenly Father, I want to live in harmony with others. Help me to be kind, patient and generous towards all people, especially those who need encouragement. Help me to also bring more unity to Your church through my service. In Jesus' blessed name, Amen.

TODAY I WILL...encourage at least five individuals with kind words or physical service.

JULY 30 **Read MATTHEW 4:1-11**

IT'S YOUR DECISION

Disney Shows – Fantasmic

"Submit yourselves therefore to God. Resist the devil, and he will flee from you."
—James 4:7

Decisions. They are a privilege but can also be scary as they are yours and yours alone to make. Nobody can make them for you. I was always told and agree that the 3 most important decisions you'll ever make are to follow Christ, your spouse and your job. In that order. But life is full of decisions, some very significant, that we must make on our own. The verse above states that one of those important decisions involves the devil and the choice to resist his evil. Fantasmic, my favorite of all Disney shows, began in 1992 at Disneyland in the Rivers of America surrounding Tom Sawyer Island. In 1998, the WDW version opened in the newly built Hollywood Hills Amphitheater at HS, which contains 6900 seats and room for 3000 additional standing guests. The two versions vary slightly in length and characters, but generally contain the same story. There was also a version in Tokyo's Disneyland, but it closed for good in early 2020.

I love everything about this show: the numerous characters and film scenes shown, the music you can't help but hum for the rest of the night and especially the ending with a nostalgic nod to the black and white Steamboat Willie who started it all. Near the climactic ending, the evil Maleficent is threatening to destroy Mickey once and for all. He then realizes it's all his imagination and shouts, "This is my dream," understanding it's ultimately his decision what happens. Dealing with the evil of Satan is not in our imagination, but it's similar in that we get to decide how our story will end. In Matthew 4, we read of Jesus tempted by Satan. Even though He was hungry and weary, He made the decision three times to resist Satan's tricks. We will also have to make that decision for ourselves many times. It's your life, your dreams, your goals and your eternity that will ultimately be affected by what you choose. What will you do when Satan comes after you? Only you can make that decision. I pray you make the right one.

PRAYER—Lord, thank You for giving me the ability to make decisions. I pray I make the right ones. Help me to firmly and boldly decide to resist the devil no matter what. In Him, Amen.

TODAY I WILL...make the decision once and for all not to let Satan affect my eternity.

JULY 31 **Read MATTHEW 16:24-28**

THE END

Disney Shows – Enchantment

"And these will go away into eternal punishment, but the righteous into eternal life."
—Matthew 25:46

The End. How many times have you seen, heard or even experienced those words? I think about significant events in my life that have ended. The last day of high school. My last night sleeping in my childhood home. Leaving my classroom the final time when my teaching career ended. As we go through life, we often experience "ends," and sometimes we don't even realize the significance of that final moment until it is gone. As we say "the end" to July, we finish with a very special show. Disney's Enchantment debuted in 2021 replacing Happily Ever After as the nighttime show that ends each day at WDW's Magic Kingdom. It consists of fireworks, multiple classic movie themes and incredible character and scene projections on Cinderella Castle.

Thankfully, this show still ends with a popular element and crowd favorite held over from previous shows as the illuminated Tinkerbell soars overhead. In the previous show, just before she flew from atop the castle, we heard these words, "And so our journey comes to an end. But yours continues on." All Disney stories end, typically with a happy conclusion and moral lesson learned. One day, Disney itself will come to an end as will each of us. But unlike everything of this world, a part of us will never die. At the end of Matthew 16, Jesus reminds us that He will one day return with His angels to collect the souls of those who have given their lives for Him. He teaches the importance of keeping our souls free and clear from the evils of the world. In the verse above, He confirms that those who are righteous and follow His commands will go on to eternal life with Him. They will never have "the end." As you continue to experience "the ends" in your life, never forget the one thing you have that won't. Make sure you have accepted Christ and don't sacrifice your soul for the temporary pleasures of the world. Ensure that the end of your earthly life is only "the beginning" of eternal salvation for your everlasting soul.

PRAYER—Lord, I want nothing more than to one day experience the beginning of my soul with You forever. Help me resist anything worldly that puts my soul in danger. In Christ, Amen.

TODAY I WILL...make sure the end of my earthly life will be the beginning of my eternal one.

AUGUST THEME

DISNEY CHARACTERS

AUGUST 1 **Read GENESIS 1:1-10**

THE BEGINNING

Disney Characters – Mickey Mouse

"I am the Alpha and the Omega, the first and the last, the beginning and the end."
—Revelation 22:13

A few weeks after our marriage, my wife and I were excited to sit down and watch our wedding video. As the video ended in a photo montage, the final words shown were "The Beginning." We thought it was a beautiful way to end our video as instead of "The End," it was recognizing the beginning of our life together. Yesterday, we talked about "The End." But what about the beginning? This month's theme is Disney characters, and I figured what better place to start than at the beginning. As mentioned, one of Walt Disney's most famous quotes was, "I only hope that we never lose sight of one thing, that it was all started by a mouse." Mickey Mouse was born November 18, 1928 and was Walt's pride and joy, starring in over 120 theatrical shorts and giving rise to the Disney name. He was one of the first talking cartoons in history and his first words were "Hot Dog," a phrase he still utters and even sings in a popular tune to this day.

So let me ask what I hope is an easy Bible trivia question. What are the first three words of the Bible? Genesis 1:1 is a verse that most can recite as it's typically taught pretty early in Sunday School. "In the beginning, God created the Heavens and the Earth." In that first verse and the next nine following, we read what God did "in the beginning." He simply spoke the world into existence with his awesome power. We know from the verse above that God was not only there at the beginning, He IS the beginning. Disney may have been started by a mouse, but everything we see and know was started by our God. He has always been and will always be, the first and the last, the Alpha and the Omega. As we begin a new month today, let us never forget who began it all. Let us recognize His power, authority and the fact that in the beginning, He spoke our world into creation. He was there when the world began, and He will be there when it ends and we begin our eternity with Him. What an awesome and mighty God we serve!

PRAYER—Almighty Father, I am in awe of Your authority and power used to speak this Earth into existence. I praise Your name and vow to serve You always. In the name of Jesus, Amen.

TODAY I WILL...fear, recognize and respect the power of God and praise Him for it.

AUGUST 2 **Read GENESIS 22:1-14**

SACRIFICE

Disney Characters – Bing-Bong

"I will offer to you the sacrifice of thanksgiving and call on the name of the Lord."
—Psalm 116:17

"Umm, Dad? We have the fire and the wood, but where is the sacrifice?" How would you respond to his question, knowing that the sacrifice was the one speaking to you and your son? When it comes to sacrifice, there are some Bible characters and a few Disney ones that come to mind. Remember Bing-Bong, Riley's imaginary friend in *Inside Out* found drifting and nearly forgotten in her long-term memory? He and Joy, one of Riley's emotions, are eventually trapped in her memory dump. They try to escape but can't quite make it until he sacrifices himself to save Joy, only to be lost from Riley's memory forever. Actor Richard Kind, who voiced Bing Bong, admitted to crying while speaking his final and one of the film's most quoted lines, "Take her to the moon for me." The scene also brought the cast and crew to tears during the recording.

What do Moses, Ruth, Mary and Jesus all have in common? Sacrifice. Moses gave much of his life to lead the people to the promised land. Ruth gave hers to care for her mother-in-law. Mary agreed to raise the Son of God. I don't think I need to explain the sacrifice of Jesus. And then there's Abraham. In Genesis 22, God asks him to sacrifice his son as a test of faith. When asked on the way about the sacrifice by his son, Abraham simply says, "God will provide." Can you imagine the pain, sadness and fear he was in when answering that question? Thankfully, God did provide, and the boy was saved, but Abraham was willing to give his son out of his devout faith and love for the Father. That same Father was not only willing, but actually gave His only Son to die out of His love for us. So it's a simple question today...what are you willing to sacrifice for God? What will you give up to return just a portion of His love? What can you sacrifice today, right now, to demonstrate your faith? Are you prepared to give Him your life?

PRAYER—Lord, thank You for the sacrifice of Your Son and the example of so many others like Abraham showing their devout faith in You. Help me to give You the same and be prepared to sacrifice whatever needed, including my life, for You. In the name of Jesus, Amen.

TODAY I WILL...sacrifice by giving up something right now that is separating me from God.

AUGUST 3 **Read 2 TIMOTHY 4:5-8**

ONE STEP AT A TIME

Disney Characters – Jaq and Gus

"But you, take courage! Do not let your hands be weak, for your work shall be rewarded."
—2 Chronicles 15:7

2,071 steps! Straight up. Without stopping. Think you could do it? Every year, that's how many are climbed to commemorate the firefighters who perished doing the same on 9/11. Have you ever climbed that many stairs at once? I've climbed a lighthouse or two and a bunch of steps inside the Egyptian pyramid, but never that many at once. Today's characters may not be as familiar, but they also ascended many steps to save one of our favorite Disney princesses. Jaq and Gus are the two main mice that helped Cinderella in her quest to try on the glass slipper. Both of these fast-talking, clumsy but hilarious mice were voiced by James MacDonald who also happened to voice Mickey Mouse and Pluto at the time of *Cinderella*'s release.

Near the end of this film, Cinderella is locked in her room, atop many flights of stairs so she won't be able to try on the slipper. Jaq and Gus manage to steal the key but then must climb what looks like about 2,071 steps to get it to Cinderella. While they initially gasp and hesitate at the sight of all those stairs, they persevere and work together to get her the key just in time. In 2 Timothy 4, Paul offers words of encouragement, telling us to work hard to endure suffering and fulfill our ministry. In verse 7, he gives one of his well-known quotes when he says, "I have fought the good fight. I have finished the race. I have kept the faith." The "race" he's referring to was definitely a marathon and not a sprint for Paul, having to endure numerous trials. Our race of faith will also be a lengthy one, way more than 2,071 steps. Like those determined mice, we can't focus on the entire staircase. We must face life one step at a time, clinging to God with each and knowing the importance of our end goal. If you become overwhelmed, remember the words above. Take courage! Your work will be rewarded. Keep climbing! You will eventually reach the top where God is waiting, and it will definitely be worth every single step!

PRAYER—Lord, please give me courage, strength and endurance to keep climbing towards You. Help me, like Paul, to keep the faith, fight the fight and finish the race. In Christ, Amen.

TODAY I WILL...keep climbing, one step at a time, focusing on my goal at the top.

AUGUST 4 **Read LUKE 10:25-37**

LIKE A GOOD NEIGHBOR

Disney Characters – Thomas O'Malley

"Let no one seek his own good, but the good of his neighbor."
—I Corinthians 10:24

I loved my neighborhood growing up as I lived on a street with kids of all ages. We would explore, have holiday parties and just hang out and play together. Who is your neighbor? Jesus was asked that very question when He told the crowd to "love your neighbor as yourself." Was He talking about those in your neighborhood? I think you know He meant more than that. Wanting to make sure they understood, Jesus told one of his most famous parables, the story of a Jewish man, beaten and robbed and then helped by a Samaritan instead of a priest and Levite who both passed him by. The people hearing this story would've been astonished, expecting both to help, and even more surprised that the Samaritan, then enemies of the Jews, was the one to give aid. Jesus was trying to teach that our neighbor includes all people, even our enemies. Everyone deserves our love and to know they are loved by the One who created them.

Did you know Thomas O'Malley when you saw today's subject? In 1970's *The Aristocats*, O'Malley is a wandering, alley cat who become the unlikely hero for the rich and prestigious Duchess and her three kittens. This film was based on an actual set of cats from the early 1900's that also inherited a huge fortune. Phil Harris not only voiced O'Malley, but also Baloo in *The Jungle Book*. Originally, he was going to be a striped cat, but animating stripes proved too difficult. Similar to the Jews and the Samaritans, a free-range, alley cat wouldn't normally associate or especially assist an elite group of "aristocats," but O'Malley wanted to make sure this lost mother and her kittens made it back home. Jesus taught us to help anyone and everyone, even those we might consider enemies, to make it back home as well. God desires that all people know Him, and it's our job to help them do that. Be a neighbor to all like O'Malley. Offer your assistance, especially to those beaten down by the world, and help them make it home.

PRAYER—Dear Lord, help me to love everyone as a neighbor. Give me the determination and courage to reach out to those in need, especially those different from me. Through Christ, Amen.

TODAY I WILL...love everyone as neighbors and not pass anyone by who is in need.

AUGUST 5 **Read JAMES 1:19-21**

TAME YOUR TEMPER

Disney Characters – Donald Duck

"Be angry and do not sin; do not let the sun go down on your anger and give no opportunity to the devil."
—Ephesians 4:26-27

Who would you say is Disney's angriest character? Certainly Anger himself (*Inside Out*) and Beast come to mind as well as many of the famed villains like Hades, Cruella, Jafar, Ursula, Scar and of course Maleficent. What about my personal favorite character, Donald Duck? Did he cross your mind? If you type "Disney's angriest character" into Google, Donald often makes the list. Donald Duck's birthday is generally accepted as June 9, 1934, the release date of his first cartoon, "The Wise Little Hen," even though he stated it as March 13 in another. Like his counterpart and often-rival, Mickey Mouse, Donald received a star on Hollywood's Walk of Fame. He's actually appeared in more short films than any other Disney character, even Mickey.

If you've ever seen a Donald Duck cartoon, you know he no doubt has a temper, easily set off by anything not going his way. It usually provides some quality humor which is maybe why I like old Donald so much. There's nothing wrong with anger if it's warranted and controlled. Remember when Jesus entered the temple and found it overtaken by the buying and selling of goods? He was quite angry and displayed it, but again, that was justified as the house of worship had become a marketplace. But anger can also be unnecessary and out of control which can lead to sin. In James 1, we're told to be slow to anger and warned that displaying unnecessary anger leads to unrighteousness with God. The above verse adds we shouldn't go to bed angry because it gives Satan an opportunity to lead us into sin. It's not always easy to avoid anger, especially when things go unexpectedly, or we are wronged in some way. If that happens, work hard to remember your goals as you strive for righteousness. Take a breath, pause and determine if your anger will accomplish anything positive. Avoid displaying a temper and influencing others negatively. Donald could probably take a lesson from these verses, and we should as well.

PRAYER—Father God, help me to avoid needless anger. Give me the willpower to think before I act on my anger so that Satan doesn't use it as an opportunity. In His Name, Amen.

TODAY I WILL...list the things that make me most angry and turn them over to God.

AUGUST 6 **Read NUMBERS 11:1-10**

AVOID THE DONKEY

Disney Characters – Eeyore

"Do all things without grumbling or disputing..."'
—Philippians 2:14

You may have heard the story. Little boy in his backyard with a baseball and bat. He shouts, "I'm the greatest hitter in the world!" before throwing the ball straight up and taking a big swing, only to miss completely. "Strike one," he sighs. He repeats the process twice more, shouting the same each time and admitting, "strike three" as the ball falls to the ground a third time. After a short pause, a huge smile begins to grow as he exclaims loud and proud, "I'm the greatest *pitcher* in the world!" It's a great lesson on optimism. There's a great YouTube version if you type "baseball optimism." Kenny Rogers even wrote a song about it called "The Greatest." There are many optimistic and cheerful Disney characters, but one stands out when speaking of the opposite. Eeyore is the very definition of a pessimist, often portrayed as gloomy, depressed and expecting the worst. He of course originated in A.A. Milne's Winnie the Pooh books, but the Disney version was first shown in a 1966 short entitled "Winnie the Pooh and the Honey Tree." He was most recently seen in the 2018 sequel, *Ralph Breaks the Internet.*

Is the glass half full or half empty? That's the classic question to determine whether one tends to be optimistic or is, to put it frankly, an Eeyore. Pessimistic folks tend to expect things to go wrong and are often vocal about it. In Numbers 11, the Israelites do a fair share of complaining as they constantly grumble both to Moses and God. They seem to forget God has been providing and protecting them all along. Philippians 2 tells us to do all things without grumbling or disputing, some versions even using the word "complaining." Focusing on the negative, complaining or leading a life of pessimism goes against God and can also discourage others. Try to always see the positive and look for the good instead of what might go wrong. In short, don't be an Eeyore. He may be cute, but his outlook on life isn't doing anyone any favors.

PRAYER—Lord, help me to realize when I'm negative, knowing that complaining does little to improve any situation. Help me to instead see the good in all situations. In Jesus I pray, Amen.

TODAY I WILL...avoid pessimism, choosing instead to focus on the positive side of things.

AUGUST 7 **Read GENESIS 18:22-33**

A DETERMINED DRAGON

Disney Characters – Elliott

"As for you, brothers, do not grow weary in doing good."
—2 Thessalonians 3:13

He knew it was coming...the city was about to be destroyed. But his nephew was there! So he begged. Please don't destroy the innocent. He even resorted to bargaining. What about 50? If there are just 50 righteous people, can you please spare it? Yes. But maybe that was too much. Can we make it 45? Ok. What about 40? 30? 20? 10? Six times he negotiated. And six times he got a yes. He refused to give up on saving the good. Today's character also refused to give up on one who was good, an innocent boy receiving destructive treatment. *Pete's Dragon*, as previously mentioned, is my favorite Disney movie. Today we focus on the dragon himself. During early planning of this 1977 film, the dragon wasn't going to be seen at all. But some lobbying from the animation department got him 22 minutes of screen time. Animators decided to make him look more like an oriental dragon since they are typically associated with good.

In this classic story, Elliott the dragon refuses to give up on Pete, knowing he can't leave the boy until the threat of danger is gone. He must make sure he is safe and in a good home. Likewise, it's our job to help save others from Satan and sin by staying with them until they find their way home through salvation in our Savior. Genesis 18 tells the story of Abraham doing the same, trying desperately to save his nephew, Lot, from destruction. He begs God, bargaining down to just 10 righteous people needed to save the whole city. And while the city does get destroyed, Lot is spared because of Abraham's persistence. Abraham didn't give up on saving Lot. Elliott didn't give up on saving Pete. We can't give up or grow weary of doing the good needed to save others. It can be discouraging when they are unreceptive or stubborn, but don't quit. Without you, they may too meet destruction by losing their soul to the evils of the world. So keep trying! Ask God for help and strength, but never give up on a soul in need of saving!

PRAYER—Dear Lord, thank You for never giving up on me. Give me strength to do the same with others. Help me find the persistence and determination to always keep trying. Amen.

TODAY I WILL...return to helping any souls I gave up on and vow to always keep trying.

AUGUST 8 **Read I SAMUEL 18:1-5**

A FRIEND TO THE END

Disney Characters – Tod and Copper

"Greater love has no one than this, that someone lay down his life for his friends."
—John 15:13

Tom and Huck. Calvin and Hobbs. Harry and Ron. The March Sisters. Holmes and Watson. Frodo and Sam. Charlotte and Wilbur. Do you recognize those famous literary best friends? I forgot Archie and Jughead. Do they count? Scooby and Shaggy? Ok, now I'm pushing it. What about Tod and Copper? They are two unlikely best friends from a 1967 novel called *The Fox and the Hound*, which Disney subsequently crafted into another timeless tale. This 1981 film of the same name was their 24th animated feature, but first to include CGI graphics. It also included some notable voices including Mickey Rooney, Sandy Duncan, Kurt Russell, Corey Feldman and even Jack Albertson in his last theatrical role as he died four months after the film's release. You may remember him as Grandpa Joe in *Willy Wonka and the Chocolate Factory.*

Tod is a wild, red fox while Copper is a domesticated, hound dog. Social cues and even their own instincts encourage them to be enemies, and they struggle to maintain a lifelong friendship. In the climactic ending, they realize how much they care for one another with one even putting his own life on the line to save the other. I failed to mention one more famous friendship. David and Jonathan had a very real and exemplary friendship in the Bible. I Samuel 18 shows just how close they were saying their souls were connected in covenant to one another. They too shared a strong bond that outlasted many struggles and pressures from outside forces as they were also willing to put their lives on the line in protection of the other. In the verse above, Jesus Himself said that's what true friendship is, being willing to lay down one's life out of love for another. Do you have friends like that? Would you give your life to save theirs, either physically or spiritually? Isn't that exactly what Jesus did for us? Be a friend to those around you. Better yet, look for someone in need of a friend to help save their spiritual life, and be that person.

PRAYER—Dear God, thanks for the gift of friendship and the bonds I share with those in my life. Help me to be a friend to those in need, seeking out ways to best help them. In Him, Amen.

TODAY I WILL...be a friend to as many as possible, especially those in desperate need of one.

AUGUST 9 **Read MARK 10:13-16**

BE MORE CHILDISH

Disney Characters – Oliver

"All your children shall be taught by the Lord, and great shall be the peace of your children."
—Isaiah 54:13

He was so sweet, cuddly and playful. And then he grew up. When we first got Boots, our family cat, he was the cutest, most loving little thing, and we adored holding and snuggling with him...until what seemed like a week later when he turned into a grouchy, independent and downright ornery adult. There was another lovable kitten who happens to be the star of Disney's 1988 film, *Oliver and Company.* Loosely based on the Charles Dickens' novel, *Oliver Twist*, this is a story of an innocent cat getting mixed up with a rag-tag, collection of canines. This fun, adventure flick featured some incredible music performed by Billy Joel, Bette Midler and Huey Lewis with one even written by Barry Manilow. Joel and Midler even voiced a couple of dogs in the film. In fact, this is the only film Billy Joel has ever acted in without playing himself. This was also the first Disney film that lyricist, Howard Ashman wrote a song for. He would of course go on to provide lyrics for some of Disney's greatest and most beloved melodies.

Though Oliver at first is completely naïve to the schemes and dangers around him, he's quickly introduced to the world by his new pack of puppy pals. Regardless, he tries his best to remain pure, not wanting to harm a soul and only wishing good things for all. Two questions from our Mark 13 reading today. Why did Jesus call the children to him? And why did He say we must receive God's kingdom like a child? Jesus loved (the little) children. He knew that, like Oliver, children are innocent, have no ill-intent and want only to please those around them. They also have an inherited, reverent fear of authority which is how we should all approach the throne of God. In short, we are to be like children because they are intrinsically good. They get along with others, desire to please, show kindness and haven't yet been negatively affected by the temptations of the world. We can all learn a lesson from the innocence and purity of a child.

PRAYER—Help me Lord to be more child-like in my fear and respect of Your authority. Give me success as I seek purity and innocence in Your sight. Through the name of Christ, Amen.

TODAY I WILL...try to see God through a child's eyes, treating Him with awe and respect.

AUGUST 10 **Read ACTS 9:36-43**

FINDING IT BY GIVING IT

Disney Characters – Minnie Mouse

"A joyful heart is good medicine..."
—Proverbs 17:22

Think about this...what in life fills you with the most happiness? Some of my answers: my relationship with God and eternal future, my family, being home, naps, traveling, Disney (shocking), music, finishing a task, leading a group and compliments. Do any of those match yours? Let me add one more...giving to others. Does that make you happy? Like her counterpart, Minnie Mouse was also created in 1928 and appeared with Mickey in "Steamboat Willie," considered to be their debut. They had actually both appeared in "Plane Crazy" earlier that year, but it was both silent and undistributed. In honor of her 90th anniversary, she recently got her star on Hollywood's Walk of Fame. In 2018, she joined five other characters (Mickey, Donald, Winnie the Pooh, Snow White and Tinkerbell) who share the honor. Her cat, Figaro, originated in the film, *Pinocchio*. Apparently, Walt loved him so much, he gave her to Minnie.

Minnie Mouse is typically shown as a cheerful and loving character. She tends to see the good in things and spreads joy to others through her vibrant spirit and sunny personality. Beginning in Acts 9:36, we meet a rarely discussed disciple of Christ named Tabitha or Dorcas. There is not much said about her, but verse 36 notes she was "full of good works and acts of charity." She was obviously a giving person who helped many because when she becomes ill and dies, many are there to mourn her. It also says many believed in God once Peter raises her from the dead. 2 Corinthians 9:7 says that God loves a cheerful giver. Typically, this verse is used for giving money back to God, but I would argue that God loves any type of charity done in joy. The verse above puts it simply saying a joyful heart is good medicine. Any happiness is good for our heart and soul, and the best way to find joy is by giving to others to bring gladness to their life. So be a Minnie. Be a Tabitha or Dorcas. Just be a cheerful giver and bring joy to others!

PRAYER—Lord, I want to be like your disciple, Tabitha and give to others. Help me to do so with joy and cheerfulness so that others may find the same through my good works. Amen.

TODAY I WILL...bring joy to just one person by giving of my time or resources.

AUGUST 11 **Read MATTHEW 23:1-12**

SERVICE OVER SELF

Disney Characters – Gaston

"Do nothing from selfish ambition or conceit, but in humility count others more significant than yourselves."
—Philippians 2:3

Who is your favorite Disney villain? Are there any you secretly like? I would say most have zero redeeming qualities, but there are also a few found intriguing, humorous and even likable at times. Gaston is certainly one of those, especially at park meet and greets. Check out the funny YouTube clip where a little girl has a verbal war with Gaston while at the parks. Gaston is an original character created by Disney. He is not present in the fairy tale on which 1991's *Beauty and the Beast* is based. Did you know that during the climactic fight scene near the end, there are skeletons shown very briefly in Gaston's eyes as he falls from the castle? These were placed to give an obvious answer to the question of if he survived the fall or not. R.I.P. Gaston!

Most of Gaston's "likeability" comes in the way of his over-the-top and dramatic arrogance and egotism. He's the very definition of overconfidence and lover of self, qualities we are warned against in Scripture. In Matthew 23, Jesus once again rebukes the Pharisees for hypocrisy, laziness and especially conceit and pride. He tells them He knows of their desire to be known and recognized by wearing fancy clothing and choosing seats of honor when possible. He ends this passage with the famous phrase, "whoever exalts himself will be humbled, and whoever humbles himself will be exalted," even saying that a servant is actually the greatest among them. We too sometimes fall into Satan's trap of selfishness and arrogance, forgetting to portray humbleness and display servanthood as Christ did. Don't forget the words above from Philippians. Work hard to put others before yourself. Gaston may be a villain you love to hate (or hate to love) with his humorous ego, but he's certainly not one to imitate. Display humility by thinking before you speak or act and by looking for ways to serve others over self. Above all, humble yourself before others and God so you can look forward to Him exalting you one day.

PRAYER—Father, I don't want to display any type of arrogance or conceit in speech or actions. Help me to instead be a servant to others and display the humility of Jesus. In His name, Amen.

TODAY I WILL...choose service over self-promotion, showing humility in all I do and say.

AUGUST 12 **Read RUTH 1:1-18**

A SELFLESS STREET-RAT

Disney Characters – Aladdin

"As each has received a gift, use it to serve one another, as good stewards of God's varied grace..."
—*I Peter 4:10*

Several years ago, I had a bicycle accident. I turned a corner, hit some loose gravel and went down hard, causing a substantial and bloody gash on my knee. I couldn't keep going without some medical attention, but I had no phone and was over a mile from home. I then noticed a man nearby in his garage and hobbled over. I'll never forget his response to my simple question. I'll finish that story shortly, but today we focus on Aladdin, subject of the 1992 smash hit. He was voiced by Scott Weinger, of *Full House* fame, although another actor did his singing. When the character was being developed, actor Michael J. Fox was used as a visual, but it was soon thought he wouldn't be appealing enough and so Tom Cruise was used instead. Rapper M.C. Hammer's baggy pants were also used as inspiration for Aladdin's famous "street-rat" attire.

Though Aladdin is shown to be intrinsically compassionate in the beginning, helping the hungry and saving the princess, he also learns great lessons along the way in humility and putting others first. In the end, not only does he admit who he truly is and risk his life to save the kingdom, but he also fulfills a promise using his final wish to free the genie. Quite the opposite of yesterday's Gaston, being a humble servant and unselfish giver should be a goal for all of us. Ruth is a wonderful, Biblical example, dedicating her life to serving her mother-in-law even though she had no real obligation after losing her husband. Back to my story...in addition to my request, the kind stranger helped completely bandage my wound and then insisted on driving me (and my bicycle!) back to my house. All I asked for was a tissue, but he went above and beyond, dedicating his time, service and resources to someone in need. Aladdin, Ruth, the kind stranger...all great examples we should strive towards. Don't forget to always show J.O.Y. in life...Jesus, Others, Yourself. In that order!

PRAYER—Dear God, help me to be a selfless person, always striving to put others first and looking for ways I can serve their needs with the gifts You've provided. Through Jesus, Amen.

TODAY I WILL...do at least one selfless act to help someone in need.

AUGUST 13 **Read MATTHEW 27:27-54**

ETERNALLY GRATEFUL

Disney Characters – Aliens

"But he was pierced for our transgressions; he was crushed for our iniquities...and with his wounds we are healed."
—Isaiah 53:5

Do you know who said these famous catchphrases? (Answers at the end.) 1."And that's the way it is." 2. "Live long and prosper." 3. "Well isn't that special." 4. "Did I do that?" 5. "Here's Johnny!" We all know certain TV and movie characters who have well-known catchphrases. Today's character, which is actually three, also have a pretty famous catchphrase. The aliens or "little green men," first seen in *Toy Story* as a single, minor character, have become important and beloved part of the whole franchise, even saving the life of the whole gang in *Toy Story 3* as mentioned in a prior devotional. The three were actually part of the 2016 Oscars assisting Buzz and Woody in presenting the Best Animated Film award to *Inside Out*.

These tiny extra-terrestrials actually have several catchphrases throughout the series including: "Oooohhhhh" and "The claw!" However, I'd like to focus on another they are known for, particularly from *Toy Story 2*. "You have saved our lives. We are eternally grateful!" is a line they repeat over and over throughout the film. Read that line again and I'm guessing you can figure out the focus of today's message. In Matthew 27 and in each of the four Gospels, we read about the pain and agony Jesus went through on that cross for each of us. The Old Testament book of Isaiah, shown above, even prophesied what He would go through as the propitiation for our sin. Do you know the word propitiation? What about atonement? Both words basically mean that He provided retribution or took on the punishment for our sin. As it says above, by His wounds, we have been healed. Because of the terrible things He suffered, our sin has been taken away so that we have hope of eternal life with God. Therefore, we can and must say to Jesus daily, "You have saved our lives. We are eternally grateful!" (Answers to catchphrases: 1. Walter Cronkite, 2. Dr. Spock, 3. SNL's church lady, 4. Steve Urkel, 5. Ed McMahon)

PRAYER—Lord God, I am eternally grateful for saving me from eternal death and providing Your only Son to atone for my numerous sins. What an incredible, matchless sacrifice! Amen.

TODAY I WILL...thank God and His Son for saving me and providing me with eternal hope.

AUGUST 14 **Read JUDE 1:17-23**

SAVE A LIFE

Disney Characters – Tramp

"...let him know that whoever brings back a sinner from his wandering will save his soul from death and will cover a multitude of sins."
—James 5:20

I've always enjoyed working with children, teaching them at school, training them at church and even treating them medically. As a paramedic, kids are my favorite patients. They are typically easier to work with than adults because they will tell you exactly what's wrong or where it hurts. It's satisfying to help a child, but have I ever saved one's life? Today's character did. In fact, he risked his own life to save a child from a lurking evil. Tramp, of *Lady and the Tramp*, is a stray mutt that becomes friends with a prestigious, Cocker Spaniel named Lady. They have their ups and downs, but eventually discover genuine care for each other. Their iconic and romantic spaghetti scene has become movie lore to the point where to "lady and the tramp it" describes the act of two people sharing food from opposite ends. Did you know the town in this film's setting is visually inspired by Walt's hometown of Marceline, Missouri? This was done at his request.

There's one pivotal scene where Tramp saves a baby from a dangerous rat, prowling near the crib. Despite risking his life and even being blamed for the ruckus, he knows it's worth it to save the child from danger. In Jude 1, we are again warned of danger in the world and advised to save others from it by "snatching them out of the fire." Like that rat, Satan prowls about, waiting to pounce. It's certainly admirable to literally save a life. But it's even more important to save one spiritually. So back to my question...have I ever saved a child's life? Not literally that I can recall. But I've certainly tried to help save them spiritually. I've taught them the Bible. I've delivered lessons and talked to some individually. I've written this and other books to inspire families and children to find Jesus and learn about God. It's our job to help save lives from Satan's worldly dominion. The verse above reminds us when we do, we save their soul from death and cover their sins. So be on the lookout and save a life! It's certainly worth any risk.

PRAYER—Lord, help me to do my part to save the lives of those who have fallen prey to the traps of the devil. Lead me to a soul today that I can assist in saving. In Jesus' name, Amen.

TODAY I WILL...work to save the life of a child (or anyone) being influenced by the world.

AUGUST 15 **Read JOHN 5:1-17**

DON'T JUST WATCH

Disney Characters – Laverne

"For the Son of man came to seek and save the lost."
—Luke 19:10

Do you like to people-watch? It's often fascinating to just sit at a crowded location and watch people with their differing mannerisms and appearances. Airports, malls and even theme parks such as Disney are typically good places to conduct this activity that some even consider an established hobby. You may not recognize today's character at first glance. Do you remember Laverne? She was one of three gargoyle friends that Quasimodo had in *The Hunchback of Notre Dame* as he also people-watched from high up in his Cathedral. Laverne was voiced by veteran actress, Mary Wickes, who you may remember as one of the older nuns from the *Sister Act* films. She actually passed away during production of this film, so another actress had to step in and finish recording her lines. Originally, Laverne was going to be voiced by singer, Cyndi Lauper, but the directors deemed her voice too youthful to be believable as a wise advisor.

We are focusing on Laverne because of a statement she makes trying to convince Quasimodo to attend the town festival instead of just watching from above as usual. She tells him, "If watching is all you're going to do, then you're going to watch your life go by without ya!" It's easy for us to fall into laziness and get caught up in doing too much watchin' and not enough doin'. In John 5, we read about Jesus healing a lame man on the Sabbath. When questioned about it, He says, "My Father is working until now, and I am working." Jesus was often chastised for doing work on the Sabbath, but He always made clear that Godly work and Christ-like service were appropriate anytime. Christ didn't come to sit and people-watch. In fact, Luke said above He came to seek and save the lost, setting an example of how to actively serve. If we just sit back and watch, we may lose the chance to help a soul in need. Choose to be active. Find a way out of any laziness so you can follow Christ in seeking and saving those who are lost.

PRAYER—God, grant me the motivation and energy to actively seek out those who are lost and need to know of Your love and promise. Keep me from laziness. In Christ's name, Amen.

TODAY I WILL...choose to be physically active as I serve God and seek out those in need.

AUGUST 16 **Read MATTHEW 3:13-17**

SAVED BY WATER

Disney Characters – Fish Out of Water

"Baptism...now saves you, not as a removal of dirt from the body but as an appeal to God for a good conscience, through the resurrection of Jesus Christ."
—I Peter 3:21

My two young sons were thrilled. My wife...not so much. It was during one of those traveling carnivals that I won two goldfish, so we headed to the store that very night and bought it all: the aquarium, the food, and all the supplies needed. 6 days later they were gone. Wait, what? Isn't there at least a week warranty on these things? Guess not, because there they were, two fish, dead in the water. Today we have a live fish, out of the water. In case you haven't noticed, we're covering a wide variety of characters here in August, some well-known and others not quite as familiar. This particular one, actually named "Fish Out of Water," was found in 2005's *Chicken Little.* In this entertaining and underrated film, Chicken Little and his misfit friends try to figure out if and why the sky is falling. One of the film's editors, Dan Molina, actually provided the voice for "Fish" by talking and screaming through a tube into a tank of water.

If you've seen this film, you know that each of Chicken Little's friends has some kind of unusual quirk. Fish Out of Water is simply that...a fish that lives out of the water, although he does wear a scuba helmet full of water so he can survive. But I highlight him today simply as a reminder that fish can't survive without water and neither can we, both physically and spiritually. In Matthew 3, we read an account referenced in all four Gospels of Jesus' baptism. Jesus was baptized in the Jordan River by John the Baptist. Once he came up out of the water, the Holy Spirit came upon Him and God spoke saying He was well-pleased with His Son. Jesus set us an example in so many things including baptism. If Jesus was immersed, received the Spirit of God and pleased God through it, why wouldn't we follow His example? If you've never taken part in this very important and symbolic act which saves you per the verse above, please consider it. Talk to someone, learn more about what it represents and follow the example of our Savior.

PRAYER—Father, I'm grateful for Christ's example of baptism. Help me to understand the importance of it and take part. Thank You for the hope of salvation it brings. In Him, Amen.

TODAY I WILL...thank God for salvation through baptism and the receiving of His Spirit.

AUGUST 17 **Read EXODUS 23:20-25**

GOD'S ANGELS

Disney Characters – Lilo

"For he will command his angels concerning you to guard you in all your ways."
—Psalm 91:11

Have you seen *It's a Wonderful Life*? I hadn't until about 5 years ago. I had heard all my life what a "wonderful" movie it was and that I had to see it, so at age 40, I gave in and finally sat down to check it out. I enjoyed it. I'm not sure it lived up to the hype, but it was a sweet and touching story. Similar to Dickens' *A Christmas Carol*, it's the story of George Bailey visited by an angel and shown his importance and how life would be without him. Today we focus on a character who asked for her own guardian angel. Maybe Lilo is a little more familiar, mainly because of her famous sidekick. Did you know that Disney promoted this 2002 film by placing Stitch into various scenes from *The Little Mermaid, Beauty and the Beast, Aladdin* and *The Lion King*? These humorous trailers can be seen on YouTube. Lilo was voiced by nine-year-old Daveigh Chase. She had also voiced the lead character in *Spirited Away* which coincidentally won the Oscar for Best Animated Film in 2003, beating none other than *Lilo and Stitch*.

Like George Bailey, Lilo needed an angel and even prayed for one. Near the beginning of the film, she kneels down and prays for a new friend saying, "Maybe send an angel, the nicest angel you have." What ends up being sent is definitely less than an angel as Stitch is quite the terror at first. However, throughout the film, he ends up being the answer to her prayers becoming a real friend and part of the family. We know that angels were sent all throughout Scripture to offer guidance and protection including in today's passage where God sends one to guide His people. But what do we know about angels for us today? Hebrews 1:14 says that angels are sent out to serve those who will inherit salvation. That's us! The verse above reconfirms this saying that He commands His angels to guard us. God is hard at work even now, using His angels to serve, watch over and protect us. Let that fact give you comfort and peace today.

PRAYER—Lord God, thank You for watching over, guiding and protecting me. I feel comfort knowing that Your angels are still at work for me today. Through the name of Jesus, Amen.

TODAY I WILL...thank God for His angels and the protection and service they provide.

AUGUST 18 **Read MATTHEW 18:21-35**

FUNDAMENTAL FORGIVENESS

Disney Characters – Pacha

"And whenever you stand praying, forgive, if you have anything against anyone, so that your Father also who is in heaven may forgive you your trespasses."
—Mark 11:25

I remember being so excited about my first apartment. My sister was moving out and I was going to be moving in. I called the landlord the day before only to be given terrible news. Due to a mix-up in communication, she had given the apartment to someone else. I was completely devastated. She had given my home away! Pacha from *The Emperor's New Groove* had to tackle that same issue when not only his house, but his entire village was to be leveled due to the Emperor's new summer home. Pacha was of course voiced by veteran actor, John Goodman who has lent his voice to several Disney characters including Sully in *Monsters, Inc.*, Baloo in *Jungle Book 2* and a minor roll in *The Princess and the Frog*. Pacha was originally going to be voiced by Owen Wilson who went on to voice Lightning McQueen in all the *Cars* films.

In one of Disney's funniest films, Pacha must decide whether or not to help the Emperor in reclaiming the throne. At first, Pacha is understandably against it, having no remorse for the one trying to take his home away. However, as the story unfolds, Pacha begins to feel sympathy for the young Emperor and forgives him. In Matthew 18, we read one of Jesus' most powerful parables about a king who forgives a servant's huge debt of twenty years' worth of wages. That same servant then refuses to forgive a fellow servant of a tiny debt of just a day's pay. When the king hears about the servant's failure to forgive, he throws him in prison until his debt is paid. Jesus assures us that God will do the same if we too fail to forgive. Forgiveness is expected of all believers. Once again, Christ set the perfect example when he forgave those crucifying Him even while agonizing in pain on the cross. The Bible is clear that God can't forgive us if we can't do the same for others. Are there individuals in your life you need to forgive? Ask God for help. Not only will it provide you relief and closure, but it will greatly please God.

PRAYER—Dear God, thank You for forgiving me of so many errors. Please help me to always do the same to others so I can continue to receive Your forgiveness unto death. In Christ, Amen.

TODAY I WILL...take the first steps toward forgiveness of anyone that needs it from me.

AUGUST 19 Read DEUTERONOMY 28:1-10

A FAITHFUL COMPANION

Disney Characters – Pluto

"Be faithful unto death, and I will give you the crown of life."
—Revelation 2:10

I felt it. I just knew she was the one. After the fish fiasco of a few devotionals back, my wife and I decided to get our boys a puppy almost 9 years ago. I made the trek to a house where a new litter was available. The owner brought out 10-15 puppies and told me to pick one. I watched them all for just a few seconds, but Molly immediately stood out to me. She has been one of our greatest decisions, is an absolute joy and is definitely the happiest and most faithful member of our family. Mickey Mouse has a similar faithful companion that we can't overlook this month. Pluto has been Mickey's dog since 1930 when he made his debut in a cartoon called "The Chain Gang" although he wasn't called "Pluto" until a 1931 cartoon. In between, he was actually called "Rover" and belonged to Minnie instead, had a wife and kids in one early cartoon and starred in another in 1940 that earned Walt Disney one of his many Oscars.

No offense to my family, but Molly has them beat on the faithful attention she always gives me. She greets me at the door, tail a-waggin', every time I come home from work and is always willing to play or love on me no matter what kind of day I've had or mood I'm in. She is a tried and true faithful companion. Pluto is the same, always by Mickey's side willing to help him through any predicament. In Deuteronomy 28, God promises blessings to the people as long as they serve Him with faithful obedience. Showing devotion to God in all situations, good or bad, is another vital characteristic we must seek to practice. God promises us the crown of eternal life in the verse above if we remain faithful to Him until death. It's okay to question or even become angry with God. I certainly have at times. We just can't allow our emotions or trials to lessen our faith in His existence, authority and power. No matter what life throws your way, NEVER lose your faith in the Father. Be like Pluto and remain a faithful companion, forever by his side.

PRAYER—Father in Heaven, I don't always understand life or like how it goes, but I know You have a plan for me. I trust You and promise to remain faithful to You forever. In Christ, Amen.

TODAY I WILL...make a vow to God out loud that I will remain faithful to Him until death.

AUGUST 20 **Read PSALM 3:1-8**

THE SHIELD OF FAITH

Disney Characters – Violet Parr

"In all circumstances take up the shield of faith, with which you can extinguish all the flaming darts of the evil one."
—Ephesians 6:16

When I taught 6th grade World History, my favorite unit was always the Middle Ages. We would talk in depth about the Medieval knights. After going over each piece of their armor individually, I would always ask the students which part they felt was most important. The answer, of course, was that it was all essential as a good knight would not want to leave any area of his body vulnerable to an enemy weapon. Every piece from the helmet to the foot coverings served as a shield for his body. It's too bad those knights didn't have the powers of one Violet Parr, the daughter and oldest child in the family of superheroes known as *The Incredibles*. Violet was voiced by Sarah Vowell who has written several non-fiction books, ironically on history and culture. New computer technology was developed specifically to animate Violet's long, black hair as it was apparently one of the most difficult parts due to the sheer quantity.

Violet's superpowers include the ability to instantly create an impenetrable shield around herself or others. Today's short psalm shows David calling God his shield, asking for His protection and saying he won't be afraid of even ten thousand enemies around him because of it. In Ephesians 6, we read about the "Armor of God." Like those Medieval knights, every piece of God's armor is vital to be protected against the world and Satan's power. One piece listed above is the shield of faith which is mentioned specifically as protecting us from Satan's darts or attempts to sway us away from God. Yesterday, we talked about the importance of remaining faithful. We may not have Violet's superpowers to create a literal shield around ourselves, but if we can keep our faith strong, we can rest assured that God will be our shield of protection. We must keep our faith strong to receive His faithful protection in return. It's a two-way street.

PRAYER—Lord, thank You for remaining faithful in Your protection offered against Satan as long as I remain faithful to You. I feel comfort in Your mighty shield. In Christ's name, Amen.

TODAY I WILL...put on the shield of faith so I can receive His faithful unwavering protection.

AUGUST 21 **Read GENESIS 2:4-15**

WORK IT AND KEEP IT

Disney Characters – Wall-E

"You shall not defile the land in which you live, in the midst of which I dwell."
—Numbers 35:34

Have you ever heard of Disney's PUSH? It is a radio-controlled, talking, robot trashcan that interacts with guests at California's Disneyland as well as the parks in Hong Kong, Paris and Tokyo. It used to also be at WDW but was retired in 2014 despite a Twitter campaign to #save-PUSH. The mechanical receptacle is operated by a plain-clothes cast member standing nearby who also has a microphone to give the robot a voice. Ever since Walt was around, Disney has been meticulous about trash collection. He made sure there were trashcans at least every 30 feet so there would be no excuse for guests to drop it elsewhere. Today's character didn't have such a luxury. Wall-E was voiced by Oscar winner and renowned sound editor, Ben Burtt, who also created the sounds for the legendary R2D2 throughout the *Star Wars* films.

If you've seen Wall-E, you know his job is to clean up the incredibly cluttered planet Earth the humans have left behind. Hour by hour without complaint, he crushes trash into cubes and stacks them in a centralized location. While this Pixar classic is fictional of course, it's a scary premise to imagine humans so careless in the future as to turn our world into basically a pile of garbage. In Genesis 2, we read the continuing story of creation and how God made man and woman and provided them with a beautiful garden to care for. Verse 15 says he put man in the garden "to work it and keep it." God has provided the same even today, allowing us to care for this beautiful Earth He made. Cluttering it up with trash or giving no care to the environment displays a lack of stewardship and is a poor example to those around us. Choose each day to show God your appreciation for life and our planet by doing your part to keep it clean. Help little Wall-E out so that we can keep our world beautiful for many generations to come.

PRAYER—Lord, Your Earth is physically beautiful, and I'm honored and blessed to live in it and be entrusted to take care of it. Help me to give time daily to do my part. In Jesus, Amen.

TODAY I WILL...find a location that needs cleaning up and spend time picking up trash. I will also vow from here on out to never walk by a piece of trash without picking it up.

AUGUST 22 **Read MATTHEW 5:33-37**

A PROMISE KEPT

Disney Characters – Carl Fredricksen

"If a man vows a vow to the Lord or swears an oath to bind himself by a pledge, he shall not break his word. He shall do according to all that proceeds out of his mouth."
—Numbers 30:2

We had just reached the summit and were resting at the top of a 14,000+ foot mountain in Colorado when he reached into his pocket, pulled out a business card and handed it to me. I couldn't believe it. He had kept his promise! A little backstory...several months before, I was eating with a buddy, and he found a random but humorous business card inside the restaurant. I knew we were scheduled to go "trekking" later that summer and said in a daring tone, "You won't keep that card and give it back to me when we get to the top of the mountain." He smiled and replied, "I promise you I will." Carl Fredricksen also keeps an important promise in the delightful, Pixar tale entitled *Up*, a rare animation story focusing on a geriatric hero. Notable actor, Ed Asner, who voiced Carl, admitted to learning a lot playing this role. Recording his lines at age 79, he even stated in a later interview that he wished he'd been more like Carl in life.

Before his beloved wife becomes ill, Carl promises they will travel to Paradise Falls together. After her passing, he decides to keep that promise no matter the cost. The final scene of the film shows their cherished home sitting proudly atop the picturesque waterfall. Carl's promise has been fulfilled. In Matthew 5, Jesus warns us about making promises we can't keep, even going so far as to say we shouldn't swear anything at all. Instead, he says our yes should mean yes and our no should mean no. Too often these days, many don't stay true to their word. They go back on promises or even lie with false intentions. In the Old Testament shown above, God was very clear about what a vow or oath meant. If you say you're going to do something, you should do it. Breaking your word is not an option in God's eyes. Make sure, like Carl, you are keeping your promises. Don't make agreements or assurances you don't intend to honor. Be a person of integrity so that others trust you and know you are true to your word.

PRAYER—Father, help me to think before I speak or act, to be honest and only make vows I am able and fully intend to keep. I want to be a person of integrity. In His holy name, Amen.

TODAY I WILL...keep my promises and not agree to anything I don't intend to do.

AUGUST 23 **Read 2 CORINTHIANS 12:5-10**

ACCEPT YOUR GLITCHES

Disney Characters – Vanellope

"...the Spirit helps us in our weakness."
—Romans 8:26

When I was in middle school, playing Super Mario Brothers on the Nintendo was all the rage. My friends and I would often compare notes during lunch on how far we had gotten in the game. I just couldn't seem to beat it with the 3 lives given. Imagine my delight when one of my friends told us about a glitch that provided an infinite amount of lives if maneuvered correctly. Once I figured that out, I was golden and went on to beat the game multiple times. Vanellope from *Wreck-It Ralph* also has a glitch. This film and its sequel, *Ralph Breaks the Internet*, together racked up almost exactly one billion dollars worldwide! In the sequel, every living Disney Princess voice actor returned with the exception of Mary Costa from *Sleeping Beauty*. She was 88 at the time and considered too old to return and voice the 16-year-old Princess Aurora.

In the original and clever "Ralph" story, Vanellope wants desperately to participate in a nightly car race but is forbidden due to her erratic, teleporting glitch. She sees this glitch as a frustrating crutch and weakness, but in the end, it's that very glitch which allows her to save the day. In 2 Corinthians 12, the Apostle Paul talks about his famous "thorn in the flesh," admitting to a very specific and unknown weakness. Paul saw his weakness as a strength, admitting it kept him from boasting and becoming conceited. He also makes clear that his weaknesses made him stronger. We all have a glitch or two, being weak or inadequate in certain areas. When we face them, we must remember that if we call on God's name, His Spirit within gives us strength and knowledge to move forward. As Paul said, weaknesses can be a blessing. They can make us stronger servants of God as we fully rely on Him and discover His power made perfect within our weakness, as it says in verse 9 of today's reading. Your glitches were put there for a purpose. Accept them as a blessing, use them and grow stronger in the power of God.

PRAYER—Lord, You know my weaknesses. Help me to rejoice in them and use them to better myself for You. I implore Your Spirit to guide me in dealing with them. Through Jesus, Amen.

TODAY I WILL...make a list of my "glitches." Accept them as blessings to make me stronger.

AUGUST 24 **Read I JOHN 2:15-18**

TOO MUCH HONEY

Disney Characters – Winnie the Pooh

"If you have found honey, eat only enough for you, lest you have your fill of it..."
—Proverbs 25:16

My dad made it best. Every Saturday during breakfast, he would slice off a square of butter, pour honey over it and mix it into a smooth spread. I longed for it and love honey-butter to this day! I know a certain bear who would most likely enjoy it also as he certainly loves one of those two ingredients. Winnie the Pooh originated in 1926 after author A.A. Milne wrote a book based on his son's teddy bear. Young Christopher Robin Milne had renamed his favorite toy "Winnie" after visiting the London Zoo and becoming infatuated with a female bear there with the same name. Since its inception, that first of many books about the bear and his friends has been translated into over 50 languages around the world. At one point, *Forbes* magazine even named Winnie as the world's most valuable character, having earned more than Mickey Mouse himself!

It's no secret that Winnie the Pooh absolutely loves honey. Even in that very first book, he eats so much of it that he gets stuck in a doorway, a story that was later retold in Disney's first film about him. I love honey too but eating as much as old Pooh does would most likely make me quite sick. We must be careful about gorging on anything pleasurable in this world...not just food, but anything that can divert our attention away from God. In I John 2, John warns us about giving in to desires of the flesh and eyes. He specifically says that these things are of the world and not of God. He reminds us that all worldly things will pass away one day but those that follow God will live forever. A little honey may seem harmless, but there are other worldly pleasures we should avoid altogether as they can lead to temptation, sin and dangerous dependances. If nothing else, getting too caught up in these cravings distracts us from serving God and putting His will first. Be diligent not to fall in love with the world or anything in it. Too much of anything worldly will cause spiritual sickness from overindulgence.

PRAYER—Father in Heaven, thank You for this world and the pleasures in it, but help me to avoid overdoing any of them so that I may keep You first in all things. In Christ I pray, Amen.

TODAY I WILL...make sure I'm not "overeating" anything worldly and losing focus on God.

AUGUST 25 **Read LUKE 6:27-36**

FACING FRUSTRATION

Disney Characters – Daisy Duck

"Whoever is slow to anger has great understanding, but he who has a hasty temper exalts folly."
—Proverbs 14:29

Think about this question for a moment...what frustrates you most in life? There are three things that pop into my head: cars, technology and other people. Cars and technology are great when they work properly, but I despise dealing with car repairs or being unable to figure out technology when it has issues. I also get frustrated with others, but more on that momentarily. Today we are focusing on an often-frustrated character in Ms. Daisy Duck. She was introduced in a 1940 cartoon entitled "Mr. Duck Steps Out." Some sources say she was actually presented earlier in 1937 as "Donna Duck," but there are conflicting reports on whether that was actually Daisy or another character altogether. Like her main squeeze, Donald, with his well-known three nephews, Daisy has three nieces of her own named April, May and June.

While Daisy has remained faithful to Donald over the years, she is typically shown to be just a bit more intelligent and mature than he is... ok, so maybe a lot more. This often causes her to show understandable frustration towards Donald and his adolescent antics. In Luke 6, Jesus stresses the importance of loving and doing good to others, even our enemies. He teaches that it's not enough to only be good to those who are good to you. As His servants, we are to work harder and do good even to those we don't like or who often frustrate us. I mentioned above being often frustrated with others. I don't like laziness, complaining or when others don't respond to texts or emails. I work hard to deal with those frustrations with patience and kindness, and I'm sure I frustrate others too. It's easy to get frustrated with others as we are all have very different personalities, but we must strive to do good to all, expecting nothing in return. Dealing with frustrations with patience, maturity and kindness takes real discipline and self-control, but if we do it correctly, as God expects, we can be pleasing to Him and a Christ-like example to all.

PRAYER—Lord, I'm sorry when I let frustrations get the best of me. Help me to control them, especially when dealing with others so that like Christ, I may do good to all. In Him, Amen.

TODAY I WILL... curb any frustrations I have with others and choose to show Christ instead.

AUGUST 26 **Read JAMES 5:13-15**

THE POWER TO HEAL

Disney Characters – Baymax

"Heal me, O Lord, and I shall be healed."
—Jeremiah 17:14

While getting my EMT and paramedic certifications, one point stressed repeatedly during classes was the importance of a complete assessment. For any patient, it's imperative to do a full-body evaluation, and we were given multiple pneumonic devices to avoid missing any potential problems. If you've seen *Big Hero 6*, you know that Baymax is a loveable, inflatable, robotic healthcare provider who also does a full-body scan to assess and heal medical issues. Baymax originally appeared in Marvel Comics in 1998 with a drastically different look. *Big Hero 6* was in fact the first animated Disney film to feature Marvel characters after they had acquired Marvel just five years earlier. In the comics, Baymax was still a robot, but served as a butler, chauffeur and personal bodyguard instead of the healthcare companion we've come to know and love.

Having a Baymax to fully assess our medical needs would be a nice piece of technology. Even with today's technology, it's often difficult to determine someone's exact medical needs. We may not have a Baymax to evaluate, assist and heal us, but we are certainly blessed with a loving and powerful Father who can and will. In James 5, we are told what to do when struggling with health issues. We are advised not only to pray, but to seek help from the church and its leaders. I'm sure you've prayed for someone's health in the past, possibly your own, but do we truly believe and trust in God's power to heal? We are told "the prayer of faith will save the one who is sick, and the Lord will raise him up." Does it always work? No, of course not. God may choose not to heal someone, and we must trust in His will and decisions. But He always listens to our prayers and will often provide healing if we ask in faith. There's no doubt that miraculous medical recoveries and healings occur daily with God at the helm. Keep your trust and faith in Him, pray without ceasing and never give up on His power to heal.

PRAYER—Dear Lord, I trust and believe in Your power to heal. I pray for my own health and for that of others. Thank You for helping us through our ailments. In Jesus' name, Amen.

TODAY I WILL...pray by name for those in need of healing with full faith that God will heal.

AUGUST 27 **Read NUMBERS 21:4-9**

A SECOND CHANCE

Disney Characters – Joe Gardner

"If we confess our sins, he is faithful and just to forgive us our sins and to cleanse us from all unrighteousness."
—I John 1:9

The Price is Right has always been one of my favorite game shows simply for the variety of games offered. "Plinko" is probably my favorite as I'm sure many would agree, but I've also always enjoyed the "Hole in One" game where contestants putt from varying distances hoping to win a big prize. What's extra exciting is that if a contestant misses the first time, the host presses a button to reveal the altered name of the game now displayed as "Hole in One OR Two," giving the contestant a thrilling second chance. It's nice to get a second chance. I'm sure Joe Gardner would agree. Do you remember Joe? He's certainly a newer Disney name being the protagonist in 2020's *Soul*. Voiced by actor, Jamie Foxx, who is himself a musician like the character, Joe was Pixar's first African American main character. Foxx was reportedly deeply invested in his character and even cried after reading his last line, referred to in the May 6th entry.

Near the end of the heart-warming story of *Soul*, Joe Gardner is given a second chance at life due to his hard work, inspiring another soul to live. In Numbers 4, God punishes His people for their complaining and lack of trust by sending deadly serpents among them. When they realize their sin and plead for their lives, God shows sympathy yet again and offers them a similar second chance at life. We may not receive a second chance at a physical life, but God offers us something better...a second chance at eternal life for our undying souls. We all sin and fall short of God's glory and any one of our sins is enough to lead us to eternal condemnation. However, our God is so forgiving and gracious, that He offers us cleansing and a second chance if we confess our sin and remain faithful to Him. There is no sin too great that God won't offer us another chance if we are sincere in our repentance and desire to come back to Him. He even longs to see us do so (2 Peter 3:9). What a loving, merciful and compassionate God we serve!

PRAYER—Father, thank You so much for giving me a second chance at eternal life with You. I'm so sorry for my sin and am so grateful for Your love and forgiveness. In Christ, Amen.

TODAY I WILL...take advantage of God's 2nd chance, repent and never leave Him again.

AUGUST 28 **Read I PETER 5:6-11**

AN OPTICAL ILLUSION

Disney Characters – Prince Hans

"...and every spirit that does not confess Jesus is not from God. This is the spirit of the antichrist, which you heard was coming and now is in the world already."
—I John 4:3

Do you like optical illusions? They've always intrigued me. My favorites are vase/face, rabbit/duck and the devil's tuning fork. Look those up if you're unfamiliar. I'm sure you're aware that an illusion appears to be one thing but can also be seen as something else if looked at from a different angle. There's a notable Disney character that fits that same description. Prince Hans, whose official name was Hans Westergaard or Prince Hans of the Southern Isles, provided quite the plot twist for *Frozen* fans in 2013. Most Disney villains are shown to be evil from the start, but not Hans. He was seen as noble and heroic until near the end of the film when his malicious intentions were dramatically revealed. According to the filmmakers, Hans, a common Scandinavian name even today, is 23 and the youngest of 13 brothers which perhaps attributed to his evil schemes to be king, knowing he would never get there through his extended bloodline.

Hans was a definite optical illusion, appearing one way while in reality being someone completely different. I Peter 5 reminds us of a real being who is also very good at illusions. We are warned that Satan sneaks around like a lion, deviously seeking his next victim. There are other verses in Scripture that say he even disguises himself in attempts to trick us. The devil is brilliant at making bad things look good. He is cunning and smart when it comes to deceiving us through our weaknesses. We may think something is pleasing and acceptable, unaware that Satan has simply disguised it because it will lead us away from God. The verse above makes it clear that Satan is alive and very active in this world. He is always looking for ways to trick you into following him and will pounce in a way and when you least expect. Like Peter advises, be always watchful and don't fall for his illusions. See him for who he truly is...a lying, devious opponent of God trying to steal as many souls as he can. Please don't be one of them!

PRAYER—Lord, please give me the knowledge and drive to recognize the devil's trucks and not be fooled by any of them. Keep him away from me! In the name of my Savior, Amen.

TODAY I WILL...be alert for Satan's schemes to confirm he isn't tricking me with an illusion.

AUGUST 29 **Read I KINGS 3:16-28**

A MOTHER'S LOVE

Disney Characters – Bambi's Mother

"As one whom his mother comforts, so I will comfort you."
—Isaiah 66:13

When I taught Bible classes, I would demonstrate today's passage with an actual doll I had cut in half. I loved watching the kids' faces when I took the doll apart showing the initial ruling of Solomon that thankfully didn't come to fruition. I know...I obviously have some psychotic tendencies. Not only does this story demonstrate his wisdom which is typically the point made, but it also shows the true love of a mother, willing to give up her child to save its life. The death scene of Bambi's mother, sacrificing herself to make sure Bambi made it to safety, is considered one of the saddest scenes in film history. Walt's own daughter begged him to change the story to keep her alive, but Walt insisted he was only following the book from which the story originated.

I also encourage you to read Proverbs 31, a beautiful passage describing a Godly woman and wife. The last few verses define an excellent mother saying she teaches wisdom, kindness and takes care of her household. There's something special about the love of a mother. I think of so many excellent Biblical examples such as Hannah, mother of Samuel; Jochebed, mother of Moses and certainly Mary, who stood by Jesus' side at all times, even as he hung in agony on the cruel cross. All of these and many others made huge sacrifices for their children due to their love and compassion. Take time today to reflect on your own mother and the gifts she provided. Not all mother-child relationships are perfect, but I'm guessing you can find a valuable lesson or two (most likely many) you learned from your mom. If you are blessed to be a mother, thank God for that privilege and put the time and effort needed into being like one of these superb examples, even that of a selfless deer. (And don't worry dads...your day is coming soon!)

PRAYER—Thank You Lord for my mother and the superb example of so many others who sacrifice daily for their children. Bless all mothers with strength, health and longevity to continue to work tirelessly and selflessly for the good of their children. Through Jesus, Amen.

TODAY I WILL... thank my mother, in person if possible, but also honor her by imitating the good qualities she gave me.

AUGUST 30 **Read PROVERBS 23:22-25**

A DEDICATED DAD

Disney Characters – Goofy

"Hear, O sons, a father's instruction, and be attentive, that you may gain insight..." – Proverbs 4:1

Well, dads...did you think your day would come this soon? I'll never forget the day I became a dad which also happened to be the first day I ever cried tears of joy. I was completely overwhelmed with emotion due to my excitement and the indescribable love I felt for my newborn son. I felt so honored and blessed by God to be given the role of a father. We've talked about many different characters this month, but we've left out a pretty important one. Most of the time, people think of Goofy as just that...goofy. But if you've seen 1995's *A Goofy Movie*, you know that he's also a pretty special and dedicated dad. The character of Goofy debuted in 1932 but was first known as "Dippy Dawg." It wasn't until later that year that he was reimagined as a younger character named Goofy. He was revealed to be a father in the 1992 television series *Goof Troop* and is the only main Disney character to have a son.

In *A Goofy Movie*, there are plenty of antics showing Goofy being his stereotypical "goofy" self. However, throughout the film, he also shows great responsibility and maturity as a father, teaching his son, Max, lessons about honesty, trust and the power of a father's love. Proverbs 23, as well as the verse from chapter 4 above, advises us to listen to our earthly father. While we obviously have a Heavenly Father who loves us immeasurably and instructs us how to live, God knew we also needed the love, discipline, wisdom and teachings of an earthly father. Once again, I advise you to spend some time today in reflection of your own dad. What lessons did you learn from him? How can you imitate or be an even better person than he was? And dads...what an incredible honor it is to be blessed with that role! Never underestimate its importance. Put your whole heart and efforts into raising children who know and love the Lord. Praise God for fathers, especially the loving One He is to us all!

PRAYER—Lord, thank you for fathers, especially the loving, generous and forgiving One You are. Help me to honor my father and reflect his good qualities in leading others. In Jesus, Amen.

TODAY I WILL...reflect on the instructions of my father and honor him, in person if possible.

AUGUST 31 **Read I CORINTHIANS 10:6-13**

NO WHISTLING REQUIRED

Disney Characters – Jiminy Cricket

"Do not be frightened, and do not be dismayed, for the Lord your God is with you wherever you go."
—Joshua 1:9

I was taught to stick my tongue directly behind my bottom teeth, pucker up and blow. It's always worked for me. What about you? Can you whistle? That's apparently all it takes to call our last character on this final day of August. Donald Duck is my favorite Disney character as mentioned, but Jiminy Cricket, one of Disney's oldest and most iconic, is a close second. In the original book from 1883, *The Adventures of Pinocchio*, there was a character named "Talking Cricket." Jiminy became Disney's version when he first appeared in 1940's *Pinocchio*. His name was actually uttered as a euphemism in *Pinocchio's* predecessor and Disney's first film, *Snow White and the Seven Dwarfs*. He is a rarely seen character in the Disney parks but does occasionally surprise guests with an appearance. Have you ever gotten to meet him?

In *Pinocchio*, Jiminy Cricket is tasked by the Blue Fairy to serve as the wooden boy's guide and conscience. In a catchy tune early on, Jiminy tells Pinocchio that he can always call him if needed by simply giving a whistle. The song specifically mentions that Jiminy will provide help in times of temptation, something we certainly face a lot of as Christians. We may not have a talking cricket to whistle for, but we do have an even greater blessing. I Corinthians 10 tells us that God is always with us when we face temptation. It assures us that He won't let us be tempted beyond our ability to withstand it. It also promises that He will always provide us a way out. We serve a faithful God. He is always with us no matter what we are doing or whatever situation we find ourselves in. Always remember He's there whenever you face temptations of any kind and look hard to find His way out. With God on our side, we really have no excuse to give in to temptation. God is there every time to help. You don't even have to whistle!

PRAYER—I need you, Lord. Help me to clearly recognize and resist temptation, evil and anything of this world that separates me from You. Thank You for being there anytime I face these difficult situations and for giving me a way out. In His holy name I pray, Amen.

TODAY I WILL...remember to always look for God's way out when facing temptation.

SEPTEMBER THEME

DISNEY RESORTS

SEPTEMBER 1 **Read GENESIS 28:10-17**

STEPPING UPWARD

Disney Resorts – Coronado Springs

"The heart of man plans his way, but the Lord establishes his steps."
—Proverbs 16:9

Welcome to September, one of my favorite months! Why? Maybe because I was born in it. Or because Fall is my favorite season. But here's another reason...we get to talk this month about all the fantastic Disney resorts. We'll begin with one I love simply because it has my favorite place on property to sit and relax. You see, I love hot tubs, and Disney's Coronado Springs Resort not only has the largest hot tub on property, but you can sit in it and have a perfect view of a picturesque waterfall slowly making its way down the 50-foot pyramid at the center of the main pool. We recently stayed here for the first time but have already stayed a 2nd time because we enjoyed it so much. The beautiful, Mayan-themed pool also features a 123-foot water slide.

Sitting at the back of that hot tub, closing my eyes and listening to the water trickle down those stone steps is one of the most peaceful and pleasant experiences I've had at WDW. That pyramid reminds me not only of Epcot's Mexico Pavilion, but also the structure it's based on at the center of Chichen Itza, an ancient archaeological site in Mexico which I had the privilege of climbing during a childhood trip. Disney won't let you climb this one except for a few steps due to strategically placed vines in the way. They also won't let you climb the one at Epcot. You can see video of a less-than-sober fellow attempting it back in 2015. Needless to say, Disney was not amused. Seeing those steep steps reminds me not only of today's reading where Jacob sees God at the top of a large ladder, but also the Proverbs verse above. Accomplishing our goal of being with God one day will sometimes, like those steps, be a difficult climb. Thankfully, we have a loving Father who leads us as long as we give Him full control. Striving to get to God without Him won't work. We must involve Him with every step. Make sure you know without a doubt that your life's path is leading upward and that you are allowing God to guide each step.

PRAYER—God, I'm determined to keep climbing upward to reach my Heavenly home with You. I know it will be a difficult ascent, but please control my steps and lead me to you. Amen.

TODAY I WILL...find determination to always keep climbing, letting God guide every step.

SEPTEMBER 2 **Read HEBREWS 11:1-40**

ICONS OF FAITH

Disney Resorts – Pop Century

"And Jesus answered them, "Have faith in God."
—Mark 11:22

A giant Rubik's Cube. A huge can of Play-doh. Massive Mr. and Mrs. Potato Heads. An enormous Sony Walkman. And a gigantic, old-school, Mickey phone. Where can you go to see all of those? The Pop Century of course! This resort celebrating all things pop-culture opened in 2003 as WDW's 4th and largest value resort. It contains five themed sections representing the decades from the 1950's through the 1990's. Each section boasts multiple, large icons mostly related to the decade itself with a few notable Disney characters thrown in. The original plans called for a sister resort across the lake to represent what would be called the "Legendary Years" or the earlier decades from 1900 through 1940. However, due to delays after the 9/11 attacks, those plans were changed to a different resort altogether that we'll look at later.

Did you know that the Bible contains some giant icons too? No, they aren't massive, visible structures like at Pop Century, but they are huge and iconic in the fact that they are listed as memorable examples of faith. The book of Hebrews groups them all together in one chapter often nicknamed the "Heroes of Faith" chapter. I encourage you to find time to read all of Hebrews 11 and really focus on each person listed, what they did for the Lord and how their faith stood out as an example. We can learn lessons from each and seek to pattern our own faith after them. The next time you stay at the Pop Century, take some time to simply walk around and enjoy the larger-than-life icons and the nostalgia they provide. Make sure to also read Hebrews 11 regularly as a reminder of our faith heroes that we can imitate to keep our faith in God strong. Jesus made it pretty simple above when he said, "have faith in God." We must never let our faith waver so that we too can be known as an icon of faith to others and especially to God.

PRAYER—God, help my faith in You to remain strong no matter what comes my way. Thank You for so many faithful examples in Your Word that I can imitate. Through Christ, Amen.

TODAY I WILL...write down my three favorite heroes of faith from Hebrews 11 and note how I can be more like them in my everyday life.

SEPTEMBER 3 **Read EXODUS 3:1-6**

FIND YOUR WILDERNESS

Disney Resorts – Fort Wilderness

"And rising very early in the morning, while it was still dark, he departed and went out to a desolate place, and there he prayed."
—Mark 1:35

My sons used to beg on occasion to set the tent up and go camping in our backyard. I relented a few times for their sake but never really had a great experience. Oh, I enjoyed spending time with them of course, but I've just never slept well outdoors. I suppose the fact that we have a train track just beyond our backyard could have been a contributing factor. If I had to camp now, I would much rather do so out in the elements of Disney's "wilderness," although I'd probably prefer one of their cozy cabins. Fort Wilderness officially opened in November of 1971, just a month after WDW's debut, making it one of the oldest "resorts" on property. The 750-acre space currently has around 800 campsites and just over 400 cabins. It also features pools, playgrounds, biking, golf carts, archery, horseback riding, and many other recreational activities.

In today's reading, Moses also found himself out in the wilderness and blessed to have a direct conversation with God where he learned about God's purpose and desires for his life. We also know that Jesus often sought time alone with God by wandering off to desolate places as in the verse above. In Matthew 4, He's even guided into the wilderness by the Holy Spirit directly after his baptism where He spends 40 days alone, fasting and bonding with God before Satan's temptation. These stories of Moses and Jesus serve as an example for each of us to possibly find our own "wilderness" in which to seek God's will for our lives. Maybe it's a spot in your backyard, a secluded park or even a quiet facility like the library, but take time to figure out a special place where you too can be alone with God. Schedule regular time there, leave your phone and any other worldly distractions behind, take only your Bible and just spend quality time meditating, talking to and listening to God. You'll be able to hear Him much clearer if you are truly there by yourself. We all need "wilderness" time with God. When's your next trip?

PRAYER—Father, I long for time alone with You. Help me to spend quality time with You regularly so I may discover Your plans and desires for my life. In the name of Jesus, Amen.

TODAY I WILL...figure out my "wilderness" spot and make plans to go there regularly.

SEPTEMBER 4 **Read LUKE 2:1-7**

A REST FOR THE WEARY

Disney Resorts – Disneyland Hotel

"For I will satisfy the weary soul, and every languishing soul I will replenish."
—Jeremiah 31:25

I think my wife and I may be a bit spoiled these days staying onsite and allowing Disney to take care of our transportation to and from resorts. When we first married, our Disney trips came from nearly an hour away in Daytona where we stayed with her parents. Therefore, we always had to drive that long trek home after a full and tiring day in the parks, and I remember being completely exhausted. We discussed how Walt chose an unknown city for Disneyland, and therefore when it first opened, there was nowhere nearby for travelers to stay. Walt knew his guests would need a place to rest after a full park day and therefore hastily arranged for his very first resort, the Disneyland Hotel, to be built in 1955. Did you know, however, that Disney didn't own it outright until 1988? Walt first sought big names such as Sheraton and Hilton to build hotels on sight and even tried convincing his friend, Art Linkletter, to invest, but they were all too skeptical of this new park's success. They have since regretted their decisions.

In Luke 2, we find the familiar story of Joseph and Mary, who were also weary travelers desperately needing a place to stay. Like Anaheim initially, rooms were very limited and the only place available for Jesus to be born was a likely filthy, animal-filled stable. While it sounds inappropriate for our Lord's birthplace, have you considered that it was God's plan all along? He wanted to show the world that even the Son of God could come from a poor and humble beginning and still grow to be recognized as the Savior of the world. As His children, He also provides a place of rest when we are desperate and weary. He told us so in Matthew 11:28-30 when Christ said to call His name when we are tired, and He will provide rest for our souls. Don't forget this offer when you feel weary and overcome. Don't let your stress or troubles cause irreparable damage to your soul. Take advantage of God's offer and come to Him for rest.

PRAYER—Lord, life can be tiring and overwhelming at times, and I don't want my soul's future to suffer because of it. Help me to remember Christ's offer for rest at all times. Amen.

TODAY I WILL...take advantage of God's offer and seek Him first if I ever feel weary in life.

SEPTEMBER 5 **Read LUKE 23:32-42**

ARE YOU A CROOK?

Disney Resorts – Contemporary Resort

"He is the propitiation for our sins, and not for ours only but also for the sins of the whole world."
—I John 2:2

"The only thing we have to fear is fear itself." You've heard that, right? What about, "Ask not what your country can do for you but what you can do for your country." Famous presidential quotes. What about, "I am not a crook!" Do you remember who said that? President Richard Nixon actually said it while standing inside today's resort. On November 17, 1973, during the height of the Watergate scandal, Nixon was addressing the Press, claiming his innocence. Of course, less than a year later, he would resign the presidency amid the same scandal, unable to maintain his "non-crook" status. The Contemporary is also known for being one of WDW's first resorts, opening with the park in 1971. Known for its A-frame design that the monorail travels right through, I remember being truly amazed seeing it for the first time as a kid and thinking it looked like something from the future. Originally planned to be named the "Tempo Bay Hotel," this resort is also very special to us as it's where we stayed on our honeymoon.

Nixon's "crook" speech in this very resort reminded me of two of the most notable "crooks" in Scripture. Jesus' interaction with the two criminals crucified beside Him is noteworthy as He not only forgave the crowd and all those contributing to his death, but he also took the time to forgive the criminal right beside him, even telling him, "Today you will be with me in paradise." Can you imagine? Suffering immensely and bearing the sin of the world but still having the compassion to forgive and give eternal salvation to a common crook. I John 2 above reminds us that Jesus is the propitiation or replacement for our sins and for those of the entire world. We are all criminals, but thankfully and graciously, His death serves as a substitute to totally eliminate our "crook" status. Never forget that sacrifice which gives us hope and blessed assurance of what's to come. Because of Christ, we can each say with confidence, "I am not a crook!"

PRAYER—Thank you Lord for sending Jesus to take the place of my sin. I praise His name!

TODAY I WILL...write down the last few "crook" things I've done, ask God in sincerity to forgive them and destroy the list, knowing His Son's death eliminates them from my record.

SEPTEMBER 6 **Read I THESSALONIANS 4:13-18**

AS CLOSE AS YOU CAN BE

Disney Resorts – Grand Californian

"...seek His kingdom and these things will be added to you."
—Luke 12:31

If you could spend the night inside any Disney attraction, which would you choose? My first thought was one of the more exciting rides like Flight of Passage or Rise of the Resistance. However, it's always been a lifelong dream to sleep inside the Cinderella Castle suite overlooking the Magic Kingdom. (Maybe I could even sneak a ride on Tinkerbell's zipline.) While that dream will most likely remain just that, did you know you can technically stay overnight inside a park as the Grand Californian Resort is technically located within Disney California Adventure. Constructed as part of a major expansion in 2001, this is the only current Disney resort with an entrance directly into a park, although there have been talks of opening similar resorts inside Epcot, and the new Star Wars Galactic Starcruiser experience will have direct access to Hollywood Studios.

Safe to say, out of all the current Disney resorts on either coast, staying at the Grand Californian gets you closest to the action. You can literally walk out of your resort and immediately be within the magic of the park. I Thessalonians 4 reminds us of Jesus coming back one day, descending from Heaven with the sounds of trumpets and angels. Those in Christ will then rise to meet Him in the air. I don't know about you, but I want to be one of those risers and be as close to the front of that line as possible to witness His return first hand. Like staying at this resort, I want to be so close that I can simply step through my door and be there ready and waiting the moment He returns As above, we are often told to seek God's kingdom first so that we are added to it. Therefore, we should be always be striving to be as close to His kingdom as possible, being ever watchful, ready and excited about His return. Stay close to the front of the action so that you don't miss His exciting call. I promise it's coming. Make sure you're ready!!

PRAYER—Father in Heaven, I'm excited and can't wait for the return of Jesus to collect us all to meet Him in the air. Help me to always be ready and watchful. In Jesus' holy name, Amen.

TODAY I WILL...seek God's kingdom first, being ready each day for His Son's return.

SEPTEMBER 7 **Read ACTS 16:19-25**

GOD'S FAVORITE MUSIC

Disney Resorts – All-Star Music

"...addressing one another in psalms and hymns and spiritual songs, singing and making melody to the Lord with your heart."
—Ephesians 5:19

During his recent Radio Practicum class, my son got to be a radio DJ each week on his college campus. As he was allowed to take song requests, I tried to be funny and texted him asking for some Taylor Swift, an artist he knows I wouldn't normally ask to hear. Imagine my surprise when he announced on the air that the next song was a request by his dad who loves Taylor Swift. Needless to say, I was a bit embarrassed. I don't mind an occasional Swift song, but "love" is a strong word. What's your favorite type of music? You can find representations and tributes to pretty much all of them at Disney's All-Star Music Resort. Built in 1994 as one of Disney's first three value resorts, this is the only one to feature a few family suites designed for larger families. The various buildings are divided into the music types of calypso, Broadway, country, jazz and rock n' roll with each, as expected, featuring large icons related to that style.

We all have styles of music we enjoy. Maybe yours even includes Taylor Swift. However, what do you think is God's favorite type of music? We find the answer in the verse above. Ephesians 5:19 tells us we are to sing and make melody in our hearts to God as He desires for us to speak to one another with songs, hymns and psalms. In today's reading, Paul and Silas had been beaten and thrown in prison, but look what they are doing at midnight. They are singing praises to God, something I think I would find a bit difficult in their situation. During a difficult and scary ordeal, they were still influencing others for God. They even converted the jailer due to their faithfulness. God created a beautiful thing in music, and He wants us to enjoy it. But He also created it to glorify Him and lift others up. It doesn't matter how well you sing. God just wants to hear you lift your voice to Him, even in difficult times like Paul and Silas. Sing praises to His name! Sing with others or even alone. Just let God hear His favorite type of music...you!

PRAYER—Lord God, thank You for music which provides entertainment and joy in life. Help me to remember to give it right back to You in the form of daily praise. In Christ's name, Amen.

TODAY I WILL...sing songs of praise to God even if alone and even if I'm having a bad day.

SEPTEMBER 8 **Read GENESIS 9:8-17**

ETERNAL PROMISES

Disney Resorts – Animal Kingdom Lodge

"Not one word of all the good promises that the Lord had made to the house of Israel had failed; all came to pass."

—Joshua 21:45

It's only the 8th day of the month and we've already gotten to see so many wonderful things at these various Disney resorts: from a beautiful waterfall flowing down a Mayan temple to giant icons of pop culture and music and even a resort door opening right into the park. But today's location has something even more exciting: live animals. At Disney's Animal Kingdom Lodge, built in 2001, there are multiple varieties of animals roaming and exploring the grounds right outside your room. This scenic resort is surrounded by three savannahs which house numerous types of animals like giraffes, zebras, wildebeests, bongos, gazelles and a large assortment of birds. The resort also features a newer section, Kidani Village, built in 2009 which includes over 300 deluxe villas with even wider views of the savannahs and even more animal species.

Animals are mentioned throughout the Bible, but perhaps nowhere as familiar as in today's reading. I actually encourage you to read the entire story of Noah's Ark in Genesis chapters 6-9 if you can. As you'll remember, Noah was instructed to take two of every species onto his ark before God destroyed the Earth by flood. Today's specific passage comes from the end of the story where God showed through His covenant how much he cared not only for Noah and his family, but for even the animals as well. When the flood was complete, He placed a rainbow in the sky to remind us all of His promise to never again destroy the Earth by flood. It has been thousands of years since that historic event and God has faithfully kept His promise. There have been floods of course, but none so great to destroy the whole world as before. God is always faithful to us and keeps His promises. The verse above reminds us of that, saying none of His promises will fail. Remember that anytime you read one of His many promises throughout Scripture. We can find great peace and comfort in the promises of God. He loves his animals, but even more so, He loves you and me and will always be there for us. And that's a promise!

PRAYER—Lord, thank You for Your faithful promises and the comfort they bring. Amen.

TODAY I WILL...focus on, reflect and find peace and rest in the promises of God.

SEPTEMBER 9 **Read LUKE 5:12-15**

BE A HUB

Disney Resorts – Caribbean Beach

"...but set the believers an example in speech, in conduct, in love, in faith and in purity."
—I Timothy 4:12b

What does the word "hub" mean to you? A wife's nickname for her spouse? The missing part of my tire? Or perhaps what I'm actually aiming for which is the center or focal point of something. For example, shopping malls used to be the "hub" for purchases, but I would argue that online sites such as Amazon have taken their place. Similarly, libraries and encyclopedias used to be the "hub" for finding information while today it's most likely Google or another online search engine. Today's resort is also called a "hub" when it comes to the fairly new, Skyliner transportation system. Disney's Caribbean Beach Resort was built in 1988 with various Caribbean-themed buildings surrounding the 45 acre "Barefoot Bay." The Skyliner was added in 2019, connecting Epcot and Hollywood Studios to this and three other resorts.

As mentioned, the Caribbean Beach serves as the Skyliner's hub meaning you must travel through its largest station and even switch gondola cars there to get to either of the two parks. For that reason, it has quickly become a very popular (and pricier) place to stay. In Luke 5, we read one of many examples of strangers coming to Jesus for a variety of reasons. In this passage, a man comes to be healed of leprosy, having heard of Jesus and knowing of His healing power. In short, Jesus was a hub or a central access point to God and His Word. People from all around knew about His reputation and came to listen, talk to and be healed by Him. We are also called to be a hub. Paul told us above to be an example to all in many areas of our Christian character. We should strive to be a hub that others use to know how to be a proper Christian, outwardly and openly demonstrating Whom we follow. Do others see you as a strong example for Jesus or do you keep your faith and beliefs hidden? Work hard to be a hub for God's Word as Christ was.

PRAYER—Father, help others to see me as a good, strong Christian example and come to me for guidance. Use me as a tool to bring many to Your kingdom. Through His name, Amen.

TODAY I WILL...become a hub! I will make myself widely available to others as a strong resource for Christ.

SEPTEMBER 10 **Read JONAH 1:1-17**

NOWHERE TO HIDE

Disney Resorts – Yacht Club

"Why do you call me 'Lord, Lord,' and not do what I tell you?"
—Luke 6:46

I'm sure everyone has played "Hide and Seek" at some point. My sons and I once played it at our church on a Saturday, and my youngest found the king of all hiding spots. We spent forever looking for him before we discovered he had gone through a vent and was actually inside the wall! In today's reading, a well-known Bible character tries to hide as well, but he chooses a boat. That reminded me of Disney's popular boat-themed resort called the Yacht Club. Opening in 1990, just 2 weeks before its sister resort, the Beach Club, next door, this deluxe resort featuring all things nautical is one of five within walking distance to Epcot and Hollywood Studios. Guests who stay at these resorts have access to Epcot's special back entrance.

In Jonah chapter 1, we read of him fleeing and attempting to hide after God commands him to go preach to the city of Nineveh. He instead boards a boat heading in the opposite direction, hoping God won't notice. I think you know the rest of the story as he certainly doesn't succeed in hiding. He is easily found, cast into the sea and swallowed by a large fish for three days as a disciplinary lesson for his disobedience. The message for us is another simple one...we can't hide from the commands of God. Remember when Adam and Eve also tried to hide in the Garden of Eden? It didn't work then either. God has directed us through His Word with several commands and instructions. As His faithful followers, we must do what He says and obey each and every one. Attempting to hide by ignoring Him or going against Him will result in His discipline and possible punishment as it did for Jonah as well as Adam and Eve. So just a reminder to work hard to do everything God instructs. Read the Bible very carefully and take it seriously. God means what He says and expects us to obey. Jonah learned that the hard way.

PRAYER—Lord, thank You again for Your Word so I know how You want me to live. Help me to read, understand and follow all You desire of me. In the name of Jesus I pray, Amen.

TODAY I WILL...vow to never hide from God's commands, instead choosing to learn His instructions and be a faithful follower at all times.

SEPTEMBER 11 **Read ROMANS 8:31-39**

INSEPARABLE LOVE

Disney Resorts – Polynesian Village

"...nor anything else in all creation, will be able to separate us from the love of God in Christ Jesus our Lord."
—*Romans 8:39*

Today is an unforgettable and historic day. Alan Jackson sang "Where were you when the world stopped turning" and one lyric suggested, "teaching a class full of innocent children." That's exactly where I was! I'll never forget their faces and my own shock and sadness as we watched the events unfold. I also remember it well because it was, and still is, my birthday, so I decided to give myself a small gift and choose my absolute favorite resort today. The theming, views, ambience and even the smell are all part of the Disney magic making this resort so very special. The Polynesian Village Resort, along with the Contemporary, were the only two resorts available when WDW opened in 1971. Since that day over 50 years ago, this resort has expanded from just under 500 rooms to nearly 900 today. A bulk of those extra accommodations came in 2015 when 20 unique and stunning, over-the-water Bungalows and 360 deluxe Villas were added.

One more fun fact about the "Poly"...it was there on December 29, 1974, where John Lennon signed the paperwork that officially broke up the legendary Beatles. After that day, the four, highly popular singers were no longer a united group. They were officially separated. Romans 8 expresses quite the opposite. In this comforting passage, Paul reminds us that God is on our side and gave His Son for us all. He concludes by emphatically stating nothing can separate us from God's love, even making a list 5 verses long of things that won't divide us. What a comforting thought knowing we can never be separated no matter what we do or how far we stray. As sad as it may be, everything on Earth, like the Beatles or those buildings on 9/11, will eventually fall. But God's love is eternal and will never perish. So where *were* you that day when the world stopped turning? Better yet, where *will* you be when it stops turning for good and God calls His chosen home? I pray you'll be firmly attached to the One who refuses to ever separate from you.

PRAYER—Lord, bless our country as we remember. Thank You for Your compassion for me. I feel such comfort knowing I can never be separated from You or that everlasting love. Amen.

TODAY I WILL...feel contentment knowing I can never be separated from God's love.

SEPTEMBER 12 **Read DEUTERONOMY 7:15-22**

BEES FOR HIS CHOSEN

Disney Resorts – Grand Floridian

"No man shall be able to stand before you all the days of your life. Just as I was with Moses, so I will be with you. I will not leave you or forsake you."
—*Joshua 1:5*

Have you ever watched a sitcom episode where the family went to Disney? I love those shows! My favorite is probably *Full House*. Do you remember when the Tanner family went to Disney World? Now there's a classic two-episode saga. Coming all the way from San Francisco, they chose to stay in the nicest and generally most expensive resort on property. The Grand Floridian not only hosted the Tanners but has also accommodated the British royal family as well as the Beach Boys while making the video for their hit song, "Kokomo," which coincidentally features John Stamos, from *Full House*, on drums. The Grand Floridian opened in 1988 and has also seen major expansion over the years including a newly opened path in 2020 which now makes it the closest resort within walking distance to WDW's Magic Kingdom. This resort is perhaps most known for its beautiful, Christmas decorations including its life-sized gingerbread house.

Did you know that bees help recycle that famous gingerbread house? The frame underneath all that gingerbread is coated with sugar after each Christmas season, and instead of power-washing it, workers take it to a tree farm and allow bees to have at it. Not only does it help the bees find a source of food within the winter months, but it helps clean off the frame for future use. In Deuteronomy 7, we read where God used bees to drive out the enemies of His people. In fact, all of chapter 7 is God telling His people they are special and chosen. He says repeatedly that He will protect and take care of them, even if it takes bees to do so. Incidentally, God also uses bees against enemies in Exodus 23 and Joshua 24. God always watches over and protects His people including you and me. He will also deliver us from our enemies including the most powerful, Satan. We are assured above that He will be with us and never leave us. Take comfort in His protection, His triumph over our enemies and His future victory over Satan's evil.

PRAYER—Dear Lord, I need Your help in conquering Satan and all his tricks, trials and temptations. Thank you for aiding me and all Your chosen. In Christ Jesus name, Amen.

TODAY I WILL...seek God's help in defeating my enemies or anything keeping me from Him.

SEPTEMBER 13 **Read JOHN 1:9-13**

JOIN THE FAMILY

Disney Resorts – Old Key West

"For whoever does the will of my Father in heaven is my brother and sister and mother."

—Matthew 12:50

What makes a Disney trip so "magical?" Is it the parks? Attractions? Resorts? Restaurants? Characters? Memories? Nostalgia? The answer is yes! All of that combines to make a Disney visit special and unique from any other vacation spot in the world. However, I would argue there's another very strong contributing factor. Being able to spend quality time with my family at a place where we share so much happiness and laughter as well as so many memories is what makes a Disney vacation so special for me. I've never stayed at Disney's Old Key West Resort, but we did visit recently for dinner and noticed numerous family pictures covering the walls. This resort was first known as Disney Vacation Club Resort when built in 1991 as it was the very first location strictly constructed for Disney's timeshare program known as Disney Vacation Club or DVC. Therefore, it was built with families in mind, hoping they would buy into the program and plan many more vacations to this very resort. For many years, those families were allowed to hang their own pictures in the resort's restaurant lobby where they still remain today.

Families are important to Disney, but even more so to God. In fact, we are told in today's reading that Jesus came here to "His own people" to "give us the right to become children of God" as long as we believe in His name and receive Him. In other words, He came to establish His family, the family of God. Unfortunately, it also says that many of His own people did not receive Him, a trend that sadly continues today even with those who claim to be in His family. God strongly desires all to join His family through Jesus. Jesus said above that whoever does God's will becomes His brother or sister. That's certainly a family I want to be in! What about you? What an honor, privilege and blessing to say we are in God's own family! If you are not a part of His family, please take steps to join. I would love to call you my brother or sister!

PRAYER—Father God, I'm so honored to be invited into Your family. Help me to remain a faithful member for life. Thank You for my brother, Jesus Christ, who made it possible. Amen.

TODAY I WILL...assure my place in God's family and encourage my brothers and sisters.

SEPTEMBER 14 **Read PSALM 11:1-7**

THE NANNY THRONE

Disney Resorts – Boardwalk

"The Lord has established his throne in the heavens, and his kingdom rules over all."
—Psalm 103:19

Do you know Todd, Paul, Alex and Carrie at WDW? After all, they've been around for years, watching guests walk by with their unblinking eyes. They have absolutely no life in them yet often move around mysteriously. Is this getting creepy or what? To be honest, these four ARE a bit creepy and can be found at today's choice destination. Opened in 1996, Disney's Boardwalk is more than just a hotel because it also includes several dining and entertainment establishments. Designed to resemble New York's Coney Island, the Boardwalk is another of the deluxe resorts found between Epcot and Hollywood Studios. In addition to the nearly 400 rooms within the main building, there are over 500 DVC villas which include larger, multi-bedroom suites.

So back to Todd, Paul, Alex and Carrie. Just who are they exactly? They are actually four, fairly famous chairs that reside at the Boardwalk. Their names are etched right on their backs while their fronts feature their undeniably strange and slightly disturbing faces. Look up a picture online if you dare! As mentioned, the chairs inexplicably tend to move around the resort from time to time and are therefore not always found in the same place. These "nanny chairs" as they are officially called, are replicas of 19th century, carousel chairs which were made for nannies to sit on while they observed the children they were watching ride the carousel. Did you know God has a chair as well? Psalm 11 is another uplifting passage assuring us that God is constantly seated on His throne watching over us too. The verse above repeats that fact. Just like those historical nannies, God is vigilantly observing His children go 'round and 'round on the carousel called "life," carefully watching to see where we get off. He allows us to make that choice while offering guidance and instructing us with His Word. Choose your stop wisely and remember He's watching, seated in His chair, waiting for you to call on Him for help.

PRAYER—Dear God, I bow before Your holy throne. I am so grateful that You are eternally seated there watching over and guiding me. Help me to make right choices. In Jesus, Amen.

TODAY I WILL...visualize the future when I kneel before the almighty throne of God.

SEPTEMBER 15 **Read 2 KINGS 2:1-11**

A HAPPY ENDING

Disney Resorts – All-Star Movies

"And if I go and prepare a place for you, I will come again and will take you to myself, that where I am you may be also."
—John 14:3

Sorry, but I'm going to go ahead and spoil next month's theme. On each day of October, we'll be discussing one of Disney's classic movies, having already looked at the Pixar films in May. What's your favorite Disney movie? I told you way back in early January that mine has always been *Pete's Dragon* because of its incredible music, wonderful story and, like most Disney films, happy ending. Speaking of movies and happy endings, Disney's All-Star Movies opened in 1999 and features five housing sections each themed around Disney films with happy endings: *Toy Story, The Mighty Ducks, 101 Dalmatians, The Love Bug* and *Fantasia*. While some of these may seem like random choices and all are quite different in their plot lines, they are alike in the fact that they all have happy endings: Woody and Buzz make it home. Charlie shoots the winning goal. Cruella is defeated and the dogs are returned. Herbie wins the race. And *Fantasia*...well, it's not much of a story, but the beautiful music concludes happily I suppose.

So what about your movie? Will it have a happy ending? I know, I know...you're probably not making a movie, but what if your life was one? I assume you would want it to have a happy ending too, right? After all, there's pretty much only two ways it can end according to Scripture. And you don't want it to be the sad ending...trust me! In 2 Kings 2, we read the end of Elijah's movie. This great prophet who did amazing things for God throughout his life got to end his story by being taken directly up to Heaven in a chariot of fire. Now that's a happy ending I wouldn't mind having myself! I'm guessing I won't get a fiery chariot, but I'm at least taking steps to assure my happy ending, meaning getting to see my Father and being reunited with family, friends and so many loved ones. Don't you want that too? I promise your story will one day have an eternal end one way or the other. Make sure your movie gets its happy ending!

PRAYER—Father, I want so badly for my life to have a happy ending like Elijah's. Please take me into Your kingdom as well. I cannot wait to be there with Your chosen. In Christ, Amen.

TODAY I WILL...write or adjust the ending to my life's "movie" to assure it is a happy one.

SEPTEMBER 16 **Read ISAIAH 44:1-5**

THE SPRING OF LIFE

Disney Resorts – Wilderness Lodge

"To the thirsty I will give from the spring of the water of life without payment."
—Revelation 21:6

Even during the hottest and driest, summer months, the creek in our backyard growing up always had water in it. Why? Because there was a natural spring there. My parents still live there, and I can report the spring still flows to this day. The Wilderness Lodge at WDW also has a spring on site...inside the lobby! This resort was patterned after the national parks of western USA. Built on the banks of Bay Lake and near the Fort Wilderness campground, this deluxe resort is accessible to the Magic Kingdom by a short boat ride. Besides the spring, the lobby includes an authentic, 55-foot totem pole and a huge, 82-foot, colorful fireplace representing the rocks of the Grand Canyon. In addition to the over 700 rooms inside the main building, there are two DVC properties on site with nearly 400 additional villas. We'll discuss one of those DVC locations in tomorrow's devotional due to an interesting and very special memento on site.

The spring inside the Wilderness Lodge lobby is actually hot, flows right up from the floor and is then strategically diverted outside. Obviously, this spring is artificial, designed and placed by Disney during construction, but it's still a neat effect that reminds me of our passage and thought for today. In Isaiah 44, God says He'll pour His water on the thirsty land and dry ground, also promising to pour His Spirit on the offspring of His chosen people. It even says because of this, those special people will "spring up" like Willow trees by flowing streams. Guess what type of tree was in my parents' yard right beside that spring? Yep, a Willow Tree! God's promise still holds true today. In the final book of the Bible above, He even promises the free water of life from His spring to anyone who is thirsty, meaning eternal life to all who seek Him. Jesus offered the same to the Samaritan woman in John 4. That special everlasting water is available to you. Just be thirsty and seek Him. There's plenty of His water to go around.

PRAYER—Eternal Father, thank You for promising the water from Your spring. I thirst for You, Lord and want to drink of that everlasting life-giving water. In the name of Christ, Amen.

TODAY I WILL...be thirsty and accept God's offer of the water of eternal life.

SEPTEMBER 17 **Read I JOHN 3:11-18**

A PRICELESS MODEL

Disney Resorts – Boulder Ridge Villas

"Therefore be imitators of God, as beloved children. And walk in love, as Christ loved us and gave himself up for us."
—Ephesians 5:1-2

One of my fondest childhood memories is a family vacation when I was a junior in high school. We flew to Chicago and then took a train all the way to Denver. It was an overnight trip, so we had a whole room to ourselves, actually sleeping on the train. It was a unique and memorable form of travel as well as a beautiful way to see the western U.S. for the first time. I've always loved trains. I even had a working, model train growing up I loved to play with. But from what I've read, as much as I enjoyed playing with and riding on trains, Walt Disney loved them even more. Yesterday, I mentioned two DVC additions at the Wilderness Lodge. One is called Copper Creek Villas, but for the ultimate Disney history lesson, you can head to the other named Boulder Ridge Villas and find the Carolwood Pacific Railroad Room located there. This room preserves the legacy of Walt's love for trains. My favorite part is that there is even a model train there with a plaque explaining it was designed by Walt himself for his family home in L.A.

What a priceless treasure to have at this resort! An actual model train that belonged to Walt Disney. As you're aware, Walt turned his love for trains and this smaller model into large, actual versions still found at each Disney park around the world. In I John 3, we are taught to love one another as Christ did. We're even told to lay down our lives for our Christian family as Christ, of course, did for us. The final verse says we should love, not in word or talk only, but in deed and truth as well. In other words, as the verse above also states, we must physically imitate Christ and actually "walk in love" as He did. Jesus was physically active, showing His love for others with good deeds, and we should do the same. Like Walt's train models, we are to be smaller versions of the immense and powerful love Jesus demonstrated and freely gave. Are you an active model of Christ, attempting to imitate Him daily in all you do? Make that a goal today!

PRAYER—Dear God, thank You for sending Your perfect Son to be our example and pattern. Help me to model Him in all I do and say so that others will know and follow Him too. Amen.

TODAY I WILL...be a model of Christ, carefully studying and imitating His every action.

SEPTEMBER 18 **Read MATTHEW 8:23-27**

A CALM FOR OUR STORMS

Disney Resorts – Beach Club

"Then he rose and rebuked the winds and the sea, and there was a great calm."
—Matthew 8:26

Know where I'd love to be right now? Relaxing in an inner tube, floating around the lazy river at Stormalong Bay. Oh, I realize that sounds a bit dicey, but that's actually the name of the peaceful and refreshing pool facility at Disney's Beach Club Resort. Considered by many to be the premier among Disney pools, it includes almost 800,000 gallons of water, a 230-foot-long waterslide inside a shipwreck replica and even a sand-bottom portion. This huge, 3-acre facility, full of aquatic activities is actually available to anyone staying at either the Yacht or Beach Club, essentially twin, side-by-side resorts, again found between Epcot and Hollywood Studios.

As mentioned, the name of this well-known, pool facility, Stormalong Bay, might bring to mind dangerous and turbulent storms which can cause worry, fear and anxiety to those involved as well as scary and costly destruction to homes and property. In fact, as I'm writing this, there was a massive, deadly storm just an hour west of us over the weekend. Numerous homes were destroyed, several are missing and over a dozen have been confirmed dead. Today's reading is likely a familiar story we actually looked at several months ago in another Gospel's account, but it's always a good reminder. Notice the vast difference between the reaction of Jesus and the Apostles to this violent storm. They are terrified, fearful of perishing and begging Jesus to save them, while He shows no fear and is actually asleep. After being awakened, He calmly rises, rebukes the storm and halts the ferocious winds and waves. Keep in mind He can do the same even today, not necessarily to immediately stop a terrifying storm we may witness, but within our own stormy and unsettling lives. Read Matthew 11:25-30 as a reminder of what Jesus can do for us when our lives are scary or out of control. He can provide sweet rest for our souls. Don't forget about this gift offered by our Savior when your own life seems impossible or unbearable.

PRAYER—Lord, You know my life is often full of storms, difficult to handle or understand. Help me to remember, request and receive the offer of Christ during these times. In Him, Amen.

TODAY I WILL...create a physical reminder of Christ's offer of peace to use when needed.

SEPTEMBER 19 **Read JOHN 17:20-26**

A ROYAL ROOM PREPARED

Disney Resorts – Port Orleans-Riverside

"In my Father's house are many rooms. If it were not so, would I have told you that I go to prepare a place for you?"
—John 14:2

In January 2015, my wife and I traveled to WDW without kids to celebrate our 15th anniversary. We got a huge surprise when we arrived to stay at the Port Orleans-Riverside Resort for the first time. Walking towards the lobby, we noticed our names on a sign being held by cast members. After introductions, they promptly told us we had been chosen as the "Royal Family of the Day" which included special treatment, balloons, a free photo and an upgrade to a "Royal Guestroom Suite." This resort opened in 1992 as "Disney's Dixie Landings Resort." The name changed in 2001 and these majestic suites were added in 2011. Imagine our delight as we entered our "regal" room to find *Princess and the Frog* theming as well as ornamental, hidden touches from several other Disney films. The entire suite was beautifully decorated with unique artwork and custom fabrics that really gave the room a "royal" feel. Our favorite part was the fiber-optic headboards that displayed a colorful, fireworks scene with the simple push of a button.

Being surprised with a stay in one of these royal suites made us feel chosen and pretty special. In John 17, we find something else special, a prayer Jesus made to the Father right before His crucifixion. Near the end, He prayed for all "who will believe in me." That's us! He continued, asking God to bring us all to Him in Heaven so that we can see His glory. A bit earlier, in the verse shown above from John 14, Jesus had talked about His Father's House with many rooms and that He would be returning there to "prepare a place" for us. One of those rooms has been chosen and prepared for you! Talk about a royal invitation! As amazing as the royal suite was on our unforgettable anniversary trip, it pales in comparison to the room awaiting us in Heaven. Make sure you accept God's invitation and follow His steps so You can one day check into your royal and eternal guest room prepared by Jesus Himself! I can't wait to see mine!

PRAYER—Thank You, holy Father, for having Jesus prepare a room for me in Your eternal home. I can't wait to get there, see His glory and bow before Your throne. In His name, Amen.

TODAY I WILL...accept my invitation and prepare to check into my room in God's house.

SEPTEMBER 20 **Read MATTHEW 13:1-9, 18-23**

PICK YOUR SOIL

Disney Resorts – Vero Beach

"As for what was sown on good soil, this is the one who hears the word and understands it."
—Matthew 13:23

I'm pretty sure my teenage sons would prefer a beach vacation at this point in their lives over Disney. (Gasp!) I'm so ashamed and apologize for their blasphemy. What is it about the beach because honestly, I kinda enjoy going myself? Maybe it's because there's so much to do while enjoying the beautiful views, stunning sand and wide-open space. As Disneyland and WDW aren't near the ocean, it's rare to find a Disney resort actually on the beach, but there are a couple which we'll discuss today and tomorrow. Disney's Vero Beach Resort opened in 1995 on Florida's east coast and houses one of two Mickey-shaped pools (the other is at WDW's Shades of Green). This resort is also known for its turtle nesting grounds nearby where at certain times of the year, guests can literally watch the baby turtles make their first steps into the ocean.

As stated, there's so much to do at the beach: reading, relaxing, tanning, sports, listening to parables, socializing or enjoying the wide variety of activities within the ocean itself. Wait...did I just say listening to parables? Well, that's what the people did in today's passage. Verse 2 says they gathered "on the beach" to hear Jesus teach a parable from a boat. Incidentally, Jesus also explains here why He used parables (read verses 10-17 and 34-35). Not only did it fulfill prophecy, but it helped the people better understand God's lessons. This parable about the sower and the four types of ground where he attempts to sow his seed is pretty simple and begs an easy question. Which ground are you? Path, rocks, thorns or good soil? It all depends on what you do when you hear God's Word. Hopefully, like the good soil, you seek to understand it and spread it to others. Good soil produces more fruit which is exactly what we are called to do throughout the world. Take time to study more parables of Christ. Seek to understand His lessons so you can be the good soil and spread the seed of God's Word.

PRAYER—Lord, thank You for Jesus' parables, making Your teachings easier to understand. Help me to be only good soil in the hearing and spreading of Your Word. In Christ, Amen.

TODAY I WILL...assure I am good soil, hearing, understanding and spreading God's Word.

SEPTEMBER 21 **Read I SAMUEL 3:1-21**

THE CHIEF MESSENGER

Disney Resorts – Aulani

"(God) saved us and called us to a holy calling, not because of our works but because of his own purpose and grace, which he gave us in Christ Jesus before the ages began."
—2 Timothy 1:9

Let's go to the beach! Again! This time, we'll have to travel a good distance, but it'll be well worth it as we're going to Hawaii! By the way, Disney actually has three resorts in the U.S. outside of park locations, but their Hilton Head Island resort is technically not on a beach, being about a mile away. But back to Hawaii! Disney's 2nd full-on beach resort is located on the Hawaiian island of Oahu. This luxurious paradise designed to celebrate the state's customs and traditions opened in 2011. The 21-acre complex includes just over 350 rooms and nearly 500 additional DVC villas. It was designed by Joe Rohde who recently retired from Disney after 40 years and spearheaded many important projects including the design of Animal Kingdom itself.

The Hawaiian word "Aulani" is translated as "messenger of great authority" or "messenger of the chief." Today's reading from I Samuel 3 is a bit lengthy, but I hope you will read the entire passage. It's the story of Samuel's first calling as a young boy. It takes a little while for him to figure out it's the voice of God calling him, but he eventually does and grows to become a great prophet for the Lord. God continues to reveal Himself to Samuel throughout his life so that he can pass on God's messages to many people. In fact, the end of today's passage says that all Israel knew of Samuel as an established prophet of God. In other words, Samuel was God's "Aulani," if you look again at what that word means. We too are called to be "Aulani" or chief messengers for God. The verse above says God calls us to a "holy calling" for His own purpose. It is our duty and mission to spread and share His words to as many as we can. Ask God to help you be more like Samuel. Seek His guidance on not only what to say, but where, when and whom to say it to. He's calling you today to fulfill this purpose. Will you listen and obey?

PRAYER—Father, I know You are calling me to be Your messenger. I accept this role and purpose and ask Your help knowing what to say and whom to say it to. Lead me to a soul that needs saving and give me the courage and knowledge to help. In the name of Jesus, Amen.

TODAY I WILL...become "Aulani" for God by seeking and spreading His messages.

SEPTEMBER 22 **Read REVELATION 2:1-7**

AN INVITATION TO PARADISE

Disney Resorts – Paradise Pier

"Truly, I say to you, today you will be with me in paradise."
—Luke 23:43

What does the word "paradise" make you think of? Perhaps it brings yesterday's Hawaiian resort to mind. That would certainly be paradise for me! Most likely, the word puts a place of bliss and supreme happiness in your mind. For whatever reason, Disney decided to name one of its resorts using the same word. Let's head back to the west coast as Disneyland only has three that are fully Disney-owned. We've already discussed the other two this month, so let's cover the final one. Paradise Pier is considered to be Disneyland's "value" resort, although its price point puts in more on the "moderate" level. It was originally known as the Emerald Hotel when first built and managed by a Japanese company in 1984. Disney purchased the property in 1995 and gave it a couple more names before settling on its current title. This tower hotel with a casual beach theme has close to 500 rooms and suites, some with excellent views of DCA Park.

So why do you think Disney finally settled on naming this resort "Paradise" Pier? Most likely because, as mentioned above, it puts visions of happiness in the minds of potential guests. Are you aware there's an actual "Paradise?" Not only did Jesus mention it (above) from the cross as a promise for the criminal beside Him, but it's also used in our reading today. At the beginning of Revelation 2, John writes to the church in Ephesus saying the "tree of life," which is the "paradise of God," is available to those who follow God and "conquer" Satan. Remember when Adam and Eve lost their paradise because they were tempted by and chose to follow Satan? Don't let that happen to you! Just as Christ gave paradise to the criminal beside Him, God offers us the chance to reside there as well. And as you well know, God's paradise will be greater than anything we can visit or even imagine here on Earth. Don't you want to see the real Paradise and experience the eternal bliss it offers? I know you do. And I know you can. Make it happen!

PRAYER—Father, I want more than anything to be in Your Paradise. I'm so grateful that it is available to criminals, either on a cross or those like me. Please bring me there! In Jesus, Amen.

TODAY I WILL...draw a picture of my vision of what God's Paradise will look like.

SEPTEMBER 23 **Read GENESIS 32:22-32**

WANNA WRESTLE?

Disney Resorts – All-Star Sports

"He will dwell with them, and they will be his people, and God himself will be with them as their God."
—Revelation 21:3

I was never much of a sports guy. In two years of little league baseball, I got one hit. One! I'll never forget that day. My eyes were closed, as usual, but I swung the bat and heard a different sound. Instead of the usual "whoosh" of a strike, I heard a "smack!" Actually, it was more like a "doink" as the ball went three feet. After the initial shock, I actually remembered to run (in the correct direction mind you) and made it first base just before the throw. Safe! It was a miracle! Little Albert got a hit! That may sound like an exaggeration but it's mostly true. Like I said, not much of a sports guy. I did decide to try and was decent at running in high school, but that's about it for me in the sports world. Regardless, I do enjoy a stay at Disney's dedicated sports resort. Built in 1994, this resort, like its neighbors, Music and Movies, is divided into 5 housing sections, this time based on various sports: surfing, baseball, basketball, tennis and football.

While those five sports may not be in the Bible, there actually is a sport in Scripture. I guess technically running could count, but did you know wrestling is there too? In today's reading, Jacob wrestles with God. While it's certainly an intriguing story, I want to focus on what Jacob says after the wrestling. In verse 30, he states, "for I have seen God face to face, and yet my life has been delivered." The reason he made this statement is because nobody was supposed to see God's face and live. Exodus 33:20 makes this clear. Even in the New Testament in I John 4:12, we are told that nobody has ever seen God. I guess John forgot about Jacob. The point is this...while nobody on Earth, save Jesus and maybe Jacob, has ever physically seen God, we are clearly told we can and WILL see Him one day. The verse above proves that as well as I John 3:2 and Matt. 5:8 which both say we WILL see God. In the meantime, let us do everything in our power to better know and understand Him so that we *can* see Him. We will most likely never wrestle with God as Jacob did, but like him, let's all strive to see God face to face.

PRAYER—Dear God, I want to see You! Help me to make that happen. Through Jesus, Amen.

TODAY I WILL...make plans to see God one day, doing what is necessary to make it happen.

SEPTEMBER 24 **Read JAMES 3:2-12**

SMALL BUT POWERFUL

Disney Resorts – Port Orleans-French Quarter

"Let no corrupting talk come out of your mouths..."
—Ephesians 4:29

Ever been to New Orleans? I've been a few times. Most recently, I was deployed there as a paramedic in August 2020 after Hurricane Laura swept through. I enjoyed the work and the opportunity to help, but it wasn't exactly the best way to see the city. We did get to visit the historical and famous French Quarter section which you can also get a taste of by heading to WDW. We discussed Port Orleans-Riverside a few days ago, but that resort has a sister next door called Port Orleans-French Quarter. If you combine them, there are over 3000 rooms making it the largest joined resorts on property. The two are connected not only by walking path, but also by boat on the Sassagoula River which connects both resorts to Disney Springs.

Besides walking and taking a boat, there's one more way to travel between the two resorts...horse carriage. My wife and I once gave this a try and had a fabulous time. Did you notice the mention of horses in today's reading? James made the point that just as a small bit in a horse's mouth can control that large animal, the small tongue in our mouths can do large things...good or bad. Our tongues can be useful for many reasons, but they can also get us into trouble. Paul gave us a good reminder in Ephesians above when he said, "Let NO corrupting talk come out of your mouths." God expects us to use our tongues for good alone, to encourage others and tell them about the Gospel. When we instead use it to curse, joke inappropriately, tear others down or say anything that goes against God, it's an abomination and disappointment to Him. James also uses analogies in this passage comparing how a large ship is controlled by a tiny rudder or a small spark can set a huge fire. He then goes back to the tongue, saying it too is a fire controlled by hell. Don't let Satan control your tongue. Use it for blessing, not cursing (v. 9-10). Don't let that tiny part of your body cause you to lose your entire soul.

PRAYER—Dear Lord, help me to focus and control my tongue, only using it for good and in ways You approve. Forgive me for when I've used it inappropriately. In Christ's name, Amen.

TODAY I WILL...be very careful to only use my tongue to encourage others and please God.

SEPTEMBER 25 **Read I TIMOTHY 2:1-8**

THE BRIDGE

Disney Resorts – Bay Lake Tower

"...there is one mediator between God and men, the man Christ Jesus..."
—I Timothy 2:5

I mentioned earlier this month how my wife and I came to Disney World on our honeymoon and stayed at the Contemporary. At the time, the main tower was unavailable, so we were given the very end room in the North Garden Wing. We absolutely loved it as we had both a balcony and most beautiful view of Bay Lake. We said then that we'd love to return one day and stay in the same room as it was now full of special beginnings and forever memories. Well, we never did. And now we can't! It's been destroyed! Thanks, Disney! That wing was removed and replaced with a brand-new DVC property in 2009. Bay Lake Tower is technically considered an addition to the Contemporary Resort even though it's a standalone structure. Most of its rooms overlook the Magic Kingdom, some even providing fireworks views from the bathtub. Now that's luxury!

While I hate that our honeymoon haven was heartlessly destroyed, I can't argue with Disney's decision to provide this luxurious location with incredible views. We stayed here once thanks to some very generous family, and it was by far the nicest room and view we've ever had. As mentioned, this resort is considered an extension of the Contemporary and actually connects to it by way of an innovative sky bridge, providing access to all features of the Contemporary such as the restaurants, shops, pools and much-needed monorail. In today's passage, you might see a similar connection in what Christ provides for us. Verse 5, shown above, states that Jesus is the mediator or "bridge" between God and man, providing access to all God has to offer. Not only did Christ's death take the place of our sin, but He is our bridge to talk to, hear from and even one day make it to God. It cannot be overstated what a gift Jesus is! Use Him constantly to learn more about God. Talk to God daily through His name. Make plans to see God through Him as the only Way (John 14:6). Jesus is our all-access bridge, so make sure to use Him.

PRAYER—Holy Father, thank You for providing a bridge to have full access to You. Help me to use Christ daily so I can know Your plan and purpose for me. In His holy name, Amen.

TODAY I WILL...use Jesus as much as possible to hear, know and one day see God.

SEPTEMBER 26 **Read I KINGS 3:5-10 AND 10:1-9**

A WISE WISH

Disney Resorts – Saratoga Springs

"What you have learned and received and heard and seen in me, practice these things, and the God of peace will be with you."
—Philippians 4:9

You've seen Aladdin so you know the drill. Rub the lamb. Get three wishes. Actually, I'm only giving you one. Sorry, times are tough. So what's your wish? More wishes? Clever, but unfair and overused. Come on. What's it going to be? While Aladdin is obviously a fairy tale, there was a man who once got to make a wish and it came true! Before we discuss that, let's travel to another magnificent resort. The Saratoga Springs Resort, inspired by the same-named city in New York, opened in 2004 as a DVC property. It's huge, 65-acre complex has 18 villa buildings containing well over 1000 guest rooms. It also includes 60 Treehouse villas which we'll discuss tomorrow. Like the Port Orleans and Old Key West Resorts, this one lies on the Sassagoula River meaning it also provides boat access to Disney Springs, although it's so close, you can actually walk. This resort was built on the site of the former Disney Institute, a resort combined with a learning center that opened in 1996. It was promoted as a way for families to vacation while learning more about Disney with interactive classes. Unfortunately, the idea flopped.

One wish. That's what he got. And he chose wisdom! In the first passage above, Solomon is given one wish by God and chooses wisdom above all else. In the second passage, the Queen of Sheba comes to test his wisdom and is thoroughly impressed. God was also impressed and very proud of Solomon's choice, blessing him with riches, power and happiness as well. God is also proud when we choose wisdom by working hard to learn more about Him. Paul encouraged the Philippians above to also use what they had learned, and we should do the same, putting into practice the knowledge and actions we learn about through His Word. I enjoy learning about Disney, but I love even more knowing as much as possible about God. Join me in learning! Like Solomon, ask God for more wisdom, especially knowledge of His Word that you can share.

PRAYER—Lord, like Solomon, I also ask for wisdom. Give me the knowledge to know what to do, how to live and what to say so that I may further Your kingdom. In Jesus' name, Amen.

TODAY I WILL...make my one wish for wisdom, asking God for it to know Him better.

SEPTEMBER 27 **Read LUKE 19:1-10**

SHOW SOME EXCITEMENT

Disney Resorts – Treehouse Villas

"And leaping up, he stood and began to walk, and entered the temple with them, walking and leaping and praising God."
—Acts 3:8

It took a few months of begging, hints and suggestions, but my dad eventually conceded. I wanted my own treehouse so badly growing up and had vivid plans of how it would look, which included a three-story, enclosed building, nestled way up in the trees. Apparently, those cards weren't on the table as mine ended up as a two-story, standalone, open structure, near the trees. Whatever. It was a treehouse. It was mine, I loved it, and it still stands over 30 years later! Did you have one? Regardless, you are welcome to book a stay at one of Disney's 60 treehouses. As mentioned yesterday, these Treehouse Villas along the Sassagoula River are considered a DVC extension of the Saratoga Springs Resort. Built during the 4th phase of construction and opened in 2009, each of the treehouses has three bedrooms and are elevated 10 feet off the ground.

Did you remember Zacchaeus from today's story? He was a wee little man, and a wee little man was he, as the Sunday School song went. Due to his "small stature" but strong desire to see Jesus, he essentially created his own treehouse, climbing up in a sycamore tree to simply catch a glimpse of the Savior. But he got a lot more than a glimpse! Jesus not only called him by name but asked to stay at his house! It's the next verse I want to focus on saying Zacchaeus hurried down from the tree and received Jesus joyfully. Zacchaeus was a tax collector and sinner which he later admitted, promising he would repent and make it right. But despite his faults, he was eager and joyful for Christ. Read Acts 3:1-10 as well where Peter and John heal a lame beggar. Look above at what he did once healed, even inside the temple! He was leaping and praising God. How often do we show that type of excitement? I'll admit I rarely see that kind of joy in others and even myself during worship. We could all stand to be more like Zacchaeus and the beggar, adding excitement and joy when we seek, get to know and praise both Father and Son.

PRAYER—God, I want to be like Zacchaeus and be eager and joyful when it comes to Christ. I want others to see my excitement and be influenced to praise You as well. In His name, Amen.

TODAY I WILL...strive to show outward joy and enthusiasm towards the Father and Son.

SEPTEMBER 28 **Read ACTS 2:1-12**

HERE'S YOUR SIGN

Disney Resorts – Riviera

"And I will show wonders in the heavens above and signs on the earth below."
—Acts 2:19

Have you traveled to another country? My first visits overseas came during high school with a school trip to Italy after 11th grade and a family vacation to France after graduation. Those just happen to be the same two countries on which today's resort is based. Disney's Riviera Resort is the newest location on our list, recently opening in late 2019. As mentioned, it is beautifully themed around the Italian and French Rivieras and specifically Walt's personal trips there and throughout Europe. In fact, some of his personal photos are used for the décor. This is also one of the four resorts with Skyliner access meaning connections to Epcot and Hollywood Studios. Being so new, I have not had the pleasure of staying here yet but have only traveled through on the Skyliner several times. I have, however, heard wonderful reviews from those who have.

There are many wonderful amenities found at this resort, but perhaps the highest reviewed is the rooftop restaurant, Topolino's Terrace. Topolino is the Italian name for Mickey Mouse, yet another way this resort celebrates a variety of European culture including the various languages. It reminded me of Acts 2 and the Day of Pentecost following Christ's death, resurrection and ascension into Heaven. The people witness and were "amazed" by some incredible things that day including the fact that each could hear the Apostles' teachings in their own language. If you keep reading to verse 19 (above), Peter quotes the prophet Joel, and therefore God, saying He will continue to show His wonders in Heaven and even through signs on Earth. Have you ever seen God's wonders or gotten a sign from Him? I believe I have several times. God speaks to us in various ways, mostly through His written Word, but also through others, His Spirit inside us and even His signs referenced here. Keep an eye out for God. He may show you your purpose, a new direction or His desires in an unexpected way. So be watchful and look for the signs!

PRAYER—O mighty Father, the many wonders You performed throughout Your Word are incredible. Help me to recognize these and other signs from You meant to guide me. Amen.

TODAY I WILL...be more watchful for God's wonders and signs and their purpose for me.

SEPTEMBER 29 **Read PSALM 37:27-34**

WAIT FOR IT

Disney Resorts – Gran Destino Tower

"But if we hope for what we do not see, we wait for it with patience."
—Romans 8:25

Remember the Fruits of the Spirit from Galatians 5? We discussed them back on April 8 when talking about the Dole Whip. Mmmm... Dole Whips...I could use one of those right about now. Anyway, if you need a reminder, the Fruits of the Spirit are love, joy, peace, patience, kindness, goodness, faithfulness, gentleness and self-control, attributes we are expected to put into practice in our Christian walk. If I asked you which of those you struggled most with, what would you say? My answer is easy. Before I share, let's get to our next to last resort, which is actually part of the previously covered Coronado Springs. In the summer of 2019, the 15-story Gran Destino Tower opened on site adding 545 guest rooms including 50 suites. On our 2nd stay at Coronado Springs, we were actually surprised with a free upgrade to this tower and thoroughly enjoyed it.

The Gran Destino Tower gets its name from a short film, *Destino*, produced through the joint efforts of Spanish painter, Salvador Dali and Walt Disney himself. What's unique about the film is that it began production in 1945 but wasn't completed and released until 2003, 58 years later. Talk about a lengthy production schedule! You probably see which Spirit fruit was most needed for this project? Hint...it's also my greatest flaw. Patience is an area where many struggle. Whether a task at work, a home-improvement project, driving (my greatest area of weakness), etc., there are many aspects of life we must approach with patience. It takes focus, discipline and certainly God's help, but it's important to demonstrate a good example of patience to those around us. Growing frustrated or showing anger when impatient can lead to sin, ungodly actions, bad choices, poor examples and damage to our relationship with God. So how's your patience? If you struggle as I do, make conscious efforts to focus, breathe and act appropriately during those times. Above all, seek God's help to find the calmness and patience needed.

PRAYER—Lord, please help me with my patience. Give me the ability to recognize dangerous thoughts, actions or words forming when I get impatient so I may stop them. In his name, Amen.

TODAY I WILL...create a plan for when I feel impatient so my words/actions don't lead to sin.

SEPTEMBER 30 **Read PSALM 100:1-5**

GIVE BACK THE NOISE

Disney Resorts – Art of Animation

"And he said to them, "Pay attention to what you hear: with the measure you use, it will be measured to you."
—Mark 4:24

Check it out on Google Images or better yet, Google Earth, because you simply must see it to believe it. It's located in Algarrobo, Chile, covers 20 acres, is 3,323 feet long and contains 66 million gallons of water. It's the world's largest swimming pool! Or at least it was until another in Egypt recently claimed the title. But it's pretty amazing to have a pool you can literally go sailing in! Disney may not have a pool quite that big, but among their many great ones, the one at today's final resort is the largest. The Art of Animation Resort finally opened in 2012 after sitting partially abandoned for many years. As we discussed earlier this month, the Pop Century had a planned extension covering the early decades of the 1900's. However, the 9/11 attacks caused a major construction delay and eventual retheming in a completely different direction. What opened instead was this celebration of animation with housing sections dedicated to four very popular animated films: *The Little Mermaid, Cars, Finding Nemo* and *The Lion King.*

In addition to many notable amenities, this resort, as mentioned, houses WDW's largest pool. The "Big Blue Pool" has zero-entry, over 300,000 gallons of water and huge *Finding Nemo* set pieces. It also has the ingenious addition of various music and sounds from speakers beneath the surface. Just another hidden touch of Disney magic if you choose to swim underwater, listen and hear. In a similar way, we are told above and throughout the Bible to listen for and hear God. He provides joyous noises in life through nature, others and the encouraging words of Scripture. While it's impossible to repay Him fully, today's psalm encourages us to return to Him a joyful noise by singing in His presence. God provides us so many wonderful things to hear. Let us return His love by singing praises right back to Him. As Psalm 104:33 says, "I will sing to the Lord as long as I live. I will sing praise to my God while I have being."

PRAYER—Holy Father, thank You for Your noise. Help me today and always to listen and hear however You speak to me. I praise You as my Father and Lord forever! In Jesus, Amen.

TODAY I WILL...listen carefully for God's noise and then give some right back to Him.

OCTOBER THEME

DISNEY CLASSIC FILMS

OCTOBER 1 **Read ACTS 15:22-26**

WILL YOU PASS THE TEST?

Disney Classic Films – Snow White and the Seven Dwarfs

"Beloved, do not be surprised at the fiery trial when it comes upon you to test you, as though something strange were happening to you."
—I Peter 4:12

Can you believe it's already October? The year is rapidly closing. As I recently spoiled, this month we will be focusing on classic Disney films, most of them made before our May theme, Pixar, even existed. And what better place to start than at the beginning. *Snow White and the Seven Dwarfs* was Disney's first, full-length film, certainly befitting the very definition of "classic." Released in 1937, it was based on the Brothers Grimm fairy tale from over a century earlier. The film was quite successful and led to one of many awards for Walt Disney when he was given an honorary Oscar consisting of one normal-sized statuette surrounded by seven mini ones. It was presented to him by famed actress, Shirley Temple who was only 11 at the time.

If you're like me, you might not have seen this classic in a while. Hello, Disney Plus! That subscription service has personally been a blessing to re-live some of these nostalgic movies. Regardless, I'm sure you remember this film's popular characters: Snow White, the Prince, the evil Queen, the Dwarfs. But what about the Huntsman? Remember him? The Queen orders him to kill Snow White in the woods, but he can't bring himself to do so. He instead begs her forgiveness and at great risk, warns her of the Queen's intentions. He knew it was the right thing to do even though it put his own life in jeopardy. Today's passage reminds us how dangerous it also was for the early Apostles, specifically calling them "men who have risked their lives for the name of our Lord Jesus Christ." We tend to assume we'll never have to face the persecution they did, but are you prepared if it happens? There are certainly Christians in other countries, even today, that are being martyred for the name of Jesus. The verse above promises "fiery trials" we will face to test our dedication, faith and righteousness. When they happen, as with the Huntsman, will you pass the test by doing what's right, even if it means your very life?

PRAYER—Lord and Father, please grant me the courage and commitment to withstand any trials that test my faith, even those that endanger my very life. In the name of my Savior, Amen.

TODAY I WILL...decide if I'm prepared to risk or even give my life for the name of Jesus.

OCTOBER 2 **Read HEBREWS 12:1-11**

DON'T GET ENTANGLED

Disney Classic Films – *Tangled*

"...let us throw off everything that hinders and the sin that so easily entangles."
—Hebrews 12:1 (NIV)

Ever gone rock climbing? I've always been impressed with those who can scale mountains with only their hands. I've only gone as far as a climbing gym which was fun and challenging. I was grateful for the multiple hand holds strategically placed. What if it was hair instead? How hard would it be to climb a rock wall, or better yet, a stone tower, using only a thick strand of hair? *Tangled* is Disney's version of Rapunzel, another timeless Brothers Grimm tale. In fact, this film was titled "Rapunzel" at first before it was changed to reflect the story's focus on multiple characters. This was Disney's 50th and most expensive animated film, costing $260 million to create. Thankfully, it was highly successful, making more than double that in box office sales.

You may not recall the entire Rapunzel story, but everyone remembers her long hair. This film makes no exception, giving her what seems like an endless supply of beautiful and even magical hair that leads to her abduction and entrapment. I've never had to deal with long hair, but I know from having sisters and a wife that it must be given frequent attention to avoid becoming tangled. Similarly, the verse above is a reminder of what else can easily "entangle" us. The verse begins today's passage which focuses on the dangers of sin and how easy it is to get caught in it. We are reminded not only to fix our eyes on Jesus as a way out but also of God's discipline when we fall into it. Our fallible minds tend to excuse small sin as no big deal, rationalizing that as long as we don't sin often or commit a "big sin," we will be fine. But this passage reminds us that sin is very deceptive and will entangle us before we know it. One small sin becomes two or three, and eventually we will justify our way into entrapment. We must be diligent and strong to rid our lives of anything going against God's instructions and wishes. Evaluate your life every day to assure you are not entangled in any kind of sin, great or small.

PRAYER—Father, I know that any sin separates us and I don't want that. Give me the strength and knowledge to get rid of anything keeping my soul from Your kingdom. In Jesus, Amen.

TODAY I WILL...get untangled from any sin, great or small, that has infiltrated my life.

OCTOBER 3 **Read PSALM 19:7-10**

YOU'VE HAD IT ALL ALONG

Disney Classic Films – Who Framed Roger Rabbit

"For the word of God is living and active, sharper than any two-edged sword..."
—Hebrews 4:12

Going non-Disney momentarily, but did you ever watch Looney Tunes? I used to watch Bugs Bunny and friends every Saturday and absolutely loved it. Of course, I loved Disney characters too so you can imagine what a dream it would've been if Disney and Warner Brothers combined their characters. Welcome to *Who Framed Roger Rabbit*! Released in 1988, this combination live action/cartoon was based on a 1981 book from which Disney purchased the film rights. They brilliantly hired producer, Steven Spielberg, who was able to convince Warner Brothers to lend their characters to the film. They only agreed with the stipulation that certain comparable characters would get equal screen time. Therefore, Bugs and Mickey and then Daffy and Donald have scenes together, the first and only time these characters shared the screen and interacted.

I loved this movie, not only for its revolutionary collaboration of characters, but also for the clever and entertaining story line. When the owner of Toontown is murdered, Roger Rabbit is accused and must therefore not only clear his name, but also find the victim's will so Toontown doesn't fall into the wrong hands. Spoiler alert...at the end, he discovers he unknowingly had the will all along. Today's short reading reminds us we too may not realize what an important treasure we've had all along. The Bible is literally God's written Word, and this psalm says it's not only perfect but also calls it sure, right, pure and true. It ends saying it's sweeter than honey and should be desired more than gold. The verse above also reminds us that the Bible is always living and active. It will never die. God's Word is eternal and it's the only way for us to know His desires and plan for our salvation. Never forget what a powerful treasure you've had all along in your Bible. Take advantage of that blessing by using it daily and even better, sharing it.

PRAYER—Lord, help me to realize what a treasure Your Word is and use it daily to guide, improve and save my life. Give me courage to share its message with others. In Jesus, Amen.

TODAY I WILL...purchase an extra Bible (or several if possible) to give away to someone who needs one. I will ask God to make that person known to me.

OCTOBER 4 **Read ACTS 11:19-26**

BE A BARNABAS

Disney Classic Films – *Dumbo*

"But encourage one another daily, as long as it is called 'Today,' so that none of you may be hardened by sin's deceitfulness."
—Hebrews 3:13 (NIV)

There is a long history of human flight attempts. As early as 400 B.C., ancient Greeks tried it by creating bird-shaped models and jumping off high places. Future attempts included human kites, homemade wings covered in feathers and even something called "balloon jumping." Needless to say, there were multiple casualties and numerous failures before the Wright Brothers finally figured it out in 1903. Researching the many creative designs, I don't recall any that were elephant-shaped. If they only knew what Disney taught us...that elephants with giant, flappy ears can fly! *Dumbo* (1941) was Disney's 4th animated feature and was created to make up financial loses of the previous two films, *Fantasia* and *Pinocchio*. Thankfully, it did just that. It is Disney's shortest film at 64 minutes and contains the only title character who doesn't speak.

You may remember Dumbo is blessed with a sidekick. Timothy Mouse becomes Dumbo's coach, advisor and eventual savior, convincing him he can fly without his magic feather just before he crashes into the ground. In short, Timothy Mouse is a constant encourager leading to Dumbo's eventual success and happiness. Our reading today introduces a man named Barnabas describing him as a "good man, full of the Holy Spirit and faith." When he is sent to the people of Antioch, he encourages them in their faith and as a result, a great number are added to the church. Earlier in Acts 4:36, we are told his name actually means "son of encouragement." Barnabas is a great example of how to follow the command above from Hebrews. We too are told to go out and encourage others daily to aid them in avoiding sin. When was the last time you asked someone about struggles or difficulties they were facing? There are many who would benefit from conversation and confession but just need someone to ask and encourage them. Be that person who listens, helps and encourages others back to a full faith and dedication to God.

PRAYER—Lord, I want to be a Barnabas. Help me to constantly encourage others, especially those in need. Give me the right words to say so they may find You. In Christ I pray, Amen.

TODAY I WILL...name one person needing encouragement who I will seek, listen to and help.

OCTOBER 5 **Read 2 SAMUEL 4:4 & 9:1-13**

ACCIDENTS HAPPEN

Disney Classic Films – *Pollyanna*

"I will restore to you all the land of Saul your father, and you shall eat at my table always."
—2 Samuel 9:7

You've probably heard the phrase, "accidents happen," and it's true. We've all experienced a few unfortunate accidents in life, some more serious than others. I've been in a few minor car wrecks and once fell down a flight of stairs but have thankfully only suffered the typical bumps and bruises. I've actually never broken a bone. Knock on wood! In short, I've been lucky with no serious accidents in life. The same can't be said for today's title character. *Pollyanna*, released in 1960, starred a young Hayley Mills who won a juvenile Oscar for the role. She's probably best known for playing both twins in the original *Parent Trap*, but this was the first of the six films she did for Disney as a child. This film is based on a 1913 novel by the same name.

Pollyanna is the story of a young girl who comes to a new town and encourages multiple citizens through her cheerful personality. She's actually a great example of a "Barnabas" from yesterday. At the end of the film, she is paralyzed due to a horrible accident and falls into depression. Thankfully, the townspeople she encouraged return the favor, aiding in her recovery. Had you heard of Mephibosheth? Today's first passage introduced him as Jonathan's son who also had a horrible accident at 5 years old, falling and becoming lame for the rest of his life. When Jonathan dies, King David wishes to honor his best friend by showing kindness to his family. Therefore, in our 2nd reading, he seeks out Mephibosheth to exalt him, give him land and invite him to always eat at the king's table, which he does. Accidents do happen. We all have or will experience difficult events that will bring us down or cause undesired struggles. When that happens, keep in mind that an unexpected good may come in time from a trial, as it did with Mephibosheth. Keep focus on God and He may use your trial to lead you in a new and even better direction. Don't ever lose faith! Accidents happen, but God is always in control.

PRAYER—Dear Lord, I pray for health and safety. When trials come, keep my faith and focus strong and use it to make me a better person or lead me to greater things. Through Jesus, Amen.

TODAY I WILL... pledge to not lose faith, knowing God can bring good from bad situations.

OCTOBER 6 **Read ROMANS 6:3-11**

A NEW CREATURE

Disney Classic Films – *Avatar*

"I have been crucified with Christ. It is no longer I who live, but Christ who lives in me."
—Galatians 2:20

A little game to start...name the superhero for each secret identity (answers at end): 1. Bruce Banner, 2. Bruce Wayne, 3. Clark Kent, 4. Diana Prince, 5. Steve Rogers, 6. Tony Stark, 7. Natasha Romanoff, 8. Peter Parker, 9. Carol Danvers, 10. Bob Parr. How many did you know? One more...Jake Sully. Remember him? Not a superhero, but his true identity was certainly unknown to the native Na'vi of Pandora. *Avatar* was produced by 20th Century Fox and released in 2009. In 2011, Fox worked out an agreement with Disney to allow theme park rides based on the film. Pandora—The World of Avatar finally opened at Animal Kingdom in 2017. Disney purchased Fox outright in 2019 meaning they now own this film and the upcoming four sequels.

This film's plot revolves around humans using "avatars" to become the native creatures of Pandora. Jake Sully, a paraplegic, can even walk and move normally when he becomes the new creature of his avatar. Today's passage explains what baptism in Christ means to us, both now and eternally. The process of baptism may seem strange at first...dunking someone underwater to save their soul? Really? How does that work? The passage explains it's symbolic, sharing in the death (to sin), burial (underwater) and resurrection (coming out of the water) of Jesus. Verse 8 provides great hope saying if we die with Christ through baptism, we'll live with Him in eternity. Finally, it makes clear that through baptism, our old self dies, and we become a new creature. The verse above echoes, saying when we are crucified with Christ (through baptism), He lives inside us, making us a new creature. I strongly encourage you to become a new creature through baptism if you haven't already. Follow Christ's example and guarantee eternal life with Him. (Answers: 1. Hulk, 2. Batman, 3. Superman, 4. Wonder Woman, 5. Captain America, 6. Ironman, 7. Black Widow, 8. Spiderman, 9. Captain Marvel, 10. Mr. Incredible)

PRAYER—Most loving Father, I'm so grateful I can share in the death, burial and resurrection of Christ through baptism. I'm also thankful it leads to eternal life with You. In Him, Amen.

TODAY I WILL...understand the symbolism of baptism to share its importance with others.

OCTOBER 7 **Read JONAH 2:1-10**

LESSONS FROM INSIDE A FISH

Disney Classic Films – *Pinocchio*

"I desire then that in every place the men should pray, lifting holy hands."
—I Timothy 2:8

Picture it. You've just been thrown from a boat into the raging sea. You try desperately to stay afloat, knowing your efforts are futile. Suddenly you see a giant, ominous shape moving slowly towards you right before everything goes dark. The blackness. The smell. The slimy feel. You can't believe you are still conscious as you wrap your mind around where you are...inside the belly of a sea creature. No escape. Why aren't you dead? What do you do? Can you believe that really happened? I'd love to ask old Jonah what was going through his mind during those 3 days. Watching today's memorable and ageless classic can at least help visualize Jonah's story as Pinocchio is also fish-swallowed near the end. *Pinocchio* was Disney's 2nd film, released in 1940 and based on an 1883 Italian book. It was the first animated feature to score an Oscar (Walt himself had won for *Snow White*). *Pinocchio* actually won two for Best Score and Song. The film sadly bombed in sales, mainly due to World War II cutting off the foreign market.

So what did Jonah do, realizing he was inside a fish's belly? While he made mistakes to start this story by disobeying God and attempting to hide, at least he made a good decision from inside the fish in today's reading. He prayed. In total darkness, with no options, in likely terror and hopelessness, he talked to God. He admitted defeat, confessed wrongdoing, vowed to do right and praised God. The best part...God heard every single word! And responded! When the prayer was done, God told the fish to spit Jonah out so he could fulfill his promise to do right. God desires us to pray. Without ceasing (I Thess. 5:17). For any reason (Php. 4:6). And with full faith it will be answered (Mark 11:24). Psalm 121 says God never sleeps or slumbers. He's always there to listen. From any place. At any time. Go to God in your darkest times. Jonah did (in his literal darkest). We can too. God is always there, ready to listen and respond.

PRAYER—Gracious Lord, thank You for being there for me no matter what time it is, where I am or what I've done. I feel peace knowing You never sleep or leave me alone. Amen.

TODAY I WILL...know I can approach God any place and time, especially my darkest ones.

OCTOBER 8 **Read I SAMUEL 13:8-14**

A PROPER APPRENTICE

Disney Classic Films – *Fantasia*

"We must obey God rather than men."
—Acts 5:29

I've mentioned before how I loved teaching the Middle Ages to my 6th graders, especially the discussion of Medieval knights and the 3 stages to become one. At first, the boy would be called a page and spend time merely observing knights in action. The 2nd step was more important. Around age 14, the boy would become a squire, assigned to one knight to learn directly how to put on armor, use weapons and ride a horse. The squire was an apprentice, learning not by watching, but by doing and imitating. Our favorite mouse was also once an apprentice. "The Sorcerer's Apprentice" is likely the most familiar portion of *Fantasia*, Disney's 3rd film from 1940. This film consisted of 8 animated segments, each set to classical music. Not only was *Fantasia* released the same year, but like *Pinocchio* it failed to make an initial profit again due to World War II as well as high production costs. However, this film has been reissued multiple times and turned into a franchise with video games, attractions and live concerts. Therefore, when adjusted for inflation, it's actually 24th overall in highest grossing films of all time.

In "The Sorcerer's Apprentice," Mickey Mouse is tasked with moving water from one source to another, and he gets the bright idea to use magic to do the work. Of course, it quickly gets out of hand and he's unable to control the ensuing floods. In I Samuel 13, we read of King Saul taking his own shortcut and making an unlawful sacrifice. Because of his disobedience, he is reprimanded and punished, losing his kingdom. We are apprentices of Jesus, tasked to follow His example in doing God's will and carrying out His instructions. But we must obey God's commands exactly as He says. We can't take shortcuts, doing things our own way. Revelation 22 warns of adding to or taking away from Scripture. We must follow His perfect Word without deviation. As Christian apprentices, we must imitate the example He set forth through His Son.

PRAYER—Dear God, I want to be an apprentice to Christ, imitating His every move. Help me to know and follow Your Word without deviation as Jesus did. In His blessed name, Amen.

TODAY I WILL...try my best to follow God's instruction exactly as He said without shortcuts.

OCTOBER 9 **Read MARK 1:2-8**

THE AUTHORITY OF CHRIST

Disney Classic Films – *Cinderella*

"Jesus came and said to them, "All authority in heaven and on earth has been given to me."
—Matthew 28:18

Remember learning to tie your shoes? That's quite the rite of passage. Which method did you learn? Loops first or knot first? I remember going through some real frustration before I finally figured it out. I just remember Velcro shoes as a Godsend. Maybe I should've just worn glass slippers like today's iconic princess. *Cinderella* came to theaters in 1950 and was an instant classic, becoming Disney's greatest box office success since *Snow White*. In the 1940's, Disney was in financial trouble after, as mentioned recently, World War II made box office bombs out of *Fantasia*, *Pinocchio* and even *Bambi*. In 1947, they were $4 million in debt and on the verge of bankruptcy. This film reversed that slump, saved the studio and even helped fund Disneyland as well as the Florida Project, which would become Walt Disney World. Thank you, *Cinderella*!

Remember this film's climactic ending? Having been imprisoned by her wicked stepmother, Cinderella escapes just in time for the Grand Duke to bend down and slide the glass slipper easily over her foot. That pivotal scene reminded me of John the Baptist's comment in today's Scripture. He is preparing the people for Jesus and says he is unworthy to even stoop down and untie His sandals. John knew the authority of the One coming and that while his own teaching was important, it was nothing compared to the message Jesus would bring. Jesus Himself even said (above) that all authority in Heaven and Earth was given to Him. We too are unworthy to untie His shoe, let alone be in His presence, know Him, follow Him and be saved by Him. But because of His great love and that of the Father, we are not only allowed but encouraged to do all those things. Recognize and respect the authority of Jesus by following His every word and example. Thank God that though we are sinful and unworthy, we still have the chance to be in His and His Son's presence one day thanks to His amazing grace and the saving blood of Christ.

PRAYER—Father, I'm a worthless sinner, unworthy of You or Your Son, but I know You offer salvation for me anyway, and I am so grateful. Through the authority of Christ alone, Amen.

TODAY I WILL...recognize Jesus' authority as the only way to know God and obtain Heaven.

OCTOBER 10 **Read ROMANS 10:14-18**

USE YOUR FEET

Disney Classic Films – *The Little Mermaid*

"...preach the word; be ready in season and out of season; reprove, rebuke, and exhort, with complete patience and teaching."
—2 Timothy 4:2

Yesterday I asked if you remembered learning to tie your shoes. What about learning to walk? You most likely don't have that memory. I certainly don't recall my own first steps, but I do remember watching my sons wobble toward me as they took theirs. I also remember a much older mermaid using her feet for the first time. Remember the beach scene when Ariel first tried to walk. She wobbled quite a bit too, and then fell into Prince Eric's arms. *The Little Mermaid* released in 1989 and began an era known as the "Disney Renaissance," a period of 10 years (and 10 films ironically) in which Disney returned to making very successful animated movies. This film, based on an 1837 fairy tale, also won Oscars for Best Original Score and Song.

The Little Mermaid had several great songs besides the Oscar winner ("Under the Sea"). Remember "Part of Your World?" Ariel sings it near the beginning as she longs to explore the human world. There's one particular lyric where she says, "I wanna be where the people are. I wanna see, wanna see 'em dancin'. Walking around on those, what do you call 'em? Oh, feet!" Ariel longs to trade in her tail for feet of her own. Feet are pretty special, a sentiment shared in Romans 10 but for a different reason. In this passage, Paul stresses the importance of preaching and sharing the Gospel. He asks a basic but important question, saying, "How are they to hear without someone preaching?" He then quotes Isaiah 52:7 and says, "How beautiful are the feet of those who preach the good news!" God gave us working feet for a reason. We can use them for so many special things, but none as important as walking to someone to share His message, especially with those who have never heard it. Praise God today for your feet and the ability to walk, move and do His good works. Make Him proud by using them to go and help those in need, encourage them and tell them how wonderful and full of hope are the promises of God.

PRAYER—Dear Lord, I am so grateful for my feet and the ability to walk and accomplish Your works. Help me to use my feet to go to others and tell them Your good news. In Jesus, Amen.

TODAY I WILL...walk on soft grass or carpet with bare feet, thanking God for all they can do.

OCTOBER 11 Read PSALM 73:1-12 & ROMANS 2:6-11

GOOD NEWS AND BAD NEWS

Disney Classic Films – *Lady and the Tramp*

"For God shows no partiality."
—Romans 2:11

"I've got good news and bad news. What do you want first?" I always ask for the bad news first to get it out of the way. What about you? Well today, I too have good news and bad news, and I'll start with that bad. Life isn't fair. But there's also good news. First, let's talk about a 1955, animated musical that also brought good and bad news to its characters. *Lady and the Tramp* was actually based on an article from *Cosmopolitan* Magazine. Years before, in 1937, one of Disney's story artists created a film idea based on his own dog, "Lady." He shared sketches with Walt who liked the idea and told him to begin working on the film. In 1945, Walt himself read the *Cosmopolitan* article titled "Happy Dan, the Cynical Dog" and thought the film would be improved if the sophisticated "Lady" met a dog like Happy Dan. Homer, Rags and Bozo were all considered as names for the "cynical dog" before "Tramp" was chosen, and the rest is history.

Remember the scene with the Siamese cats who cause all kinds of damage that Lady is blamed for. I remember being angry the first time thinking "that's not fair!" Thankfully, the good news comes at the end when Lady and Tramp get their happy ending. I asked you to read two passages. The first is a psalm basically proclaiming that life isn't fair. The psalmist admits jealousy of the arrogant who are thriving and the wicked who are rich. It's difficult to see bad people become happy and successful. But again, life will never be fair and sometimes evil will prosper while good is suppressed. That's the bad news. The good news comes about in our 2nd passage from Romans 2 teaching us that God is ALWAYS fair. He shows "no partiality" or favoritism and "will render to each one according to his works." This passage makes clear that God will be fair in rewarding the good and punishing evil. Life may not be fair now, but just wait, as it certainly will be on Judgement Day. Which side of God's fairness will you be on?

PRAYER—Father, thank You for being fair and showing no partiality when You send Christ to bring us home. Help me to be among those You reward with eternity. Through Him, Amen.

TODAY I WILL...accept life's unfairness and prepare instead for the eternal fairness of God.

OCTOBER 12 **Read PSALM 91:1-16**

THE PERFECT PROTECTOR

Disney Classic Films – *Old Yeller*

"But the Lord is faithful. He will establish you and guard you against the evil one."
—2 Thessalonians 3:3

She's quite small so she could never take down an intruder, but we would definitely know one was coming! Our dog, Molly, weighs about 10 pounds and is barely higher than the floor, but anytime the mailman comes, someone jogs by or even the wind blows, she lets us know with her "fearsome" bark. She's our little protector. *Old Yeller* was a 1957, live-action, drama about an impressive and very effective protector of the farm-living Coates family. Unsurprisingly, this film was based on a 1956 novel of the same name which won a Newbery Honor Award and led to the author actually writing this film's screenplay. The success of both book and film led to a sequel novel and film entitled *Savage Sam*. Sadly, it did not enjoy the success of the first.

This was one of my favorite films growing up. If you've never seen it, you've got something to watch on Disney Plus! Hint...have tissues ready. It's a wonderful, heart-warming story, full of action. Old Yeller is a stray dog, so it takes the family a little while to warm up to him. But eventually he becomes a full-fledged, family member and serves them well. Most importantly, he provides protection on several occasion, saving their lives repeatedly. Today's message is a simple reminder that Psalm 91 illustrates beautifully. In this psalm, God is called our shelter, our refuge, our fortress, our deliverer and our dwelling place. It says He will cover us and protect us under His wings. It also provides great hope and comfort saying He will command His angels to guard us, and that no evil will befall us. There are so many reassuring and comforting descriptions of God in this psalm. I suggest you keep this one bookmarked to re-read from time to time. God is our perfect protector. As long as we are faithful, He will not let evil prevail against us. The verse above reassures us of that. He will guard us and keep us close to His side. What an uplifting and encouraging promise that we can all take comfort and find peace in!

PRAYER—Holy Father, thank You for Your promise of protection. I feel peace and comfort knowing You are there at all times, watching over and guarding me. In His Holy name, Amen.

TODAY I WILL...bookmark or print Psalm 91 to read often and praise God for His protection.

OCTOBER 13 **Read LUKE 15:1-7**

ONE OVER NINETY-NINE

Disney Classic Films – *101 Dalmatians*

"The times of ignorance God overlooked, but now he commands all people everywhere to repent."
—Acts 17:30

Yesterday I discussed Molly, our family's fearless, furball of fortification. Other than her occasional bark at anything that moves, she's pretty laid-back and easy to care for. That wasn't the case 9 years ago when we got her as a puppy. If you've had a puppy, you know what I mean. They end up being worth it but take a lot of initial work! What if you had to care for 99 instead?! I can't imagine caring for 99 pet rocks, let alone high-spirited puppies. But there's one family who was apparently up for it. By the end of *101 Dalmatians,* there are 99 puppies to care for. This 1961 animated classic was based on a 5-year-old novel (shocking). It was also quite successful financially, pulling Disney out of another slump caused by the high production costs and lackluster sales two years earlier of a film we'll discuss soon, *Sleeping Beauty.*

Remembering the 99 puppies counted at the end of this film immediately brought today's story to mind. And that's just what it was...a parable or story of Christ. In this one, a shepherd is watching over 100 sheep but loses 1. That leaves 99. Isn't that enough? Shouldn't we be proud of this shepherd for successful care of 99% of his sheep? I mean, that's as close to perfect as you can get! But the point is not the 99... it's the 1! God, as our Shepherd, isn't satisfied with 99%. He cares for every single sheep and goes after the 1. The final verse sums it up saying, "There will be more joy in Heaven over one sinner who repents than over ninety-nine righteous persons who need no repentance." God cares deeply for the one and wants it to turn around, change its ways and come home. He's always there, watching and waiting for his lost to repent. The verse above is more direct saying He commands us to do so. Are you lost? Are you "the one?" Do you need to repent and come back home? If so, you are the most important to God right now, and He is anxiously awaiting your return. Remember, it's never too late.

PRAYER—Most caring Lord, thank You for being my attentive Shepherd. Help me not to stray but to stay among the righteous. If I ever need to repent, give me the strength to do so. Amen.

TODAY I WILL...not be the one. If I need to repent of anything, I will do so and come home.

OCTOBER 14 **Read MARK 10:17-22**

FEED THE BIRDS

Disney Classic Films – *Mary Poppins*

"Whoever is generous to the poor lends to the Lord, and he will repay him for his deed."
—Proverbs 19:17

I love all musicals, but especially ones from Disney. What about you? If you think about it, many of Disney's most successful films are musicals. Today's film is certainly no exception! *Mary Poppins* (1964) was the first major project of the infamous Sherman Brothers and their musical expertise. Their hard work, along with that of the entire cast and crew paid off as this was not only Disney's highest grossing film to date, but it also won 5 of 13 Oscar nominations! This film is said to be Walt Disney's crowning achievement as it received the only Best Picture nomination of his lifetime. The 2013 film, *Saving Mr. Banks* chronicles the creation of this film and Walt's efforts to secure the rights from P.L. Travers who wrote the *Mary Poppins* books.

You may recall this film's "Feed the Birds" as Walt's favorite song. Near the end, young Michael is encouraged to invest his money in the bank, but he wishes to help the poor woman who "feeds the birds" instead. Good choice, Michael! In Mark 10, another young man asks what he must do to go to Heaven. Jesus tells him to not only follow God's commands, but also sell all he has and give to the poor. Unfortunately, the man is too attached to his treasures and walks away sad. So are we supposed to give all we have to the poor? Not necessarily, but we should certainly be willing. Jesus was trying to instill a greater focus on treasures in Heaven. There's a problem when our possessions here matter more than what we seek above. Nothing we have belongs to us anyway. The proverb above says God will repay those who are generous to the poor. Matthew 5:42 says give to those who beg, and Hebrews 13:2 tells us we might just be helping God's angels in disguise. Consider how much of God's money you give to the poor. Could you give even more? Are you holding your earthly treasures too tightly? Would you give it all up if God asked? Don't forget about the poor woman who did just that! (Mark 12:41-44)

PRAYER—Oh generous Father, thank You for so many material things. Help me to remember they all belong to You, and I should give away as much as I can to the poor. In Christ, Amen.

TODAY I WILL...determine how much I give to the poor and consider giving more regularly.

OCTOBER 15 **Read I CORINTHIANS 12:12-27**

SWITCH PLACES

Disney Classic Films – *Freaky Friday*

"So whatever you wish that others would do to you, do also to them."
—Matthew 7:12

What's your favorite day of the week? Mine is Sunday because not only do I not work Sundays or Mondays, but I love going to church and sharing fellowship with my family. I might've said Friday as a former teacher as it meant the end of a long school week and beginning of a restful weekend, but now I work 24 hours most Fridays, meaning they are hectic and tiring. I guess I could call them freaky too, but I'll leave that to today's film. It takes place on a Friday, and on the 13th too, so the story is definitely a bit freaky. *Freaky Friday* was a successful comedy, making $36 million on just a $5 million budget. It starred eventual Oscar winner, Jodie Foster who was only 14 when this film was released in 1976. It has had three different remakes, all produced by Disney, the most famous of which starred Jamie Lee Curtis and Lindsay Lohan.

Based on a 1972 novel, this film is about a mother and daughter who inadvertently switch places after they simultaneously wish to do so. Switching bodies but not minds, they are forced to see what the other must deal with daily, giving each a renewed understanding and appreciation for the other. In I Corinthians 12, Paul reminds the church they were all baptized into one body, but there are still many different nationalities, cultures, and even mindsets. In other words, it takes work to unify the church as we're often told to do (I Cor. 1:10, Gal. 3:28, Php 2:2, Psalm 133:1). What do we do when we don't agree with a fellow Christian? How do we unify with someone who thinks differently? The "Golden Rule" above is once again the best answer. Treat them how you want to be treated. Like this film, switch places by getting into their mindset and seeing things from their perspective so a Biblical compromise can be reached. We shouldn't let petty differences divide the family of God. Strive to maintain unity by putting yourself in others' shoes. Above all, treat others with respect and kindness, just as you desire to be treated.

PRAYER—God, I'm sorry for our selfishness and division within the body of Christ. Help me to see things from all angles and work hard to bring more unity to Your church. In Him, Amen.

TODAY I WILL...put myself in others' shoes if a disagreement arises among God's family.

OCTOBER 16 **Read I JOHN 2:1-6**

WHO IS YOUR NAVIGATOR?

Disney Classic Films – Flight of the Navigator

"For I have given you an example, that you also should do just as I have done to you."
—John 13:15

What if you could travel anywhere in the world in minutes? Instant vacations! Wouldn't that be nice? Where would you go? I'd be heading to Australia, a bucket-list dream. 12-year-old David finds a machine that does just that in *Flight of the Navigator*, a 1986, sci-fi adventure. This film is noted for being one of the first films to not only use extensive CGI effects but also electronic music in its soundtrack. One of its smaller spaceship props was refurbished and now sits on top of a Tomorrowland drink station in WDW's Magic Kingdom. If you're a fan, you might check out "Life After the Navigator," a 2020 documentary about the film and troubled past of its star.

I've always loved this movie too, another fantastic and exciting story in my humble opinion. Young David eventually figures out this machine that can travel anywhere in record time, is an alien spaceship. Once on board, he is told by the robotic computer that he is now its navigator due to reasons later discovered. As navigator, he controls when and where they go leading to adventures around the globe and even a short trip to outer space. Unfortunately, as fun as that would be, there are no machines like that available for us to navigate. Actually, we shouldn't be navigating our lives at all. The beginning of I John 2 reminds us of who our Navigator should be. We are not only told to follow the commandments of Jesus Christ, but also to "walk in the same way in which He walked." In another verse above, Jesus Himself says we should do just as He did. Jesus came here to be our example and demonstrate exactly how we should live. HE is our navigator. We should only do, say and act as He did, allowing his example to be a pattern for our life. Allow Christ to navigate your life. Don't try and take over the controls. Just sit in the passenger seat and let Him guide all that you do. Study His life daily and thoroughly so you can imitate Him and allow Him to navigate you to the eternal home we're all striving for.

PRAYER—Dear Lord, thank you for sending the perfect Example and Navigator. Help me to study and know Him well so I can follow His pattern and make it home. In His name, Amen.

TODAY I WILL...allow Christ alone to navigate my flight home by imitating His every move.

OCTOBER 17 **Read NUMBERS 14:1-12**

IT JUST TAKES TRUST

Disney Classic Films – Raya and the Last Dragon

"And those who know your name put their trust in you, for you, O Lord, have not forsaken those who seek you."
—Psalm 9:10

Dragons...who or what does that make you think of? I've mentioned my love for Pete's. I also like the song about Puff. Of course, there's Figment, Mushu, Maleficent and a host of others, mostly from literature or visual media. There's even a dragon on the Animal Kingdom logo. Ever noticed? Originally there was to be a "Beastly Kingdom" section at AK dedicated to mythological creatures. That never materialized, but the dragon remains on the logo to this day. Disney's latest dragon was introduced simultaneously to theaters and Disney Plus in 2021. *Raya and the Last Dragon* is Disney's latest "classic film" as of this writing and became the 2nd most streamed title ever upon its release. Raya is only the 3rd Disney princess not based on a fairy tale or story. Do you know the first two? Hint...they both start with "M." I'll tell you at the end.

If you missed this one, let me summarize the story. (Spoiler alert!) During a power struggle, five Asian tribes destroy an important gem that fights off evil spirits, breaking it into pieces. Raya, one tribal chief's daughter, must find the last dragon and travel to each tribe to retrieve and unite the pieces before it's too late. Sound confusing? Sorry. Just watch it. It's good! The point is, Raya learns that trust between the tribes is the only way to fight against the evil spirits and that she too must learn to trust others before spreading the same message. In Numbers 14, we again read of the Israelites distrust in God. This time, they also refuse to trust Joshua and Caleb after they spy out the Promised Land, deeming it safe. The people are forced to wander the wilderness for many years because of their lack of trust in the two men who even warned them not to rebel against God and His promise of protection. We too must learn to trust in God no matter the circumstance. That can be difficult when we can't see the outcome, but the psalm above reminds us He will not forsake us if we will only trust. As the old hymn says, "Trust and Obey, for there's no other way! (The 2 other original princesses are Merida and Moana!)

PRAYER—Faithful Father, help me to trust in You always, no matter what. In Christ, Amen.

TODAY I WILL...make a promise to trust in God no matter what direction life takes me.

OCTOBER 18 **Read PSALM 8:1-9**

YOU ARE SMALL

Disney Classic Films – Honey, I Shrunk the Kids

"It is he who sits above the circle of the earth and its inhabitants are like grasshoppers."
—Isaiah 40:22

You are small. No, you are tiny. Actually, make that miniscule. The verse above says you are like grasshoppers, but honestly you can't even be seen. It's impossible to put into words just how small you are, but I do know the shrunken kids in today's film were ¼ inch tall according to one line. *Honey, I Shrunk the Kids* was a surprise, comedy hit when it came out in 1989. In fact, for 5 years it held the record for highest grossing, live-action, Disney film. The original director came up with the story and was going to call it "Teeny Weenies." (Ugh!) However, he became ill during production and had to be replaced. The new director changed the name to "Grounded" and then "The Big Backyard" before this title was chosen based on an actual line from the film.

Wanna know why you are so small? You are one of nearly 8 billion people on a single planet in our solar system of 9. (I'm counting Pluto. Sue me.) Our biggest planet, Jupiter, is 1,300 times bigger than Earth while our sun is 1.3 million times larger. It's estimated that our Milky Way Galaxy alone has between 100 and 400 billion stars in it with at least that many planets. A light year is how far light travels in a year or 5.8 trillion miles! Our galaxy is 100,000 light years across. To top it off, there are 2 trillion galaxies in the observable universe. Observable! How much more is out there that can't be seen? So do you see what I mean when I say you are small or basically non-existent? But are you really? David wonders the same question in Psalm 8, asking God as he gazes into the universe, "what is man, that you are mindful of him?" He then answers his own question saying God has created us only lower than those in Heaven, crowning each of us with glory and honor. He knows you by name (Isa. 43:1). He knows the number of hairs on your head (Matt. 10:30.) You may be practically invisible compared to the size of the God's universe, but He sees you. He knows you. And he loves you. And that's all that matters!

PRAYER—O Lord, my Lord, how majestic is Your name in all the Earth. I am invisible and insignificant, yet You know and love me. I praise Your Holy name forever! In Jesus, Amen.

~~TODAY~~ TONIGHT I WILL...gaze at the stars and try to comprehend how small I really am.

OCTOBER 19 **Read GENESIS 12:1-9**

MORE THAN A MARATHON

Disney Classic Films – Homeward Bound: The Incredible Journey

"I have fought the good fight, I have finished the race, I have kept the faith."
—2 Timothy 4:7

Ever run an organized race? 5K? 10K? Marathon? Yesterday's film mentions that due to the kids' ¼ inch height, traveling the 64 feet of their backyard, a bulk of the plot, is the equivalent of 3.2 miles. That's almost exactly a 5K (3.1 miles). Does that seem far? What about a marathon (26.2 miles)? Yesterday's characters got the 5K. Today's much furrier ones get the marathon. *Homeward Bound: The Incredible Journey* is a remake of a film based on a book. Say what? In 1961, a book was released simply called *The Incredible Journey*. It was a fictional story based on the author's actual cat and 2 dogs. In 1963, Disney released a live-action film of the same name based on the book. The first version had only narration and the pets didn't talk. In this more popular 1993 film, the title became a bit longer, and the pets were given celebrity voices.

This remake doesn't clarify how far the pets travel to get home, but the book says 300 miles. Wow! That's several marathons combined, which may seem far, but I know of someone who went even further to get home. In Genesis 12, we see God's first call to Abram (later Abraham), telling him to leave home and travel to a better land. Abram packs up his family and begins a long, dangerous journey, hundreds of miles and full of difficulties. But he never turns back due to his obedience and faith. Guess what? You're on the same journey. God may not have called you to move physically, but He has asked you to endure the path to Heaven. And believe me...it will be a long, difficult journey. Definitely not a 5K... or even a marathon! Paul also knew life was a long race, mentioning it above. The writer of Hebrews, possibly Paul as well, refers to it saying, "let us run with perseverance the race marked out for us." (12:1) If you're going to make it to Heaven, you must stay in the race despite the trials presented. It will be an incredible journey, and the prize will be well worth it, so keep running! You are homeward bound!

PRAYER—Lord, help me to stay in the race no matter what. I realize it will be more than a marathon but give me the strength to endure. I want the prize I've been called for. Amen.

TODAY I WILL...endure the long race and journey home to be with my Father forever.

OCTOBER 20 **Read MATTHEW 21:18-22**

THROW OUT THE DOUBT

Disney Classic Films – *Cool Runnings*

"But let him ask in faith, with no doubting, for the one who doubts is like a wave of the sea that is driven and tossed by the wind."
—James 1:6

Don't you love an underdog story? I think of Jim Abbott, successful in pro-baseball, yet born without a hand. Or college football's Rudy Ruettiger, whose story was chronicled in one of my favorite films. Or the famed Olympic victory of the 1980 U.S. Hockey team. But perhaps one of the greatest underdog stories involves a bobsled team from the frigid, snowy nation of Jamaica. Wait, where? *Cool Runnings* is the 1993 true story of the Caribbean nation's team and their determination to compete with the best in the 1988 Winter Olympics. While the film tweaked the story a bit to enhance the drama, the team truly did gain media fame and notoriety among viewers as inexperienced underdogs from a unlikely nation with a tropical climate. The team has since competed in several Olympics, even beating the U.S. team during the 1992 Winter games.

Not all underdog stories are sports related. Remember David and Goliath? Read I Samuel 17 if you need a refresher. David was certainly the underdog but claimed victory due to his refusal to doubt in God's power. God can do anything (Mark 10:27), and nothing is impossible for Him (Luke 1:37). The Jamaican team went further than anyone could've imagined due to doubtless determination. In Matthew 21, the disciples question a miracle of Christ and are told that those who have faith without doubt will be able to move even mountains. Jesus was attempting to teach them a lesson in the importance of trust and truly believing God that listens to and answers our prayers. James tells us above we should pray in faith and with absolutely no doubt. Evaluate your faith right now. Do you truly believe God hears your requests and has the power to grant them? Make sure before you even speak to Him, you have no doubt of who He is or what He can do. God is real and will do great things for you, even miracles, if you ask and it's within His will for you. Be diligent in prayer! Trust! Believe! Have faith! And throw out the doubt!

PRAYER—Dear God, help me to truly trust in Your power and ability to do all things. Aid me in getting rid of all doubt or lack of faith in what You can do. In the name of Jesus, Amen.

TODAY I WILL...add doubtless belief and faithful trust to all the requests I make of God.

OCTOBER 21 **Read MALACHI 3:6-12**

GO AHEAD, TEST HIM!

Disney Classic Films – *National Treasure*

"Give, and it will be given to you. For with the measure you use it will be measured back to you."
—*Luke 6:38*

They laughed! They actually laughed as they dropped the check into the collection plate. We had been challenged to follow the verse above, trust God and give more money than our comfort zone allowed. I'll be honest...my wife and I gave a little more but nothing like my friend and his wife. They decided to just go for it and basically gave their entire checking account. So they laughed, not knowing how they were going to make it financially. I'll finish that story, but first, let's talk treasure...*National Treasure*! This 2004 surprise blockbuster spawned a 2007 sequel that raked in even more "treasure" for Disney. As of this writing, there's a 3rd film as well as a Disney Plus series in the works. This original story about a treasure hunt throughout historical U.S. landmarks was filmed mostly on location. The exception was the Independence Hall scenes which were actually filmed at its replica at Knott's Berry Farm theme park in California.

Spoiler alert for the film, but our heroes do eventually find the "national treasure" they are seeking. You may not think you have treasure, but most of you are rich compared to the world. So do you give some back weekly as commanded? (I Cor. 16:2) What if you gave more? You know, we are told not to test God (Deut. 6:16). Jesus even said so Himself (Matt. 4:7). But did you read today's passage? In verse 10, He actually tells us we're allowed to test Him in this one thing, challenging us to give more, a lot more! God basically dares us to test Him, saying if we will just trust and try it, He will "open the windows of heaven for you and pour down for you a blessing until there is no more need." Do you trust Him enough to try it? My friend later told me they could not believe what God did for them after that day and how much they got back. Put God to the test. It works! Give Him more. A lot more! He will give it back and then some. Trust and give it a shot! I guarantee you'll be blessed and amazed with what God does in return.

PRAYER—Lord, help me to trust Your promise and give back more than I ever have. Please use it to further Your kingdom. I can't wait to see what You'll do for me in return. Amen

TODAY I WILL...test God by giving more than I'm comfortable with for a set amount of time.

OCTOBER 22 **Read GALATIANS 3:10-14**

A BROKEN CURSE

Disney Classic Films – The Princess and the Frog

"Christ redeemed us from the curse of the law by becoming a curse for us..."
—Galatians 3:13

It's pretty much been around since the beginning of mankind. The first Biblical reference is in Genesis 27 between Isaac and his son, Jacob. A couple chapters later, Jacob does it again, this time in meeting his future wife, Rachel and then a couple verses later with his uncle Laban, no doubt with different feelings. Historians aren't exactly sure why the practice originated. Some think it was just instinctive or evolved from prehistoric activities like the premastication of food or even checking another person's health. Have you figured it out yet? We're talking about kissing! Why? Because *The Princess and the Frog* (2009) has the most kisses of any other Disney film, not to mention the fact that the whole plot begins and ends with a kiss. This film was based on a novel which in itself was based on another Brothers Grimm folk tale. It was also notable because it marked Disney's brief return to traditional animation as opposed to CGI.

So why are we talking about kissing and what's the spiritual message? Good question...glad I asked. There are many kisses throughout the Bible of all different types and reasons, even one of deception between Jesus and his betrayer, Judas. However, I'd rather focus on what the kiss in this film accomplished. It broke the curse. Actually, the first kiss started the curse, but it was eventually broken with another. We were also once under a curse, broken not by a kiss but by a cross. Galatians 3 tells us the original law cursed those who didn't follow it and doomed them to eternal damnation. Thankfully, it goes on to say that Jesus redeemed us and actually became the curse for us when He was hung on that cross. Because of that generous act, we are now saved by our faith and not cursed and condemned by our sin. What a powerful, life-saving sacrifice of Jesus to break a curse set to condemn us forever with His pain and suffering! Never forget what Christ did for you. His blood broke a terrible curse, providing us hope of eternal salvation.

PRAYER—God, thank You for giving Your Son to break the curse on me. In His name, Amen.

TODAY I WILL... focus on the incredible sacrifice of the cross and what it means for me. I will also take advantage of the now broken curse and strengthen my faith in God and His Son.

OCTOBER 23 **Read JEREMIAH 1:6-10**

YOUTH IS NO EXCUSE

Disney Classic Films – *Zootopia*

"Let no one despise you for your youth..."
—I Timothy 4:12a

It was like having a home security system...for free! When we first moved into our house, we were thrilled to learn our new neighbor was a police officer. For years, his patrol car in the driveway served as a protector and deterrent for any shenanigans in and around our humble habitat. I've always had high respect for those in law enforcement, even before joining the first responder team myself. Maybe that's why I enjoyed *Zootopia* from 2016 so much as it focused on the life of a young, rookie police officer. Extensive research for this film took place not only in Disney's own Animal Kingdom, but also at the San Diego Zoo and even Kenya to study the walk cycle and fur colors of various animals. Animators used 64 different species of animals in this film and created over 800,000 separate character models to choose from. Wow!

As mentioned, the plot here revolves around young rabbit, Judy Hopps and her lifelong goal to become a police officer. She finds it quite difficult initially, not only having to relocate from country life to the bustling metropolis, but especially because of her youthfulness and innocence among an older and advanced police force. In the end, her drive and determination win out and she doesn't let her youth stop her from accomplishing her dream and doing her job effectively. In the first chapter of Jeremiah, God rebukes the young prophet for making excuses about his own youth, telling him directly, "Do not say, 'I am only a youth;' for to all to whom I send you, you shall go, and whatever I command you, you shall speak. Do not be afraid of them, for I am with you to deliver you, declares the Lord." If you are young or just feel inexperienced in evangelism, take these words of God to heart. This is one of many times where God tells us not to fear for He will be with us and deliver us. If you are doing God's work, He will be there to guide and protect you. Don't let youth, inexperience, excuses, doubt or fear stand in your way.

PRAYER—Father God, give me the drive and courage to do Your work and spread Your message despite any fears, immaturity or inexperience I may have. In Christ's name, Amen.

TODAY I WILL...not allow my youth or inexperience to stand in the way of doing His work.

OCTOBER 24 **Read EZEKIEL 11:14-21**

A NEW HEART

Disney Classic Films – *Moana*

"Every way of a man is right in his own eyes, but the Lord weighs the heart."
—Proverbs 21:2

Ever heard of Kosrae? It's a remote island and state of Micronesia in the Northern Pacific Ocean. It is 42 square miles in size and has a population of around 6,600 people. It's also nicknamed "the island of the sleeping lady" as its distinctive shape viewed from the ocean resembles a female sleeping on her back. Disney's *Moana* also featured an island shaped like a sleeping woman, the fictional "Te Fiti." This instantaneous blockbuster was released in 2016, the same year as yesterday's film, *Zootopia*, marking the first time since 2002 that Disney released two feature films in the same year. Together they grossed well over $1.5 billion worldwide! As of this writing, Moana is the 12th and most recent official, Disney princess.

So do you remember Moana's mission and the role that Te Fiti played? Moana learns a blight on her native island has been caused by the removal of the "heart" or power source of Te Fiti. She follows her calling to leave her island, find the heart and restore it. When she succeeds, the island is no longer corrupted, and the ocean and surrounding islands are healed. Through the prophet, Ezekiel, we read of the Lord Himself also restoring a heart to His chosen people. God speaks and promises to remove their old hearts of stone and give them a new one along with His Spirit, assuring it will lead to righteousness and the following of His ways. He ends by saying, "And they shall be my people and I will be their God." Being one of God's chosen means serving Him with the pure heart He provides. In verse 21, God rebukes those with corrupt hearts that only serve their own pleasures. The verse above sums it up well. God will judge us not on outward appearance, but on the purity of the heart He provides when we become His child. We must be sure to always follow His ways over our own. Seek the pure heart and Spirit of God so that you may serve Him properly, seek Him first and follow His ways above all others.

PRAYER—Faithful Father, thank You for restoring the hearts of Your chosen so that they seek righteousness over evil and worldly desires. Fill me with Your heart and Spirit! In Jesus, Amen.

TODAY I WILL... ensure I possess the Spirit and heart of God, seeking His will over my own.

OCTOBER 25 **Read PSALM 4:1-8**

REST IN PEACE

Disney Classic Films – *Sleeping Beauty*

"Behold, he who keeps Israel will neither slumber nor sleep."
—Psalm 121:4

I love naps! What about you? That wasn't the case growing up as I remember dreading them both at home and in pre-school. But times have certainly changed, and with my current busy life and paramedic sleep schedule, or lack thereof, I cherish any chance I get to just close my eyes and sleep. We can't leave this month's classic films without talking about the famous sleeping princess. *Sleeping Beauty* from 1959 was Disney's last animated film based on a fairy tale until *The Little Mermaid* 30 years later. This film took a while to make, over 8 years to be exact. Disneyland was even built and opened during its production with the centerpiece castle being named after the princess to promote the future film. Its musical score was adapted from the 1890 Sleeping Beauty ballet by famed, Russian composer, Tchaikovsky. As mentioned earlier, this film did not do well initially but has succeeded greatly in re-releases, adaptations and sequels.

Today we are looking at yet another comforting and uplifting psalm of David, reassuring us of the Lord's protection and faithfulness, especially when we need Him in times of distress. Did you notice the word "Selah" a couple times? That is a Hebrew word you'll find over 70 times throughout many psalms asking the reader to simply pause and reflect on the words just read. Take some time to pause and reflect on this psalm today. Verse 4 asks us to do just that, telling us to "ponder in your own hearts on your beds and be silent." Our God is forever faithful, day and night, 24/7, without breaks or holidays. According to another psalm above, He never naps or even pauses from watching over and guarding us. Because of His unconditional love and constant, dedicated protection, the final verse of this psalm says that unlike Him, we can lie down and sleep in peace, knowing that we dwell in the safety of our Father's loving embrace.

PRAYER—Lord, I'm thankful for sleep and any chance I get to rest and recharge my body. Thank You for not sleeping and instead keeping watch over me at all times. In Jesus, Amen.

TODAY I WILL...take a nap or at least find some time to rest comfortably knowing my God is awake and watching over me.

OCTOBER 26 **Read ACTS 12:1-11**

A PROMISE OF RESCUE

Disney Classic Films – *The Rescuers*

"I will rescue them from all places where they have been scattered on a day of clouds and thick darkness."
—Ezekiel 34:12

I remember it well. I was 12, and we were at a Friday night, high school football game. The announcer came on the PA system between plays and said, "Ladies and gentlemen, I just wanted to let you know that Baby Jessica has just been rescued." For a few minutes, everyone forgot about the game and cheered, celebrated, hugged and cried tears of joy. You can read Jessica McClure's story online if you aren't familiar, but for two days in October 1987, that 18-month-old captured the heart of the entire country which united in celebration at her rescue. Today's film focuses on the rescue of another little girl named Penny. *The Rescuers* actually began development in 1962, but Walt disliked the project and had it shelved. When it finally released in 1977, its success led to a 1990 sequel, the first Disney animated film to ever have one.

It's heartwarming to read of someone rescued from a dangerous situation like the true story of Baby Jessica or even the fictitious rescue of Penny by a couple of eager mice. Acts 12 tells another true story of the rescue of Peter from prison by an angel of God. Peter says in verse 11, "Now I am sure that the Lord has sent his angel and rescued me..." There are other Biblical stories, even in Acts, of the Lord rescuing His disciples from danger so that their important work may continue. The Lord also promises to rescue us. The reassuring verse above shows His promise through the prophet, Ezekiel, to rescue us when we are in danger or uncertain about our surroundings. He will not only provide rescue in times of danger, but also when Satan works to distract our missions of faith with temptation. In I Corinthians 10:13 it says that God provides a rescue or way of escape when temptation seeps into our lives. Seek God's rescue anytime you are in danger, either physically or spiritually. He will provide protection or even a way out and be there to help get you back on your feet so His mission can continue through your good work.

PRAYER—God in Heaven, I'm so grateful for Your love, protection and promise of rescue, especially in scary times or when I'm tempted to sin. Save me if it be Your will. In Him, Amen.

TODAY I WILL...remember to go to God and seek Him first, anytime I'm in need of rescue.

OCTOBER 27 **Read PHILIPPIANS 4:15-20**

COUNT YOUR BLESSINGS

Disney Classic Films – *The Aristocats*

"Every good gift and every perfect gift is from above."
—James 1:17

"Let them eat cake!" That famous, historical line is most often associated with Marie Antoinette, the final queen of France before the Revolution. It was thought she uttered the phrase making fun of the peasants complaining of starvation, but historians now agree it originated elsewhere and she most likely never said it. Regardless, she was highly unpopular, except among the high-class Aristocracy, whom she favored. Today's film focuses not on an elite group of citizens, but on some privileged and prosperous cats. *The Aristocats,* like yesterday's film, also had a lengthy production period. It began in 1962 as an original script for the TV program, *Walt Disney's Wonderful World of Color.* After a couple years of development, Walt suggested it would be more suitable as an animated film. It finally released the day before Christmas in 1970.

This story of a wealthy cat and her 3 kittens living a life of luxury takes a turn for the worse when they are kidnapped and abandoned in the countryside. Thankfully, they meet a kind alley cat who leads them home as they learn to appreciate their blessings along the way. In today's reading, Paul tells the Philippian church they alone helped him financially, even repeatedly throughout his missionary journeys. Despite no other churches helping him in that way, he reminds them that God will supply all our needs. Paul wasn't worried. It didn't matter that only one church helped because He knew God was on his side and would provide. James tells us above that every financial blessing we have is from God. Hebrews 13:5 reminds us to be content with what we've been given and refrain from loving money. We've all been blessed at different levels, but compared with most of the world, we could all belong to the Aristocracy. We must learn to be content with whatever God decides to give us, knowing He will always provide for our basic needs and most likely give us much, much more. Count your blessings and be content!

PRAYER—Father, thank You for my plentiful blessings. Help me to be content and not let worry or the love of money damage my faith or focus on You. In the name of Jesus, Amen.

TODAY I WILL...no longer worry about money because I know God will take care of me.

OCTOBER 28 **Read PROVERBS 6:16-19**

GOD HATES IT...TWICE!

Disney Classic Films – *A Goofy Movie*

"No one who practices deceit shall dwell in my house; no one who utters lies shall continue before my eyes."
—Psalm 101:7

George Washington had wooden teeth. Red makes bulls angry. Gum takes 7 years to digest. You should wait an hour after eating to go swimming. Humans only use 10% of their brains. Sharks can smell a drop of blood a mile away. How many of those do you believe to be true? Well, guess what? They're all lies! Maybe "myths" is a nicer word. Today's underrated film about our pal, Goofy and his son, Max, revolves around a lie and the mess it causes. *A Goofy Movie* (1995) was released as a follow-up to the once popular, TV series, *Goof Troop*. A goal of this film was to expand Goofy's character and show his emotional side. While the film resulted in average sales initially, it developed a cult following and got a direct-to-video sequel in 2000. Bill Farmer, the voice of Goofy since 1987, was at first told to drop Goofy's traditional sounding drawl and give him a regular voice. Thankfully, the one who made that decision was fired and CEO Michael Eisner and Walt's nephew, Roy E. Disney, told Farmer to retain the classic voice.

The plot of this entertaining story begins when Goofy wants to take his son on a fishing trip. Max lies to a girl he likes about where he's going which leads to a world of trouble along the way. Did you know there are seven things God says He hates? That's a strong word. I certainly want to avoid doing anything God hates. Today's proverb lists those seven things and lying is on there. Twice! It's #2 and #6! So apparently God hates lying. A lot. Colossians 3:9 says, "do not lie to one another." That's pretty clear. Revelation 21:8 says liars will go to hell. Also clear...and blunt...and scary! The verse above tops it off saying nobody who lies will dwell with God or even continue to be His child. It's pretty obvious...God hates lying. He wants us to use our words for good and honesty instead of deceit or betrayal. Think hard before you speak. Avoid lying at all times, no matter the reason. Make honesty a regular part of your vocabulary so that you please God first and foremost but are also known to others as a truthful person.

PRAYER—Lord, help me to be an honest person and refrain from lying at all times. Amen.

TODAY I WILL...avoid lying for any reason and instead be known as a person of integrity.

OCTOBER 29 **Read I PETER 2:4-10**

DESTINED FOR GREATNESS

Disney Classic Films – Star Wars: The Force Awakens

"And we know that for those who love God all things work together for good, for those who are called according to his purpose."
—Romans 8:28

I know, I know...some of you may be confused by the title of today's "classic" Disney movie. I don't know if this film fits the category or not, but I can't ignore the hype, success, influence or 45-year franchise that has become a part of our lives whether we like it or not. *Star Wars: The Force Awakens* opened in 2015 and was the first Star Wars film distributed by Disney since they purchased the franchise in 2012. It all began in 1977 with three very successful films known as the original trilogy. In 1999, three more films were released as prequels to the originals. Finally, Disney released three films, known as the sequels, beginning with this one. Altogether, the Star Wars franchise is the second most profitable in history raking in over $10 billion! The franchise has also led to Galaxy's Edge and several attractions on both coasts, allowing park guests to be totally immersed in the world of Star Wars. Side note – the most successful film franchise in history is the Marvel series ($23 billion!) and yes, I realize it also now belongs to Disney and should probably be included. However, it doesn't have as long of a history, and I really don't have room. Sorry. But yay Marvel! I love those films too. (even more than Star Wars – gasp!)

Through this first film of the sequels trilogy, we meet a host of new characters and see the return of many favorites. Rey becomes the new lead character and quickly learns she is destined for greatness. In today's reading, Peter teaches we too are meant for greatness, saying that while we may be rejected by men, we are chosen and precious in the sight of God. He also says we belong to God and are royal and holy. When you dedicate your life to God and become His follower, He chooses you to be His and guides you to do great things for Him. Like Rey, you simply must be willing to put forth the effort. Ask God to show you His purpose and the great things you can do. All things will work together for good if you love God and seek His calling.

PRAYER—Father, I want to live up to being chosen by You and do incredible things for Your kingdom. Make my purpose known and help me to work diligently to achieve it. In Him, Amen.

TODAY I WILL...admit I can do great things for God, seek His calling and my purpose.

OCTOBER 30 **Read DANIEL 6:6-24**

HOW BOLD ARE YOU?

Disney Classic Films – *The Lion King*

"...proclaiming the kingdom of God and teaching about the Lord Jesus Christ with all boldness and without hindrance."
—Acts 28:31

That's how good the opening scene was as it alone served as the film's trailer. The original first scene for *The Lion King* was a dialogue introducing the characters. However, when the directors heard the song, "Circle of Life," they scrapped that scene and wrote the one we are all familiar with. Not only that, but they used it as the film's trailer. I would argue it's the best opening scene in a Disney film and possibly in movie history. It also makes for a great Broadway opening if you've seen the stage show. The Lion King (1994) is one of Disney's most classic films and set all kinds of box office records, earning nearly $1 billion to date. This film is widely known for being Disney's first ever original storyline with the filmmakers claiming they based the story on the Biblical stories of Joseph and Moses as well as Shakespeare's Hamlet.

Today we read the Bible's original lion story. While the miracle of God saving Daniel by literally "shutting the lions' mouths" (v. 22) makes a great story, don't forget what got him thrown in there in the first place. When Daniel heard the new law forbidding the worship of God and specifically designed to eliminate him, look at what he did in response. Verse 10 says he knelt in front of his windows three times daily and prayed to God, just as he had done before. Daniel wasn't dumb. He knew he'd be seen and caught. He knew he was going into that lions' den. But he also knew that praying and worshipping God was more important than anything, even his life. Daniel showed tremendous boldness in putting his dedication to God above all else. We are also told to proclaim the name of the Father and worship Him with boldness. There are some even today that pay the ultimate price for their faith. Is your commitment to God that strong? The final verse of Acts above shows that Paul proclaimed His name and taught Christ's message with "all boldness and without hindrance." Will you do the same, no matter the cost?

PRAYER—Give me the courage and boldness, O Lord, to proclaim Your name above any persons or laws that try to hinder me. Help me to be a Daniel in my outward faith. Amen.

TODAY I WILL...show boldness in proclaiming my Godly faith and exemplifying Christ.

OCTOBER 31 **Read 2 CORINTHIANS 11:12-15**

DEVIL IN DISGUISE

Disney Classic Films – *Bambi*

"...even Satan disguises himself as an angel of light."
—2 Corinthians 11:14

Happy Halloween! I've always loved this holiday. Growing up, Halloween was an event in my neighborhood. Several families would go all-out and set up a haunted cul-de-sac, complete with ominous fog, spooky music and a flying ghost (via zipline). We would go out in costume for hours collecting candy until our bags were overflowing. Disney puts on a pretty good Halloween party themselves, and I'm always impressed with the elaborate costumes presented by adults and children alike. Our final classic movie is *Bambi* from 1942. This was Disney's 5th animated film and based on a 1923 book that was actually intended for adults and therefore initially deemed too "grim and somber" for a family film. In early 2020, a CGI remake was said to be in the works.

So what does Halloween have to do with *Bambi* and a spiritual message? Good question, again. As discussed in February, the "man in the forest" who kills Bambi's mother is never seen but still considered one of Disney's greatest villains. In fact, he was ranked #20 on AFI's list of worst movie villains. *Snow White's* evil queen was the only Disney villain ranked higher (#10). In a similar way, Paul warns us in today's few verses there are many real-life, costumed villains in the world trying to deceive us, calling them "false apostles and deceitful workmen, disguising themselves as apostles of Christ." It's no surprise he mentions Satan himself as also wearing a costume by "disguising himself as an angel of light." As you know, Satan is tricky and quite good at what he does. He doesn't make himself obvious or easy to see. Like the *Bambi* villain, he stays hidden and even disguises himself in something more pleasing to our eyes to trick and deceive us. So on this fun-filled holiday and going forward, don't be fooled by the disguises of the devil or his minions. Check under the mask carefully to make sure those around you are not false teachers or workers of Satan, attempting to steal you away from the Father.

PRAYER—Lord, I do not want to be deceived by Satan or his false teachers. Help me to be alert, careful and knowledgeable so I don't fall for his disguises or deceptions. In Jesus, Amen.

TODAY I WILL...be alert and watchful for the devil in disguise trying to trick and trap me.

NOVEMBER THEME

DISNEY FUN FACTS

NOVEMBER 1 **Read GENESIS 11:1-9**

NEVER EQUAL

Disney Fun Facts – Structural Height Restrictions

"...though he was in the form of God, did not count equality with God a thing to be grasped..."
—Philippians 2:6

Welcome to November! This month we'll look at some fun facts about the Disney parks, films or history. Question...what's the highest altitude you've ever reached (not counting flying)? I think mine would be the top of the World Trade Center pre 9/11 at around 1300 feet, although technically I was much higher summiting a 13,000-foot peak in Colorado with a church group. Dubai's "Burj Khalifa" (2,722 feet) is the highest one could currently reach going the skyscraper route, and obviously the 29,032-foot Mt. Everest would be the ultimate in altitude. One thing is certain, you won't get near those heights in the Disney parks as no structure is over 200 feet tall. FAA regulations say anything taller must have a light for planes. Wanting to avoid unnecessary lights, Disney has kept all park attractions below 200 feet, although several are close. Cinderella Castle reaches 189', Big Thunder Mountain stretches 197', Tower of Terror is 199' and Expedition Everest tops them all at 199.5'. Technically, there is a structure taller than 200 feet, but outside the parks, as the Dolphin Hotel reaches 257' and does indeed have a beacon on top.

So why all this talk about tall structures? In Genesis 11, the misguided people attempt to build a tower reaching all the way into the heavens. The Lord looks down and sees their intentions to become equal with Him, so He creates new languages, baffling them and halting their project, which becomes known as the "Tower of Babel" due to their confusion. Ecclesiastes 12:13 says our main job is to fear God and keep his commandments. The verse above states that even Jesus knew equality with God wasn't possible. We are to fear and respect God as the highest authority and not one with whom we can be equal. God is over all the Earth and everything on it. We could never do anything nor build anything on Earth to reach His equal. We can only see Him after death through our continued faith, His loving grace and that powerful sacrifice of Christ.

PRAYER—Righteous Father, You are above all. I recognize Your authority and fear Your holy name. I deeply desire to be with You that I may see Your greatness and power. In Jesus, Amen.

TODAY I WILL...move one step closer to God each day, knowing I can never be equal.

NOVEMBER 2 **Read JEREMIAH 2:1-7**

TAKE OUT THE TRASH

Disney Fun Facts – Secret Trash System

"Show yourself in all respects to be a model of good works..."
—Titus 2:7a

Oscar the Grouch sang, "I love trash!" Let's briefly share his sentiments and dig through some trashy facts. The average U.S. citizen creates 4 lbs. of trash daily and up to 56 tons per year. Americans alone generate 40% of the world's total waste. Unfortunately, that trend doesn't stop at Disney with more than 80,000 lbs. of trash discarded daily at just the Magic Kingdom alone. Needless to say, we are trashy people. Walt Disney was very particular about trash. Not only did he insist on a trash can at least every 30 feet, but he invented the rectangular cans with enclosed flaps to prevent spillage and curb the smell. Today, most Disney cans are colorfully decorated and even themed to entice guests to use them. Small replicas are even popular as merchandise. Most impressively, Disney has a hidden, vacuum-powered, trash collection system that moves all garbage through a series of underground tubes to a centralized location. There are 13 collection sites throughout the Magic Kingdom, and every 20 minutes the 200-horsepower exhausters thrust the garbage through the tubes at 35 mph directly below the feet of guests.

In today's reading, the Lord speaks again through Jeremiah the prophet, reminding us of the plentiful land he brought his people to, despite their complaints. Unfortunately, the people disappointed the Lord once again and defiled the beautiful land He brought them to. We are now His chosen people, blessed with good and bountiful land. Most of us have homes and property with bountiful grass, trees and landscaping. God wants us to be good stewards of the land He has given (Gen. 2:15) and model good works (above verse) to others. It's a shame how much disregard is shown and how much trash is produced daily, even at Disney, when we all could do more to show appreciation for His gifts. What can you do today to be a better steward of God's blessings, especially the wonderful land and surroundings He has entrusted to you?

PRAYER—Father, I'm very grateful for all Your gifts, especially this Earth and its beautiful land You've entrusted to us. Help me to be a good steward and care for it. In His name, Amen.

TODAY I WILL...figure out at least one new way I can be a good steward of God's gifts.

NOVEMBER 3 **Read PHILIPPIANS 3:7-11**

PUT AWAY THE FILTH

Disney Fun Facts – Unavailable for Purchase

"Therefore put away all filthiness and rampant wickedness and receive with meekness the implanted word, which is able to save your souls."

—James 1:21

Pepsi products, toy guns, shot glasses, newspapers, selfie sticks and Avengers characters. Know what all those have in common? You won't find them at WDW. Coke has exclusive rights to sell their products. No guns, not even bubble ones, for obvious reasons. You may see shot glasses, but they ring up as "toothpick holders" to keep it family friendly. Newspapers are scarce at best as Disney wants you to forget about the outside world. (No problem...happy to!) Selfie sticks equals safety risk. And while Avengers characters are seen in Disneyland, especially at their new Marvel Campus, a licensing agreement keeps them from appearing on the east coast. There's one more item you won't find for sale. Gum is unavailable for purchase anywhere on WDW property including parks, resorts, Disney Springs and even the Orlando airport! You're allowed to bring it yourself of course, but you definitely can't buy it. It's simply too messy as cast members are constantly having to scrape it off the ground and from underneath furniture.

Don't get me wrong...I love gum, but I also understand Disney's policy as it can be downright yucky when not disposed of properly. It's no fun finding it on the bottom of your shoe, right? In the verse above, we are told to put away all filth and wickedness. In Philippians 3, Paul calls it "rubbish," saying it includes anything not of Christ. His point is that knowing Christ and gaining our reward through Him makes everything else meaningless, unimportant and basically filth. He refers to it all as "loss," saying it doesn't matter what he might have gained in the past. It's all loss compared to his faith and sharing in Christ's death, burial and resurrection through baptism so that he can one day be with Him eternally. So yes, you can chew gum, even at Disney. Just don't leave a filthy mess. More importantly, don't get involved in anything disgusting or wicked so you can remain one with Christ, the only "gain" in life that will ever matter.

PRAYER—Lord, give me the willpower to avoid anything disgusting or wicked in my life. I want only to share in Christ's sufferings so I may follow Him to You one day. In Him, Amen.

TODAY I WILL...keep filth from my life and put my relationship with Christ as top priority.

NOVEMBER 4 **Read ACTS 23:1-11**

A HEFTY PUSH

Disney Fun Facts – Tinkerbell's Flight

"Cry aloud; do not hold back; lift up your voice like a trumpet; declare to my people their transgression, to the house of Jacob their sins."
—Isaiah 58:1

Ever tried ziplining? We've tried some local courses, but I long to experience those long, exotic ziplines above beautiful landscapes. Disney doesn't have ziplining except for some small water park versions. Actually, there is a super long and high zipline on both coasts, but not for the public. Surely you've seen Tinker Bell soar above the crowd during the nightly fireworks. I would love to try that zipline, but unfortunately that ain't happening as she (or he at times) must be between 4'11" and 5'2" and weigh no more than 105 lbs. So close! The first "Tink" was a 98-pound, circus performer Walt hired to fly over Sleeping Beauty Castle...at the age of 71! At WDW, there is only room for tiny Tink and one other to take an elevator and then ladder up to the petite space near the top of Cinderella Castle. At the right moment, Tinker Bell gets a hefty push so she can travel the 850 feet in 30 seconds at 30mph. If she fails to make the full distance, which is rare, she must pull herself hand over hand to her Tomorrowland roof landing spot.

Sometimes we must give others a little, or even a hefty, push as well. In Acts 23, Paul is unapologetically direct, even using anger and bluntness to "push" the council into believing the truth, and God commends Paul for his courageous testimony. We're called to give our own testimony in teaching Christ, and it may take harsh truths to get the message across, especially if unsuccessful at first. Yes, Col. 4:6 says to be gracious with others, and Eph. 4:15 says to speak the truth in love, but the believers also prayed for and received the ability to speak with boldness in Acts 4. The verse above advises us to "cry aloud" and "not hold back" when talking to others about past sin. There's a delicate balance in teaching others, helping them see past mistakes and aiding them in finding faith in God through Christ. After showing initial grace and love, we may need to be more direct in "pushing" them to see the truth so as to eternally save their soul.

PRAYER—God, give me the courage and right words to be open and honest with those who need You. Help them to see and understand before it's too late. Through Jesus I pray, Amen.

TODAY I WILL...be bold and direct if necessary to those I'm attempting to bring to Christ.

NOVEMBER 5 **Read I JOHN 4:1-6**

FOLLOW THE RULES

Disney Fun Facts – Flag Rules

"...there will be false teachers among you, who will secretly bring in destructive heresies, even denying the Master who bought them, bringing upon themselves swift destruction."
—2 Peter 2:1

A major highlight chaperoning my son's 8th grade, Washington trip was visiting the Smithsonian and seeing "The Star-Spangled Banner," the original flag that inspired Francis Scott Key in 1814 to write what would become our national anthem. The flag is a great symbol of our freedom, and I'm reminded of its rules of etiquette. For example, the U.S. flag should never touch the ground and must be illuminated if flown at night. The flag shouldn't be flown during inclement weather, and if it becomes tattered, it should be repaired or destroyed properly. There are several others, including flying it at half-staff during an official period of national mourning. It's no surprise Disney has several U.S. flags on display, and I'm happy they have a traditional flag lowering ceremony nightly with the Pledge of Allegiance and national anthem. But did you know that all Disney flags are purposely made incorrectly with perhaps a star or stripe missing?

Disney does this because it technically makes them "pennants," meaning they don't have to follow the above rules. Disney isn't always able to see to it that the rules are followed, so to make it easier, they get around them by not raising official flags. In I John 4, we are cautioned to be wary of rule breakers. The Bible actually warns us many times to watch out for those who appear sound and knowledgeable but are actually false prophets set up to lead us astray. John advises us to test every soul to make sure it is led by God's Spirit and not a spirit of error. God's laws must be followed, and we can't be swayed by the pleasing look of those who break or even bend His rules. The verse above is clear that false teachers will be sneaky and secretive in their methods, but they will in fact be denying Christ and dooming themselves for eternity. Don't get caught up with rule breakers and end up on their popular path to destruction. Carefully test everyone against the truth of Scripture and stay firmly planted on the smaller path to salvation.

PRAYER—Father, I want to know and live Your Word so I will be able to properly test anything I see or hear against Your truth. Help me to avoid those who break Your rules. In Jesus, Amen.

TODAY I WILL...not be enticed or swayed by anyone who breaks God's rules.

NOVEMBER 6 **Read ISAIAH 55:6-11**

THE GIFT OF WATER

Disney Fun Facts – Channeling the Rain

"He gives rain on the earth and sends waters on the fields."
—Job 5:10

Do you ever struggle packing for your Disney trips? Sometimes it's hard to predict the weather, making it easy to overpack in anticipation of every possible scenario. I know the WDW forecast in particular typically calls for rain every afternoon. In actuality, it rarely does rain, and we normally have pretty decent weather throughout our vacation. I do remember one time when we got off Epcot's Test Track and exited into a monsoon. I have never seen rain that hard. For some crazy reason, we decided to brave it and run to our next attraction. Needless to say, we were thoroughly drenched. It's too bad we hadn't departed Epcot's giant icon instead. Did you know Spaceship Earth was designed so that no rain ever pours off the 16-million-ton sphere? Instead, all water is channeled through passages within the structure and funneled into the World Showcase Lagoon, meaning you can stand directly underneath during a storm and stay dry.

Disney Imagineers are so clever. How do they figure out a system that keeps rain from falling off a giant, round ball and channel it into a lagoon a quarter-mile away? The lack of rain under Spaceship Earth reminds me of I Kings 17-18 where God stopped the rain for three years causing severe drought and famine because of King Ahab's sin. But I also remember today's passage from Isaiah which encourages us to seek the Lord who brings forth rain to replenish the Earth. As the book of Job says above, God controls everything we have and see, even the rain that so often keeps us from drought and despair. It is He who decides when it rains and how much we will receive. Even the simple but essential blessing of water comes from above. Take time today to thank God for the basic necessities of life such as food, water, shelter and clothing, items we too often take for granted. The all-powerful, all-knowing, ever-present Father provides us daily with the constant blessings we need to survive and deserves our praise and thanksgiving.

PRAYER—Thank You, O Lord for the rain. I am so blessed to have water available whenever I need it. You always provide life's basic necessities, and I am ever grateful. In His name, Amen.

TODAY I WILL...stop and thank God every time I use water, realizing what a blessing it is.

NOVEMBER 7 **Read JAMES 1:12-15**

WITHSTAND THE WIND

Disney Fun Facts – The Mighty Fortress

"Be strong in the Lord and in the strength of his might. Put on the whole armor of God, that you may be able to stand against the schemes of the devil."
—Ephesians 6:10-11

Do you remember story of the "Three Little Pigs," all trying to escape the evil wolf and his powerful "huff n'puff?" One pig elects to build his house of straw while the second chooses sticks. It's no surprise when those two houses fall with ease. But the third pig is wise, selecting bricks which easily withstand the mighty winds of the wolf's blow. Today we are focusing once again on the image that most often represents not only the Magic Kingdom, but typically the entirety of WDW. Cinderella Castle is surrounded by a moat of over 3.3 million gallons of water. For WDW's 25th anniversary, it was famously and unpopularly made over to look like a giant birthday cake. Check out that picture. Yikes! When the now-extinct Stitch attraction first opened, the castle was covered in toilet paper and graffitied with the words "Stitch is King!" A common misconception is that this castle is made of bricks or stone as it appears, but it was actually designed to be even stronger. Constructed of fiberglass and plaster surrounding a 600-ton steel-based frame, Cinderella Castle can withstand hurricane winds up to 125 mph.

This iconic structure was obviously designed to be a mighty fortress, virtually indestructible by the typical speed of hurricane winds. In James 1, those who remain strong and steadfast during trials and temptations are called "blessed." The verse above commands us to show strength in the Lord's power by putting on the whole armor of God. Every piece listed after that (truth, righteousness, readiness, faith, salvation and the Word of God) is vital to withstand the devil's tricks. Satan's first priority is to tempt you with worldly pleasures and draw you away from a relationship with God. We must seek, ask for and receive the strength of God so we too can be a mighty fortress. Having a sturdy foundation in God's Word will allow us to withstand Satan's schemes which are more powerful than a wolf's blow or even mighty, hurricane winds.

PRAYER—Dear Lord, I ask for Your mighty strength so I may be firmly planted in Your Word and therefore withstand the devil and his sneaky schemes. Through the loving Savior, Amen.

TODAY I WILL...fortify my foundation and build myself out of God's impenetrable strength.

NOVEMBER 8 **Read 2 TIMOTHY 2:14-26**

RAISE YOUR BRIDGE

Disney Fun Facts – The Drawbridge

"Finally, brothers, whatever is true, whatever is honorable, whatever is just, whatever is pure, whatever is lovely, whatever is commendable...think about these things."
—Philippians 4:8

It was an absolute dream house! For some reason related to my dad's work, our family once got to spend a weekend at a luxury mansion when I was a child. This east Tennessee mountain home had a fireman's pole between multiple stories, a lookout perch way above the roof, triple bunk beds, secret passageways between floors, a huge model train, a giant hot tub and an inside basketball court! And that's just what I remember. Oh yeah, it also had a working drawbridge at the front entrance. Yesterday we discussed Cinderella Castle, an impressive structure no doubt, but the original Sleeping Beauty Castle in Disneyland has something it doesn't. Not only was its construction overseen by Walt himself, but it has the only operational drawbridge of any Disney castle in the world. This drawbridge has been raised only twice, during the 1955 opening of the park itself and for the 1983 reopening of Fantasyland. Railings have since been added to prevent guests from toppling off the side, making it unlikely to ever be raised again.

Drawbridges were used during Medieval times to keep enemies out of castles. In 2 Timothy 2, Paul lists several things we must also keep out of our lives: unnecessary arguments, irreverent or foolish talk, lies, youthful passions and ignorant controversies. Instead we're told to pursue righteousness, faith, love, peace and a pure heart. He says if we keep out dishonorable things, we will be a useful vessel for God, set apart as holy and ready for every good work. We all have a working drawbridge we can raise at any time to keep out unholy, shameful or dangerous things. You get to decide what you let in and out of your mind and body. As suggested above, choose to only think about and do noble, Godly things. Don't allow evil to cross your bridge and enter your mighty fortress. Be an honorable tool that only feeds on proper, righteous qualities. Pray again for God's strength to recognize things not of Him and raise your bridge when needed.

PRAYER—Holy Lord, thank You for allowing me to make choices. Help me to be aware and consciously decide to allow only righteous things to influence my thoughts and actions. Amen.

TODAY I WILL...control what enters my mind and body, preventing anything not of God.

NOVEMBER 9 **Read PSALM 1:1-6**

BE A TREE

Disney Fun Facts – Green Space

"For as the earth brings forth its sprouts...so the Lord God will cause righteousness and praise to sprout up before all the nations."
—Isaiah 61:11

My city is growing way too fast! Living in Nashville since birth, I've seen massive and dramatic changes over the years. Particularly in the last decade, we've grown exponentially in population and construction. Stop coming to Nashville people! We're full!! I'm kidding. Sortof. While I'm honored to live in an admired city, the rapid changes have caused some undesired results, not the least of which is the drastic decline in green space. It's sad to see public parks and grassy fields taken over by apartment buildings and office towers. This is one area where Disney has consciously kept control, making sure progress isn't just about rides, resorts and restaurants. In fact, more than 12 percent of WDW, around 4,000 acres, is made up of gardens, greenery and other landscapes. In addition, Disney adds around three million plants and trees annually.

I love the Bible's first psalm. Read it carefully and consider the blessed one it refers to. It says they will delight only in God's Word, meditate on it constantly and keep away from sinners. That's the goal we should all be striving for. To achieve that "blessed" status from God, it says we must be like a prosperous tree, firmly planted by a stream of water that brings forth fruit at all times and doesn't ever wither. Let's break that down. "Firmly planted" means rooted in God's Word. The "stream of water" is our life source, the living water God offers that gives eternal life. "Bringing forth fruit" means we share that offer and message with others to multiply the numbers of saved souls. And "not withering" means we don't give up. We keep our faith strong and endure the race no matter the trials or temptations that come. I'm grateful that despite their fast-paced progress, Disney continues to make green space a priority. As you and I grow in maturity and faith, let us remember to keep some green space so we can be like that tree with all its important components necessary to live forever in that holy and beautiful city He is preparing.

PRAYER—Heavenly Father, I want to be a tree for You. Strengthen me to stay rooted in Your Word and never give up on getting myself and many others into Your eternal kingdom. Amen.

TODAY I WILL...find a tree to sit under to meditate on Psalm 1 and pray to be a tree for God.

NOVEMBER 10 **Read 2 CORINTHIANS 6:14-18**

SET YOUR BOUNDARIES

Disney Fun Facts – Animal Barriers

"Therefore go out from their midst, and be separate from them, says the Lord."
—2 Corinthians 6:17

I've got another YouTube video you should check out. It's called "Battle at Kruger." The 8-minute video was shot in 2004 during a safari at Kruger National Park in South Africa and depicts a battle between a herd of buffalo, a group of young lions and a surprise visitor. I don't want to spoil it too much. Violent encounters between animals can be a powerful and intense visual. Thankfully, you won't see anything like that at Disney's Animal Kingdom where multiple species dwell and roam. I realize a Disney vacation is supposed to be exciting and full of surprises, but we don't really want to see animals attacking each other, do we? Well Disney doesn't, so they have placed specifically designed, hidden barriers throughout the Kilimanjaro Safari attraction. Many of these electric barriers are plant-shaped making it look like the animals are free-ranging, while they are secretly well guarded against each other.

Our reading from 2 Corinthians 6 warns us to set up some carefully-designed boundaries in our lives as well. We are told not to be "equally yoked" with unbelievers as righteousness has no place with those who break the Law of God. We are reminded that our bodies are the temple of God and therefore anything unclean cannot be allowed to enter it. Yes, we are to be like Jesus, spread God's message and bring unbelievers to the Father. However, we can't allow their unbelief or worldly ways to infiltrate our lives in the process. It's a delicate balance that requires God's guidance and some firm boundaries. The real animal kingdom can be brutal and dangerous if certain creatures are allowed to cross paths. In the same way, God won't allow His kingdom to be penetrated with any evil from this world. If we want to enter His home one day, we must make sure we keep our lives pure and have the proper boundaries in place to keep out the practices of the most wicked creature still roaming the Earth, seeking to steal our salvation.

PRAYER—Dear Lord, help me find the balance between spreading Your message to those who need it and separating myself from any evil that attempts to cross into my path. In Christ, Amen.

TODAY I WILL...set my boundaries and separate myself from anyone that breaks God's laws.

NOVEMBER 11 **Read MATTHEW 25:14-30**

SECRET SKILLS

Disney Fun Facts – The Hidden Court

"Having gifts that differ according to the grace given to us, let us use them..."
—Romans 12:6

I enjoy college basketball's "March Madness" Tournament. It's thrilling to watch that 68-team bracket whittled down to one champion. My family always does a friendly bracket competition, as I know many do, and I look forward each year to "making my picks." I can watch basketball like a champ, but I was never too good at playing it. However, I wouldn't mind taking a few shots on Disneyland's secret court. Yes, you read that right. There's a hidden basketball court inside the Matterhorn Bobsleds ride. The half-court, backboard and hoop were placed in a room near the top for professional climbers to use during breaks, as they have scaled the summit during peak crowds to entertain guests, a tradition that occasionally still continues. For safety reasons, the internal door was locked, so the court was only accessible to the climbers from the outside. According to cast members, the court is still there, and you can see a picture online.

While basketball is certainly not my talent, it definitely is for some, like those "March Madness" participants. Thankfully, God has blessed me with other skills, some of which I didn't know about and have discovered over time. No doubt He has blessed you with the same. In Matthew 25, we read what is actually called the "parable of the talents," although it's referring to an amount of money. A master entrusts money to his three servants, expecting them to work hard and multiply it. The first two do, but the third fears the risk and buries his talent, angering the master. Jesus was teaching us to use our God-given talents for Him, even if it means taking a risk. Just like that secret court, you may have a hidden talent you can use for His glory. Take time to explore possible skills you may be unaware of. Discipline yourself to use those to further His kingdom and serve others as best you can. Whatever you do, don't waste, bury or hide them in fear of the risk. Ask God for the courage to use them in service to Him and others.

PRAYER—Thank You Lord for my strengths and talents. Help me to use those for your glory. Help me to also discover new ones and give me the courage to try them. In His name, Amen.

TODAY I WILL...list my known talents and at least one new one I will explore without fear.

NOVEMBER 12 **Read JAMES 2:18-26**

MOVE ALREADY!

Disney Fun Facts – The Broken Monster

"For as the body apart from the spirit is dead, so also faith apart from works is dead."
—James 2:26

Are they really real? Even Nessie?! They gotta be with all the eyewitness accounts, testimonies and proof (insert air quotes). They even have pictures! (air quotes again.) Whether it's Bigfoot, the Loch Ness Monster (a.k.a. Nessie) or even the scary Chupacabra from Puerto Rico, there are several legendary creatures that many swear exist. There's even a Skunk Ape in Florida? Oh, come on! Oh yeah, I did forget the most important one...the terrifying Yeti! And I know just where to find him. If you really take your time in the queue of Animal Kingdom's Expedition Everest, reading the plethora of information and checking out the photos, you may actually start to believe yourself. And then when you ride, which you must do of course, you may just catch a glimpse of the creature, roaring up a storm, but not moving an inch. Why won't he move? Just a few months after this ride debuted, his supportive framing split meaning he couldn't perform his normal 5-foot horizontal and 18-inch vertical movement safely. Since that day, over 15 years ago, the Yeti has remained stationary. He appears to move a little due to a strobe light which has earned him the nickname, "Disco Yeti." At 25 ft. tall, he's the largest, most complex audio-animatronic ever built. Joe Rohde, the Imagineer in charge of the ride, swore in 2013 he would get the Yeti moving someday, but as he's now retired from Disney, don't get your hopes up.

Today's message from James 2 is simple. We can't please God and do His will by remaining stationary like that broken Yeti. James reminds us that faith is not enough, saying even demons believe in God. But we must combine our belief with works. We must be active, get up, go out and physically serve Him and others. James gives the example of Abraham demonstrating his love by climbing a mountain and physically placing his own son on an altar as a sacrifice. The verse above sums it up fairly directly. Faith without works is dead. Don't be stationary in your service to the Father. Demonstrate your conviction and devotion to Him through works.

PRAYER—Lord, help me to show my love for You through faith AND works. In Jesus, Amen.

TODAY I WILL...list ways I can demonstrate my love for God through action and get moving!

NOVEMBER 13 **Read PROVERBS 22:17-21**

DO YOU HEAR THAT?

Disney Fun Facts – Most Popular Souvenir

"He who has ears to hear, let him hear."
—Matthew 11:15

So what's your go-to souvenir on a Disney trip? T-shirt? Mug? Christmas ornament? Pin? Pressed penny? Stuffed animal? All good choices and all quite popular. For me, it's usually a figures set or snow globe to add to my collection. However, none of those can claim best-selling souvenir of all time. That honor belongs to the coveted Mickey ears. In fact, around 100 million have been sold since Disneyland opened in 1955. These days, as you may know, there are numerous colors, styles and variations of both those and the Minnie headbands making them very popular products. You can also get your name engraved on them at several park locations.

So let's talk about ears. Maybe not Mickey's ears in particular, but the ones God gave each of us and what they are best used for. Solomon had a good idea in Proverbs 22 when he said, "Incline your ear, and hear the words of the wise." He then advised we keep the wise words we hear with us so we can have them ready to pass along to others when needed. He speaks of trusting in God and knowing which words are "right and true" so that we may "give a true answer" when asked. Solomon was the wisest man who ever lived, receiving his wisdom directly from God. He knew that our ears were best used listening to His words and letting His instructions enter through our ears and into our minds so that we may follow them and tell them to others who need to hear. Romans 10:17 says our faith comes from hearing, and in John 6:45, Jesus said all who hear and learn from God will come to Him. We can use our ears for a lot of things, some good and some bad. Try to avoid listening to worldly things. Instead, choose to use your ears to hear and listen to what God is trying to tell you. This is the first step in getting to know Him and His Son so that you can learn what to do to be saved. As Jesus said above, if you have ears, then hear! Take the time to just be quiet, listen and hear. His words will come.

PRAYER—Father God, I'm grateful for the ability to hear what You want me to hear. Speak to me and increase my faith and knowledge of You by what I hear today. In His holy name, Amen.

TODAY I WILL...resolve to only use my ears for good and for God. I will listen for Him.

NOVEMBER 14 **Read JOHN 9:1-7**

TIME'S A WASTIN'

Disney Fun Facts – Building Disneyland

"Look carefully then how you walk, not as unwise but as wise, making the best use of the time, because the days are evil."
—Ephesians 5:15-16

Remember the show, "Minute to Win it?" It offered $1 million for the contestants that could complete ten games in 60 seconds each. Many of the games involved building a tower of some sort out of household items like cups. What if they had been told to build a theme park? How long would that have taken? More than a minute of course. But what? A year? Two years? Five? Ten? Go back to the first option. Hard to believe, but the entirety of Disneyland took just one year to build. Construction began on July 16, 1954, and the park opened on July 17, 1955, a year and a day later. It opened with 20 attractions, shops and eateries, so it was no small feat to get the land cleared and all completed in just a year, not to mention parking and other logistics.

If a new theme park was announced today, can you imagine how long it would take to build? Certainly more than a year! Walt obviously wasted no time and was very proficient in leading, delegating and choosing the best crews for the job. We looked at Jesus healing the blind man in January, but I want to focus on verse 4 where Christ says, "We must work the works of Him who sent me while it is day; night is coming, when no one can work." Jesus knew His time and ministry were limited and He had a lot of work to do. Every minute he had to teach and spread the Gospel was important and valuable, and it should be to us as well. The verse above says we should make the best use of our time. Colossians 4:5 says the same. Most people by human nature are pretty good at procrastination. We have every intention of serving and teaching Christ to others, but we assume we'll get to it eventually and there's plenty of time. But there may not be. Your life, the life of the one in need of Christ or the world may end in the next 60 seconds, and you may have only a minute to win it...it being the soul of someone heading the wrong way. Use your time wisely. Don't waste it and don't wait. The time to act and work for God is now!

PRAYER—Dear God, only You know how much time I or those in need of You have left. Help me to avoid procrastination when it comes to doing Your work. Through Christ's name, Amen.

TODAY I WILL...make the best use of my time for God, even making a schedule if necessary.

NOVEMBER 15 **Read MATTHEW 24:3-14**

SNEAKY CATS

Disney Fun Facts – Disneyland's Pets

"Be sober-minded; be watchful. Your adversary the devil prowls around like a roaring lion, seeking someone to devour."
—I Peter 5:8

Do you remember *The Lion King* scene where Mufasa gives young Simba a pouncing lesson? He lets him practice on Zazu, telling him to stay quiet and low to the ground. Our cat would do the same growing up, sneaking very slowly, in full view of course, before harmlessly attacking our legs. Cats can be funny but also quite sly and effective in procuring their prey. Disneyland uses this to their advantage, allowing up to 200 cats to roam the park, especially at night, to help control the rodent population? It's often assumed the cats are "feral" or untamed, but Disney assigns cast members to feed and care for them, so they're not exactly wild and pose no real threat to guests. Disney keeps them around to aid in keeping the park neat and tidy. There's even a website, disneylandcats.com, that profiles each cat, giving updates and information on them.

How do you see the devil? Is he the little red guy with horns, a spiked tail and pitchfork? Is he a snake like in the Garden? Or is he perhaps a cat or lion as the above verse describes? The truth is it doesn't matter what he looks like. The important thing to remember is that he exists, he's active and he still works to steal us from God. Matthew 24 describes his work and strategy to lead us astray, especially as we approach the end of the world and Christ's return. Jesus warns that the devil will use others to teach false messages that will sound convincing and true. There will also be wars, disasters and betrayals of all kinds. Many are convinced that time is now, but no one truly knows if the end is soon or many years away. We just have to be ready at all times and make sure we are on the side of right and the actual truth. Like those sneaky, "employed" cats, the devil is always prowling, quietly sneaking up behind us and preparing to pounce. Be forever watchful, ready to catch him in the act and determined to resist. We know God will defeat him in the end, but he will sadly win many souls before then. Don't let him win yours!

PRAYER—Father, help me to be alert and recognize the sneaky attacks of Satan and those he uses against me. Give me the strength to always resist him boldly. Through Jesus Christ, Amen.

TODAY I WILL...be watchful for the devil's attacks, likely through the influence of others.

NOVEMBER 16 **Read DEUTERONOMY 6:1-9**

NANNY'S NOTE

Disney Fun Facts – The Time Capsule

"The memory of the righteous is a blessing, but the name of the wicked will rot."
—Proverbs 10:7

It was dated September 11, 1982, my 7th birthday and read, "Dear Albert, keep this note as your ticket to a movie of your choice. Love, Nanny." After receiving that gift from my grandmother, I tucked it away and basically forgot about it until finding it in my old desk nearly 30 years later. At that point, she wasn't well enough to redeem my "ticket," and she passed soon after. Finding that note was like digging up a time capsule, bringing back memories of not only receiving it, but of the fun I always had with my Nanny and what a blessing she was. Disneyland has a couple of time capsules as well. On their 40th anniversary in 1995, they buried one near Sleeping Beauty's Castle. It's scheduled to be opened on their 80th anniversary, July 17, 2035, and supposedly contains photos, newspapers and other items of the day. Disney California Adventure also buried one at a 2012 rededication. It's scheduled to be extracted a couple years later in 2037.

If others, through their memories, unearth a time capsule about you in the future, what will they see? In Deut. 6, we're taught the importance of passing God's instructions on to future generations by talking about them at home, when we walk, when we lie down and rise up. In other words, our children should be immersed in God's words as we discuss them throughout their lives. Hopefully, they will then do the same with their own children. My grandmother did this both with my mom and directly with me, so her "time capsule" was full of Godly lessons and examples. Will future generations know of your faith and love for God? The verse above says memories of the righteous are a blessing. Be a blessing now and always by teaching and demonstrating God's ways. Nanny's note reminded me of her strong example of Godly faith. I plan to see her again one day so I can finally redeem my ticket. I realize there may not be movies in Heaven, but viewing the glory of God while seated next to her will be even better.

PRAYER—Eternal Father, I want others, my family in particular, to remember me as a moral example of Christ's love, Godly faith and knowledge of Your truth. In His blessed name, Amen.

TODAY I WILL...be a blessing to my family by demonstrating righteousness and passing it on.

NOVEMBER 17 **Read JOHN 4:1-15**

A DRINK OF WATER

Disney Fun Facts – Free Stuff

"Whoever believes in me, as the Scripture has said, 'Out of his heart will flow rivers of living water.'"
—John 7:38

You wouldn't think "free" and "Disney" would ever appear in the same sentence, but here are a few free things WDW offers: monorail, boat and Skyliner rides, buttons, sodas at Club Cool, fireworks, the Water Pageant or a movie under the stars from several resorts, crafts for kids at Epcot and best of all...free Wi-Fi! You might can even score free samples at certain eateries, and of course the famous "Disney magic" often surprising guests with upgrades, perks or special gifts. And there's one more item always free...water! No, not bottled. Let's not go crazy. But you can always receive a free cup of ice water anywhere serving drinks. Now, keep in mind it's Florida tap water so it may not be your cup of tea...err, water...but at least it's free. I've taken advantage, especially when I'm enjoying a delicious Disney snack (which is not free of course).

A simple cup of water can quench a dying thirst or satisfy one in need. Jesus Himself asked for a drink twice. The first time was in John 4. He is weary from a journey, stops to rest by a well and asks a Samaritan woman for a drink. She hesitates out of fear as Jews and Samaritans at that time didn't associate. Jesus tells her if she only knew who was asking, she would in turn receive a special "living water" back from Him. He speaks of the same gift above in John 7. The 2nd time Jesus asked for a drink was from the cross. He received sour wine on a sponge instead. Jesus was rejected twice asking for a simple drink of water, but we can give Him that drink and provide others His living water too. In Matthew 25:35, Jesus said when we provide a drink to those in need, we are really giving it to Him and will be rewarded. His living water is special. He told the woman whoever drinks of it will never thirst again. She didn't understand, but we know He meant eternal life. Find the courage and drive to go out today and offer Christ's living water to those in need of it. It will be the most rewarding drink of water they ever receive.

PRAYER—Lord, thank You for a drink of water to quench my thirst. Thank You even more for the living water You offer through Your Son that means I'll never thirst again. In Him, Amen.

TODAY I WILL...give away bottled water and use the chance to tell others about living water.

NOVEMBER 18 **Read JOHN 4:16-42**

SOMETHING FROM NOTHING

Disney Fun Facts – The Parking Lot

"...whoever believes in me will also do the works that I do; and greater works than these will he do, because I am going to the Father."
—John 14:12

In 1970, Canadian singer, Joni Mitchell, released "Big Yellow Taxi," a song later covered by artists such as Amy Grant and Counting Crows. The song speaks of environmental concerns with its most famous line, "they paved paradise and put up a parking lot." Disneyland actually did the opposite. They took a parking lot and put up a paradise...in the form of a 2nd park! Disney California Adventure opened in 2001, bringing new thrills and excitement, but before it was DCA, it was simply a parking lot for the original Disneyland Park. DCA is 72-acres and themed around the history and culture of California. Originally, it was going to be a west coast version of Epcot called WestCOT with an even larger version of the spherical Spaceship Earth.

Joni Mitchell wrote the song in Hawaii after seeing beautiful mountains in the distance but parking lots all around. I'm all for protecting green space, and we've discussed how Disney does just that, but they also take parking lots and barren land and create incredible parks that provide magic and memories to so many families, truly making it the "happiest place on Earth." Today's reading finished yesterday's story of Jesus and the Samaritan woman. After Jesus tells her who she is, even recalling her sins, she is finally convinced He is the Christ. She then runs into town telling everyone about Him, and verse 39 says many believed because of her testimony. Do you see what God can do? He took a sinful woman and made her a witness for Christ. He changed Zacchaeus from a deceitful tax collector into a repentant, saved soul. And of course, He even took a murderer named Saul and transformed him into Paul, the greatest Christian missionary in history. Disney can turn a parking lot into a "paradise," but God can turn a sinful soul into a faithful follower. He can do the same for you. If you've wandered away, turn around and let Him change you into one who does great things for both Him and those who need His message.

PRAYER—Father, take control! I am Yours to use however You best need me. Change me into a faithful servant who does great things for You, Your chosen and Your kingdom. Amen.

TODAY I WILL...allow God to change me from a parking lot into a future paradise with Him.

NOVEMBER 19 **Read 2 KINGS 22:8-13**

WORDS WORTH REPEATING

Disney Fun Facts – The Train Message

"Man shall not live by bread alone, but by every word that comes from the mouth of God."
—Matthew 4:4

This will age me, but do you remember those old commercials for S.O.S. cleaning pads? The dirty pots and pans would all bang and clang in unison, begging to be cleaned. It took me a long time to figure out they were all clanking out S.O.S. in Morse Code, dot dot dot, dash dash dash, dot dot dot. This early form of communication, named for the inventor of the telegraph, Samuel Morse, is actually broadcast repeatedly at Disneyland. If you visit the New Orleans Square train station, there's a small telegraph office in the waiting area where you can hear constant dots and dashes, repeating over and over the first two lines of Walt Disney's opening day speech.

Walt began his speech on that 1955 day with these words, "To all who come to Disneyland, welcome. Here age relives fond memories of the past, and here youth may savor the challenge and promise of the future." Those powerful words have now been repeated thousands of times through the train station's telegraph clicks. In 2 Kings 22, a surprise discovery is made when King Josiah orders the repair of God's temple. They find the Book of the Law and realize it hasn't been followed properly for years. If you read the next chapter, King Josiah himself reads the Book aloud to make sure the people will begin following God's instructions. Some words bear repeating. Jesus said above that it's not food that truly sustains us in life. It's hearing the words from God's mouth repeatedly, which help us not only here on Earth, but in finding eternity as well. If we fail to read or hear His words on a regular basis, we won't know how to live properly and will fall into disobedience like the people under Josiah. Read God's Word today. Repeat tomorrow. Keep that pattern going indefinitely. There's no such thing as overreading Scripture. Its words will help us in our own S.O.S. They will Save Our Soul!

PRAYER—Father, help me to nourish my life both now and eternally by repeating Your words daily. I never want to fall into sin or disobedience, so help me to get into the daily habit of studying Scripture so I can know how You want me to live. In the name of Christ I pray, Amen.

TODAY I WILL...begin an unending pattern of reading or hearing His words on a daily basis.

NOVEMBER 20 **Read LUKE 12:4-9**

WHAT'S MY NAME?

Disney Fun Facts – First Names Only

"I am the good shepherd. I know my own and my own know me, just as the Father knows me and I know the Father..."
—John 10:14-15

Since we're nearing the end of this book, allow me to finally introduce (and likely embarrass) myself. Hi, my name is Albert Thweatt. I have a weird last name that's been pronounced eleventy zillion different ways. (It rhymes with "sweet" by the way.) Also, my middle name is Ashley, which never ever got made fun of. (Sense the sarcasm?) It was my grandfather's name and apparently used to be more popular with boys. Not so much anymore! Thanks parents! Finally, my dad is Albert too, so I'm a junior. He goes by Al, so many assume I want the same. Wrong! I can't stand when people call me Al. Paul Simon's famous song was definitely not written for me. Sorry, just some of my name pet peeves. Walt Disney had one too. He liked to be informal and despised when people called him "Mr. Disney," insisting that everyone call him by his first name. This is why cast members have first names only on their name tags to this day.

Have you ever heard of the Life360 app? Let me tell you...it's a Godsend, especially if you have teenagers. It tracks through their phone so you can see where they are at all times. Did you know God has the same app on us? Well, maybe not an actual app, but He always knows where we are and much more. Today's passage confirms God knows and cares for each of every one of us, saying He even knows the number of hairs on our heads. Isaiah 43:1 says He knows our name. Jeremiah 1:5 says He knew us before we were even conceived. God knows our actions, our words, and even our thoughts. He hears us when we pray, either out loud or silently. The verse above says God knows all the sheep who are following the good Shepherd in Jesus Christ. I hope you like your name, but perhaps you have some issues (as I clearly do) or prefer to be called something specific like Walt did. What truly matters is that God knows you by name and everything about you. Trust in His undying love as you praise and call Him by name as well!

PRAYER—Loving Father, I praise and worship Your holy name. Thank You for knowing my name and everything about me. Please call my name home one day. In Jesus' name, Amen.

TODAY I WILL...list at least 10 names for God and use them to call on and praise Him.

NOVEMBER 21 **Read JOHN 15:1-11**

THE VINE AND THE BRANCHES

Disney Fun Facts – The Liberty Tree

"By this my Father is glorified, that you bear much fruit and so prove to be my disciples."
—John 15:8

It weighed 35 tons and was 60 feet tall but was nearly 8 miles from where they wanted it to be. Could they actually move it? After all, it had been firmly rooted for at least 130 years. Rumors say Walt himself found the tree and requested it be relocated as the centerpiece of one of six themed lands soon to be under construction in his new park. The giant oak was transplanted over several months by horticulturalists by drilling holes through its massive trunk, placing in steel pins and lifting it with a 100-ton crane. Once replanted at Magic Kingdom's Liberty Square, the holes were refilled with hardwood and the "wounds" healed. It was named "Liberty Tree" after the famous elm that once stood in Boston and sheltered strategic Colonist meetings in planning against the British. MK's colossal replica is now nearly 200 years old and holds 13 lanterns to signify the original colonies. Over 500 trees have since been planted by Disney from its acorns.

In John 15, Jesus clarifies our purpose using a tree analogy, explaining that we must first be rooted in the Father as the giver of all life. He calls us "branches" that grow off of Him as the "true vine." You know how trees work. They get water and nutrients through the roots, firmly planted in the soil. Those vital sources of life then make their way to the branches through the vine or trunk. The branches then produce fruit or new seeds to repeat the whole process. We can't grow as branches if we aren't attached to Jesus as the vine and firmly rooted in the truth of God's Word. Once we accept and follow Christ, we can then begin to bear fruit for God's kingdom. That great oak in Liberty Square has produced over 500 new trees from its acorns. How many trees, or new followers, have you produced? 500? 50? 1? It's not too late. Start today! Don't just be an empty branch. What good is that? Contribute to God's kingdom and fulfill His purpose for you. Bear fruit! Produce seeds! Plant some new trees for the Father!

PRAYER—Lord, I'm so thankful I can be firmly attached to You and rooted in truth through Your Son. Help me to bear seeds and plant new trees. Send me a soul to save. In Him, Amen.

TODAY I WILL...make plans to fulfill my purpose of bearing fruit through Jesus Christ.

NOVEMBER 22 **Read MATTHEW 13:24-29**

SHALLOW WEEDS

Disney Fun Facts – Fantasmic Lake

"Therefore, as you received Christ Jesus the Lord, so walk in him, rooted and built up in him and established in the faith, just as you were taught..."
—Colossians 2:6-7

There's a memorable scene in Disney's original *Parent Trap* where one twin is in the lake, trying to convince her dad's snooty fiancé that it's shallow. What she can't see, of course, is that the clever girl is standing on the shoulders of her twin sister, completely submerged underwater. The villainous woman falls, both for the prank and into the lake, creating a humorous scene. It's often hard to determine a lake's depth, especially when you can't see the bottom, which is also true of the "lake" surrounding Fantasmic, my favorite WDW show. That specific body of water which houses three giant water screens, pyrotechnics and multiple watercrafts including the giant steamboat at the end full of characters also holds 1.9 million gallons of water. That's enough to fill every bathtub on WDW property...twice! One would think a lake with that much water and activity would be fairly deep. However, Fantasmic Lake is only one foot deep on average. It was designed that way for safety reasons in case a performer accidently falls in during the show.

Today we read a parable in which Jesus told of a field of good crops plagued with weeds placed by an enemy. To avoid uprooting the good plants, the master instructs his servants to wait until harvest time to gather, bind and burn the weeds while the good crops will then be gathered to the master's barn. Yesterday we saw the importance of being firmly rooted in the Father. Have you ever picked weeds? It's not a fun chore, but they typically come up easily as their roots are shallow. So which crop are you? A firmly-rooted, thriving plant or a shallow weed, easily uprooted to be gathered and burned? Fantasmic lake is deceptively shallow. Don't make the same mistake of being an ungrounded weed mixed in among the good chosen crops. There are too many weeds in this world already! Make sure your roots run deep in Godly faith and truth so you will one day be chosen and gathered by the Master into his barn for all eternity.

PRAYER—Lord, I don't want to be a shallow weed, planted by the devil to destroy Your good crops. Help my roots to run deep in Your truth so I can grow into great things for You. Amen.

TODAY I WILL...confirm that I am good crop, deeply rooted in faith, and not a shallow weed.

NOVEMBER 23 **Read ECCLESIASTES 3:1-8**

WHAT TIME IS IT?

Disney Fun Facts – The Mickey Watch

"Watch therefore, for you know neither the day nor the hour."
—Matthew 25:13

As a typical child of the 80's, the best decade ever of course, I remember a few times I wanted to join the latest fashion fad. I wore my "Members Only" jacket too much. I begged for and received parachute pants. Ray Bans...had 'em. Acid-washed jeans...check. And there was one more craze I just had to be a part of. I couldn't wait to get my own Swatch watch, complete with the rubber "swatch guard." The Swiss Swatch company, founded in 1983, skyrocketed from $3 million to $105 million in sales by 1985, but there was another very popular watch many years earlier. In 1930, the Waterbury Clock Company reached an deal with Walt Disney to produce a Mickey Mouse watch. Introduced at the 1933 Chicago World's Fair for $3 each, the watch was very successful, becoming the company's first million-dollar line and saving it from financial ruin. In 1957, the 25 millionth watch was presented to Walt himself. By the way, Waterbury Clocks went on to become Timex, one of the most successful watch companies to this day.

Time. It's important. Think about it. The world runs on it. We base our lives around it, rely on it and stress about not having enough of it. According to Ecclesiastes, there is a time for all things, and God has a purpose for everything we see or experience. As His faithful followers, we must remember to trust His judgement and be ready for all things. For example, there will be many times of happiness, but also those of great sadness. There will be periods of peace mixed in with times of war. The joy of birth will be matched with the pain and sorrow of death. It all has a purpose and is the will of God, so be patient and give Him your trust at all times. After all, the only time that really matters is one we don't even know according to the above verse. At some unknown point, time will stop, the world will end, and Christ will return. We must be always ready for that special moment when our forever begins, and time will never matter again.

PRAYER—Holy Father, Your will be done. Help me to trust You at all times, no matter what I'm facing or emotion I'm feeling. I just want to be prepared always for the end of time. Amen.

TODAY I WILL...give God control of all my time, understanding He has a purpose for it all.

NOVEMBER 24 **Read I CORINTHIANS 2:6-13**

THE UNIMAGINABLE STREETS

Disney Fun Facts – The Small World Secret

"...and the street of the city was pure gold, like transparent glass."
—Revelation 21:21

It all started on January 24, 1848, when James Marshall found a few specks of metal near the lumber mill he was building. He took the pieces to John Sutter, the mill's owner, and the two privately tested and confirmed it was gold. They agreed to keep it quiet but told a 3rd man while securing the land rights who blabbed the news leading to the famous California Gold Rush. In the nearly 200 years since that event, the price of gold has risen from $20 to around $1800 per ounce. It is arguably the rarest and most coveted of our precious metals and is therefore used sparingly, especially as a building material. Therefore, you may be surprised to know you can find it on the outside of one of Disneyland's most iconic attractions. The façade of the "Small World" boat ride is covered in 22 carat gold leaf. The original plan was simply to paint it gold, but it was determined the upkeep over time would be more costly than using the real thing.

Have you ever driven on an old or worn-out street? If you live in Nashville, TN, you do it every day as we have more potholes than people. If you're like me, you've driven on all types of roads from asphalt to gravel to dirt and even cobblestone. However, I doubt anyone can say they've driven on, walked on or even seen a street made of gold. But you can! The verse above from Revelation confirms the streets in Heaven are pure gold...and that's just the start of how amazing and glorious it will be. In I Corinthians 2, Paul says if the people had only known what is awaiting them there, they never would have crucified Christ. He emphasizes it well in verse 9 saying no eye has seen, no ear has heard and no heart can ever imagine what God has prepared for those who love Him. The structure around Disneyland's "Small World" attraction is beautiful, but nothing we've ever seen or could even dream can compare with the majesty of what is waiting for us. I want to walk those golden streets. I want to see it all. Don't you?

PRAYER—Lord, I want to walk Your streets of gold. Please bring me there. In Jesus, Amen.

TODAY I WILL...read all of Revelation 21 while trying to picture what Heaven will look like, knowing it will be so much better than I could ever imagine.

NOVEMBER 25 **Read I PETER 1:13-21**

WASN'T WORTH IT

Disney Fun Facts – Snow White's Payment

"As you come to him, a living stone rejected by men but in the sight of God chosen and precious."

—I Peter 2:4

How did you first earn money? And grandma doesn't count. Did you get an allowance? Have a job? I remember my first allowance being $1 per week, mainly to take out the trash and clean my room. Wasn't worth it, although the amount slowly rose over time...inflation I guess. I also remember getting $2 an hour to babysit. Also wasn't worth it. My first real job was good ole Mickey D's for minimum wage of $4.25 per hour. Again, wasn't worth it...even with the free McNuggets. Wanna guess how much Adriana Caselotti, voice actress for Snow White, made for her iconic role? $20 per day! Granted it was 1937 and this was Disney's first film, but that still only amounted to $970 total or the equivalent of $17,000 today. I wonder if Ms. Caselotti thought, 'wasn't worth it' as she also had trouble finding work afterwards. She did play a background singer in *It's a Wonderful Life* and had one offscreen line in *The Wizard of Oz*.

We all do things in life that we feel weren't worth it, whether there's money involved or not. Sometimes the value of working just doesn't match that of the outcome. So let me ask this question...are you "worth it" to God. After all, He has put a lot of work into you. Not only did He create you, but He's watched over, guided and protected you since birth. And now He's working desperately every day to keep you on the righteous path. Once your life is done, will He then say about you, "wasn't worth it." I hope you know the answer. Of course you are worth it! Today's passage from I Peter says you are more valuable than silver or gold because you were bought with the precious blood of Jesus. The verse above echoes saying that though you may be rejected on Earth, you are precious and chosen by God. Never doubt your worth to God. You are obviously invaluable seeing what He gave up for you. While we could never live up to that cost, work hard to repay just a small fraction by making Him proud and returning His love.

PRAYER—Father, I'm so grateful You place such great value and never give up on me despite my many faults. Thank You for Your love and the incredible price You paid to prove it. Amen.

TODAY I WILL...realize I'm invaluable to God and do my best to return a portion of His love.

NOVEMBER 26 **Read GALATIANS 1:11-17**

LIVE UP TO YOUR CLAIM

Disney Fun Facts – Peter Pan's Voice

"Watch yourselves, so that you may not lose what we have worked for but may win a full reward."
—2 John 1:8

Macaulay Culkin, Drew Barrymore, Corey Feldman, Britney Spears and Lindsay Lohan. Know what those child actors have in common? They all battled drug addiction at some point and fortunately lived to tell about it. For other child stars like Corey Haim, Jonathan Brandis, Brad Renfro and River Phoenix, the drugs won the battle. Yesterday we discussed Snow White's young voice actress. Today we look at the young man who not only voiced Peter Pan but also starred in the Disney films *Song of the South* and *Treasure Island*. Bobby Driscoll was 15 when he gave Peter Pan a voice. He became a very successful child actor, winning an Oscar in 1950 and receiving his Hollywood Walk of Fame star in 1960. In 1968, however, his 31-year-old body was found dead due to drug use. At that point, he was homeless, penniless and without any identification. His body went unidentified and unclaimed for over a year before his mom finally sought his whereabouts and a fingerprint match confirmed who was in the unmarked grave.

We mentioned yesterday how invaluable you are to God, having been bought with His Son's blood. In Galatians 1, Paul again gives His testimony of being chosen by God despite his former life persecuting Christians. He even admits being a zealous follower of Judaism. However, being called directly by Jesus and given the command to preach the Gospel instead, he became immediately zealous for Christ who became his new passion. I know you don't need the reminder, but you too were chosen and called by God. He paid a great price for you. It is therefore your responsibility, and should be your desire, to find your passion and live up to that calling. Bobby Driscoll was a successful child actor, but in the end, what did he have to show for it? He was unclaimed and unknown. You have been claimed and are completely known by God. Hear His calling and run with zeal, as Paul did, to tell others what God has done for you.

PRAYER—Lord, thank You for choosing, claiming and calling on me. I want to repay you but know I never could. Help me to be zealous in telling others all You've done for me. Amen.

TODAY I WILL... Live up to God's honorable calling by telling others what He's done for me.

NOVEMBER 27 **Read MATTHEW 10:16-23**

SHEEP AMONG WOLVES

Disney Fun Facts – Walt's Failures

"...and you will be hated by all for my name's sake. But the one who endures to the end will be saved."
—Matthew 10:22

You've probably heard stories of individuals who achieved greatness but faced a rough start. Michael Jordan was cut from his high school basketball team. Henry Ford went bankrupt twice before establishing the Ford Motor Company. Thomas Edison was told by teachers he was "too stupid to learn anything." Even the great Walt Disney faced many trials and rejections on the road to success: He had a strained relationship with his father. He made poor grades in school. He was fired from an early newspaper job. His first cartoon business went bankrupt. He lost his first character, Oswald the Lucky Rabbit. He dealt with anxiety keeping his business afloat. His animators went on strike during WW2. And finally, we spent 4 devotionals in February talking about the disaster of Disneyland's opening day. It's a wonder Walt still had hair when he died.

We've discussed it before, but we all face trials, rejection and failure in our own journeys for success. In Matthew 10, Jesus makes it clear we will face the same in true service to Him. He gives His Apostles a warning that is meant for us too, saying He is sending us out as His sheep, but we are facing a world full of wolves. We all know what wolves do to sheep. Coincidentally, Matthew 7:15 says, "Beware of false prophets, who come to you in sheep's clothing but inwardly are ravenous wolves." Jesus says we should expect to be persecuted, mocked, hated, betrayed by even family and forced to answer for our faith and Christian works. When that happens, we are told not to be anxious, for God will give us the strength and knowledge through His Spirit to know what to do and say. Living a true, open and righteous life for God will not be easy. There will be times we will ask the question from a couple days ago...is it really worth it? Jesus answers that question above. "The one who endures to the end will be saved." Oh yeah, it'll be worth it. Trust me. Stand firm in any rejections or trials you face. The reward is coming!

PRAYER—Righteous Lord, I'm so grateful to be one of Your sheep, but I know the wolves will come. Help me know how best to handle the persecution, hatred and betrayals. In Him, Amen.

TODAY I WILL...ask God for strength to prepare for the inevitable trials coming my way.

NOVEMBER 28 **Read MATTHEW 5:21-26**

HOW RUDE!

Disney Fun Facts – Cast Member Rules (Part 1)

"So put away all malice and all deceit and hypocrisy and envy and all slander."
—I Peter 2:1

A 2019 article on pairedlife.com lists the top 25 rudest behaviors in people, something they say is on the rise. I don't have room all 25, but here are the top 5: blocking the grocery aisle with your cart, leaving a mess in a public bathroom, driving slow in the fast lane, talking or texting during a movie and not picking up after your dog. (Come on folks, that's gross!) Are you guilty of any of those behaviors? What about pointing with one finger? (GASP!) How dare you! Did you know Disney cast members aren't allowed to point with one finger? It is considered rude by their standards so they must always do a two-fingered point. Check it out next trip. There are actually many specific rules cast members must follow, and we'll look at a few others tomorrow.

I'm thrilled that Disney stresses the importance of avoiding rudeness and displaying kindness. It definitely shows as we rarely encounter a rude cast member. Sure it happens, but it's obvious what their standards are which makes them stand out above other similar parks. As Christians, we should also stand out as creatures of kindness, avoiding rudeness at all costs. It all comes down to self-control, focusing on our thoughts and actions, managing our anger and putting the needs of others ahead of our own (Php. 2:3). In today's passage from Matthew 5, Jesus stresses the importance of controlling our anger as it can easily lead to improper thoughts, dangerous actions and sin. He says if we ever feel angry toward anyone, we should go to that person and work it out before anything else, including the worship of God. Peter adds to the suggestions above by teaching us to get rid of feelings of anger, deception, unfairness, jealousy and revenge. All of these qualities would fall under the umbrella of rude behaviors and general selfishness. Keep in mind that you are striving to be an example of Christ in all things. Work hard to avoid rudeness or anything that would tarnish your reputation or especially that of Jesus Christ.

PRAYER—Dear God, I want to exemplify Christ in all I say and do. Give me the self-control to avoid rudeness towards others. Help me to put others' needs above my own. In Christ, Amen.

TODAY I WILL...write down at least 3 rude behaviors I struggle with and will improve.

NOVEMBER 29 **Read REVELATION 22:18-21**

GOD RULES

Disney Fun Facts – Cast Member Rules (Part 2)

"With my whole heart I seek you; let me not wander from your commandments."
—Psalm 119:10

Donkeys aren't allowed to sleep in bathtubs in Arizona. You can't whistle for your lost canary before 7 a.m. in Berekley, CA. Never sell dyed chickens in Akron, OH or sit on the sidewalk in Reno, NV. And definitely avoid sleeping in a South Dakota cheese factory. Those are all actual written laws, although some are clearly outdated, and none are likely enforced. Every state has some weird laws. Even the Bible has a few under the old law like no tearing your clothes (Lev. 10:6), eating fat (Lev. 3:17), letting anyone fall off your roof (Deut. 22:8) or boiling a baby goat in its mother's milk (Exodus 23:19). Umm, what? As mentioned, Disney cast members have rules too, in addition to the two-fingered point. They can't chew gum or make guests feel stupid. They can't take pictures "backstage" or even look at their phones "on stage." They must pick up trash but aren't allowed to bend over to do so. They must scoop as they walk. And the words "I don't know" are a big no-no as they are always required to either give an answer or figure it out.

There will always be rules whether from governments, jobs, schools or businesses. We even make rules for our own homes. And of course, God has rules too. Sometimes we may not like the rules, even God's. We may disagree, think they are too harsh or even outdated. We've discussed the importance of following His rules regardless. However, in the last few verses of the Bible, we're also told how serious God is about them. These verses must be important if God saved them for last. Verses 18 and 19 specifically say we are forbidden to add to or take away anything from the Bible. It's very easy to want to bend or alter one of God's laws to suit our desires. But we must be very careful not to do so. This is why concentrated reading and daily study of the Scriptures is so important. Make every effort to know and follow every law of God. He knows what's best for us and His rules will discipline and guide us right into His loving arms.

PRAYER—Almighty God, You know what is best for me and what I must do to keep my life focused. Help me in following all the laws You have set forth. In Jesus I pray, Amen.

TODAY I WILL...work to follow every rule God has without bending or altering it.

NOVEMBER 30 **Read MATTHEW 7:21-23**

THE TWO TRAINS

Disney Fun Facts – The Disney Railroad

"For the gate is narrow and the way is hard that leads to life, and those who find it are few."
—Matthew 7:14

Sure, it was occasionally loud when we played outside, but I always thought it was kind of neat that my grandparents had a train track just across their street. Ironically, my wife and I chose a home with an even closer train track, directly behind our backyard. Again, it can be loud at times, but only for a moment as it passes, and we don't even notice it inside anymore. And I still think it's neat to watch the trains go by, prompting great memories of my grandparents. We've already looked at how much Walt loved trains. Remember he too had one in his backyard, a working model he and his guests could ride around on. His love of trains led to a railroad in all but one worldwide Disney location, carrying millions of guests every year. The one in the Magic Kingdom at WDW for example, carries 1.5 million passengers annually. The four trains there were originally built between 1916 and 1928 and have been fully restored to run in tip-top shape.

Do you like riding the Disney trains? I do! It's such a long, soothing and peaceful ride full of much to see and enjoy. As we move into the final month of the year, I simply want to remind you we are all riding the railroad of life, and there are actually two trains available. One has plenty of seats, an easy track, no rules and is very popular and attractive. The other train is much smaller. Seating is very limited, the track is hard and there are definite rules. It takes dedication, discipline and focus to even keep your seat. Both trains follow parallel tracks, but at some point, those tracks will split. 1.5 million a year on the WDW train may seem like a lot, but it's nothing compared to how many have ridden, are currently riding and will ride life's trains. Sadly, so many will choose the large, easy train, but it has a devastating destination. Jesus makes this clear in Matthew 7. We must do the will of God to obtain a ticket and stay on the small train. Its track is difficult and narrow, but the destination is an unimaginable paradise. Which train are you on?

PRAYER—Holy Father and Creator, I want to be one of the few on the narrow path. Keep me firmly fixed and give me strength to avoid the easy and popular way. In Christ's name, Amen.

TODAY I WILL...ensure my seat with the few passengers and remain firm on the small train.

DECEMBER THEME

MISCELLANEOUS MOUSEDOM

DECEMBER 1 **Read HEBREWS 11:8-16**

A TOUCH OF HOME

Miscellaneous Mousedom – Main Street

"For here we have no lasting city, but we seek the city that is to come."
—Hebrews 13:14

Its land area is a measly 3.3 square miles with a population of only around 2,000. It boasts a handful of local restaurants, two hotels and a public library. Oh, and a Dollar General. But for this north central Missouri town, that's about it. Well, except for also being the one and only, self-proclaimed, hometown of a Mr. Walter Elias Disney. Walt was actually born in Chicago, but his parents moved him and his siblings to Marceline, Missouri when he was just four years old. While they only lived there for four years, Walt treasured his time there, calling it the best of his life. For this reason, he went back to visit on several occasions and even patterned Main Street in Disneyland after Marceline's downtown streets. If you visit the city today, you can see both his family's farm and home as well as a downtown museum dedicated to his life.

All six park locations around the world have some form or variation of Main Street as tribute to Walt's original vision and desire to remember his beloved childhood home. Back in October, we looked at Genesis 12 and God's original call to Abraham, asking him to leave his home and travel to a new land. In today's passage from Hebrews, we get a bit more to the story. We are told that not only was Abraham a great example of Godly faith, having no idea where he was being told to go, but that he also knew good and well that it truly didn't matter. Verse 10 says that Abraham was "looking forward to the city that has foundations, whose designer and builder is God." Abraham knew what the old hymn says and what we must remember..."This world is not my home. I'm just a passing through." Walt chose to pattern Main Street after Marceline so he could enjoy and share just a touch of what he called home. But we know better. God's world is beautiful, and we have many blessings here, but this is not home. As the verse above says, our true home is yet to come, and that is what we should be seeking every day of our lives.

PRAYER—Dear Lord, thank You for my temporary home and many blessings here, but help me to remember my true home is yet to be. I can't wait to see what You've prepared. Amen.

TODAY I WILL...remember anytime I'm struggling that the best is always yet to come.

DECEMBER 2 **Read ISAIAH 1:16-20**

WHITE WITH BLOOD

Miscellaneous Mousedom – Disney "Snow"

"...the blood of Jesus his Son cleanses us from all sin."
—I John 1:7

It's the eternal question humans have been debating for centuries. Everyone has their answer and there's typically no middle ground. So what's your choice? You must pick a side. Would you rather be too hot or too cold? I'm team hot! Don't get me wrong, I don't enjoy being hot, but I absolutely despise being cold. The only time I feel otherwise is while sleeping. I don't like waking up hot. I'd much rather be a little cold and grab another blanket to snuggle with. So maybe I do ride the fence on the hot/cold debate. It's a hard question! I just know you can experience aspects of both while at Disney, even at the same time! Disney has the ability to make snow for guests to enjoy, sometimes when it's not even cold. Of course, Disney "snow" is actually a form of soap that is harmless and leaves no residue on clothing or surfaces. They produce it for several occasions such as during the Christmas parties, at Disney Springs during the holidays and even during certain shows like Hollywood Studios' Frozen Sing-a-long.

I may hate being cold, but I still enjoy a good snow on occasion. It's a beautiful sight and brings back wonderful childhood memories of playing, sledding and missing school (the best part). The Bible talks of snow a few times, but today's passage uses it to make a tremendous comparison. As humans, we are weak, fallible and basically filthy with sin. In fact, God says through the prophet Isaiah that our sins are like a scarlet stain on our soul. But He also reminds us the blood of Christ, poured out for us on the cross, cleanses that sin and makes us as white as snow. Do me a favor. Type "B.C. blood of the cross" in Google Images and check out the comic strip that pops up. It's an excellent illustration of this very passage. The sacrifice of Jesus was incredibly powerful, enough to transform our sin-stained, guilty sentence of eternal death into one of a forgiven, snowy-white, innocent soul that has been gifted a life with God forever.

PRAYER—Gracious Father, I am so weak, and I hate that I sin against You. Thank You for loving me regardless and using Your own Son's blood to cleanse me of that sin. In Him, Amen.

TODAY I WILL...vow to remember, when I see snow, what Christ's blood does for me.

DECEMBER 3 **Read GENESIS 3:8-13**

YOU CAN RUN BUT...

Miscellaneous Mousedom – The Utilidors

"...be sure your sin will find you out."
—Numbers 32:23

Let's see...I'm gonna guess it was Colonel Mustard...in the kitchen.... with the...revolver! Am I right? Ever play Clue? Or see the film? Great movie! I always thought it was both neat and clever that the game (and film alike) had secret passages that could instantly take you between rooms. I always wished my own house had hidden passages like that. It's no surprise where the most elaborate system of secret passages can be found. The story goes that Walt was very disturbed one day to see a cowboy cast member at Disneyland walking through Tomorrowland on his way to Frontierland as he felt it ruined the whole illusion. Therefore, the entire Magic Kingdom at WDW was purposely built up on a second level so that a series of utility corridors, or "Utilidors," could be built at ground level. This not only provides a place for cast members to eat, change and prepare, but also allows them to move between lands unseen. Incidentally, the Seven Seas Lagoon in front of the MK was a result of all the dirt moved to create the two levels. You can see an online map of the Utilidors to see that they practically run under the entire park!

Disney may have created an incredibly clever way to keep the magic hidden, but even those Utilidors aren't good enough to hide from God. Today we read the story of Adam and Eve right after they ate the fruit, directly disobeying God. It's almost laughable that they attempt to hide when they hear God walking through the garden soon after. God even humors them Himself asking, "Where are you?" As if He didn't know. As mentioned before, God is very powerful, all-knowing and all-seeing. We can't hide from Him. We can't even hide our sins from Him according to the verse above. But that's not a threat. It's actually a good thing! Knowing we can't hide and God is constantly watching helps keep us righteous and on that narrow path. It's also comforting knowing He's always there when we need Him, especially in troubled times.

PRAYER—Dear Lord, I know I can't hide from You. I don't want to hide from You. I want to make you proud by keeping Your commandments in everything I do. Through Jesus, Amen.

TODAY I WILL...do, say and even think all things with the mindset that God is beside me.

DECEMBER 4 **Read GENESIS 6:1-8**

A FAVORABLE CRUISE

Miscellaneous Mousedom – Disney Cruising

"And Jesus increased in wisdom and in stature and in favor with God and man."
—Luke 2:52

If money was no object, what would be your dream vacation? For me, the destination wouldn't be as important as the form of travel. I would be cruising! I love cruising, and I daresay Disney does it best. Two of my four cruises have been with Disney, both outstanding and memorable. Somehow, they still capture the magic on board those giant ships. As of this writing, Disney has four active cruise ships: Magic, Wonder, Dream and Fantasy. The plan is to add three more by 2025. The 5th ship will be the Disney Wish with the others yet to be named. Disney cruising began in 1998 when the Magic took its first voyage to the Bahamas. Disney cruising is unique in many ways of course, but they pioneered "rotational dining" in which guests alternate between restaurants providing a unique experience each night with varying decorations and themes.

After discussing Abraham, Adam and Eve in December, we continue our look at the Genesis characters by cruising with Noah today. But can you really call it "cruising?" I'm not sure what Noah did would qualify. Can you imagine a one-windowed, wooden cruise ship filled to the brim with animals? Not exactly luxury accommodations. At the beginning of Genesis 6, we see why God chose to flood and destroy the Earth. He regretted making man as there was rampant corruption and evil. Except for one. Verse 8 confirms that "Noah found favor in the eyes of the Lord." Because of his righteous virtues and faith, Noah and his family were saved on that "cruise ship." Thousands of years later, someone else "found favor" in the eyes of God. Check above if you're unsure. If we are to imitate the life of Christ as instructed, we too must find favor with God by honoring His wishes and having the faith and morals of both Noah and Jesus. We know God will one day destroy the Earth again, next time with fire. Compared with the world, those saved by Him will once again be few. Will you be among the few in His favor?

PRAYER—Almighty Father, I want to be like Noah and especially Jesus in finding favor with You. Help me to remain among the few, chosen and saved by Your grace. In Jesus, Amen.

TODAY I WILL...do whatever it takes to be favorable in the eyes of my Father.

DECEMBER 5 **Read LUKE 16:19-31**

AVOIDING THE CASTAWAY

Miscellaneous Mousedom – Disney's Private Island

"In that place there will be weeping and gnashing of teeth, when you see... all the prophets in the kingdom of God but you yourselves cast out."
—Luke 13:28

Did you see *Cast Away*. with Tom Hanks alone on a deserted island for years? While that film isn't true, there have been a few real-life "castaways." The longest by far was Jose Alvarenga who spent 438 days adrift at sea. Read his incredible story online. Can you imagine being "cast away" for that long...alone? Disney has a "Castaway" island, but it's certainly not deserted. In 1997, Disney purchased a 99-year lease on a 1000-acre island from the Bahamian government and named it Castaway Cay (pronounced "key"). Only 55 of those acres have been developed, but it still serves as an exclusive port for thousands of cruisers annually, including those on the maiden voyage of the Disney Magic in 1998. Incidentally, Disney has recently purchased part of another island they've named "Lighthouse Point," which will be another exclusive cruise port.

Having been blessed to visit the paradise that is Castaway Cay a few times, I wouldn't mind being stranded there, even alone, for maybe a couple weeks, but certainly not as long as Mr. Hanks or Mr. Alvarenga. But I'd even suffer that long to avoid being a "cast away" as described in John 15:6 or in the verse above that begins by defining hell with "weeping" and "gnashing of teeth" and ends saying those sent there will be cast away from God. In Luke 16, Jesus gives a more realistic description of hell's torment by illustrating what it's like for a rich man sent there. Not only does the man plead for just one drop of water to cool his burning tongue but begs to warn his family of his agony. He is denied both. Christ told this story to warn us of the anguish and suffering to come for those who deny Him and reject the Father. Unfortunately, many will not heed this warning and will instead be "cast away" into this dark place of eternal pain. The time to warn your family, others and even yourself is now. Don't wait until it's too late.

PRAYER—Lord, I do NOT want to be cast away to eternal weeping, agony and torture. Please keep me from hell's misery and help me in warning as many as possible. In Christ, Amen.

TODAY I WILL...realize the reality and truth of hell and do whatever it takes to avoid it. I will also find the courage to warn others of the danger they are in if they continue to reject God.

DECEMBER 6 **Read 2 JOHN 1:4-11**

DON'T CUT IN LINE

Miscellaneous Mousedom – The FastPass System

"Everyone who goes on ahead and does not abide in the teaching of Christ, does not have God."
—2 John 1:9

I never explained December's theme, but hopefully you've figured out that we're ending the year with some miscellaneous topics that didn't necessarily fit anywhere else. And yes, "Mousedom" is a word...or at least an accepted Disney slang. So did you hear about the man caught skipping lines and giving unauthorized tours at Hollywood Studios? In June of 2021, he was discovered using a stolen Disney iPad to jump to the front of lines. Shame on him! There is a legal way, of course, to get to the front of Disney lines. For many years, Fastpass was a free "line-cutting" service given to all who purchased park tickets. Disney began the service in 1999, basing it on reservation systems already in place at various world's fairs. At first, they used paper tickets but gradually moved to an online reservation system called Fastpass Plus. In 2021, a new "Genie Plus" and "Lightning Lane" system was announced, which is a paid reservation system.

While the Disney Parks provide happiness, laughter, fun and lasting memories, they can also sadly bring out selfish actions of cheating when it comes to long lines and impatience. You may be able to cut lines at Disney and get away with it, but there's no skipping line when it comes to God. Today's passage gives us yet another warning about the importance of following God's commands and avoiding being deceived by those who don't. Verse 9 specifically (above) tells us not to try and get ahead by methods other than those following the teachings of Christ. The passage goes on telling us to not even welcome non-believers into our homes as we risk being deceived by their evil ways. This world is unfortunately full of people who try to cheat and get ahead using their own methods without following the path God has set up. Be carefully cautious when it comes to choosing leaders. Make sure they are abiding in every teaching of Christ, not using their own methods and definitely not taking shortcuts when it comes to God's commands.

PRAYER—Father, help me not to be deceived by those who take shortcuts in following Your commands. Help me to do all things Your way and not my own. In Jesus' holy name, Amen.

TODAY I WILL...vow to test all methods and teachings against the one constant, God's Word.

DECEMBER 7 **Read ROMANS 10:9-13**

CUT IN LINE

Miscellaneous Mousedom – Year of a Million Dreams

"For everyone who calls on the name of the Lord will be saved."
—Romans 10:13

I'll never forget the moment. We had just gotten off our first ride of the day, Kilimanjaro Safari at AK, and were met by two cast members in the exit line. They presented us all with a "Dream Fastpass," a placard with a detachable Fastpass to every ride in the park. We were thrilled to discover we got to go to the front of every attraction's line that day. The "Year of a Million Dreams" was a promotion on both coasts that ran from October 2006 to December 2008. During that time, one million guests, including us, were selected randomly and surprised with prizes ranging from a single Fastpass or Disney hat all the way to another Disney trip or, the ultimate prize, a stay in the Cinderella Castle Suite, which was supposedly given away each night during the promotion. What a gift!? Don't you wish Disney would bring that promotion back?!

You may be a bit confused by today's title, especially when compared with yesterday's title and message. Yesterday, we discussed the importance of not "cutting line" when it comes to the commands of God and getting to Him only through a genuine belief in Christ and His teachings. However, there is a God-approved way to get to the front of a line. Not Disney's lines of course, but the much more important, salvation line, which doesn't take money or online reservations. Instead, Romans 10 says we must verbally confess Jesus as Lord and believe in our hearts that God raised Him from the dead. Do you accept those things as truth? Are you willing to say aloud and to others that Jesus is Lord? Do you truly believe He died and was raised alive again? God says if you do then you get to move to the front of the salvation line! You will be saved! Of course, we must remember other verses instructing us to follow Christ in baptism and remain faithful throughout life, but confessing the name of Jesus and believing in all he said and did are the first steps in obtaining that Heavenly Fastpass and moving to the front of God's line forever.

PRAYER—Lord, I confess Jesus Christ as Your Son and Lord of my life, and I believe that He died for me and was raised again. Help me to follow all He did and assure my salvation. Amen.

TODAY I WILL...move to the front of God's salvation line by believing and confessing Christ.

DECEMBER 8 **Read MATTHEW 18:1-6**

BECOME A CHILD

Miscellaneous Mousedom – Kidcot

"...do not provoke your children to anger but bring them up in the discipline and instruction of the Lord."
—Ephesians 6:4

It's super fun to watch YouTube videos of kids being surprised with a Disney trip. Our family has one on there too! We used a scavenger hunt in 2009 to surprise our boys, and it went great, that is until my youngest realized he'd be missing school, which he was apparently sad about. Weird child. He's certainly changed his tune there! It's fun taking kids to Disney as they do an excellent job catering to them in so many ways. Even Epcot, which may seem like more of an adult park, has a wonderful (and free!) program for kids in the World Showcase section. For many years, they've offered a service called "Kidcot" where kids of all ages can currently collect a card from each country with facts on one side and a coloring picture on the other. Each station has markers if the kids want to do their artwork there. Ziploc, the current sponsor, even offers a free suitcase-shaped, plastic bag to keep all the cards in. If all 11 are collected, they also get a special postcard from Mickey himself. There is also typically a native of that country there at the station to teach the children further information about the history and culture of that nation.

Watching kids' reactions as they experience Disney, especially the first time, is absolutely priceless. When it comes to learning, kids are clean slates. Their brains are fresh and anxious to be filled with new information. Jesus knew this as He encouraged us to become more like them, saying it in today's passage and several times throughout the Gospels. Christ knew that kids are innocent, eager to learn and respectful of authority, so He said we must humble ourselves and become the same in our relationship with God. Picture a child's face seeing Disney for the first time. Try to have that same reaction every moment you get to spend with God. Humble yourself before Him. Be eager to soak up as much knowledge as you can. Respect His authority, discipline and instruction. Become like a child in His presence...because you are His child!

PRAYER—Dear Father, I am humbled and honored to be Your child. Help me to act more like one in the way I approach Your throne and seek to know more about You. In His name, Amen.

TODAY I WILL...write down 5 ways I can better become like a child in the presence of God.

DECEMBER 9 **Read JOHN 8:21-38**

TRAVEL METHODS

Miscellaneous Mousedom – Disney Transportation

"I am the door. If anyone enters by me, he will be saved."
—John 10:9

Try to think of the most unusual method you've used to travel. Planes, trains and automobiles (sounds like a good movie title) are likely the most common forms, but have you ever used a different, and perhaps unique, method? I traveled via mule to the bottom of the Grand Canyon, through Venice, Italy on a gondola and even across the English Channel on a hovercraft. Disney certainly offers some unique forms of travel too. During a trip there, one can travel by bus, boat, Skyliner, monorail, roller coaster and all sorts of other ride vehicles. Did you know the Disney bus system is the 3rd largest in Florida? The number of miles logged by the WDW monorails since 1971 is enough to make 30 trips to the moon and back! Disney has over 750 boats and 8 submarines making it the 5th largest "navy" and 8th largest submarine fleet in the world. Also, did you know that at one time, you could fly straight to Walt Disney World? There is a small airport near the MK that is no longer used. Guests that once flew there would hear "When You Wish Upon a Star" played out as the small planes drove over special grooves in the pavement.

Today we read an important lesson from Jesus Himself in which He basically tells us that due to our sins, we are condemned to eternal death and unworthy to go to Him. Thankfully, he also confirms that by believing in Him, we can avoid this condemnation and eternal death sentence. He says if we will abide in Him and His words, we will be His disciples and be set free from sin by knowing the truth of who He was and what He said. He ends by saying those who continue to practice sin are slaves to it, but believing in Him as God's Son frees us from that slavery. This is yet another passage confirming the above verse. Jesus is the one and only door to Heaven, and we must enter through Him. We can travel many ways here on Earth and even at Disney, but the ONLY way to travel to Heaven is through Christ. No other method will get you there. He is the only way to be freed from sin and therefore eligible for entrance through those glorious gates.

PRAYER—Lord, help me to use Jesus as the only door to Your kingdom. Through Him, Amen.

TODAY I WILL...confirm my method of travel as Jesus alone in my quest for Heaven.

DECEMBER 10 **Read ACTS 8:26-38**

WHY WAIT?

Miscellaneous Mousedom – The Disney App

"See, here is water! What prevents me from being baptized?"
—Acts 8:36

So here's a question that's no fun...what's your LEAST favorite part of a Disney trip? Many of you will say "going home" which is both clever and accurate. But is there anything else you don't like about going to Disney? The prices? The heat? Exhaustion? Crowds? Lines? Ugh! All of those can certainly be troubling, but Disney has taken steps to try and ease some of those burdens. Not so much with the prices (of course), but with crowds and lines. In 2008, they began development of the My Disney Experience App. This app has many helpful features like dining reservations, mobile food ordering, park hours and reservations, and the all-important wait times. While one used to have to physically go to an attraction to see its wait time or at least find that one centralized display board, now those times are given instantly via your phone.

Nobody likes to wait in line. We certainly try to avoid it in many ways including arriving before rope drop and checking wait times about... oh...492 times per day! Despite every effort, we sometimes just have to wait. When Flight of Passage first opened, we rope dropped it of course, but our oldest loved it so much, he chose to get back in line alone and wait again...for 3 hours! Sometimes you just can't avoid the lines. However, there is something more important you don't have to wait for. In Acts 8, Philip is guided to minister to an Ethiopian official. He tells Him the good news of Jesus and obviously talks to Him about baptism because the official sees a body of water and proclaims verse 36 above. Baptism is an important step in following both the commands of God and in the footsteps of Christ. If you haven't taken part, I'll ask the same question he did. Why wait? What's preventing you? This man was baptized immediately when he realized its importance. What's your excuse? If you need to study it more, go ahead. Read about it. Study it. Ask a mentor about it. But why wait? There's no line for baptism.

PRAYER—Dear Lord, I know baptism is an important step in my walk with You. Help me to follow Christ in taking part or help others to understand its importance if I already have. Amen.

TODAY I WILL...choose one person I can share with and discuss the importance of baptism.

DECEMBER 11 **Read I CORINTHIANS 10:23-33**

WHAT SHOULD WE EAT?

Miscellaneous Mousedom – Disney Dining

"...I try to please everyone in everything I do, not seeking my own advantage, but that of many, that they may be saved."
—I Corinthians 10:33

I only went to Disney 2 or 3 times as a kid. I remember being just as excited then as I still get today...but for different reasons. Back then, it was pretty much just about the rides, but now I see it is about so much more, and the magic lies in finding new experiences each and every time. Besides the rides, which I still love, there's are shows, tours, hidden secrets. new learning and discoveries, and of course, the food. Oh, the food! I didn't really care much as a child. Just get me my chicken nuggets, and I was a happy camper. But today, the overabundance of choices, tastes and settings when it comes to food makes that part just as exciting as the rides, if not more. Disneyland serves over 24 million meals a year with over 15,000 different food items offered, while WDW boasts over 400 places to eat with over 90 being full-service establishments.

Who doesn't love to eat? I only wish my metabolism still worked like it did when I ate those nuggets. But alas, it checked out a long time ago. The Apostle Paul used food as an example in today's reading to make a valid point when it comes to offending and saving others. He stated above that his goal was to please everyone, putting their needs and even their opinions above his own. He mentioned the importance of eating anything put before us as God's blessing...unless it somehow offends another. His lesson was the importance of putting our own feelings aside and catering to another's beliefs in hopes of winning their soul. Obviously, if their opinions go against God, that's a different issue. But if it's just a petty difference that doesn't really matter, we should strive to avoid offending them. Working towards unity with others is vital in achieving our goal and purpose of bringing them to Christ. Work hard to bond and connect with others, especially those who are lost or need a reminder of God's love and gift. Think before you speak or react. Are your differences really more important than the salvation of another's soul?

PRAYER—God, give me the ability to think and weigh the importance of disputes before I pass judgment or offend. I want more than anything to aid others in finding You. In Christ, Amen.

TODAY I WILL...not let my feelings or trivial conflicts hinder me in helping another find God.

DECEMBER 12 **Read REVELATION 7:9-17**

JOIN THE CLUB

Miscellaneous Mousedom – Club 33

"After this I looked, and behold, a great multitude that no one could number, from every nation, from all tribes and peoples and languages, standing before the throne and before the Lamb..."
—*Revelation 7:9*

My son recently joined a fraternity at his university. It's probably good I don't know the details about his initiation, but I do know he got very little sleep and had to perform a lot of petty tasks. I never joined a "frat." The only club I ever tried for was Costco, and that initiation was tough enough. Waiting in line. Getting approved. Supplying my credit card. Brutal! There is another club I'd love to join, but I ain't forking over my credit card for it. It would be way over the limit anyways. Club 33 is an elite and private organization that began at Disneyland in 1967. As of 2018, it's also now found in Tokyo, Shanghai and 3 of the 4 WDW parks. The original location was Walt's idea and is still open in Disneyland's New Orleans Square. It consists of a private lounge, fine-dining restaurant and excellent views of the park. As of this writing, the wait list is closed, and the last known wait was around 14 years! If you ever did make it into the club, the initial charge is said to be around $25,000 with annual dues of $10,000. I'll stick with Costco!

I'll never be able to join Club 33. I don't even expect to ever see inside the door. However, I'm proud to say I'm part of a way better club that has a much easier door to get into. Joining the family of God by following His commands and one day entering His kingdom is a "club" open to all. Our passage not only describes how glorious and amazing it will be, but also says that it's for "a great multitude, from every nation, and from all tribes, peoples and languages." All who join and enter God's holy gates will get to stand before His throne, see His face and that of His Son. It says we will never hunger, thirst, be scorched by the sun or be sad. We will wear robes of white, washed clean by the blood of Jesus and spend eternity on our knees praising the name of God. Better yet, it costs nothing. There's no waiting list. And it's not elite or private. It's for everyone! So what are you waiting for? Follow the steps God has given! Join the club!

PRAYER—Oh Lord, I am so excited and thankful I can be saved in Your club forever! Thank You for telling me exactly how to join. I can't wait for Heaven's promises. In His name, Amen.

TODAY I WILL...assure my place in God's club and never let my membership expire!

DECEMBER 13 **Read ROMANS 13:1-7**

GOD'S APPOINTED LEADERS

Miscellaneous Mousedom – Disney Leadership

"Therefore whoever resists the authorities resists what God has appointed, and those who resist will incur judgment."
—Romans 13:2

Have you ever held a position of leadership, maybe in school, work or another capacity? It's an honor to be chosen, elected or promoted to lead, but it often comes with greater responsibilities and accountability and can even involve extra time, stress and difficult decisions. I'm sure being a leader within the Disney company would bring the same. There have been numerous Disney leaders in many capacities over the years. Walt, as President and Board Chair and his brother, Roy, as Vice-Chair and CEO, were the first official leaders, but today there are hundreds of names on the list which can be found online. There is still a Board of Directors at the top of the chain which then breaks into branches over the corporation, each park, resort, the media, content, international operations and a host of other divisions. There have been 10 Board Chairs in Disney history from Walt all the way down to the current (as of this writing), Bob Chapek.

As you well know, the Disney name, brand and company has grown immensely since it began nearly a hundred years ago and is today well-known for its entertainment, progression, value and success. However, it's also known for change, something that even Walt was a big proponent of. Walt thought the parks in particular should always be changing, becoming fresh and new each time a guest returned. Sometimes the changes work out and we grow to enjoy them, but others seem unnecessary, and we don't understand the reasoning or just miss the way it was. Today's passage instructs us to respect those in leadership positions, even when we don't agree. I don't always agree with my leaders, whether at work, in government or even at church, but I try to respect their position and treat them kindly as commanded. Verse 2 above says God Himself has appointed our leaders, so we must remember He's ultimately in control, and we should trust both His judgement and ability to take care of us in all things. He is, after all, our ultimate leader.

PRAYER—Lord, help me to trust your plan and strive to always show kindness and respect for my leaders. Give them wisdom and help them to seek You in their decisions. In Christ, Amen.

TODAY I WILL...respect those in leadership positions, even if I disagree with them.

DECEMBER 14 **Read REVELATION 3:14-22**

LEAVING LUKEWARM

Miscellaneous Mousedom – Disney Construction

"So, because you are lukewarm, and neither hot nor cold, I will spit you out of my mouth."
—Revelation 3:16

As a boy, I remember wanting to be a carpenter as I thought it would be fun to build things. Plus, it was Jesus' job (Mark 6:3), so how could I go wrong? I quickly found the answer when I spent a summer working construction as a teenager. I got nervous on the ladders, fell through an unfinished deck and even stepped on a nail, requiring a tetanus shot. Construction was neither my forte nor my purpose, but I admire those who do it, especially at Disney where they build beautiful, architectural structures and construct a wide variety of attractions. As mentioned yesterday, the parks are ever changing and there always seems to be construction. Some projects move fast, like the entirety of Disneyland as discussed exactly one month ago, while others, and I daresay most, seem to take forever. As I'm writing this, there is construction in all 4 WDW parks, much of it being done in correlation with the 18-month, 50th anniversary celebration.

I recall a powerful sermon in which our minister placed 5 chairs on stage. He described a "person" sitting in each in various stages of spirituality from atheism to full dedication to God. But it was that 4th chair that stood out...the lukewarm chair. In Revelation 3, Jesus accuses a church of being lukewarm and says He will spit them out because of their half-hearted works and lackluster service. In other words, they won't be saved. Our minister said the same of chair #4. Disney construction may be lengthy and frustrating, but at least they are striving for progress and always adding to the magic. We must do the same. We can't just be lukewarm in our service to God without works, actions, progress and the sharing of our faith. We must be "constructing" ourselves at all times into better Christians. If you describe your faith, works, service and dedication as "okay" or "fine," then you are likely lukewarm and are risking being "spit out." Strive to be greater, a stronger disciple of Christ, always seeking improvement and perfection.

PRAYER—Lord, I don't want to just be lukewarm in my service and devotion to You. Help me to construct myself into something greater and constantly improve to be better for You. Amen.

TODAY I WILL...leave lukewarm behind, building myself into a strong, ever-growing servant.

DECEMBER 15 **Read REVELATION 22:1-5**

YOUR DREAM SUITE AWAITS

Miscellaneous Mousedom – Cinderella Castle Suite

"Rejoice in that day, and leap for joy, for behold, your reward is great in heaven."
—Luke 6:23

I think she was serious. She really wanted me to bid! I was observing the online auction with the price rapidly rising, and my wife was watching intently over my shoulder, asking questions about our bank account! But unless we were going to sell the house or perhaps a teenager, we weren't gonna win. It was July 2019 and ESPN was hosting an online charity auction. The coveted item up for bid was a trip for four to WDW with airfare, two nights in a Disney resort, four-day Park Hoppers, a $2000 gift card, a VIP guide, and breakfast in the MK. And oh yeah, just one more tiny prize...a one-night stay in the Cinderella Castle Suite!! The ultimate in lodgings! The winning bid was $75,600! The well-known, but rarely-visited suite is small but superbly decorated with incredible park views. Originally envisioned for Walt's family to stay, the space remained mostly empty after he passed and was only occasionally used for storage or even Disney telephone operators. That is until 2006 when it was refurbished for the previously mentioned "Year of a Million Dreams." It is now only offered very rarely for charity or prizes, although it's rumored some celebrities have weaseled their way in...for a pretty penny no doubt.

Just like Club 33, a stay in this pinnacle of rooms will likely never happen, for me or you, but there is a destination awaiting our stay that makes this suite look like a boarding house. Much more space. Way better views. Completely free. No online auction or sweepstakes needed. And the best part...you never have to check out! The final chapter of the Bible begins by describing Heaven's beauty, also confirming we will see the face of God, have His name on our foreheads and remain there with Him forever. It will never be night because it will be bright with the light of God, unimaginably beautiful and majestic. Even Christ told us above to rejoice and leap for joy at the reward coming our way. Make sure you are on track to obtain your forever stay in this ultimate of accommodations. Your suite is awaiting! (John 14:2)

PRAYER—Father, I can't wait to see the views from the room You've prepared for me. Amen.

TODAY I WILL...view online pictures of the castle suite, imagining Heaven's superiority.

DECEMBER 16 **Read PROVERBS 4:1-13**

SEEK TO LEARN

Miscellaneous Mousedom – Disney College Program

"An intelligent heart acquires knowledge, and the ear of the wise seeks knowledge."
—Proverbs 18:15

My wife insisted, "You really ought to read this book about two sisters who worked in Disney's College Program." She has dreams of our sons joining the same, finding careers at Disney and one day owning the place. (Maybe that's how I'll get my castle suite stay!) I reluctantly agreed to read it, having no idea where it would lead. I enjoyed it, decided to check out the publisher's website and found a link seeking book ideas. So it was that very book about the Disney College Program that led to my 3 devotional books as well as the one you are reading now. The program began in 1981 and enlists students globally to participate in a paid internship on either coast. Each semester, over 4000 students are put in multiple positions throughout the properties. Most work either the spring or fall semester, although some extend a full year. Although the program doesn't pay greatly, Disney does provide housing, a few perks and quality work experience, bringing great value to future resumes. Disney is well-known for promoting from within, so if there's a desire to advance up the Disney chain, the college program is a great place to start.

I wish I had my current Disney passion in college. I would've pursued a spot in this program in a second. Not only would it be fun, but the experience would've proven highly profitable in future work endeavors. Proverbs 4 stresses the value of wisdom, education and instruction, listing multiple benefits in gaining knowledge. And it doesn't just profit grade school or college students. We are never too old to grow in the knowledge of God's Word. Another proverb above calls us intelligent when we do so. While some of you, including myself, may be too old to join Disney's College Program and learn more about our happy place, it's never too late to seek knowledge about God, His plan and His Son. That information will lead us to an even happier place. "Keep hold of instruction; do not let go; guard her, for she is your life." (v. 13)

PRAYER—Eternal Father, I desire to know as much as possible about You and Your Word. Help me to gain proper and correct information about You daily. In the name of Christ, Amen.

TODAY I WILL...show wisdom by seeking more knowledge of God, His Son and instructions.

DECEMBER 17 **Read LUKE 22:39-44**

YOU'RE CLEAR TO FEAR

Miscellaneous Mousedom – Halloween Party

"But when he saw the wind, he was afraid, and beginning to sink he cried out, 'Lord, save me.'"
—Matthew 14:30

What's the scariest movie you've ever seen? Disney actually produced one of mine. It's called *Watcher in the Woods*, and it terrified me as a kid. I chose to watch it again recently for my third devotional book, and it still gave me the creeps! I don't watch those type of films often, but I still do enjoy a good scare...occasionally. Maybe that's why I like Halloween. And yes, I know it's December, but I didn't get a chance on Halloween to elaborate on today's topic. Disney has had a special, Halloween event since 1995 at WDW and has since expanded it to California and even Paris. This quality event encourages guests to dress up in creative costumes, provides candy for the kids and has special parades, displays and goodies. The event closed due to the pandemic and a smaller scale party is currently offered. It began in response to a similar event at Universal Studios, which is more centered on horror and fright whereas Disney's is more family friendly.

Maybe you don't like being scared, but true fear is a natural emotion found even within the Son of God Himself. In Luke 22, Jesus is praying the night before His death and displays fear because of the suffering and pain He knows is imminent. He even sweated drops of blood due to his agony, a medical phenomenon that can occur during high levels of stress. Thankfully, God was with Him as expected and sent an angel of comfort and strength so He could face His fear and complete the necessary task at hand. In the verse above, we see Peter showing fear, and even David, "a man after God's own heart," showed great fear often as evidenced by several psalms. It's okay to be afraid. We will all experience this emotion due to actual life events and not just scary movies or Halloween. When it happens, remember to seek God who will also send you an angel, His Spirit or even His own loving arms to comfort you and ease your burden. "I sought the Lord, and he answered me and delivered me from all my fears." (Psalm 34:4)

PRAYER—Lord, thank You for the examples of so many in Scripture, even Christ, showing fear and leaning on Your comfort and peace. Please give me the same when I'm afraid. Amen.

TODAY I WILL...readdress any worries or fears I have and verbally give them to God.

DECEMBER 18 **Read JOHN 18:33-37**

CUT THE ROPE

Miscellaneous Mousedom – Aerophile

"They are not of the world, just as I am not of the world."
—John 17:16

For my parents' 30th anniversary, my sisters and I decided to do something special and gave them a hot-air balloon ride. I'll never forget watching them soar into the air and then trying to follow by car, winding through the city streets, as we were their ride home. I've never taken a hot-air balloon ride myself, but I have enjoyed the tethered version at WDW's Disney Springs. Aerophile, once known as "Characters in Flight," is operated by a French company specializing in tethered balloon rides, hosting one in Disneyland Paris as well. The 19-foot balloon is filled with helium (not hot air) and can accommodate 30 guests at a time, lifting them into the air for 8-10 minutes. We really enjoyed our ride and could see for miles including all four WDW parks.

While riding in Disney's balloon is fun, it's not the same as taking a true, hot-air balloon ride. My parents rose to around 3000 feet in their ride, while Disney's only goes to 400 being tethered to the Earth's ground. In John 18, Jesus talks to the Roman Governor, Pilate, who asks Him questions trying to figure out just who He is and the motives behind His work. Jesus answers by making it clear that His kingdom is not of this world. He even says He and the Apostles didn't fight back but allowed His arrest (and eventual death) calmly, knowing it was necessary to move on to His true kingdom. He ends by saying the only reason He came into the world was to "bear witness to the truth." Jesus was not of this world and made clear in His prayer above from John 17 that we aren't either. God has granted us life on Earth just briefly with the same purpose as Christ, to proclaim the truth to all who will listen. But our true residence is awaiting us in Heaven, so make sure you are not attached or "tethered" to the world in any way. Don't give in to its evil pleasures, temptations or sin. Choose instead to cut the rope and make it obvious to everyone where you are headed as you prepare to soar away to your true home with God.

PRAYER—Father, I know You have a purpose for me, and I'm grateful for my life. However, I'm also thankful to not be of this world as I'm ready to soar home to You. In Jesus, Amen.

TODAY I WILL...cut the rope and stay untethered to the world, ready to fly home when called.

DECEMBER 19 **Read PROVERBS 2:1-15**

HIDDEN TREASURES

Miscellaneous Mousedom – Hidden Mickeys

"The kingdom of heaven is like treasure hidden in a field..."
—Matthew 13:44

The first time my name was published was actually not in these now four devotional books. It was in a popular book called *Hidden Mickeys* by Steven Barrett. I'll never forget seeing that tiny Mickey, randomly-placed inside Spaceship Earth and wondering, 'Is that a hidden Mickey?' I submitted it, and Barrett told me that while a few others had recently found the same, he would give me credit too. Wow! I was so eager to purchase the next edition and see my name in print. We later found a few others and my boys got their names printed too, much to their excitement. The history of hidden Mickeys goes back to the construction of Epcot in the late 1970's. That park was originally to be more adult-oriented without characters, so some Imagineers saw it as a challenge to "sneak" a hidden character (mostly Mickeys) into the artwork or attraction designs. Since then, finding hidden Mickeys has become an attraction within itself as there are around 1000 at WDW alone. You can also find them in the resorts, restaurants, in films or even off property. See if you can find the largest one, made of trees, using Google Earth or a similar site.

I love finding hidden Mickeys. My favorite, which can only be seen from the monorail, is the full-body Mickey just sittin' on top of the Contemporary Resort. It's fun to find something secret or hidden, almost like a treasure. Today's proverb refers to finding God's wisdom and understanding as a "hidden treasure." It also confirms God gives it freely if we will but only ask. As Christians, we should constantly be seeking hidden treasure by thirsting for the knowledge of God so we can know how to receive our Heavenly reward, which incidentally is also referred to as a hidden treasure in the beginning of the parable above, which goes on to say a man finds the treasure, sells all he has and buys the field joyfully. That's how wonderful the treasure of Heaven will be, and we should seek it daily by first finding treasure in the words of God.

PRAYER—Lord, help me to complete my treasure hunts, both here on Earth with your instruction and eternally by gaining entrance into Your kingdom. In Christ's name, Amen.

TODAY I WILL...begin my treasure hunt by seeking more wisdom and knowledge of God.

DECEMBER 20 **Read PROVERBS 3:1-6**

A STRAIGHT AND DIRECT PATH

Miscellaneous Mousedom – Skyliner

"Ponder the path of your feet; then all your ways will be sure. Do not swerve to the right or to the left; turn your foot away from evil."
—Proverbs 4:26-27

There are several Disney attractions that have come and gone over the years. Can you think of any you really miss? Did you know there used to be a "Skyway" attraction in three of the parks including Disneyland in California, Tokyo and the MK in Florida. They closed in 1994, 1998 and 1999 respectively due to expansion, cost maintenance or just plain aging and were missed by many. All 3 transported guests between Fantasyland and Tomorrowland with the California version even traveling through the mountain of the Matterhorn ride. Thankfully, in September of 2019, WDW debuted the Disney Skyliner, an extensive transportation system consisting of 300 gondolas and 5 stations connecting both Epcot and Hollywood Studios to four different resorts. Each gondola can hold up to ten people and plays onboard music and announcements. Many of them are decorated on the outside with characters from various Disney and Pixar films.

Yesterday, we looked at Proverbs 2 and the importance of seeking the wisdom of God. In the next proverb, we are again told the value in keeping His commandments and remembering His teachings. We are then given a well-known instruction in verses 5 and 6 telling us to trust God completely, lean not on our own understand and acknowledge Him in all things. We're told if we do so, He will make our paths straight. Another proverb above has similar advice telling us to focus on our path and not to swerve right or left. The Disney Skyliner is not only fun to ride, but it's also very convenient. If you are staying at one of the four resorts it services, it can get you to the parks quickly, taking a straight path and not having to deal with stoplights, traffic or gates. Trusting in God does the same, giving you a direct path to Him without curves in the path caused by evil. Sure, we will still have obstacles and sporadic bumps in the road, but trusting in His ways and not relying on our own methods is the most direct route to His love and guidance.

PRAYER—Gracious and loving Lord, help me to trust in You at all times and not try to "fix life" on my own. I want to remain on the direct path to you always. In the name of Jesus, Amen.

TODAY I WILL...find the straight line to God by trusting and letting Him guide my paths.

DECEMBER 21 **Read I KINGS 18:20-40**

GOD'S FIREWORKS

Miscellaneous Mousedom –Disney Fireworks

"...for our God is a consuming fire."
—Hebrews 12:29

I promise it was an accident. I had set up a small bottle rocket in a bush and it was facing up, but when the fuse burned, it caused the whole thing to go off balance and it shot off across our yard just as my friend and neighbor happened to be walking by. It hit her square in the stomach and exploded at her feet. She screamed and ran off crying, and I instantly felt terrible. I also cried that day when my mom made me go to her house and apologize. Eventually all was forgiven, and we remain friends to this day. I guess I was a minor pyromaniac as I loved fireworks as a kid...and still do! Therefore it's no secret I enjoy the many pyrotechnics used throughout the Disney parks. Over the years, there have been dozens of shows involving fireworks. Disney doesn't disclose exactly how much they spend, but in 2020, it was estimated that Disneyland spent $50,000 per day on fireworks. Another estimate put the annual fireworks bill for WDW alone at $45-$50 million! That's a lot of bucks for the bang! (Ha!—Did I just make that up?)

Today's reading is one of my favorite Bible stories where God demonstrates His own fireworks. Well, maybe not fire "works" per se, but certainly fire, sent straight from Heaven. After Elijah challenges the prophets of Baal to see which "god" will ignite their altars, God proves His existence and power by consuming not only the offering, but the wood, stones and even surrounding water as well. The verse above states God is a consuming fire. If you read the previous verse, it commands us to be grateful His kingdom cannot be shaken and to worship Him with reverence and awe. Fireworks are loud and powerful, but also beautiful and mesmerizing. The "fire" of our one and only God is the same. We can be fascinated by His creation and beauty, but we must also respect His power and authority. Aren't you grateful the true and living God who created everything, but will one day consume it all with fire, is on your side?

PRAYER—Almighty God, I am grateful for Your tender love and care as well as Your power and dominion over Heaven and Earth. I praise Your name with respect and awe. In Him, Amen.

TODAY I WILL...see God as caring and beautiful while respecting His authority and might.

DECEMBER 22 **Read JOHN 3:1-6**

THE POWER OF WATER

Miscellaneous Mousedom – Disney Water Parks

"Repent and be baptized every one of you in the name of Jesus Christ for the forgiveness of your sins, and you will receive the gift of the Holy Spirit."
—Acts 2:38

There was nobody in sight, and the attractions sat empty and dilapidated. Yet supposedly the water fountains still worked, and music still played over the speakers. Talk about creepy! There are several, likely unauthorized, YouTube videos exploring this deserted waterpark, back when it still existed. Disney's River Country operated from 1976 to 2001 and then sat empty until 2019 when it was finally demolished for a new resort (currently on hold due to Covid). River Country is the only full-fledged Disney park to shut down indefinitely. Thankfully, WDW still has two larger water parks that have remained in place. Typhoon Lagoon opened in 1989 and Blizzard Beach came soon after in 1995. Both have expanded over time and remain popular, typically being the 2nd and 3rd most visited water parks globally with a park in China winning the prize.

I never experienced River Country, although my wife has fond memories of it. I do enjoy a good water park though. There's just something fun about it, especially on a hot day when the water feels so cool and refreshing. Think again about how much we use and rely on water, even as a step in God's plan of salvation. We've talked before about baptism, even this month, but just a reminder of its importance and what it provides. According to John 3, we must be "born again" or baptized by water and the Spirit to enter God's kingdom. Being immersed, as Jesus was, not only symbolizes our dedication, representing His death, burial and resurrection, but it also fills us with the Holy Spirit. The verse above confirms this as do Acts 1:5 and Matt. 3:11. Receiving the Spirit is essential in our faith walk as it helps us in our weaknesses and prayers (Romans 8:36), aids us in witnessing to others (Acts 1:8), and teaches and helps us remember the words of Christ (John 14:26). Water is an amazing and powerful gift from God as the waters of baptism can both save our souls and fill us with the Holy Spirit to guide us throughout life.

PRAYER—Loving God, I am forever grateful You offer Your Spirit to guide and help me in my walk with You, especially in difficult times. I ask for its continued presence in my life. Amen.

TODAY I WILL...reflect on Romans 8:9, Ezekiel 36:26-27, Gal. 5:22-23 and I Cor. 6:19-20.

DECEMBER 23 **Read 2 CORINTHIANS 1:3-7**

PASSES FOR PEACE

Miscellaneous Mousedom – Annual Passes

"For as we share abundantly in Christ's sufferings, so through Christ we share abundantly in comfort too."
—2 Corinthians 1:5

We are considering it. We've never had them before, but we'd love to try it. We've had season passes to our zoo and a local water park. And growing up, we bought yearly passes to Opryland, our local theme park (R.I.P.). But we've never taken the plunge into Disney Annual Passes. A.P.s were introduced in the 1980's when ticket books were eliminated. As you may know, both Disneyland and WDW first used an admission fee combined with ticket books allowing a certain number of rides. When those went away and attractions became unlimited, the fee shot up as expected and many guests were upset they couldn't get into the park simply to eat or shop unless they paid the high rate. Therefore, Disney introduced A.P.s as an option for park regulars. The original A.P. was around $100 for adults (Wouldn't that be nice!?), while the current price is well over $1000 depending on which level you choose. By the way, there's also a "Golden Pass" only given to Disney Legends, Board members and a rare guest, like the first ever visitor to Disneyland. The Golden Pass allows lifetime entry into all 9 Disney parks around the world.

I would love to have a Disney A.P.! I'm just not sure my bank account would love it. But it would be so nice to just come and go as I pleased, sit on a bench, people watch and not worry about time crunches. Read today's passage from 2 Corinthians carefully. Read it twice! Count how many times "comfort" is used. Our God is great and gives us so many blessings, including comfort and peace, especially when needed most. Yes, we have times of suffering that we share with Christ as indicated above, but we also get to share in His comfort as well. Just like having those A.P.s and the freedom to take it slow, sit and rest, God's comfort provides that same relief and calmness. Do you feel relaxed and calm? If not, ask God for relief, take a deep breath, sit down and remember that God's got this. He's holding you and the whole world in His hands.

PRAYER—Father, I am ready and willing to do Your work and remain active in this world, but I am also very grateful for times of peace. Please send me Your comfort. Through Jesus, Amen.

TODAY I WILL...sit, relax and take some deep breaths while asking d for His comfort.

DECEMBER 24 **Read MATTHEW 3:1-6**

WHERE DO YOU DECORATE?

Miscellaneous Mousedom – Christmas Decorations

"You blind Pharisee! First clean the inside of the cup and the plate, that the outside also may be clean."
—*Matthew 23:26*

Hey, have you noticed tomorrow is Christmas?? You probably have. So I guess we better start talking about it, especially at Disney! I've always loved Christmas. I remember growing up with so many wonderful traditions, especially in preparation: picking out our tree, hanging ornaments, putting lights outside, adjusting the countdown calendar, searching the house for hidden gifts (just kidding mom... sortof). In fact, I think I enjoyed the prep and decorating more than I did the actual holiday. Our house was (and still is) always pretty decked out, but there's no way we, or I daresay anyone, could compete with Disney's decorations. For example, just at WDW: 1300 decorated trees, 15 miles of garland, 8.5 million lights, 300,000 yards of ribbon, a 25-foot wreath at Disney Springs, a 70-foot tree at the Contemporary, 150 semi-trucks full of decorations and of course, a full-size gingerbread house at the Grand Floridian. Just...WOW!

There's nothing like seeing decorations galore to get you in that Christmas spirit. But what about you? How well, or better yet, how much do you decorate yourself? In Matthew 3, we get our first glimpse of John the Baptist who was sent to prepare the way for the coming of Christ. This passage actually gives him a physical description saying he wore camel's hair and survived on a diet of locusts and honey. Yum! It seems John was not too worried about his outward appearance or how he "decorated" himself, despite being sent to introduce Christ! We are told throughout the Bible (I Peter 3:3-4, I Chron. 28:9, Luke 16:15) that it's what's inside and not out that matters most to God. Jesus tried to stress this with the Pharisees above in a pretty blunt and direct way. While decorations are great for Christmas, we need not be so concerned about our own. We should instead focus on our thoughts, attitude, actions and good works, making sure to keep Jesus inside (our hearts) as well, so that we can better imitate Him on the outside.

PRAYER—Dear Lord, help me focus more on what You see inside and not worry about what others see outside. I want my heart, actions and even thoughts to be pure. In His name, Amen.

TODAY I WILL...focus on decorating my inside, making sure my heart is right with God.

DECEMBER 25 **Read LUKE 2:8-20**

GOD IS WITH US!

Miscellaneous Mousedom – Candlelight Processional

"Behold, the virgin shall conceive and bear a son, and they shall call his name Immanuel" (which means, God with us).
—Matthew 1:23

HO, HO, HO!! Merry Christmas!! I pray today brings you and your family much joy, love and laughter. As you celebrate, consider this question...what's the greatest story you've ever heard? Maybe you read a phenomenal work of literature or saw a remarkable, inspiring film. Or maybe someone just sat you down, perhaps as a kid, and told you a captivating story you'll never forget. I've heard many great stories, but one most definitely stands out above them all. In 1965, an epic American film came into theaters about the life of Jesus from birth to ascension. It was entitled *The Greatest Story Ever Told*, and I would have to agree with its title. I'm so grateful that Disney continues to tell this story each year through its Candlelight Processional. This show was first performed at Disneyland in 1958 and then at WDW during its opening year of 1971. In 1994, it relocated to the current venue at Epcot's American Gardens Theater. The show features an orchestra and choir singing Christmas songs while a celebrity host retells the Biblical story of Christmas. This show typically runs each night between Thanksgiving and the end of December.

There are many great stories, but the story of Jesus, which really starts at the Bible's beginning with His genealogy, the prophecies and all the events leading up to His life, is by far the greatest story of all time. And it's all non-fiction. It truly happened! Today you read only His birth from Luke 2, but I hope you will choose to read something about Him each day. He was the greatest man who ever lived. He was God in the flesh. He was sent to show us how to live, to prepare us for our journey and give His life so that we can reach our final destination. A man like that deserves to be celebrated not just today, but every single day of the year. Praise God for Jesus! Praise God for sending Him to live among us and remain alive in our hearts! Praise God that through His indwelling, we shall forever praise His name as Immanuel, meaning God is with us!

PRAYER—Holy Father, thank You for giving us the greatest gift we could ever receive in Your Son. Thank You for His story which includes Him in my heart and my salvation. In Him, Amen.

TODAY I WILL...take time out of the holiday hustle and bustle to ·ect and celebrate Jesus.

DECEMBER 26 **Read COLOSSIANS 2:8-17**

KEEP CELEBRATING

Miscellaneous Mousedom – Christmas Party

"One person esteems one day as better than another, while another esteems all days alike...The one who observes the day, observes it in honor of the Lord."
—Romans 14:5-6

Well, it's now the day after Christmas. Ready to go back to normal life? I'm certainly not! It's kinda like a Disney trip. The preparation, anticipation and vacation are wonderful, but when the trip is done, it's so hard to go back to the routine! Therefore, we're going to spend just one more day talking about Christmas, and today we focus on what Disney does best... parties! Disney has been celebrating "Mickey's Very Merry Christmas Party" since December of 1983 with some slight alterations recently due to the pandemic. The Christmas party, like Halloween, is typically a ticketed event and includes specially themed stage shows, parades, fireworks and attractions as well as dance parties, character meet and greets, holiday treats, snow from Main Street to the castle and so much more. The event runs on select nights throughout November and December.

Did you have fun celebrating yesterday? I hope you allowed some time to celebrate Jesus too. This is one area where I disagree with how I was raised. I was taught we don't celebrate Christ's birth on Christmas day because we don't truly know what day He was born and should be celebrating Him every day anyway. And while I agree with both, I disagree with neglecting to celebrate Him at all. In Colossians 2, we are told what Christ's life means to us and how we share in His baptism, making us alive, forgiving our debt and filling us with the Spirit. Verse 16 specifically says there should be no judgement in celebration of Him, even referring to a festival. The verse above also states it's acceptable if someone chooses to celebrate one day over another. So it's true we don't know Jesus exact birthdate. And Yes, He should be celebrated every day. But I see nothing wrong with choosing a day to specifically remember His birth and celebrate with family and friends. I for one am glad that the world still chooses to remember our Savior through Christmas. So keep on celebrating! Today and every day. Celebrate Jesus forever!

PRAYER—Blessed Lord, I celebrate Your Son today, yesterday and every day. Help more in the world to know and recognize Jesus and what His life means to all of us. In His name, Amen.

TODAY I WILL...celebrate the life of Jesus with praise, reverence and study of His teachings.

DECEMBER 27 **Read ACTS 1:6-11**

LET YOUR LIGHT SHINE

Miscellaneous Mousedom – Disney Tours

"Let your light shine before others, so that they may see your good works and give glory to your Father who is in heaven."
—Matthew 5:16

Well, Christmas is officially over. Bah humbug. Do kids these days even know "bah humbug?" Hey, here's a question as we begin to wrap up our daily dates with Disney...if you had to work in a Disney park, what position would you choose? I think I would be a VIP or tour guide. While it might be fun working a ride or show, I think I would enjoy even more getting to meet people and share Disney facts and history. A VIP tour guide hosts up to 10 people with prices ranging between $400-$850 per hour (depending on the season) and a 7-hour minimum. For that hefty price, you receive limited backstage access at all four parks and a virtual Fastpass to the front of most lines. If that doesn't quite fit your budget, there are multiple tours offered on both coasts with prices ranging from $20-$300 per person. Each WDW park offers various tours, taking you backstage and even underground in the Utilidors. There are several at Disneyland too including one that allows access into Walt's private apartment above the Main Street fire station.

I enjoy telling others about Disney, like with these books, so I know I would enjoy doing it in person. But even more important than sharing Disney facts is a duty we all have in spreading the facts about God and our faith. In Acts 22-26, Paul is arrested and allowed several times to speak and give his defense. Each time, he chooses to share his own testimony of how he came to know and love God through his Christ-assisted conversion. Just a few years before, in Acts 1, Christ Himself gave us a charge to be His witnesses to the "ends of the Earth," His last words before ascending into Heaven. We are called to be daily tour guides for Jesus by sharing our testimony as Paul did and letting our light shine. At our church, our Children's Ministry assembly room is named "The Lighthouse" and the verse above is painted on the wall, inspiring the kids to be a light. Choose to be one yourself by telling others your story and the good news of Jesus that has hopefully changed your life. Be the beginning of their forever change too! Let your light shine!

PRAYER—Lord, help me in witnessing to others and spreading Christ's good news. Amen.

TODAY I WILL...be a tour guide for Jesus by sharing my story and re importantly, His!

DECEMBER 28 **Read JOHN 1:1-14**

THE WHOLE STORY

Miscellaneous Mousedom – Disney Plus

"For God so loved the world, that he gave his only Son, that whoever believes in him should not perish but have eternal life."
—John 3:16

How about some random Bible facts: A ball is mentioned once (Isaiah 22:18); God prevented the Israelites' clothes and shoes from wearing out for 40 years (Deut. 29:5); God sings (Zeph. 3:17); A man has 24 fingers and toes (2 Sam. 21:20); A donkey talked (Numbers 22:28); A woman was cut into 12 pieces (Judges 19:29). Sorry, that last one was a bit gruesome, but did you know those true facts? Most of them surprised me! You can always learn something new in the Bible. To learn new facts about Disney, I suggest its own streaming service as a great source. Disney Plus launched in November of 2019 and currently has well over 100 million subscribers. It contains an absolute surplus of content, both fictional and informational, including virtually every film and TV show Disney has ever made. There's also a plethora of original programing from new films and series to nature documentaries to extensive coverage of Disney history, its films and theme parks. There's even a series covering many of the individual attractions.

Can you see why this streaming service is an excellent source for Disney history, facts and entertainment? It's virtually the whole Disney story in one place. The same holds true for the Bible. It contains the whole story of God, and as mentioned, you can learn something new every time you open it. The beginning of John 1 takes us back to the beginning when the Word (Jesus) was with God and the world was created. From then on, God's story continued, progressing to the life of Jesus which led to us being a part of His story as well. I said the Bible is God's whole story, but that's actually not true. His story lives on and continues today through you. Strive to know His whole story by opening your Bible daily. Keep His story going by telling others so they can spread it too. John 3:16, likely the Bible's most famous verse, is also a good summary of God's story, but the word "eternal" proves one important fact. His story will never end!

PRAYER—Eternal Father, thank You for giving me Your story through the written Word. I'm so grateful to be a part of that story. Help me to learn more of it each day. In Christ, Amen.

TODAY I WILL...take time to read one additional passage or Bible story I'm unfamiliar with.

DECEMBER 29 **Read I THESSALONIANS 2:1-8**

END PICTURE

Miscellaneous Mousedom – Skywriting

"For I am not ashamed of the gospel, for it is the power of God for salvation to everyone who believes."
—Romans 1:16

There were ten of us dads, each with a 12-year-old son. We took the boys to "End Picture" farm for a weekend of bonding and spiritual growth, using the time to discuss God, life and becoming a man. One dad, the farm's owner, used a session to explain the reasoning behind his farm's name as buying the property was a lifelong goal or part of his "end picture." He then challenged each of us to draw our own "end picture," putting onto paper how we envisioned our future with God to look. Today's topic can often be seen at WDW but has no connection to the company as it takes place not IN the parks, but 10,000 feet above them. Since 1998, retired pilot Jerry Stevens, has been flying his crop duster over Orlando and spelling out encouraging messages about God, Jesus and love. He calls it the "Holy Smokes" ministry and his messages can be seen for up to 50 miles depending on the clarity of the day. Stevens volunteers his time with no payment, saying that God has always provided, and that he prays for Jesus to guide each flight.

I'm not sure how Disney feels about the spiritual messages high above their parks, but I love them! I've seen it several times on our trips and it's always a fascinating, inspiring and creative way to spread God's message. As you know, we are all called to share the Gospel of Christ, and we too must occasionally be creative in doing so. In I Thess. 2, Paul says he didn't preach for greed or glory but did it with gentleness to appeal to more individuals. Teaching Christ is very important, as evidenced in the verse above, but sometimes we must do so creatively to better reach others. Having boys (and their dads) create their "end picture" was also creative and really helped us each think about what Christ and His Gospel meant for our future. Let us each try to meet others where they are and be patient and considerate in telling them about Christ. By the way, my end picture still sits on my nightstand and shows my reunited family, standing before the light of God, singing His praises with all the saved. What does your end picture look like?

PRAYER—Lord, help me to be creative in spreading the Gospel to others. In His name, Amen.

TODAY I WILL...take the time to draw my own end picture. What will r future look like?

DECEMBER 30 **Read JOB 42:10-17**

THE BEST IS YET TO BE

Miscellaneous Mousedom – Magical Express

"What no eye has seen, nor ear heard, nor the heart of man imagined what God has prepared for those who love him."
—I Corinthians 2:9

Horatio Spafford was an American lawyer and church elder who lost most of his investments in the Chicago Fire of 1871. Two years later, his wife and daughters were crossing the Atlantic when their ship crashed into another vessel. All four daughters, ranging from 18 months to 12 years, were killed. His wife survived and sent him a telegram with the simple words, "Saved alone." Separated due to business, Spafford rushed to reunite with his wife, sailing the same route his family had taken. When he came to the spot at sea where his daughters had perished, he wrote the familiar hymn, "It is Well with my Soul." While it certainly doesn't compare to that tragic story, riding Disney's Magical Express can mean either devastation or joy, depending on which way you are going. Beginning in 2005, Disney began offering free bus service to and from the airport for those staying on property. While exciting to ride upon arrival, it was playfully dubbed the "Tragical Express" by returning guests as it meant the end of their vacation. Giving another meaning to the "tragical" label, the service was discontinued at the end of 2021.

Seven years after losing his four daughters, Spafford lost a three-year-old son to scarlet fever. Needless to say, he faced great tragedy and pain during his lifetime. One might even compare him to Job, who faced similar losses of family and property and was encouraged by friends and even his own wife to "curse God and die" (Job 2:9). In chapter 42, Job is rewarded by God who is proud of his unwavering faith despite his tragic losses. All his fortunes are restored, and he is given "twice as much as he had before." Each of our lives at times can feel tragic, like we're riding a real "Tragical Express" full of trials, suffering and pain. However, the verse above assures us we can't even imagine what God has in store for those who love Him and remain faithful like Job and even Mr. Spafford. Don't ever lose your faith and trust in God no matter how difficult life becomes. Remember what's coming. The best is most definitely yet to be.

PRAYER—Father, help me to always remain faithful to You no matter what. In Him, Amen.

TODAY I WILL...look up the lyrics to Spafford's hymn and reflect on his faith vs my own.

DECEMBER 31 **Read PSALM 84:1-12**

NEVER A KISS GOODBYE

Miscellaneous Mousedom – The Kiss Goodnight

"...this is God, our God forever and ever. He will guide us forever."
—Psalm 48:14

Happy New Year! If you've read all the way through, congratulations and thank you! I pray this book has helped you both in your personal walk of faith and in growing closer to God.

His name is Mr. King, and he was my chorus director for three years in high school. He has been the same for my sons, having obviously taught several years. He is firm and demanding but was one of the most effective and successful teachers I ever had. As we sang the last note of our final concert each year, Mr. King would transition his hand from conducting into a blown kiss goodbye, a tradition that continues to this day. While most of the audience watches the chorus, I still watch his kiss goodbye as it always puts a lump in my throat. Cinderella Castle also tells its guests goodbye on most nights. Approximately 30 minutes after the Magic Kingdom closes, the castle magically begins twinkling, "When You Wish Upon a Star" begins playing and a final goodbye announcement is made. This brief presentation is called "The Kiss Goodnight."

We all have to say goodbye many times throughout life, but there is One who never will. Psalm 84 today gave us one final glimpse of how wonderful Heaven will be, saying "Blessed are those who dwell in Your house, ever singing Your praise!" It says a day in His house is better than a thousand anywhere else, and that God withholds nothing good from those who remain faithful. Revelation 1:7 assures us Christ IS coming to begin our forever, and as the psalm above states, God will be our guide forever and ever. The castle says goodbye to guests with a kiss as does Mr. King to his chorus. But with our eternal King, there will never be a kiss goodbye. His kingdom will never end. NEVER. I assure you God is real, Heaven is truth and forever will be a reality. Where will you spend it? Are you sure of your salvation? If not, find your assurance in the only possible place, through our Lord and Savior, Jesus Christ. Praise be to God FOREVER!

PRAYER—Eternal and loving Father, thank You for a blessed year, full of Your love and care. Help me to be sure of my salvation in Jesus and remain faithful to You forever and ever. Amen.

TODAY I WILL...make definite plans to continue my daily time with God in the new year.

Made in the USA
Columbia, SC
15 February 2022